CHANGES IN THE AIR

The Environment in History: International Perspectives

Series Editors: Dolly Jørgensen, *University of Stavanger;* Christof Mauch, *LMU Munich;* Kieko Matteson, *University of Hawai'i at Mānoa;* Helmuth Trischler, *Deutsches Museum, Munich*

Rachel
Carson
Center
ENVIRONMENT AND SOCIETY

Changes in the Air

*Hurricanes in New Orleans
from 1718 to the Present*

Eleonora Rohland

berghahn
NEW YORK · OXFORD
www.berghahnbooks.com

First published in 2019 by

Berghahn Books

www.berghahnbooks.com

© 2019 Eleonora Rohland

Library of Congress Cataloging-in-Publication Data

A C.I.P. cataloging record is available from the Library of Congress

British Library Cataloguing in Publication Data

A catalogue record for this book is available from the British Library

ISBN 978–1-78533-931-8 hardback
ISBN 978–1-78533-932-5 ebook

To my parents, who laid the groundwork.

And to Franz, with all my love.

Contents

Figures and Maps

Figures

Maps

Acknowledgments

This book is the result of a string of journeys—physical, mental, and emotional. It would not have been written without the helping hands and clear-sighted minds of dear friends, colleagues, family, and often of complete strangers. The first leg of this journey involved moving from one country to another. The second brought me to New Orleans in December 2009 and January 2010. Interviewing forty New Orleanian citizens and ten experts (politicians, economists, architects, city planners, and scientists) on their experience of Hurricane Katrina was an extraordinary, immersive, and life-changing experience. Therefore, I would like to first thank all my interviewees for their trust and extraordinary openness in sharing their memories and reliving often painful experiences. It is they who let me glimpse the many facets that make New Orleans what it was and is. Even if I quote only a small number of interviews out of the sample, their (hi-)stories are at the background of this book's narrative.

I would never have been able to reach such a diverse group of private citizens and experts, nor got to know the city and its environs without the invaluable help and expert knowledge of Craig Colten, Richard Campanella, Jim Amdahl, and Barry Keim. Jim Amdahl introduced me to Rita Legrand, an incredibly well-connected and politically active New Orleanian, then in her early seventies, who took me under her wing and to many political events, and who connected me with her extended network all over the city. Another irreplaceable contact and lasting friendship I owe to my dear friend Lisa Stalder, who brought me together with a fellow Swiss woman in New Orleans, Regula Keith. Rea, Chuck, and their son Jackson Keith became my family and village in all possible and impossible situations (like pulling my car out of the mud of the sidewalk on which I had parked it to avoid flooding from heavy rains), fed me delicious dinners, and generously provided contacts. I had the extraordinary luck to get to know and interview Jan Garbers, the 2005 director of operations of the German Federal Agency for Technical Relief (THW) who was responsible for pumping the water out of New Orleans after Hurricane Katrina. Love had found him in New Orleans after "the Storm": he married his wife Laura and, hence, luckily was still there when I came to do my interview study. They both have become dear friends and kindly helped me find further interviewees.

Yet, those two months of interviews were only the beginning. As the historian in an interdisciplinary research project on "Memory of Disasters," I was going to search for further layers of 'disaster memory' farther back in time. With the excellent advice of my mentor Cornel Zwierlein, my research focus evolved, bringing me back to New Orleans three more times to rummage through the city's various archives. My research trips would not have been possible without the generous funding of the Schweizerische Studienstiftung (Swiss Study Foundation) and without the fellowships at the German Historical Institutes (GHI) in Washington and Paris. I thank Hartmut Berghoff, then Director of the GHI Washington, for his insightful comments on questions of research and for many inspiring conversations. And I thank Rainer Babel, director of the early modern history section of the GHI Paris and my temporary adviser for his warm welcome and support during my six-week stint researching French colonial New Orleans at the National Archives in Paris.

Researching a period of almost three hundred years in archives all over the United States and Europe is impossible without the expert help of archivists and library staff. Greg Lambousy, director of collections at the Louisiana State Museum and Sarah-Elizabeth Gundlach, curator at the Historical Center of the Louisiana State Museum, provided excellent sustained support and guidance throughout my stay at the institution. My gratitude also goes to Daniel Hammer, deputy director of the Historic New Orleans Collection who was of invaluable help for my research there, and to the staff at the New Orleans Public Library. Further thanks are due to the staff of the Library of Congress in Washington, DC, and to the staff at the National Archives in College Park, Maryland.

Throughout all this transatlantic to and fro, the Institute for Advanced Study in the Humanities Essen (KWI) under the direction of Claus Leggewie provided the roof, research framework and a critical discussion forum for the stages of this research endeavor. Particularly, my colleagues, Gitte Cullmann, Maike Böcker, and Ingo Haltermann proved critical, patient and benevolent discussants of a diverse set of problems and questions. Principal Investigators Harald Welzer and Dietmar Rost were a continuing guiding presence, assisting this research process wherever possible.

I am grateful to Christof Mauch for his consistent support and friendship over the years and for his helpful recommendations on structuring this book's narrative. Two anonymous reviewers equally provided invaluable advice and suggestions for the improvement of the content and structure of this book. Furthermore, I would like to thank Cary Mock and Mike Chenoweth for generously sharing their knowledge about hurricanes and their historical reconstructions in personal conversations and email exchanges. Also, special thanks to Cary for freely sharing historical records and painstakingly collected data with me. My heartfelt gratitude goes to John Davis and Gareth Davies for spending their precious time reading through this text and making helpful suggestions for changes. I thank the Berghahn editorial team, Lizzie Martinez, and Alison Hope, for their meticulousness and patience in giving the manuscript the finishing touch.

I am furthermore blessed with many excellent colleagues and friends who have helped shape the thought process of this book in conversations and after presentations of chapters, most prominently Tony Oliver-Smith, Craig Colten, Richard Campanella, Greg Bankoff, John McNeill, Jim Fleming, Jim Rice, Richard Tucker, Joyce Chaplin, Marcy Rockman, Virginia García-Acosta, Raymundo Padilla Lozoya, Luis Arrioja Díaz, Cécile Vidal, Jean-François Mouhot, Grégory Quenet, Welf Werner, David Bresch, Mark Stoneman, Sherry Johnson, William O'Reilly, Ted Beatty, and George Adamson and Matthew Hannaford, who share my interest in connecting historical research with questions of the present, in particular.

My very deep and affectionate gratitude, of course, goes to my parents, Hans and Petra Rohland, who supported this journey in so many ways and to all my wonderful friends in Zurich, Bern, and Basel (you know who you are!), who accompanied this process with dinner invitations, emotional support, and great conversations.

Without my husband, Franz Mauelshagen, his nerves of steel, and his humorous and loving support, this book would not be what it has become. He kept me fed, even-tempered, and proofread throughout. Thank you for putting up with the long stretches of separation during archival leaves and for being my partner in this and all else that we share.

Abbreviations

AANO   Archdiocesan Archives of New Orleans

AGI   Archivo General de Indias

AMO   Atlantic Multi-decadal Oscillation

ANF   Archives Nationales de France

ANOM   Archives Nationales d'Outre-Mer

BOB   Bureau of the Budget

CCSRC   Citizens' Central Storm Relief Committee

ENSO   El Niño/Southern Oscillation

HNOC   Historic New Orleans Collection

HTML   Howard Tilton Memorial Library, Tulane University

HUD   Department for Housing and Urban Development

IPCC   Intergovernmental Panel on Climate Change

ITCZ   Intertropical Convergence Zone

LSM   Louisiana State Museum

NARA   National Archives and Records Administration

n.d.   no date

NFIP   National Flood Insurance Program

NHC   National Hurricane Center

NOAA   National Oceanic and Atmospheric Administration

NOPL   New Orleans Public Library

OEP   Office of Emergency Planning

SRCA   Swiss Re Company Archive

Hurricane Katrina and the Future of the Past

It started over the Bahamas. A tropical depression began forming on Tuesday 23 August 2005, and the National Hurricane Center (NHC) assigned it the name Katrina. It took until Thursday 25 August until people along the Gulf Coast of the United States and in New Orleans really started taking notice. Early evacuees began leaving the city on Friday 26 August. The city's mayor, Ray Nagin, addressed the public on TV and declared a state of emergency, calling for a voluntary evacuation on the evening of Saturday 27 August. Consequently, more citizens packed their cars with a few days' worth of clothes and their most important belongings and took to the evacuation routes. Those who had set their minds on staying went about boarding up their houses to protect against the hurricane winds. On the morning of Sunday 28 August Mayor Nagin addressed the public on TV again, this time calling for the extraordinary measure of a mandatory evacuation, after Katrina had intensified to a Category 4 storm overnight. The first feeder bends, the outermost cirrus clouds of a hurricane vortex and harbingers of the system's approach, appeared in the sky over New Orleans on Sunday evening. The winds picked up during the night and roared with increasing intensity. Katrina made landfall as a Category 3 storm in St. Bernard and St. Tammany Parish below the city in the early morning hours of Monday 29 August 2005, after having kept most citizens who stayed behind awake or tossing in an uneasy sleep. At around 8:00 A.M. the first levee breach at the Industrial Canal was recorded and water started flowing into the city. One eyewitness from Tremé who had stayed in the city described this moment: "You've seen white caps, on the lakes, or in the ocean? That's how the water's rushing in. You look down the street there and you see the water coming, and it's just rushing in and stuff is floating in it."[1] Additional levee breaches followed during the morning and noon of 29 August until eventually 85 percent of the city was under various depths of water. The toll was enormous: 1,800 people died as a result of Hurricane Katrina. Those who had remained in New Orleans were evacuated—and displaced—eventually, after trying to survive for five days in a city whose systems had broken down completely due to the hurricane.[2]

On a cold December day in Germany, four years and a few months after Hurricane Katrina had flooded and almost destroyed New Orleans, I flew to the city in order to interview forty New Orleans citizens (those who stayed as well as those who evacuated) and ten experts (scientists, economists, city planners, and politicians) on their disaster memory of Katrina. The goal was, ultimately, to find out how people remember a disaster and whether they learn from their experience—in short: whether and how memory/knowledge translates into action.[3] My interview guideline covered all aspects of the actual hurricane experience, from preparedness to whether interviewees remembered Hurricane Betsy in 1965—the last big one before Katrina—and whether they thought Katrina was a "natural" or a human-made (social) disaster. However, the question which ultimately inspired this book's extended journey from the recent past of Katrina in 2005 to the comparatively deep past of New Orleans's founding years in 1718 was about the future.

The answers to my question whether interviewees were afraid that a hurricane like Katrina could reoccur can be neatly partitioned into two groups: First were those who feared and thought it possible (or were even certain) that a Katrina-like disaster could repeat itself. Those also agreed that if such a disaster *did* happen again they would not be able to go through the emotional stress again, that this would be the end of the city of New Orleans.

> *I mean, you know, yes, it can happen again. Hopefully there are things being put in place that will protect us more but I know that we're still very vulnerable, that we're still walking a tight rope, somewhat. But it's still our home. I think if it happened again, that would be it. I know, and not just myself, everybody I talk to: 'Could you go through it again?'—'No way.' I don't think we have the physical or emotional energy to go through this again.*[4]

Those in the other group were often categorical in their dismissal of the possibility that such a disaster could reoccur, at least within their lifetime.

> *That's not gonna happen no more. You take out a whole population of people, how many times that's gonna happen? They had to move a million people. That's gonna happen no more. That's why I say it should be recorded. It's a once-in-a-life-time-thing.*[5]

It is almost an anthropological constant that humans draw on the past in order to form an opinion about the future.[6] German historian Reinhard Koselleck conceptualized this phenomenon for historical time under the term "future of the past."[7] He diagnosed a shortening period between the experienced past and the expected future due to the acceleration of events during modernity. Hand in hand with this acceleration went the element of the unknown, which, hence, meant breaking out of the erstwhile cyclical understanding of history.[8] To interview people affected by Hurricane Katrina about their expectations of the future was therefore an eerie experience of seeing the future of the past in the making—albeit in a still-open time horizon that will hopefully remain unconsumed for a long time to come. Extending the gaze back into the city's hurricane history (see figures 1.1 and 1.2 in chapter 1) gave those very contextual Katrina-statements an uncanny timelessness. Both groups thus drew on their experience, but with different outcomes and possibly different implications for individual, future action. Representatives of the second group in some cases freely admitted that they wanted or had to believe that a Katrina-like event would not reoccur within their lifetime so as to be able to move on in life.[9]

The scientifically informed perspective, however, is on the first group's side and it paints a bleak picture of the future. Richard Campanella, historical geographer and New Orleanian by choice, belonged to my group of experts. He had studied the city geographically and historically for twenty years and stayed during Hurricane Katrina. His answer to my question was that

> it will definitely happen again. Other disasters, like earthquakes or volcanoes, have roughly the same chance of happening tomorrow as yesterday. But what's different about a hurricane striking lower Louisiana is that tomorrow is *riskier* than yesterday. Why? Because the soils are sinking, the coast is eroding, the sea is rising, and all indications are that global temperatures are warming, thus further increasing sea level and likely the frequency or severity of tropical storms. Thus, tomorrow is riskier. Many advocates of New Orleans often say: "Well you know, there are disasters in other cities, too, so why are we saying 'we must evacuate, we must move.'" As someone who loves this city, I too am tempted make that argument. But it's comparing a broken leg to cancer. A broken leg could happen any time and it's bad and you're out of commission but it heals; whereas the cancer—the geological cancer that we have here—might well prove fatal. It will definitely reduce the eventual lifespan of the city. We will not be here a thousand years from now. If we do things properly we might be able to squeeze out a few hundred years.[10]

Campanella's reference to an extended future in the interview and his deep-past perspective in *Bienville's Dilemma* were the first instances that made me think about Katrina in a historically much larger context than just Hurricane Betsy (1965) or the twentieth and twenty-first centuries.[11] With the sentence "if we do things properly, we might be able to squeeze out a few hundred years," Campanella was referring to what he had said about wetland loss in Louisiana and to the problem of sinking soils and the increasing flood risk New Orleans is exposed to in the context of ongoing anthropogenic climate change. In post-Katrina New Orleans, "doing things properly" had, among many other programs to rebuild the city, taken shape as the Dutch Dialogues, a group of delegates (architects, scientists, policymakers) from New Orleans visiting the Netherlands to see the world-leading flood management systems of the Rhine-Meuse-Scheldt Delta, and, in turn, inviting a Dutch delegation to New Orleans to acquire direct advice on how to develop the city's flood protection in a resilient way.[12]

Doing things properly with regard to sustaining New Orleans under conditions of global warming, then, is what climate change research calls "adaptation to climate change." While climate change on the global scale is described in terms of increasing temperatures due to rising carbon dioxide levels in the atmosphere, the effects of these temperature changes on the local scale may be variegated and certainly not uniform. One aspect that has emerged from climate science over the past decade with near certainty, however, is that climatic extreme events (i.e., tropical cyclones, flood events, hailstorms, droughts, etc.) will become more frequent and/or more intense in a warming climate.[13] While earthquakes and volcanoes are geological phenomena that, to our current knowledge, are not connected with changes in the climate system[14] and do not occur with any apparent regularity or in cycles, tropical cyclones are seasonally occurring climatic phenomena whose fluctuation is connected to larger-scale systems such as El Niño/Southern Oscillation (ENSO), the Atlantic Multi-decadal Oscillation (AMO), and the Intertropical Convergence Zone (ITCZ), which are predicted to shift with ongoing anthropogenic climate change.[15] While no single hurricane event can be directly attributed to climate change, tropical climatologists are predicting an increase in activity—if not in number then in the intensity of future hurricanes under warming conditions, because hurricanes are chiefly fueled by warm sea surface temperatures.[16]

Ostensibly, adaptation to present-day and future climate change means reacting to those global and local, long-term and rapid-onset changes in the environment. Encapsulated in this simple understanding of adaptation is, again, how knowledge and experience translate into action. Clearly, in the context of the field of climate change adaptation research, pioneered by the Intergovernmental Panel on Climate Change (IPCC), adaptation is treated as a conscious and target-focused and plannable process on the local, regional and national policy-making level of countries. This seems to be self-evident and taken as a matter of course.[17] Yet, judging from the relatively recent history of global and national climate policy, it is clear that this particular understanding of adaptation is a historically new development.[18]

Looking at the disastrous aftermath of Hurricane Katrina, my focus thus started shifting from disaster memory of one discrete event to adaptation to the hurricane hazard in general. In particular, adaptation *before* anthropogenic global warming had become a globally pressing issue and a major field of research and policy production. How had societies adapted to climatic extreme events such as hurricanes in the past and before the term even existed? Could the disaster that was Katrina just be the symptom of a much longer history of (non-)adaptation of the city of New Orleans? Was Katrina New Orleans's Three Hundred Year Hurricane, in the same sense as the American anthropologist Anthony Oliver-Smith had diagnosed the 1970 Ancash earthquake as Peru's Five Hundred Year Earthquake in his seminal 1994 study?

Oliver-Smith takes the Peruvian earthquake disaster that caused seventy thousand deaths and destroyed 80 percent of the built infrastructure of the affected Department of Ancash as an opportunity to unravel the area's long-term history of social vulnerability and adaptation to natural hazards. The anthropologist turns to the beginning of the Spanish colonial period, showing how the conquerors disrupted time-tested adaptive practices of the indigenous population by imposing unsustainable Castilian architectural styles, settlement patterns and surplus-extraction oriented food production.[19] Throughout Oliver-Smith's article, the social vulnerability of the Peruvians seems unbroken and continuous across the five-hundred years of his study.

While this book's focus is inspired by Oliver-Smith's long-term perspective, it departs from that model in important ways. On the one hand, adaptation, not vulnerability is at its center—though the two concepts are evidently related. On the other hand, the continuity suggested in Oliver-Smith's Peru-study may be difficult to transfer to New Orleans. Apart from the fact that the socio-environmental conditions in the Mississippi Delta prior to French settlement were very different from those of Spanish-conquest Peru in the early sixteenth century, the city's history is characterized by three distinct political regimes. Louisiana was claimed for France by the French explorer Robert Cavelier de la Salle in 1682, the first forts (Mobile and Biloxi) were set up along the Gulf Coast in 1699 and 1700, and the cornerstones for New Orleans were laid in 1718; in 1762 the colony was ceded to Spain in the Treaty of Fontainebleau, in 1800 Spain handed Louisiana back to France, and in 1803, the Jefferson administration bought it in the Louisiana Purchase. Added to this rather eventful political history is the relatively high (physical) mobility of the non-enslaved parts of colonial societies, enabling them to choose *not* to settle and adapt to the recurring threat of hurricanes on the Gulf Coast but to move to friendlier environments devoid of this hazard. Thus, clearly, when extending the focus on adaptation from Hurricane Katrina in 2005 back to New Orleans's colonial beginnings, the question whether any kind of continuity in adaptation to hurricanes in fact existed, must remain open to scrutiny.

However, is it necessary to go so far back in time to learn about adaptation to the hurricane hazard in New Orleans? Would it not be enough to stick with the time period between, say, Hurricane Betsy in 1965 and Katrina in 2005? In terms of the question how memory/experience transforms into action, the temporal distance between those two hurricane events, forty years—a human generation—is significant. Disaster researchers have found that the average half-life of disaster memory was about one to one-and-a-half generations. In other words, if natural disasters occur less frequently, risk-awareness and preparedness decrease and a "disaster gap" ensues.[20] In addition, considering that cultural practices and risk-management institutions arose from the experience of disasters over time, it makes sense to go back farther in time in order to form a viable perspective on how societies adapted to the hazard of hurricanes. Implicit in this perspective—as well as in the problem of the disaster gap— is the factor of repetition. Climate historian Franz Mauelshagen has called it a key concept in historical disaster research as "it is the link between the past and future, or, more precisely, between past experience and future societies."[21] Prevention and risk management require forecasts and these usually rely on data of the past, or in other words, on the future of the past.

New Orleans, as so many other North American cities, with its comparatively short but well-recorded history, is an ideal case to study the socio-environmental dynamics of a city and its societies from its inception. Colonial authorities left abundant written evidence of their reasoning for the choice or abandonment of a settlement site, of learning about new environments and environmental hazards. In order to be able to draw conclusions about New Orleans's long-term adaptedness or non-adaptedness to hurricanes, it is therefore important to first establish what the French founding fathers of the city as well as the settlers might have known about hurricanes when settling between the Mississippi and Lake Pontchartrain in 1718. Most fundamentally, were they even aware of the risk of hurricanes to the region? From a present-day perspective, one might easily take for granted that they were, as European colonies in the Caribbean had been battered by hurricanes since Columbus' arrival in 1492 and hurricanes were no novel occurrence at the beginning of the eighteenth century. However, could colonials perceive hurricanes as moving systems that, after touching Cuba or Saint-Domingue, might also make landfall at the Louisiana Gulf Coast? These questions about the beginning of New Orleans's hurricane history concern knowledge as a precondition for adaptation. These aspects need to be clarified before the historical development of specific adaptation options and practices can be considered.

Environmental archaeologist Marcy Rockman suggested that it takes humans who move into unfamiliar environments at least one generation (thirty-five years) to acquire robust knowledge about local climatic patterns, the carrying capacity of a given soil or the flood regime of a river.[22] In other words, adaptation options are embedded in time and, in the case of Louisiana, in a wider local, national, and transatlantic historical context. However, there is no determinism in technological and scientific development with regard to adaptation. As the long-term perspective in this book will show, the availability of adaptation options through the interplay of science and technology does not guarantee what has been called successful adaptation. Time and again, political priorities and cultural values got in the way of what with hindsight may appear to have been obvious choices.

This book thus explores how New Orleans's societies have adapted to the recurring threat of hurricanes from the French colonial foundation of the city in 1718 across three political regimes, French colonial, Spanish colonial, and American to hurricane Betsy in 1965 and touching on Hurricane Katrina in 2005. While the general geographical focus is on the city and the downriver parishes of St. Bernard, Jefferson, and Plaquemines, the question about the evolution of hurricane knowledge includes the wider geographical and cultural contexts of the Caribbean and the transatlantic republic of letters within which notable phenomena such as hurricanes were discussed. This book considers adaptation to the hurricane hazard in the wider social, cultural, and political context that emerged from the historical record. That is, I understand adaptation as the result of social practices that develop in the aftermath of repeated natural extreme events over time. Yet, hurricane events also affected social practices that had no connection to the hazard whatsoever. Clearly, hurricane adaptation can be and is influenced by decisions, social processes and vulnerabilities which are not directly related to the hazard. In other words, in some of the case studies that follow, the historical context becomes more important than the actual story of the hurricane disaster. This fact points to the enigmatic and complex character of the concept of adaptation and of disasters as the entanglement of "processes and events, social, environmental, cultural, political, economic, physical, technological, transpiring over varying lengths of time."[23]

The insights we may gain on adaptive practices on the individual level and through interview studies is unfortunately not sustainable throughout the whole period of time that is covered by this book as there are no comparable historical sources that span several generations, let alone centuries. In other words, researching adaptive practices in the aftermath of hurricanes over a time period of three hundred years, it was necessary to search for answers on the more macro-level of institutions in order to reach a certain measure of homogeneity in the source material. Records at this level of society not only facilitate a long-term perspective on possible institutional change in the aftermath of hurricane disasters, but also on the effect that general institutional change (unrelated to hurricane impacts) has on the capacity of a society to cope with and adapt to the hurricane hazard. Evidently, and to some extent, inevitably, in an initially colonial setting such as New Orleans with its long history of slavery, this leads to a documentary bias toward a European, white, and predominantly male perspective that is difficult to circumvent other than through the reflexive application of *adaptation as a relative concept* as outlined in chapter 1.

The information on adaptive practices throughout the eighteenth century was derived from documents generated by the local colonial authorities. In the French case this refers to the correspondence of the governor and/or intendant, the two highest ranking officials in the colony, and to the correspondence of the royal engineers with the Company of the Indies or the minister of the marine, depending on whether the colony was administered by the company (1717–31) or by the French crown (1731–62). The Spanish colonial period is based on the correspondence of the Spanish governor and/or intendant with the minister of the Indies in Seville and on the Spanish city council (the *cabildo*) records for the eighteenth century. The case studies of the nineteenth century are based on the New Orleans Conseil de Ville (City Council) records, which continued to be written in French until the mid-1830s; on newspapers, which, in New Orleans only started to be printed at the beginning of the nineteenth century; and on federal state level records for the nineteenth and twentieth centuries. In those few cases, where English editions of French or Spanish primary sources were available, I have indicated this in the notes; otherwise all translations from French and Spanish records into English are by me.

Studying adaptation to extreme events such as hurricanes historically, and over the long term is an interdisciplinary endeavor that draws on several fields of historical and climatological research. Understanding the physical aspects of the hazard of hurricanes and how they relate to the climate system is key for grasping its complexity which, in turn, is part of the history of hurricane knowledge and science and ultimately for the question of adaptation to this hazard.[24] The long-term natural scientific history of hurricanes, in which the three hundred years of this study is embedded, is covered by paleotempestologists. They reconstruct the frequency and intensity of past tropical cyclones from the archives of nature—that is, from sea floor and lagoon sediments as well as tree rings. This field intersects with paleoclimatology working on long-term data series of ENSO cycles, which are crucial for understanding the (multi-) decadal variation of hurricane frequencies in the Gulf of Mexico. Paleoclimatology is capable of reconstructing ENSO and hurricane events for time periods that exceed the human archives (written historical records) by far, particularly in the Americas.[25] In turn, where human and natural archives overlap, historical records are usually more accurate with regard to dates and, crucially, they contain detailed information about the impacts of extremes on societies.[26]

Its focus on historical hurricanes and their societal repercussions place this book in environmental history, and, more specifically, in disaster history. For the past twenty years, historical disaster studies have developed as a sub-field of environmental history insofar as they have been dealing with natural rather than technological disasters. The majority of studies that have emerged from historical disaster research have concentrated on discrete catastrophic events that acted as caesurae for the affected societies.[27] Thus, researching a long-term perspective that takes into account repeated impacts of natural extreme events based on historical records is still a new approach for which, so far, there exist only a few instances.[28] A notable example with regard to hurricanes is Stuart Schwartz's recent Sea of Storms, which does for the (Circum-)Caribbean what this book does for New Orleans and the Mississippi Delta region.[29] Considering the wealth of literature that has emerged in the aftermath of hurricane Katrina, and considering the general disaster-proneness of New Orleans it is surprising that only two articles with a specific focus on disasters (in general) and one on the hurricanes of the city's French colonial period have been published so far.[30] While not focusing on disasters exclusively, Christopher Morris's and Richard Campanella's excellent long-term environmental histories of the Lower Mississippi Valley and the Mississippi Delta, provide a wealth of geological, environmental and socio-cultural information on which this study draws throughout.[31]

The narrative of this book is structured along five adaptive practices and one effect (political vulnerability) of a practice wholly unconnected to hurricanes and adaptation, namely, slavery. The five practices—*levee building, evacuation, disaster migration, disaster relief,* and *insurance*—appear at different points in time in the historical record and require shifting narrative strategies. That is, although most of the book is structured chronologically, some chapters look at developments over the long term, while others concentrate on specific hurricane events. I intermittently draw on the city's full hurricane chronology (see figures 1.1 and 1.2) in order to show parallels or to highlight differences in coping and adaptation between events.

In the following, chapter 1 starts by briefly inquiring into the present-day understanding of adaptation as outlined by the IPCC. This institution's definition has acquired somewhat of a benchmark status and hence merits a closer look. Based on a critical reading and reappraisal of the IPCC's definition from a historical perspective I argue for understanding adaptation as a relative concept. With this slightly altered lens with which to track adaptive practices through time, we first return to knowledge as a precondition for adaptation. The chapter thus shifts focus between our twenty-first-century knowledge of hurricanes and the state of hurricane knowledge at the time of Louisiana's first settlements in 1699 and 1700 and of the foundation of New Orleans in 1718. By zooming in on seventeenth- and early-eighteenth-century tracts on hurricanes in the French and British Caribbean, a clearer picture emerges of how eighteenth-century contemporaries understood hurricanes (*ouragans* in French). With this tableau of Caribbean hurricane knowledge context we are hence able to assess the reactions to New Orleans's first hurricane experience in 1722, four years after the foundation of the city. Based on this first glance into the history of hurricane knowledge, the remainder of chapter 1 is dedicated to outlining how hurricanes can be chased safely through historical archival material.

Chapter 2 follows Louisiana's founding fathers, the Canadian brothers Jean-Baptiste Le Moyne de Bienville and Pierre Le Moyne d'Iberville, in their early exploration of the Mississippi Delta and their later quest, starting in 1718, for a site to build New Orleans in order to establish their state of knowledge about the hazard-proneness of the area. Their correspondence with the metropole, together with the letters of the royal engineers who came to oversee the building of Louisiana's capital, shed light on the question of environmental learning, the role of indigenous knowledge, and the early technological adaptation of the French to the Mississippi environment.

Levee building is chronologically one of the first adaptive practices that appears in the historical records. The fact that the French imported their own levee-building technology with all its virtues and flaws from France to the Mississippi Delta is highly significant for the question of adaptation, as we will see by following this practice through the French and Spanish dominion of Louisiana and to the Great Mississippi Flood of 1927. In and around New Orleans levee building protected both life as well as property from river floods and hurricane storm surge that was pushed upriver and temporarily reversed the Mississippi's current. Yet the plans to build levees in front of New Orleans were driven by the much more frequent experience of river floods. Therefore, the first part of chapter 2 focuses more strongly on technological adaptation in New Orleans and the plantations that were located up and down river from the city. The second part zooms in on La Balize (the beacon), a strategic military and trading post set up at the mouths of the Mississippi in 1723. Here, chapter 2 returns to the question of environmental learning, showing how difficult it was not only for the French, but also for the Spanish, to interpret the Mississippi Delta environment properly, to judge its inherent long-term risks, and on how technology was thought to solve the obstacles they encountered. In chapter 2 we hence travel through all three of New Orleans's political phases: French, Spanish, and American.

The intimate connection of the adaptive practices of *evacuation* and *disaster migration* with environmental knowledge emerges as the undercurrent of chapter 3. Both practices prevent harm to human life but are different in scope. Evacuation is usually a short-term measure to remove people temporarily from harm's way and is either externally or self-administrated.[32] Disaster migration, on the other hand, is when people move from a disaster-prone environment to a different, ideally less-disaster-prone place of settlement without returning. If this process is administered top-down, it can turn into forced migration, or displacement. The focus of this chapter is on voluntary—that is, self-administered—disaster migration. In chapter 3 the geographical focus shifts again between the Caribbean and the Louisiana Gulf Coast, as well as between the two practices. In early-eighteenth-century New Orleans disaster migration occurred frequently in the aftermath of hurricanes, which were usually followed by prolonged periods of food scarcity and a consequent price inflation. The loss of frustrated settlers who decided to move to less-disaster-prone places upriver from New Orleans jeopardized the economic prosperity of the colony throughout its French and Spanish periods. Economic anxieties due to population loss in the aftermath of a hurricane reappear even in chapter 5, at the end of the nineteenth century, though, of course in a politically different context. Evacuation follows its own historical chronology that includes multiple factors such as the geographical vulnerability of New Orleans to hurricanes, population growth, the evolution of meteorology as a scientific field, and the development of several unrelated technologies. The second half of chapter 3 will hence shed light on those crucial moments in time during the 1870s and, again, during the 1940s when it became possible to forecast hurricanes and to warn at-risk populations in the Caribbean and on the Louisiana Gulf Coast, thus enabling the securing of life and property in these areas on a new scale.

In chapter 4 New Orleans's enslaved population and slavery as a systemic factor of political vulnerability in a natural hazard situation come into focus. That is, chapter 4 explores in more detail one of the instances in which aspects that are unconnected with hurricanes and adaptation become magnified by the extreme event and suddenly take center stage. While slavery had been part of New Orleans's and thus French and Spanish Louisiana's fabric from the start, the colony turned into a fully fledged slave society later than any of its Caribbean counterparts. This transition occurred precisely around the time of the geographically close-by Haitian Revolution and the Louisiana Purchase in 1804 and 1803, respectively. The explosive situation with regard to the growing population of enslaved Africans in and around New Orleans, the social tensions among whites and free people of color in Louisiana's process of acquiring statehood, as well as the War of 1812 form the backdrop—or rather, the foreground—of the hurricane of 1812. On the night of 19 August 1812 the uproar of the natural elements was apparently used by New Orleans slaves to coincide with an attempt at overturning the social order, through a revolt in the city. By centering on political vulnerability in connection with war and revolution, chapter 4 stands in the wider context of subjects such as national security and state(s) of emergency.[33] Both of these subjects have received scholarly attention from historians, though usually not with a strong focus on natural hazards and disasters.[34]

Chapter 5, then, returns to adaptive practices but to one that is less directly linked to technological and scientific developments than chapters 2 and 3. Rather, it is connected to factors such as population growth and economic development. From the point of view of governance, *disaster relief* as an adaptive practice to relieve social hardship in the aftermath of a disaster becomes a more pressing issue because increasing numbers of people could potentially fall into poverty as a result of property loss and loss of livelihood through a disaster. In 1893, in the middle of a U.S.-wide economic depression, the devastating Cheniere Caminada Hurricane hit the barrier islands Grand Isle and Cheniere Caminada below New Orleans. Two thousand people were killed in the states of Louisiana and Mississippi, some seven hundred (half of the population) on Cheniere Caminada alone. Thus, chapter 5 follows the hurricane's aftermath and the emergence and centralization of a local hurricane disaster relief institution in New Orleans, the Citizens' Central Storm Relief Committee. At the same time, Louisiana representatives introduced a bill to the House of Representatives asking for federal disaster relief from the hurricane that had hit their state. This interplay of the local, state, and federal levels in the provision of disaster relief comes into view in chapter 5. Here we oscillate between the sphere of adaptive practices on the local institutional level on the one hand, and a more systemic view that includes political culture and decision-making on the federal level on the other.

This local–federal shift in perspective continues in chapter 6, which focuses on *insurance* as an adaptive practice and brings us to Hurricane Betsy in 1965, also known as Billion Dollar Betsy. It was the last hurricane to flood New Orleans (i.e., the Lower Ninth Ward and Gentilly) in a major way before Hurricane Katrina hit the city forty years later. We start again from a local perspective on the impact of the hurricane on New Orleans. A set of letters to President Lyndon B. Johnson provides insight on the social effects of the existing, unequal system of federal disaster relief. The fact that this system had reached its financial limits by the mid-1960s was recognized and discussed by politicians in Washington, DC, at the time. By focusing on the attempt to transition from the overdrawn disaster relief provisions to a disaster insurance program, chapter 6 sheds light on a pivotal point of systemic change with regard to hurricane (and flood) adaptation in the aftermath of Hurricane Betsy. Throughout the chapter, our gaze shifts from New Orleans to the level of federal politics and to the discussion about the form that this new program was to acquire.

The influence of natural hazard insurance on individual as well as national adaptive capacity is often subtle and hidden. It seems that, precisely because of this hidden nature of insurance, the political process of negotiation between the different governmental agencies has so far largely remained in the dark.[35] Yet the question as to the specific structure of an insurance program (i.e., whether it is mandatory or voluntary, and whether it is a purely private industry program or a public–private partnership, etc.) is crucial with regard to the program's functionality, and ultimately, for people's adaptation and vulnerability on the ground. While all of these factors seem to belong to the rational realm of economic and political decision-making, chapter 6 shows how the deeply ingrained legal and political traditions together with ideas of American identity influenced the process that led to the implementation of the National Flood Insurance Program (NFIP) in 1968.

In conclusion, chapter 7 pulls the different strings of this book together and attempts to distill more general points from the overview over the *longue durée* of hurricane adaptation in New Orleans.

Notes

1. As I agreed with the interviewees, they will remain anonymous. Interviewee No. 12, male African American from Treme, New Orleans, age 57, on 18 December 2009.
2. See Richard Campanella's chapter on Hurricane Katrina in Richard Campanella, Bienville's Dilemma: A Historical Geography of New Orleans (Lafayette: Center for Louisiana Studies, University of Louisiana at Lafayette, 2008), 329–39.
3. The interview study was conducted in the context of the program "Climate and Culture" within the research group "Memory of Disasters" at the Institute for Advanced Study in the Humanities Essen (KWI). Nonexpert interviewees were chosen primarily with regard to whether they had stayed (13) or evacuated (27) during Hurricane Katrina. An even count between African American (19) and white (21) interviewees was attempted and almost reached. The age of interviewees ranged from twenty-three to eighty-seven, and the social stratification ranged from transient worker to taxi driver, social worker, business owner, musician, church rector, graduate student, professor, and attorney. The interviews were qualitative, biographical interviews that started with an open entry question and that then followed an interview guideline. Statistical data (i.e., age, income, profession etc.) were collected with a questionnaire. For a more detailed description of the interview method—that we called the "enviro-biographical interview"—and more Katrina-interview excerpts see Eleonora Rohland et al., "Woven Together: Attachment to Place in the Aftermath of Disaster: Perspectives from Four Continents," in Listening on the Edge, ed. Stephen Sloan and Mark Cave (New York: Oxford University Press, 2014).
4. Interviewee No. 7, female, white New Orleanian from Lakeview, age 55, on December 11, 2009.
5. Interviewee No. 19, male African American New Orleanian, age 56, on 8 January 2010.
6. One of the most important reference works from the field of neurobiology is still David H. Ingvar, "'Memory of the Future': An Essay on the Temporal Organization of Conscious Awareness," Human Neurobiology 4, no. 3 (1985).
7. For the English version of the book see Reinhart Koselleck, Futures Past: On the Semantics of Historical Time, Studies in Contemporary German Social Thought (Cambridge, MA: MIT Press, 1985).
8. Reinhart Koselleck, Vergangene Zukunft. Zur Semantik geschichtlicher Zeiten (Frankfurt am Main: Suhrkamp, 1989), 33–34.
9. E.g., interviewee No. 3, female white New Orleanina from Lakeview, 73 years old, December 8, 2009.
10. Richard Campanella, Tulane University, New Orleans, expert interview on December 10, 2009.
11. Campanella, *Dilemma.*
12. U.S. Green Building Council, "Dutch Dialogues: New Orleans architects look to the Netherlands for ideas on living with water," http://plus.usgbc.org/dutch-dialogues/ accessed 17 March 2017.
13. Dim Coumou and Stefan Rahmstorf, "A Decade of Weather Extremes," *Nature Climate Change* 2 (2012); Stefan Rahmstorf and Dim Coumou, "Increase of Weather Extremes in a Warming World," *Proceedings of the National Academy of Sciences* 108, no. 44 (2011); Andra J. Reed et al., "Increased Threat of Tropical Cyclones and Coastal

Flooding to New York City during the Anthropogenic Era," *Proceedings of the National Academy of Sciences* 112, no. 41 (2015).

14. Although there is speculation that expanding (warming) ocean watermasses might push plate tectonics. C.f. Simon Lamb and Paul Davis, "Cenozoic Climate Change as a Possible Cause for the Rise of the Andes," *Nature* 425 (2003); Maya Tolstoy, "Mid-ocean ridge eruptions as a climate valve," *Geophysical Research Letters* 42, no. 5 (2015).

15. Kevin J. E. Walsh et al., "Tropical Cyclones and Climate Change," *Wiley Interdisciplinary Reviews: Climate Change* 7, no. 1 (2016), 71–73.

16. Kerry A. Emanuel, "Downscaling CMIP5 Climate Models Shows Increased Tropical Cyclone Activity over the 21st Century," *Proceedings of the National Academy of Sciences* 110, no. 30 (2013), 12219.

17. See, e.g., the early stages of the debate on adaptation to climate change: W. Neil Adger, Nigel W. Arnell, and Emma L. Tompkins, "Adapting to Climate Change: Perspectives across Scales," *Global Environmental Change* 15, no. 2 (2005).

18. The IPCC, an international congregation of scientists assessing the science on climate change, was founded in 1988 to provide a scientific basis for policymaking with regard to climate change. It informs the international process of negotiating climate change policy through the United Nations Framework Convention on Climate Change (UNFCCC), which was founded in 1992. Adaptation to climate change as a policy-relevant subject has arisen within this context and time. IPCC, "IPCC Factsheet. What Is the IPCC?," World Meteorological Organization (WMO). Retrieved 16 July 2018 from https://www.ipcc.ch/news_and_events/docs/factsheets/FS_what_ipcc.pdf. See also Eleonora Rohland, "Adapting to Hurricanes: A Historical Perspective on New Orleans from Its Foundation to Hurricane Katrina, 1718–2005," *Wiley Interdisciplinary Reviews: Climate Change* OnlineFirst (2017), 2.

19. Anthony Oliver-Smith, "Peru's Five Hundred Year Earthquake: Vulnerability in Historical Context," in *Disasters, Development and Environment,* ed. Ann Varley (Chichester, UK: John Wiley & Sons, 1994), 34–40. A further important influence for the scope of this book was Greg Bankoff, *Cultures of Disaster: Society and Natural Hazard in the Philippines* (London: Routledge Curzon, 2003).

20. Karl Fuchs and Friedemann Wenzel, *Erdbeben. Instabilität von Megastädten. Eine wissenschaftlich-technische Herausforderung für das 21. Jahrhundert,* Schriften der Mathematisch-naturwissenschaftlichen Klasse der Heidelberger Akademie der Wissenschaften (Berlin: Springer-Verlag, 2000), 22; Christian Pfister, "'The Monster Swallows You': Disaster Memory and Risk Culture in Western Europe, 1500–2000," *RCC Perspectives* 1 (2011), 15–16.

21. Franz Mauelshagen, "Disaster and Political Culture in Germany since 1500," in Mauch and Pfister, *Natural Disasters,* 44.

22. Marcy Rockman, "New World with a New Sky: Climatic Variability, Environmental Expectations, and the Historical Period Colonization of Eastern North Carolina," *Historical Archaeology* 44 (2010), 4–5; Marcy Rockman, "Knowledge and Learning in the Archaeology of Colonization," in *Colonization of Unfamiliar Landscapes: The Archaeology of Adaptation,* ed. Marcy Rockman and James Steele (New York: Routledge, 2003), 15.

23. Anthony Oliver-Smith, "Global Changes and the Definition of Disaster," in *What Is a Disaster: Perspectives on the Question,* ed. Enrico L. Quarantelli (London: Routledge, 1998), 178.

24. Kerry Emanuel, *Divine Wind: The History and Science of Hurricanes* (Oxford: Oxford University Press, 2005).
25. Jeffrey P. Donnelly et al., "Climate forcing of unprecedented intense-hurricane activity in the last 2000 years," *Earth's Future* 3, no. 2 (2015); Michael E. Mann et al., "Atlantic Hurricanes and Climate over the Past 1500 Years," *Nature* 460, no. August 13 (2009).
26. For a research summary of the field of climate impact research see Franz Mauelshagen, *Klimageschichte der Neuzeit 1500—1900,* Geschichte kompakt (Darmstadt, Germany: WBG, 2010), 19–20.
27. Caesurae have been marked by societal learning processes, in particular. See Christian Pfister, "Learning from Nature-Induced Disasters. Theoretical Considerations and Case Studies from Western Europe," in Mauch and Pfister, *Natural Disasters.*
28. For studies from historians see Mauelshagen, "Disaster," Bankoff, *Cultures,* and Raymundo Padilla Lozoya and Myriam de la Parra Arellano, " Metodología, métodos, técnicas. Sistematización de la recurrencia de amenazas naturales y desastres en el estado de Colima, México," *Estudios sobre las Culturas Contemporáneas* 21, no. 3 (2015). For an anthropological perspective see Oliver-Smith, "Earthquake"; for studies by historical geographers see Georgina H. Endfield and Isabel Fernández Tejedo, "Decades of Drought, Years of Hunger: Archival Investigations of Multiple Year Droughts in Late Colonial Chihuahua," *Climatic Change* 75, no. 4 (2006); Karl W. Butzer and Georgina H. Endfield, "Critical perspectives on historical collapse," *Proceedings of the National Academy of Sciences* 109, no. 10 (2012); Matthew J. Hannaford and David J. Nash, "Climate, history, society over the last millennium in southeast Africa," *Wiley Interdisciplinary Reviews: Climate Change* (2016); George Adamson, "Institutional and community adaptation from the archives: A study of drought in western India, 1790–1860," *Geoforum* 55 (2014); James L. Wescoat, "Water, Climate, and the Limits of Human Wisdom: Historical-Geographic Analogies Between Early Mughal and Modern South Asia," *Professional Geographer* 66, no. 3 (2014).
29. Stuart B. Schwartz, *Sea of Storms: A History of Hurricanes in the Greater Caribbean from Columbus to Katrina* (Princeton, NJ: Princeton University Press, 2015).
30. Richard Campanella, "Disaster and Response in an Experiment Called New Orleans, 1700s–2000s," *Oxford Research Encyclopedias: Natural Hazard Science* (2016); J. Donald Hughes, "New Orleans: An Environmental History of Disaster," in *Natural Resources, Sustainability and Humanity: A Comprehensive View,* ed. Angela Mendonca, Ana Cunha, and Ranjan Chakrabarti (Dordrecht, Netherlands: Springer, 2012); Paulette Guilbert Martin, "Les Ouragans de Louisiane de 1717 à 1750 et Leurs Effets sur la Vie des Colons," *Revue de Louisiane/Louisiana Review* 4, no. 2 (1975).
31. Christopher Morris, *The Big Muddy: An Environmental History of the Mississippi and its Peoples, from Hernando de Soto to Hurricane Katrina* (Oxford: Oxford University Press, 2012); Campanella, *Dilemma.*
32. The term "disaster migration" gained prominence in the aftermath of Hurricane Katrina in 2005. Anthropologist Anthony Oliver-Smith used it in in his article "Disasters and Forced Migration," cf. Anthony Oliver-Smith, "Disasters and Forced Migration in the 21st Century," *Understanding Katrina: Perspectives from the Social Sciences* [website] (2006), http://understandingkatrina.ssrc.org/Oliver-Smith/.
33. For the United States, William O. Walker III noted that many scholarly works dealing with national security and foreign relations from a historical point of view tended to

concentrate on World War II exclusively. Walker challenges this scholarship by taking the history of national security back to the very formation of the United States. William O. Walker, *National Security and Core Values in American History* (New York: Cambridge University Press, 2009), xi. For foundational texts on states of emergency see Jacques Derrida, "Force of Law: The Mystical Foundation of Authority," in *Deconstruction and the Possibility of Justice,* ed. Cornell Drucilla, Michael Rosenfeld, and David Gray Carlson (New York: Routledge, 1992); Michel Foucault, "Governmentality," in *The Foucault Effect: Studies in Governmentality,* ed. Graham Burchell, Colin Gordon, and Peter Miller (Chicago: Univeristy of Chicago Press, 1991); Giorgio Agamben, *State of Exception* (Chicago: University of Chicago Press, 2005).

34. Existing studies have focused on the role of Roman emperors in recreating order in the aftermath of disasters; "good government" in medieval Italian city republics and German imperial cities after the occurrence of flood disasters; the role of the bubonic plague in early modern European state building, and in a wider sense also the formation of a "secure society" in relation to fire disasters and insurance in the early modern German territories. Cf. Martin Dinges, "Pest und Staat," in *Neue Wege in der Seuchengeschichte,* ed. Martin Dinges and Thomas Schlich (Stuttgart, Germany: Steiner, 1995); Mischa Meier, "Roman Emperors and 'Natural Disasters' in the First Century A.D.," in *Historical Disasters in Context: Science, Religion, and Politics,* ed. Andrea Janku, Gerrit Jasper Schenk, and Franz Mauelshagen (New York: Routledge, 2012); Gerrit Jasper Schenk, "Managing Natural Hazards: Environment, Society, and Politics in Tuscany and the Upper Rhine Valley in the Renaissance (ca. 1270–1570)," in Janku, Schenk, and Mauelshagen, *Historical Disasters in Context*; Cornel Zwierlein, *Der gezähmte Prometheus. Feuer und Sicherheit zwischen Früher Neuzeit und Moderne* (Göttingen, Germany: Vandenhöck und Ruprecht, 2011).

35. The German environmental historian Uwe Lübken is one of the few historians who has worked extensively on the history of the National Flood Insurance Program (NFIP), see Uwe Lübken, "Die Natur der Gefahr. Zur Geschichte der Überschwemmungsversicherung in Deutschland und den USA," *Behemoth: A Journal on Civilisation* 1, no. 3. Special Issue: Surviving Catastrophes (Anne Dölemeyer, Hg.) (2008); Uwe Lübken, *Die Natur der Gefahr. Überschwemmungen am Ohio River im neunzehnten und zwanzigsten Jahrhundert* (Göttingen, Germany: Vandenhoeck & Ruprecht, 2014), 278–91. There is a chapter on the NFIP in Robert Hinshaw's biography of Gilbert F. White, which focuses on White's role in the evolution of the program. Robert E. Hinshaw, *Living with Nature's Extremes: The Life of Gilbert Fowler White* (Boulder, CO: Johnson Books, 2006), 153–70. See also Craig Colten's chapter on the development of flood insurance and the NFIP. Craig E. Colten, *Southern Waters: The Limits to Abundance* (Baton Rouge: Louisiana State University Press, 2014), chap. 3.

CHAPTER 1

Adaptation, Knowledge, and Hurricanes in History

Adaptation as a Relative Concept

Although today adaptation is being used in a variety of scientific and every-day contexts, the concept has gained prominence mainly in climate change research during the past fifteen years or so.[1] That is, it has been most commonly used by the natural and social sciences and less so by the humanities. If they engaged with the term at all, environmental historians so far have either used adaptation synonymously with adjustment, or have refrained entirely from using the concept, owing, it seems, to a certain unease with its roots in evolutionary biology. Specifically, the unease in applying the concept to human societies or cultures has been directed toward the problem of free will and the environmental determinism perceived to be inherent in adaptation's nineteenth-century, biological understanding. And although not determinist in the nineteenth-century sense just mentioned, climate change adaptation and social scientific disaster research, in particular, today operate with a pre-conception of adaptation as inherently positive and/or successful that renders the concept inoperable for historical research.[2]

It is important to note that the IPCC and climate change adaptation research's understanding of adaptation usually assume a global perspective that encompasses a large variety of climatic phenomena (i.e., the novel occurrence or increase of slow- as well as rapid-onset extreme events, changing rainfall patterns and temperatures) and, consequently, an equally large set of adaptation options. In this book I focus on adaptation to a recurring natural hazard (that could be influenced by global climate change) rather than on historical climate variability itself. However, since climate change may express itself locally in an increase or intensification in extreme events such as hurricanes, the two perspectives are obviously related.

The 2007 IPCC report defined adaptation as "the adjustment in natural or human systems in response to actual or expected climatic stimuli or their effects, which moderates harm or exploits beneficial opportunities."[3] While the 2014 update of the report added that adaptation may also occur as "unplanned actions,"[4] the most striking lacuna in the IPCC's definition of adaptation, however, is its lack of a notion of time and adaptation as a process. In other words, the fact that those "adjustments . . . to climatic stimuli" do not occur in a temporal vacuum but with reference to past experiences (the future of the past) is blanked out entirely. Including adaptation as unplanned actions almost as an afterthought, the 2014 report has not changed the main definition or the research focus on adaptation as a conscious, planned, and policy-driven process. Applied to the past, it will capture only a fraction of adaptive processes and practices and it will certainly only superficially answer the question of limits and barriers to adaptation.[5] Part of the problem is that the IPCC's definition is based on challenge-and-response and rational choice theory, two approaches with a very limited understanding of individual—let alone societal or collective—action. Adjustments to stimuli (challenge-and-response theory) assumes a linear, sequential understanding of time and human action with no room for synchronicity or contingency, which is often involved in societal coping with the effects of extreme events, as I will show throughout this book. It might be difficult to identify beneficial opportunities (rational choice theory) unambiguously across time since norms and values are subject to change and because they differ according to social stratification, race, and ethnicity.

I thus propose to expand the current, present-focused understanding of adaptation to *adaptation as a relative concept* with regard to time, space, and sociocultural context (including social stratification). While the most basic tenement of wanting to preserve life and property from harm probably holds true across all levels of society, the ways in which different strata of society— and even different genders within society—could and can exploit beneficial opportunities to protect themselves is at the core of a relative conception of adaptation.[6] Moreover, attention to the fact that disaster impacts and our perception of them can vary with regard to social stratification, ethnic, cultural, and religious background helps solve the problem of teleology.

According to the IPCC's understanding, if adaptation is successful—that is, harm is moderated and beneficial opportunities are exploited—society is improving. History, in countless studies, belies this linear narrative, however. In the 1970s historical ecologists introduced the term "maladaptation" to account for unsuccessful endeavors to adjust to a changing environment.[7] Yet, this binary again introduces an underlying value framework that is temporally and culturally bound into the analysis that historians should refrain from in order to avoid anachronistic analyses in their narratives. Thus, in order not to introduce another normative term but still be able to account for the "negative" outcomes of adaptation, following William H. McNeill, I suggest considering vulnerability the flipside of adaptation in such a way that one cannot exist without the other. In *The Global Condition*, McNeill expressed this interdependence of adaptation and vulnerability by suggesting this nexus worked almost like a natural law. He called it the "conservation of catastrophe," explaining that "every gain in precision in the coordination of human activity and every heightening of efficiency in production were matched by a new vulnerability to breakdown."[8] Considering adaptation and vulnerability as coevolving phenomena may prevent linear success narratives of adaptation and helps highlighting the complexity and contingency of human–environment interaction over time.

"Hurricane Knowledge" and "Hurricane Science" across Time

As mentioned above, the IPCC definition of adaptation does not include a notion of knowledge, experience, or learning. By dislodging the concept from its current climate change environment and taking it to a historical–colonial first contact situation, the centrality of knowledge for adaptation becomes immediately apparent, however. In the case of Louisiana (as in many other cases in the colonial Americas) we have ample record of such a first contact situation by European colonials with the native population and the unfamiliar environment and climate of the New World.[9] The Canadian brothers Pierre Le Moyne d'Iberville and Jean-Baptiste Le Moyne de Bienville (hereafter Iberville and Bienville) led the first small groups of settlers from France to the Gulf Coast, founding Biloxi and Mobile in 1699 and 1702.[10] From the documents they left behind, we learn about their interactions with the indigenous population regarding provisions as well as suitable sites for settlement. In the case of New Orleans (1718) and the Mississippi Delta, these communications also included information about the flood hazard and the flood-proneness of specific sites.[11] These historical records make evident the importance of local environmental knowledge for the establishment of European colonies in the New World—regardless of the fact that Louisiana was a comparatively late colonial endeavor.

As far as this local environmental knowledge concerns hurricanes, I am referring to this specific body of knowledge with the term "hurricane knowledge," since until the early nineteenth century it remained just that, the local and practical knowledge of specific groups of people, rather than a science sustained by experts. It is only in the 1950s that meteorologist Herbert Riehl called the field "tropical meteorology."[12] The distinction between hurricane knowledge and science is crucial for a history of adaptation to hurricanes, since it helps to make visible the role of indigenous or local knowledge.[13] In the case of European colonists in the Caribbean and on the Gulf Coast, this body of knowledge became the basis from which a scientific treatment of the phenomenon could grow in the first place.

It is not by coincidence that I have mentioned the Caribbean and Louisiana in one breath several times already. The two regions were connected by the

mercantilist trading system of the Spanish and French empires, in particular. In *Building the Devil's Empire,* Shannon Dawdy even speaks of the Mississippi–Caribbean world. According to the anthropologist, the colonial trade
(and smuggling) system that evolved between New Orleans and the Caribbean
ports was using the same routes as ancient indigenous trade networks.[14] The
importance of this wider (Circum-) Caribbean trade context in the aftermath
of hurricane impacts for provisioning the city of New Orleans will be explored
in more detail in chapters 2 and 3. However, with regard to knowledge and
adaptation, the Caribbean indigenous people's knowledge about hurricanes
was the cradle for the European understanding of the phenomenon. The Dominican friar Bartolomé de las Casas, for example, in his *Historia de las Indias*
recorded the second hurricane that affected the island of Hispaniola in October 1495, in which four ships were lost by "a great tempest which the Indians
in their language call huracán, and which we now all call huracanes, which we
have, at sea or on the ground, almost all of us experienced."[15] Hence, the beginnings of the adoption of the term *"huracán"* into first the Spanish and later
the French, English, and even German languages.

Apart from borrowing the Taíno term to describe these violent storms,
the Spanish and French colonists of the Caribbean also relied on indigenous
knowledge in order to know if a hurricane was approaching. With regard to
adaptation to hurricanes and reducing harm to life and property, being able to
tell the signs of approaching cyclones was of course a desirable thing. According to a seventeenth-century account by French Dominican friar Jean-Baptiste
du Tertre, French settlers in the Antilles believed "that the savages notice it
[the coming of a hurricane] a long time in advance & that they are warned by
their *Rioches* or *Maboyas*;[16] so much so that since these Islands were settled,
there has hardly been a hurricane, which the savages did not predict. For me,
I believe these are pure fables; . . . salty rainwater is an infallible prognostic for
[hurricanes]."[17]

Clearly, as a Dominican missionary, du Tertre had to distance himself from
what he saw as the Amerindian practice of consulting spirits in order to predict hurricanes and instead based his observations on the careful examination of natural phenomena. Yet, it emerges from du Tertre's description that
colonizers of the Caribbean at the end of the seventeenth century were still
strongly relying on the local environmental knowledge held by the indigenous
population.

Today, the globally used term for hurricanes is "tropical cyclone," which is
different from mid-latitude cyclones or low-pressure systems of the temperate
zones. The word "hurricane" is hence the regional term for tropical cyclones,
in use mainly in the tropical North Atlantic. "Typhoon" is the regional name
used in the western North Pacific and "tropical cyclone" or "cyclonic storm" in
the South Pacific and the Indian Oceans. Today, a tropical cyclone is defined

as a "nonfrontal synoptic-scale (200–2000 km in diameter) low-pressure system originating over tropical or subtropical waters with organized convection (i.e., rain shower or thunderstorm activity) and definite cyclonic surface wind circulation."[18] The latter has to be at least 74 miles per hour (120 kilometers per hour) in order for the system to qualify as a tropical cyclone/hurricane and for the Saffir/Simpson scale to come into play.[19] Civil engineer Herbert Saffir developed the hurricane intensity scale in 1969 in order to assess hurricane damage and provide a comparison between different hurricane strengths in different locations around the world. The scale consists of five levels of storm intensity that are based on the increasing structural damage that occurs with growing wind speeds. To these five categories Robert Simpson, then director of the National Hurricane Center, added storm surge potential and the central air pressures that are related with different wind speeds—hence the name Saffir/Simpson scale.[20] Within the Saffir/Simpson scale a differentiation is usually made by tropical meteorologists, hurricane forecasters, and (re-)insurers between hurricanes and major hurricanes, a status assigned to hurricanes that are Categories 3 to 5.[21]

Considering the above, the present-day definition of hurricanes appears to be rather straightforward. However, what are the specific challenges of dealing with tropical cyclones, or, to put it differently, what differentiates hurricanes from other natural hazards, such as floods, fires, or earthquakes? As opposed to floods and fires, but very much like earthquakes, hurricanes cannot be prevented. That is, humans cannot modify them in such a way as to stop them from occurring.[22] This may sound banal, but it is an important fact with regard to the understanding of adaptation to natural hazards. In their book chapter "Social Choice in Dealing with Hurricanes," Mary Frances Myers and Gilbert F. White suggest three approaches to coping with hurricanes: modifying the hazard, modifying susceptibility to the hazard, and modifying the impact of the hazard.[23] Myers's and White's options two and three in fact represent instances of adaptation, even though they do not use the term. If modifying a hazard is impossible—as with hurricanes—humans adapt by changing their own behavior.

Furthermore, before radar or satellite imagery and upper air measuring networks were developed, it was impossible to see hurricanes as we do today. Tropical cyclones are such large-scale systems that they cannot be observed in the same way as tornadoes or water spouts. Such smaller whirlwind phenomena are observable in their paths over land or water. The vortex of a hurricane, which looks so awe-inspiring on aerial photography or satellite images, is not visible as a whole from the ground due to its scale. Of course, its effect is physically noticeable as changing wind directions, and—at the passing of the eye across the observer—as an eerie and deceptive stillness of wind and sound, sometimes accompanied by glimpses of a blue sky, followed by a sudden recommencement of the storm. In other words, before the technological advances of the twentieth and twenty-first centuries, long-term experience with the specific tropical environment in which hurricanes occur was required in order for people to single out the meteorological signs that indicated the approach of such storms. It took Caribbean colonial societies (Cuban Jesuits of Spanish origin, to be precise) until the 1870s to produce their first accurate hurricane forecast that was capable of saving lives. The indigenous Taíno and Arawak people, on the other hand, seem to have had an intricate understanding of hurricanes that even included their counterclockwise gyration—a factor Europeans only started discussing in the 1830s. It became known and published under the name of Buys Ballot's Law in 1857.[24] Unfortunately, the Jesuits' skill—a combination of physical theory, calculations, and meticulous meteorological observation—was lost to their American contemporaries until the technology spawned by two world wars allowed for the real-time detection and tracking of hurricanes. Only the making visible of the phenomenon of hurricanes enabled their forecast and hence the most important impact mitigation strategy with regard to hurricanes—evacuation.

A second challenge for past as well as present societies is that hurricanes are a multi-hazard. That is, apart from producing wind velocities of more than 155 miles per hour (250 kilometers per hour) and corresponding damage at Category 5, hurricanes, through their forward motion, also produce a storm surge the size of which depends on the cyclone's wind speed.[25] Considering the low-lying (and in the twenty-first century densely populated) coastlines of the Gulf of Mexico, storm surge is almost more of a threat to the built environment than are the high winds.[26] As if those two hazards were not enough, hurricanes also generate torrential and long-lasting rainfall in the course of their condensation process. Hurricane precipitation does not impact only the coastal area where a hurricane made landfall, but often also occurs farther inland, causing flash floods in rivers and landslides in mountain valleys. In other words, inland floods caused by hurricane precipitation are secondary hazards (and disasters) that may significantly enlarge the impact area of a tropical cyclone. Last, hurricanes can also spawn tornadoes, which are short-lived but very destructive whirlwinds that are capable of leveling entire towns in a few minutes.[27]

A third problem is the seasonality, and thus ultimately the frequency of hurricane events; the latter is key for the question of adaptation. The recognition that Atlantic hurricanes occur during the summer months of the year was only firmly established among Europeans after a long-term presence of European colonists in the Antilles. For example, Charles de Rochefort, a French Protestant minister stationed on Tobago during the mid-seventeenth century, noted that hurricanes usually occurred in July, August, and September. He observed furthermore that they used to arrive every seven years or even less frequently, and that since a few years however, they had started to return every two years.[28] Ralph Bohun, an English clergyman who wrote a treatise on winds and hurricanes in 1671, provided the same seasonality as de Rochefort. He found a hurricane that had occurred in October to be "very unusual."[29] On the other hand, Edmund Halley, an English astronomer, stated that they occurred in August, "not much before or after," and that hurricanes were not an annual phenomenon, since sometimes several hit during the same year and sometimes none hit for several years.[30]

So, while it was relatively straight-forward to observe the months of the hurricane season, it was historically much more difficult for scholars to explain why there were years when only few hurricanes occurred and others where a high number of them was recorded. We know today—that is, since about the 1980s—that these shifting patterns are connected to changes in climatic phenomena such as the ENSO, the ITCZ, and the AMO. However, even though eighteenth-century colonists in the Caribbean had noted these shifting frequencies, they could not explain, let alone foresee, them. The fluctuation between seasons with high frequencies of major land-falling hurricanes and those with fewer or none is closely linked to the societal questions of disaster memory and loss mitigation practices. As we will see throughout this book, both, high- as well as low-impact frequencies presented a problem during the first century of Louisiana's existence under French and Spanish rule.

A further factor that was historically difficult to understand was the origin and causation of hurricanes. Early French and Spanish travelers and chroniclers of the Indies all essentially used theories based on the Aristotelian ideas of conflicting winds.[31] Although Ralph Bohun himself called hurricanes a "conspiracy of the winds," his treatise provided an almost encyclopedic overview over the then-existing explanations for the causes of hurricanes.[32] For example, he cited Francis Bacon who had put forth the hypothesis that some "expansive spirits contained in some Minerals," in particular in niter, could exceed the force of hurricanes. Since some French sources Bohun had read mentioned that a hurricane had moved rocks from the top of a mountain "as if they had been blown up with gunpowder," the Englishman surmised that "such wonderfull effects" could not be produced by niter alone but only by a reaction of niter with sulfur. Bohun concluded his treatise by stating that he could not determine for certain the cause of hurricanes, yet, that they could hardly be produced by "the agitation of common vapours or air" alone.[33]

Little progress was made in explaining the generation of tropical cyclones throughout the following century. Buffon's *Histoire Naturelle*, published between 1749 and 1789, featured a chapter on "irregular winds, hurricanes, whirlwinds and other phenomena caused by the agitation of the sea and the air" in its first volume. It was entirely based on Aristotelian meteorology and did not mention Bacon's mineral theory.[34] Similarly, Denis Diderot and Jean le Rond d'Alembert's *Encyclopédie ou dictionnaire raisonné des sciences, des arts et des métiers* (1751–80) had an entry for *ouragan* that explained that it was a very violent storm and that there were different sorts of hurricanes differentiated by the names of *prester, typho, vortex, exhydria,* and *ecnephis*.[35] The first two and the last of those were, in fact, the different sorts of winds described in Aristotle's *Meteorologica*.[36] By reintroducing the terms for meteorological phenomena the ancients had observed in the Mediterranean and in Asia Minor, and by quoting Buffon's rather blurry description of hurricanes, equally based on Aristotelian meteorology, the two encyclopedists demonstrated the difficulty of capturing clearly what those violent phenomena were and how they originated. It is quite striking that Buffon as well as Diderot and D'Alembert, whose publications reflected the state of the art of natural history in the eighteenth century, staunchly represented tropical cyclones in terms of Greek antiquity. This perception started to shift only with what historian Jim Fleming called the American storm controversy during the early nineteenth century (see chapter 3).[37]

The difficulty of defining clearly what a hurricane was, before the instrumental era of the nineteenth century, is also expressed in the term's shifting geographical context of use. A comparative review of three major scientific journals that were founded in the mid-seventeenth century, the *Journal des Sçavans* (1665 to 1933), the *Histoire et mémoires de l'académie royale des sciences* (founded in 1666), and the *Philosophical Transactions of the Royal Society* (1665 to present), showed that, throughout the eighteenth century, in the majority of cases when the term *ouragan* or hurricane was used in those journals, it described a continental European storm and not a tropical cyclone of the Atlantic.[38] In fact, between 1665 and 1780 only one article of the *Transactions* used the term for a scientific analysis of a tropical cyclone.[39] It seems, hence, that on the European continent the term "*ouragan*" or "hurricane" acquired the meaning of a strong (mid-latitude) storm. On the American continent, however, where it had originated, the word "hurricane," though obviously still far from being defined in the same way as today, had kept the definition that winds were blowing from "different points of the compass during the same storm."[40]

With this general state of hurricane knowledge at hand, we could assume that Louisiana's colonial personnel, as well as the first generations of settlers had some knowledge of the phenomenon of hurricanes. However, despite the fact that the French colonials had had twenty years to gather environmental knowledge on the Gulf Coast and in the Mississippi Delta, and despite the fact that they had experienced a hurricane that had hit Dauphin Island (off Mobile Bay) in 1715, the hurricane that hit New Orleans on 12 September 1722 apparently came as a surprise for the colonial officials, planters, and even more so for a large part of the only recently arrived German settlers and enslaved Africans. While the French term for hurricane, *ouragan,* was used in the colonial correspondence,[41] the Natchez planter Antoine Simon Le Page du Pratz, an eyewitness to the 1722 hurricane, described it as a "phenomenon . . . that frightened the whole province" and that "no one could guess its cause nor foresee its effects."[42]

Thus, even after establishing the general state of knowledge about hurricanes in the late seventeenth and early eighteenth centuries, French Caribbean and the European republic of letters, Le Page du Pratz's statement of surprise, again raises the question as to what the French colonial officials and settlers who came to the shores of the Gulf Coast at the beginning of the eighteenth century actually knew about hurricanes. Did the vicinity to the hurricane-prone Antilles influence this knowledge? And what role did local (indigenous) knowledge play for the advancement of hurricane knowledge in the eighteenth century?

With regard to the first question it is important to briefly zoom in on New Orleans's demographic composition in order to establish the possible knowledge backgrounds of historical agents present in the colony at the time of the hurricane. The label "French" in the widely used term "French colonial Louisiana" is in fact quite misleading, since a large part of the first settlers who had come to the Gulf Coast with the Iberville expeditions in 1699 and 1700 came from New France.[43] In addition, the colony was populated by (continental) French convicts between 1717 and 1719, a first shipment of enslaved Africans from the Ivory and Gold Coasts in 1719, as well as by German settlers between 1720 and 1721 as a result of John Law's settlement campaign.[44] The 1721 census counted 1,095 people in the colony, including white men, women, and children; white indentured servants; and African and Indian slaves.[45] This count did not include the circa 1,600 Germans who had come to the colony and part of whom had settled at Les Allemands, also known as the German Coast, thirty miles upriver from New Orleans. And of course, about 90 percent of the vast stretch of land the French had named La Louisiane was inhabited by various native nations.[46]

While some of the continental French newcomers, who were mostly from Atlantic port cities such as Caen, Lorient, La Rochelle, Brest, Nantes, and Bordeaux, may have heard of *ouragans* from hear-say, it is quite evident that none of the European colonist groups (nor the 514 enslaved Africans) came from geographical locations that would have prepared them for or made them familiar with the phenomenon of hurricanes.[47] Louisiana's colonial officials, usually drawn from the aristocracy, on the other hand, had completed a military education that included French naval schools. Early-eighteenth-century instruction in navigation would almost certainly have prepared them to recognize tropical cyclones on land and at sea. Hence, the colonial officials' familiarity with and ability to refer to the 1722 storm as an *ouragan*.

The Canadian and French newcomers and the indigenous populations of the Gulf Coast and Mississippi Delta interacted frequently throughout the early eighteenth century in exchanging and trading food and in intercolonial warfare.[48] Also, the French colonial sources clearly indicate that the explorers and early colonists learned from the local indigenous peoples about the Mississippi River's flood regime, however no references were made regarding the transmission of hurricane knowledge from one group to the other. This situation contrasts markedly with the Caribbean islands. This difference in the circulation of environmental knowledge may be obvious considering the fact that the Caribbean archipelago is much more exposed to Atlantic hurricanes than the Gulf Coast around the Mississippi Delta.[49] Given the hurricane experience of the geographically close Caribbean islands, would it not have been possible for contemporaries to infer that if hurricanes could occur there, they might also hit the Louisiana Gulf Coast?

The fact that the historical sources yield no information on the communication of hurricane knowledge between the indigenous population and the French colonials before 1722 could of course merely be a problem of historical records. Maybe such communication did take place but was deemed unimportant because there was no immediate context in which it could have been applied and so it never made it into written correspondence. However, considering that no major hurricane had hit the Mississippi Delta since the arrival of Iberville in 1699,[50] it is possible that, even though the colonial personnel knew of hurricanes occurring in the Caribbean, they simply did not know that these storms might also affect the Gulf Coast. Clearly, if hurricanes were not considered a hazard that could threaten the new colony, there was no reason to communicate about them.

The assumption that contemporaries of the early eighteenth century imagined hurricanes as phenomena restricted to a geographical region is confirmed by seventeenth-century tracts on the climate of the Caribbean islands, some of which we have already encountered. The French Catholic missionary Antoine Biet, who had traveled to French Guyana and Barbados in 1652, for example, stated, "These hurricanes are furious tempests . . . and they reign only around these Antillean islands and in the seas, that surround them." Edmund Halley, in a contribution to the "Philosophical Transactions of the Royal Society" of 1686, also assigned hurricanes geographically to the Caribbean islands, while Ralph Bohun, in his "Origine and Properties of Wind" also included the Philippines into the known realm of hurricane occurrence.[51] Fast-forwarding to an *early-nineteenth-century* statement made by meteorologist William Redfield, we learn that seventeenth- and eighteenth-century Europeans could not yet conceive of hurricanes as forward-moving storm systems. "When accounts of hurricanes were formerly received as occurring at different islands, on various dates, with marked differences also in the direction of the wind it was taken for granted . . . that such accounts, in most cases related to different storms," Redfield remarked in an 1831 article in the *American Journal of Science and Arts*.[52] In other words, until the beginning of the nineteenth century hurricanes were considered discrete, localized events. While it was clear to early-eighteenth-century contemporaries that such storms were typical for the Caribbean islands, no theory or terminology yet existed that could have connected the archipelago and the North American Gulf Coast as a climatic region and hence a common risk zone. Hence, neither early-eighteenth-century settlers on the ground such as Le Page du Pratz, nor European scholars interested in the science of winds and hurricanes could draw the conclusion that hurricanes occurring in the Caribbean might also threaten the newly settled North American coast of the Gulf of Mexico.

Hurricanes in New Orleans

While eighteenth-century contemporaries puzzled about the shifting frequencies of hurricane occurrences, today we have the advantage of being able to draw on serial observations that were made since the 1850s. This allows for establishing the average hurricane frequency of a place such as New Orleans and provides basic information about the city's risk-proneness. Louisiana climatologists Barry Keim and Robert Muller state that the specific geographical setting of New Orleans, mostly below sea level and between Lake Pontchartrain and the Mississippi River, makes it "more prone for hurricane disasters than any other major American city." On the other hand, New Orleans is situated fifty miles inland so that hurricanes and tropical storms are usually weakened when they hit the city.[53] Historically, the wetlands that surround New Orleans were more extensive than they are today, and they were, in fact, growing through sedimentation. Hence, they added to the coastline's brake effect against hurricanes. Keim and Muller established that for the 157-year period between 1851 and 2007 ninety-six tropical storms and hurricanes threatened New Orleans, which amounts, on average, to slightly more than once every other year. Of those ninety-six threats, thirty-eight were tropical storms (less than 74 mph wind speeds) that struck New Orleans directly, and fifteen were Category 1 and 2 hurricanes that affected the city. No major hurricanes—Categories 3 to 5—hit New Orleans during this period, likely a result of the city's relatively protected inland location.[54] As a comparison, the coastal town of Boothville, Louisiana—southeast below New Orleans—was struck by forty-two tropical storms, eighteen Category 1 and 2 hurricanes, and seven major hurricanes in the same period.[55] The fact that no major hurricanes and "only" Category 1 and 2 hurricanes hit New Orleans should not be taken as evidence that those events were easily dealt with. Hurricane Katrina was "merely" a

Category 2 storm at landfall and it did not even strike New Orleans directly. In other words, such statistical data are helpful to gain an overview over the hazard-proneness of an area, but in order to assess the actual societal impact of a historical hurricane event, we need to research individual cases up close.

The official meteorological hurricane record reaches back only to 1850, meaning that meteorologists and climatologists rely on the work of historians, historical climatologists, and paleotempestologists to uncover earlier hurricane events from human and natural archives in order to complete their data series. However, these historical reconstructions are fraught with their own problems of homogenizing and calibrating diverse sets of data. For historians dealing with human archives, the question how people, before the technological advancements of the twentieth century, determined that they were experiencing a hurricane and not an ordinary storm, is crucial. Precisely because of the relatively long-lasting definitional blurriness, it is important to verify whether what is called a hurricane in historical observations (in particular for the pre-instrumental era)[56] was in fact a hurricane. Such verification can be obtained from historical hurricane chronologies compiled by historical climatologists.[57] The most recent chronology by Michael Chenoweth is based on historical data from ship logs, diaries, and newspaper reports that he cross-referenced with three earlier chronologies[58] as well as with data from two contemporary researchers.[59] In particular, ship log data are a valuable source for verification since on-ship measurements of wind speed and, after the invention of barometers, air pressure were taken three times a day by experienced personnel trained in using a relatively consistent vocabulary for their observations.[60] Land observations of hurricanes, on the other hand, are usually made after the fact and with a focus on losses rather than on the storm's meteorological properties. Descriptions of damage to houses, ships, and trees, nevertheless, can be useful for historical climatologists and climate historians for estimations of hurricane strength. Yet it is the historical nautical vocabulary that can readily be translated into the Beaufort scale, and that ultimately allows for a transformation of descriptive into numerical data.[61]

Thus, the following is a brief walk through New Orleans's eighteenth-century hurricane timeline (figure 1.1) with data gleaned from the French and Spanish colonial records and tested against the existing chronologies mentioned above. The first hurricane recorded by French colonials on the Louisiana Gulf Coast occurred in October 1715 at Dauphin Island, which is a barrier island before Mobile Bay, while the first hurricane to affect New Orleans made landfall seven years later on 12 September 1722.[62] In her article on the French period hurricanes, Paulette Guilbert Martin finds a 1717 hurricane that I cannot confirm, either from the manuscripts or from Chenoweth's or Millas's hurricane chronologies.[63] As we can see in figure 1.1, the hurricanes that occurred

Figure 1.1. Chronology of hurricanes that hit New Orleans during the eighteenth century, with other important extreme events and disasters.

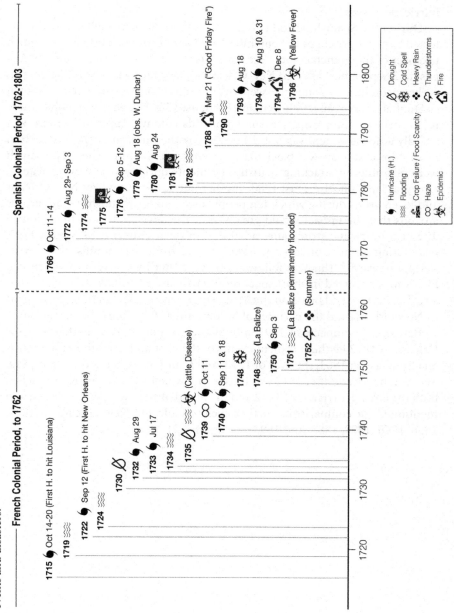

under French rule (1718–62) are on average spaced out by a decade each, except for the occasional back-to-back event, or seasons with several consecutive hurricane strikes.[64]

During the Spanish period (1762–1800), the Louisiana Gulf Coast was affected by two hurricanes in September and October 1766, hampering Spanish takeover of the French colony. Six years later, a late August hurricane (29 August to 3 September) affected New Orleans and Mobile, while in 1776 it was an early season June cyclone that swept over the city.[65] A severe hurricane, known as Dunbar's Hurricane, followed on 18 August 1779.[66] It was "so terrible, there is no memory [of a similar calamity] in this colony." Apparently, there was "hardly a house which was not destroyed" by the hurricane. The destruction of all ships and boats was particularly severely felt at a time when the Spanish were planning on attacking British settlements upriver from New Orleans.[67] One year later, on 24 August 1780, another hurricane swept over New Orleans and its environs during which ten people died and the Spanish Intendant was anxious that the impact would greatly slow the development of the colony.[68] The next hurricane struck after a lapse of thirteen years, on 18 August 1793, devastating an area of seventy-seven leagues from the mouths of the Mississippi upward.[69] This was followed one year later by a season in which two hurricanes occurred in short succession on 10 and 31 August 1794, again destroying harvest and boats on the Mississippi, causing devastation and despair in New Orleans and the parishes of St. Bernard and Barataria below the city.[70]

Between the impacts of 1793 and 94 and the next hurricane that hit New Orleans in 1812 lie the turbulent events of the Haitian Revolution, the Louisiana Purchase in 1803, the War of 1812, and Louisiana statehood, also in 1812. The next hurricane after 1812 was the Great Barbados Hurricane of 1831 when both the Great Hurricane of 1812 and the Flood of 1816 were remembered and mentioned for comparison. Further cyclones affected New Orleans in 1837, 1856, 1860, 1879, 1888, and 1893 (see figure 1.2).

Figure 1.2. Chronology of hurricanes that hit New Orleans during the nineteenth and twentieth centuries, as well as other important extreme events and disasters.

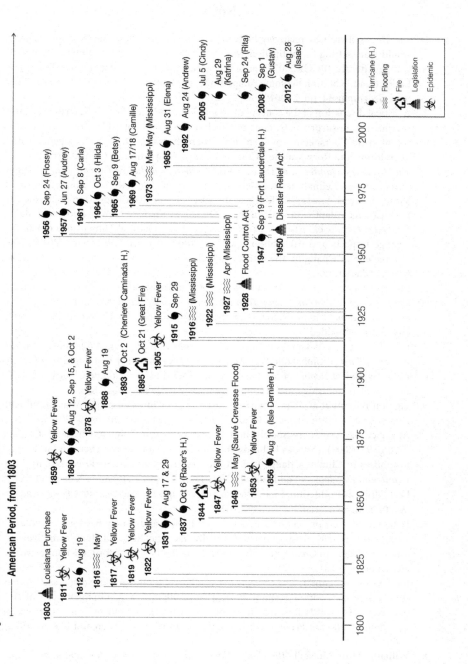

Notes

1. As long as there was relatively high uncertainty as to when exactly climate change would start setting in, mitigation was the prominent concept of climate change research. After the IPCC's 2007 Report, however, a shift toward adaptation is discernible. Lesley Head, "Cultural Ecology: Adaptation—Retrofitting a Concept?," *Progress in Human Geography* 34, no. 2 (2010), 4.

2. A critical discussion of the concept of adaptation in relation to climate change is rather recent, and, unsurprisingly, does not include environmental historians. For a most recent critical perspective by historical geographers, see Stavros Mavrogenis, Petros Theodorou, and Rory Walshe, "Climate Change Adaptation: A Critical Approach," in *The Routledge Handbook of Disaster Risk Reduction Including Climate Change Adaptation*, ed. Ilan Kelman, Jessica Mercer, and JC Gaillard (New York: Routledge, 2017); Virginia García Acosta, "Building on the Past. Disaster Risk Reduction Including Climate Change Adaptation in the Longue Durée," in Kelman, Mercer, and Gaillard, *The Routledge Handbook*. Also see W. Neil Adger et al., "Cultural Dimensions of Climate Change Impacts and Adaptation," *Nature Climate Change* 3, February (2013); Noel Castree et al., "Changing the Intellectual Climate," *Nature Climate Change* 4 (2014); Head, "Adaptation."

3. Martin Parry et al., eds., *Climate Change 2007: Impacts, Adaptation and Vulnerability: Contribution of Working Group II to the Fourth Assessment Report of the Intergovernmental Panel on Climate Change* (Cambridge, UK: Cambridge University Press, 2007), 869 (emphasis added).

4. I. R. Noble et al., "Adaptation Needs and Options," in *Impacts, Adaptation, and Vulnerability. Part A: Global and Sectoral Aspects. Contribution of Working Group II to the Fifth Assessment Report of the Intergovernmental Panel on Climate Change*, ed. C. B. Field, et al. (Cambridge, UK: Cambridge University Press, 2014), 838.

5. E.g. Jon Barnett et al., "From Barriers to Limits to Climate Change Adaptation: Path Dependency and the Speed of Change," *Ecology and Society* 20, no. 3 (2015); W. Neil Adger et al., "Are There Social Limits to Adaptation to Climate Change?," *Climatic Change* 93 (2009); Douglas K. Bardsley, "Limits to Adaptation or a Second Modernity? Responses to Climate Change Risk in the Context of Failing Socio-ecosystems," *Environment, Development and Sustainability* 17, no. 1 (2015); Johanna Nalau and Walter Leal Filho, "Introduction: Limits to Adaptation," in *Limits to Climate Change Adaptation* (Cham, Switzerland: Springer, 2018).

6. For a recent, Katrina-related article see Paul Kadetz and Nancy B. Mock, "Problematizing Vulnerability: Unpacking Gender, Intersectionality, and the Normative Disaster Paradigm," in *Creating Katrina, Rebuilding Resilience* (Oxford, UK: Butterworth-Heinemann, 2018).

7. John William Bennett, *The Ecological Transition: Cultural Anthropology and Human Adaptation* (New York: Pergamon Press, 1976), 260; M. Watts, "On the Poverty of Theory: Natural Hazards Research in Context," in *Interpretations of Calamity from the Viewpoint of Human Ecology*, ed. Kenneth Hewitt (Boston: Allen and Unwin, 1983), 236.

8. William Hardy McNeill, *The Global Condition: Conquerors, Catastrophes, and Community* (Princeton, NJ: Princeton University Press, 1992), 148.

9. Karen Ordahl Kupperman, "Apathy and Death in Early Jamestown," *Journal of American History* 66, no. 1 (1979); Sam White, "'Shewing the Difference betweene Their Conjuration, and Our Invocation on the Name of God for Rayne': Weather, Prayer, and Magic in Early American Encounters," *William and Mary Quarterly* 72, no. 1 (2015); Rockman, "New Sky."

10. Jay Higginbotham, *Old Mobile: Fort Louis de la Louisiane, 1702–1711* (Mobile, AL: Museum of the City of Mobile, 1977), 454–55.

11. Pierre Le Moyne d'Iberville, "Mémoire de D'Iberville sur le pays du Mississipi, La Mobile et ses environs, leurs rivières, les peuples qui les habitent, et du commerce qui se pourra faire dans moins de cinq ou six années, en établissant ce pays," in *Découverte par Mer des Bouches du Mississippi et Établissments de Le Moyne D'Iberville sur Le Golfe Du Mexique (1694–1703)* (hereafter *Découverte*), ed. Pierre Margry (Paris: Maisonneuve et Cie., 1881), *Quatrième Partie*, 603ff. See also Commander Sauvole's journal, Sauvole, "Journal Historique de l'établissement des Francais à la Louisiane. Recueil que j'ai pris sur mon journal de ce qui s'est passé de plus remarquable depuis le départ de M. d'Iberville du 3 mai 1699 jusqu'en 1700. [Lettre de Sauvole. Commandant au Biloxi, sur ce qui s'est passé dans l'intervalle du 1er au 2ème voyage de D'Iberville, et Instructions qui lui sont laissées par ce dernier en Mai 1700]," in Magry, *Découverte*, 449ff.

12. Herbert Riehl, *Tropical Meteorology* (New York, : McGraw-Hill, 1954).

13. There seems to be no clear-cut boundary between those different concepts, according to Roy Ellen; Roy F. Ellen and Holly Harris, "Introduction," in *Indigenous Environmental Knowledge and its Transformations: Critical Anthropological Perspectives*, ed. Roy F. Ellen, Peter Parkes, and Alan Bicker (Amsterdam: Harwood, 2000), 2.

14. Shannon Lee Dawdy, *Building the Devil's Empire: French Colonial New Orleans* (Chicago: University of Chicago Press, 2008), 107–10.

15. Bartolomé de las Casas, Feliciano Ramírez de Arellano Fuensanta del Valle, and José León Sancho Rayón, Historia de las Indias, 5 vols., vol. 2 (Madrid: Imprenta de Miguel Ginesta, 1575/1875), 114–15. For the dating of the hurricane see José Carlos Millás and Leonard Pardue, Hurricanes of the Caribbean and adjacent regions, 1492–1800 (Miami, FL: Academy of the Arts and Sciences of the Americas, 1968), 31–35. For an excellent summary of the development of early Spanish colonial hurricane knowledge see Schwartz, Storms, 1–33.

16. Maboya or Mabuya is a Caribbean deity associated with hurricanes; it is sometimes also called the god Huracán or by extension a spirit associated with Huracán. Fernando Ortiz Fernández, *El Huracán, su Mitología y sus Símbolos*, 1st ed. (Mexico City: Fondo de Cultura Económica, 1947), 665. However, in his *Histoire*, du Tertre has a chapter on the "Maboüyas," which turn out to be lizards. He reports that they are called "Maboüyas" (Maboyas) because "it is a name they [the Indians] usually give to everything that scares them." Jean-Baptiste du Tertre, *Histoire générale des Antilles, habitées par les François*, 2 vols., vol. 2 (Paris: Thomas Iolly, 1667), 315.

17. Du Tertre, *Histoire*, 73. A similar account of the English settlers consulting the Indian population on the matter of hurricanes is provided by Captain Langford. Captain Langford and Mr Bonavert, "Captain Langford's Observations of His Own Experience upon Huricanes, and Their Prognosticks. Communicated by Mr. Bonavert," *Philosophical Transactions (1683–1775)* 20 (1698), 407.

18. Barry D. Keim and Robert A. Muller, *Hurricanes of the Gulf of Mexico* (Baton Rouge: Louisiana State University Press, 2009), 56; Emanuel, *Wind*, 21.

19. Keim and Muller, *Hurricanes*, 58, 60. For a detailed description of the generation of hurricanes see ibid., 56–67.

20. Herbert S. Saffir, "Communicating Damage Potentials and Minimizing Hurricane Damage," in *Hurricane! Coping with Disaster: Progress and Challenges Since Galveston, 1900*, ed. Robert Simpson, Richard A. Anthes, Michael Garstang, and Joanne Simpson (Washington, DC: American Geophysical Union, 2003), 155–56.

21. Keim and Muller, *Hurricanes*, 45.

22. An attempt at modifying hurricanes was made during the 1960s when the National Oceanic and Atmospheric Administration (NOAA) carried out project Stormfury, using silver iodide particles to seed hurricane clouds under the assumption that those storms would then disintegrate. The project was discontinued due to a lack of measurable results. Mary Frances Myers and Gilbert F. White, "Social Choice in Dealing with Hurricanes," in Simpson et al., *Coping with Disaster*, 145. See also H. E. Willoughby, D. P. Jorgensen, R. A. Black, and S. L. Rosenthal, "Project STORMFURY. A Scientific Chronicle 1962–1983," *Bulletin of the American Meteorological Society* 66, no. 5 (1985); Joanne Simpson, R. H. Simpson, J. R. Stinson, and J. W. Kidd, "Stormfury Cumulus Experiments. Preliminary Results 1965," *Journal of Applied Meteorology* 5, no. 4 (1966).

23. Myers and White, "Social Choice," 144–47.

24. Ortiz Fernández, *Huracán*, 28–31; *Encyclopedia Britannica Online*, "Buys Ballot's Law," http://www.britannica.com/EBchecked/topic/86881/Buys-Ballots-Law. Before William Ferrel and Buys-Ballot formulated the law, sailors all over the globe over the centuries had noted the general rotation of hurricanes in the northern and southern hemisphere and recorded it in their logbooks, Henry Piddington published it in 1848 in his *Sailor's Hornbook* under the heading "The Law of Storms." Henry Piddington, *The Sailor's Horn-Book for the Law of Storms*, 7th ed. (London: Frederic Norgate, 1848), 6.

25. Saffir, "Damage Potentials," 157.

26. Between 1960 and 2008 the population of the U.S. Gulf Coast increased by 150.2 percent. See Steven G. Wilson and Thomas R. Fischetti, "Coastline Population Trends in the United States: 1960–2008," in *Current Population Reports* (2010), http://www.census.gov/newsroom/releases/archives/population/cb10-76.html., 4.

27. During the 2004 hurricane season several hundred tornadoes were generated by hurricanes. However, tornadoes can also occur as the result of shifting synoptic scale climate patterns such as strong La Niña events (they create cold equatorial Pacific Ocean temperatures, which in turn favor the generation of thunderstorms and tornadoes in the United States) as in April 2011 and March 2012. See Munich Re, *Topics Geo: Natural Catastrophes 2011. Earthquake, Flood, Nuclear Accident. Analyses, Assessments, Positions* (Munich, Germany: Munich Re, 2011), 32–33; Swiss Re, *Sigma: Natural Catastrophes and Man-Made Disasters in 2012. A Year of Extreme Weather Events in the US*, vol. 2 (Zurich, Switzerland: Swiss Re, 2013), 6.

28. Charles de Rochefort, *Histoire Naturelle et Morale des Iles Antilles de l'Amerique. Enrichie de Plusieurs Belles Figures des Raretez les Plus Considerables Qui y Sont d'écrites. Avec un Vocabulaire Caraïbe*, 1st ed. (Rotterdam, Netherlands: Arnout Leers, 1658), 243.

29. Ralph Bohun, *A Discourse Concerning the Origine and Properties of Wind with an Historicall Account of Hurricanes, and other Tempestuous Winds* (Oxford, UK: Printed by W. Hall for Tho. Bowman, 1671), 294.

30. Edmund Halley, "An Historical Account of the Trade Winds, and Monsoons, Observable in the Seas between and Near the Tropicks, with an Attempt to Assign the Phisical Cause of the Said Winds, By E. Halley," *Philosophical Transactions* 16, no. 179–91 (1686), 157.

31. Lopez Medel for example, describes hurricanes as "a competition and antagonism of diverse and opposing winds . . . which happens when from various and opposing parts many and diverse winds concur." Tomás Lopez Medel, De los Tres Elementos. Tratado Sobre la Naturaleza y el Hombre del Nuevo Mundo, ed. Berta Ares Quejia, 1570 ed. (Madrid: Quinto Centenario, 1990), 31. Antoine Biet explains the generation of hurricanes in the same vein: "The four principal [winds] are at the same time in such a strong battle, blowing with such impetuosity each from its side, that the sea . . . is assembled from all four quarters of the earth." Père Antoine Biet, Voyage de la France Equinoxiale en l'Île de Cayenne, Entrepris par les Francais en l'Anné 1652 (Paris: Francois Clouzier, 1664), 286.

32. Bohun, Discourse, 302; Rochefort, Histoire Naturelle, 243.

33. Bohun, Discourse, 299–302.

34. Georges-Louis Leclerc Compte of Buffon, "Preuves de la Théorie de la Terre. Article 15. Des Vents Irréguliers, des Ouragans, des Trombes, et de Quelques Autres Phénomènes Causez par l'Agitation de la Mer et de l'Air," in Buffon, Histoire Naturelle, Générale Et Particulière, Avec La Déscription Du Cabinet Du Roy 1 (1749): 478–501. Accessed 5 April 2013, http://www.buffon.cnrs.fr/. See esp. pp. 487–90.

35. Denis Diderot and Jean le Rond d'Alembert, Encyclopédie, ou Dictionnaire Raisonné des Sciences, des Arts et des Métiers, etc. Chicago: University of Chicago: ARTFL Encyclopédie Project (Spring 2011), (1751–80), http://encyclopedie.uchicago.edu/

36. Aristotle, *Meteorologica*, trans. Erwin Wentworth Webster (Oxford at the Clarendon Press, UK: Oxford University Press, 1923), Book 3.1, 370b, 371a.

37. James Rodger Fleming, Meteorology in America, 1800–1870 (Baltimore: Johns Hopkins University Press, 1990), chap. 2, 23–54. For a discussion of cyclonic winds in Europe see Gisela Kutzbach, The Thermal Theory of Cyclones: A History of Meteorological thought in the Nineteenth Century, ed. Society American Meteorological, Historical Monograph Series (Lancaster, PA: Lancaster Press, 1979), 15.

38. The search was conducted using the full-text digitized versions (on www.gallica.bnf.fr and of the *Transactions* at www.jstor.org) of those journals. However, since not all letters sent from abroad were printed, an in-depth study of the manuscripts as well as the print versions of the journals would be required to reinforce this point. Frank R. Freemon, "American Colonial Scientists Who Published in the 'Philosophical Transactions' of the Royal Society," *Notes and Records of the Royal Society of London* 39, no. 2 (1985), 191.

39. Langford and Bonavert, "Observations." The index of the 1780 supplement to the Philosophical Transactions that covers the issues from the beginning of publication in 1665 to 1780 shows three entries for the key word "hurricane," one of which refers to Captain Langford's "Observations" and the other two of which concern severe storms in Europe. Philosophical Transactions of the Royal Society of London, "Supplement: A

General Index to the Philosophical Transactions, from the First to the End of the Seventieth Volume," *Philosophical Transactions of the Royal Society of London* 70 (1780), 232.

40. William Charles Redfield, "Remarks on the Prevailing Storms of the Atlantic Coast of the North American States," *American Journal of Science and Arts* 20, no. July (1831), 19.

41. Le Blond de La Tour to Directors, 30 September 1722, HNOC, ANOM, Colonies, C13 C 6, fol. 339r; Delorme to Directors, 30 October 1722, HNOC, ANOM, Colonies, C13 C 6, fol. 403r.

42. Antoine Simon Le Page du Pratz, *Histoire de la Louisiane* (Paris: De Bure, la Veuve Delaguette, et Lambert, 1758), 174.

43. In particular, the tables of the first two censuses taken in 1699 and 1700 contain the category "Canadiens." However, later censuses, even if they do not provide lists of Canadian residents, still state the New France origin of individuals. Charles R. Maduell, *The Census Tables for the French Colony of Louisiana from 1699 Through 1732* (Baltimore: Genealogical Pub. Co., 1972), 1–5.

44. Cécile Vidal and Gilles Havard, eds., *Histoire de l'Amérique Française*, revised ed. (Paris: Flammarion, 2008), 151–52; Henry P. Dart, "The First Cargo of African Slaves for Louisiana, 1718," *Louisiana Historical Quarterly* 14, no. 2 (1931), 167. René Le Conte and Glenn R. Conrad, "The Germans in Louisiana in the Eighteenth Century," *Louisiana History: Journal of the Louisiana Historical Association* 8, no. 1 (1967), 68.

45. Diron D'Artaguiette's 1721 Louisiana census encompassed New Orleans, the village of Bayou St. John, the village of Colapissas, the village of Chapitoulas, the village of Gentilly, the village of Cannes Brulées, Petit Dezert, English Turn and Chaouchas. Jay K. Ditchy, "Census of Louisiana in 1721," *Louisiana Historical Quarterly* (1930), 140–41, 176.

46. Conte and Conrad, "Germans," 73, 75, 77; Paul A. Kunkel, "The Indians of Louisiana, about 1700. Their Customs and Manner of Living," in *The French Experience in Louisiana*, ed. Glenn R. Conrad (Lafayette: Center for Louisiana Studies, University of Southwestern Louisiana, 1995). For population estimates of Indian nations in the Mississippi Delta, see Daniel H. Usner, *Indians, Settlers & Slaves in a Frontier Exchange Economy: The Lower Mississippi Valley before 1783* (Chapel Hill: Published for the Institute of Early American History and Culture, Williamsburg, Virginia, by the University of North Carolina Press, 1992), 20–21; James S. Pritchard, *In Search of Empire: The French in the Americas, 1670–1730* (New York: Cambridge University Press, 2004), 7–8.

47. Vidal and Havard, *Amérique Française*, 144.

48. The French were allied with the Choctaw, the Cherokee, the Alabama (including the Talapoosa and the Abihka), the Kawita, the Tunica, the Apalachee, the Houma, and the Arkansas. By the mid-eighteenth century some of those nations had been reduced to as few as sixty warriors, such as the Tunica. Gwendolyn Midlo Hall, *Africans in Colonial Louisiana: The Development of Afro-Creole Culture in the Eighteenth Century* (Baton Rouge: Louisiana State University Press, 1992), 19.

49. Only 31 percent of the hurricanes that occur in the North Atlantic basin are hurricanes that enter the Gulf of Mexico. Keim and Muller, *Hurricanes,* 56.

50. Michael Chenoweth, "A Reasessment of Historical Atlantic Basin Tropical Cyclone Activity, 1700 to 1855," *Climatic Change* 76 (2006), 169–240.
51. Biet, *Voyage,* 285; Halley, "Trade Winds," 157; Bohun, *Discourse,* 256.
52. William Charles Redfield, "Hurricane of August 1831," *American Journal of Science and Arts* 21, no. Oct (1832), 191.
53. Keim and Muller, *Hurricanes,* 131.
54. Ibid., 132. For the hurricane strike model employed by the authors, see ibid., x.
55. Ibid., 135.
56. The general date given for the beginning of the era of instrumental meteorological measurements is ca. 1850 for the European context, when the first national meteorological networks were set up. Mauelshagen, *Klimageschichte der Neuzeit 1500—1900,* 50.
57. Chenoweth, "Reassessment." For hurricanes before 1700 see Millás and Pardue, *Hurricanes.*
58. Andrés Poey y Aguirre, "A Chronological Table Comprising 400 Cyclonic Hurricanes Which Have Occurred in the West Indies and in the North Atlantic within 362 years, from 1493 to 1855," *Journal of the Royal Geographical Society* (London) 25 (1855); Millás and Pardue, *Hurricanes*; David McWilliams Ludlum, *Early American Hurricanes, 1492–1870* (Boston: American Meteorological Society, 1963).
59. Cary J. Mock, "Tropical Cyclone Reconstructions from Documentary Records. Examples for South Carolina, United States," in *Hurricanes and Typhoons: Past, Present, and Future,* ed. R. J. Murnane and K.-B. Liu (New York: Columbia University Press, 2004); Ricardo García-Herrera et al., "New Records of Atlantic Hurricanes from Spanish Documentary Sources," *Journal of Geophysical Research* 110 (2005).
60. Already in 1727, New England mathematician Isaac Greenwood pointed to the value of observations from ship logbooks for hurricane histories. Isaac Greenwood, "A New Method for Composing a Natural History of Meteors Communicated in a Letter to Dr. Jurin, R. S. & Coll. Med. Lond. Soc. By Mr. Isaac Greenwood, Professor of Mathematicks at Cambridge, New-England," *Philosophical Transactions* 35 (1727), 398.
61. On the accuracy of ship log data see Dennis Wheeler, "An Examination of the Accuracy and Consistency of Ships' Logbook Weather Observations and Records," *Climatic Change* 73, no. 1 (2005). On the use of nautical language before the Beaufort Scale, see Dennis Wheeler and Clive Wilkinson, "The Determination of Logbook Wind Force and Weather Terms: The English Case," *Climatic Change* 73, no. 1 (2005); and M. Prieto et al., "Deriving Wind Force Terms from Nautical Reports Through Content Analysis. The Spanish and French Cases," *Climatic Change* 73, no. 1 (2005). For an example of a hurricane reconstruction from (written) historical sources see Cary J. Mock et al., "The Great Louisiana Hurricane of August 1812," *Bulletin of the American Meteorological Society* 91, no. 12 (2010).
62. The colony of Louisiana was hit by at least seven hurricanes between 1715 and 1750. There probably were also tropical storms or weaker hurricanes, but those seven were destructive enough to be recorded. For the Dauphin Island hurricane (which occurred between 14 and 20 October, according to Chenoweth, "Reassessment" (no page no.) in 1715, see Journal de Diron D'Artaguiette, ANF, Colonies, C13 C 2, fol. 198v. For 12 September 1722, see Le Blond de La Tour to Directors, 30 September 1722, HNOC, ANF, Colonies, C13A 6, fol. 339r.

63. However, Governor Jean-Michel de l'Epinay wrote in a 1717 letter to the Superior Council of Louisiana that there had been two *"coups du vent"* (storms) in March, one of which lasted twenty-four hours. The term "hurricane" is not used, however. De l'Epinay further reports that the "ancient habitants" could not remember having experienced such bad winds. It is unlikely that those two storms were hurricanes, since March would be extremely early for tropical cyclones to form. L'Epinay to the Conseil de Ville, 10 May 1717, ANF, Colonies, C13 A 5, fol. 37r and 38r. Under *ouragan*, Menier, Taillemite, and de Forges provide no entry later than 1750 in their index to Louisiana's French Colonial records. Cf. Marie-Antoinette Menier, Etienne Taillemite, and Gilberte de Forges, eds., *Inventaire des Archives Coloniales. Correspondance à l'Arrivée en Provenance de la Louisiane*, 2 vols., vol. 1 (Paris: Archives Nationales, 1976).
64. The hurricane chronology in figure 1.1 is based on the French and Spanish colonial records, thus contains a bias for hurricanes that actually made landfall and were recorded in New Orleans. Hurricanes that occurred at sea and were recorded by sailors' ship logs are not included here.
65. Sherry Johnson, *Climate and Catastrophe in Cuba and the Atlantic World in the Age of Revolution*, Envisioning Cuba (Chapel Hill: University of North Carolina Press, 2011), appx. 1, 204.
66. William Dunbar, "Meteorological Observations, Made by William Dunbar, Esq, at the Forest, Four Miles East of the River Mississippi, in Lat. 31 degrees 28 minutes North, and in Long. 91 degrees 30 minutes West of Greenwich, for the Year 1800," *Transactions of the American Philosophical Society* 6 (1809).
67. Galvez to Navarro, 19 August 1779, HNOC AGI, Papeles de Cuba, Leg. 1232, Ed. 145, Reel 6, doc. 202, fol. 659.
68. Navarro to Galvez, 29 August 1780, HNOC AGI, Papeles de Cuba, Leg. 593, Ed. 87, Reel 107, fol. 52–57; Carondelet to Aranda, n.d. [1793], HNOC AGI, Papeles de Cuba, Leg. 178, Ed. 144, Reel 166, doc. 92.
69. Carondelet to Aranda, n.d. [1793], HNOC AGI, Papeles de Cuba, Leg. 178, Ed. 144, Reel 166, doc. 92, No. 14.
70. Rendon to Alcudia, 16 September 1794, HNOC AGI, Papeles de Cuba, Leg. 638, Ed. 141, Reel 6, doc. 1. See also Rendon to Alcudia, 11 December 1794, HNOC AGI, Papeles de Cuba, Leg. 638, Ed. 141, Reel 6, doc. 2, 3; de las Casas to Campo de Alange, 15 September 1794, HNOC AGI, Audiencia de Santo Domingo, Leg. 2643, Ind. 845, fol. 597–604; Pedro Pedesclaux, 19 December 1794, NOPL, Acts and Deliberations of the Cabildo, 25 May 1792–10 April 1795, AB 301 1779–1795, vol. 3 No. 3, fol. 180.

CHAPTER 2

Environmental Learning and Path Dependence

At the close of the seventeenth century, Jean-Baptiste Colbert, Marquis de Saignelay, King Louis XIV's minister of finance and simultaneously minister of the marine, was acting on a policy of colonial containment. Under the impression that the French colonial empire had reached its maximum expansion, he did not want more exploration but rather favored drawing together and developing existing settlements.[1] Neither the French king nor his minister was interested in starting a new colonizing adventure. Despite this fact, the explorer Robert Cavelier de la Salle embarked on his expedition down the Mississippi River in search of a warm water port for the Canadian fur trade. This venture culminated in his claiming the large swath of territory from the Great Lakes to the mouths of the Mississippi for France in 1682 and in naming it after the Sun King. It took almost another twenty years from that time, however, until an actual French presence was established on the Gulf Coast because the attention and resources of the French regent were occupied by warfare on the European continent.

When the French crown finally did launch a Mississippi expedition in 1699, it was a purely reactive and strategic venture. For two years rumors had reached Paris that the English were interested in the Mississippi and even that they were establishing a colony there. Finally, the new minister of the marine sent a group of soldiers, headed by Pierre Le Moyne d'Iberville, to investigate the matter.[2] Minister Pontchartrain admitted that he was not interested in forming a colony in Louisiana, but merely in keeping the English from doing so. The proponents of the republic of letters (scholars, scientists, and members of the academies), however, as well as French discoverers were eager to explore the vast, unknown territory.[3]

In April 1699 Iberville reached the Gulf of Mexico and set up a small fort called Biloxi. In a chain of memoirs subsequently written to the minister, he skillfully intertwined the strategic and commercial advantages of keeping Biloxi and strengthening the French foothold at the mouths of the Mississippi.[4] The minister of the marine gave the Canadian a green light to explore further the potential of trade in buffalo skins and in particular to search for lead mines, factors that were to inform the crown's decision on whether to establish a more permanent French presence in Louisiana.[5] Yet even then the French idea was not one of a settlement colony with a plantation economy or agriculture. According to general mercantilist practice, the vision of French colonial policy was that colonies existed for the exploitation of the mother-country, to provide it with raw materials and serve as markets for finished products.[6] Consequently, settlers and settlement of Louisiana were not on the initial agenda. The plan was, rather, to send over a cost-saving minimum of colonial personnel and soldiers who would secure the French posts. This attitude contributed significantly to the difficult situation the early French colonists faced who joined Iberville. The settler's hardship—in part resulting from French colonial policy—prevailed not only during the first years after their arrival at the shores of the Gulf Coast and Mississippi, but well into the first half-century of settlement.

Indigenous Knowledge and French Engineering

At the time of the 1715 hurricane, the Louisiana settlers had already "enjoyed" the regime of Antoine Crozat's Compagnie de la Louisiane (Louisiana Company) for two years. That is, for lack of funds to sustain Louisiana, Louis XIV had ceded it to a private entrepreneur who was granted property rights and the trade monopoly over the colony for fifteen years by letters patent.[7] The new company government was hardly an improvement to the colony's strained situation during the years of the War of the Spanish Succession (1701–14), when ships from France either failed to reach the Gulf Coast or had been stocked insufficiently to supply the starving settlers. Crozat's aim was to make profits from the colony as quickly as possible, regardless of the actual reality of the settlers. His rigid price politics and application of his monopoly stifled the burgeoning economic activity that had emerged between the French Gulf Coast settlements, Biloxi and Mobile, and the French Caribbean colonies Martinique and Saint-Domingue.[8] The company failed in 1717 and the Louisiana monopoly was ceded to the Scottish merchant John Law.

Under the aegis of John Law's Compagnie d'Occident (Company of the West), Louisiana was to become a proper settlement colony. In August or September of 1717, a resolution was issued to build "thirty leagues upriver, a town to be called New Orleans."[9] The first time the advantages of a settlement on the Mississippi River had been mentioned was by the early explorer of Louisiana, Robert Cavelier de la Salle. He had suggested that one single post near the mouths of the Mississippi would suffice in order to control a vast expanse of hinterlands while at the same time serving as a port to ship to France the (mostly imaginary) riches from the new colony.[10] The strategic and commercial advantages of such a settlement apparently remained part of the geopolitical imaginary of the French colonial officials throughout the first two decades of settlement on the Gulf Coast and the Mississippi River.

However, what were the motives for placing Louisiana's new capital in such a hazard-prone environment? Were French colonial officials aware of the potential flood and hurricane risks? It was, apparently, by no means clear from the beginning that the new city was to be placed at its present site. The company merely specified that the settlement should be approachable by the river as well as by Lake Pontchartrain. To royal engineer Perrier, the company had suggested the area where Bayou Manchac and the Mississippi meet.[11] Several other options were discussed controversially by colonial officials. Establishing a new city and redistributing the seat of colonial government was no small political matter. In a sparsely populated area the capital city was sure to receive the largest share of attention from the royal (or company) government; it attracted trade and laborers and thus provided the basis for the settlers to carve out at least a modest living. To have these opportunities taken away from them through the reestablishment of the settlement for many colonists meant the abandonment of just-finished houses and their rebuilding in a new location. To make matters worse, it was not the first time such a transfer was to happen in the Louisiana colony. In 1711 the location of Fort Mobile had to be changed to its present-day site due to a lack of resources and poor site selection. Biloxi had experienced the same fate. Even contemporaries thought such ordeals to be detrimental for the advancement of the colony.[12]

As early as 1708 Bienville had described the area between Lake Pontchartrain and the Mississippi River as annually inundated in spring in a letter to the French secretary of the marine, Jérome Phélipeaux de Pontchartrain.[13] Bienville and his brother Iberville had passed through this area several times during their early exploration trips in 1700. In his journal, recording his second Louisiana journey (1699–1700), Iberville wrote that he and Bienville had gone to "the portage from Lake Pontchartrain to the Mississippi" to see whether their feluccas could navigate "the river that leads to the portage."[14] They found the portage—a stretch of land between that river and the Mississippi—to be one league (2.5 miles) long and half of the way knee-high under water.[15] They had been led to this location on a previous occasion by Indian guides who showed them how they crossed the land, carrying their boats and goods—hence the term "portage." The colonists later called that stream St. Jean, in honor of Bienville, and adapted the indigenous term for the river, as "bayouque," into French.[16] As early as 1700 the strategic advantage of this site was evident to Iberville and Bienville. It provided a shortcut from the Gulf of Mexico through the Mississippi Sound into Lake Borgne, from there through the Rigolets to Lake Pontchartrain and via Bayou St. John to the Mississippi River. This route was much shorter and easier to navigate than it would be to sail ships up the meandering Mississippi, against the river's current and with changing wind directions from the mouth to the same site (see map 2.1).[17]

Bienville, who had just been appointed governor of Louisiana in March 1718, is suspected to have made the ultimate decision for the exact location of New Orleans on the natural levee of the Mississippi River, close to the portage and Lake Pontchartrain. In May 1718 the clearing of the present-day French Quarter site began. While the process of cutting wood and reed to make space for buildings was under way, Jean-Baptiste Bénard de la Harpe, a French officer and *concessionaire* (license-holder) in the Company of the West, harbored doubts about this choice of site. He estimated that it was too close to the river and suggested a removal of the future seat of government upriver to the higher-ground Natchez area.[18] Two years later, in 1720, de la Harpe voiced these concerns again in a memoir "on the present state of the province of Louisiana." He "feared that they [the administrative council of the Company of the West] were not informed of the true geographical situation" of New Orleans and about the fact that "the land is flooded, impractical, unhealthy," and in his opinion "unfit for the cultivation of rice [. . .]."[19] While the city was in fact flooded and frequently had to deal with diseases, New Orleans's environs were not, in fact, unfit for growing rice. Enslaved Africans started planting the crop below New Orleans after they were first brought to Louisiana in 1719.[20]

Similarly, Drouot de Valdeterre who had been commander at Dauphin Island and at Biloxi, provided a list of existing French posts and what should be done with them (i.e., whether they were to be relocated or to be continued). New Orleans, marked as "capital," was followed by a short note: "Established at the mouth of the river subject to inundation, to be changed and reestablished in the plain of Manchac." He further remarked that "the city of New Orleans is situated . . . in marshy terrain and adjacent to waters which overflow twice a year."[21] Clearly, at least the colonial officials on location were aware of the flood risk and frequency and of the marshy nature of the designated site for the city. Hurricanes, as a possible additional hazard, however, do not appear anywhere in the administrative correspondence or Iberville's and Commander Sauvole's journals of the early exploration and settlement phase.[22]

Despite the concerns about the suitability of the site and despite the flooding of large parts of New Orleans's terrain in 1719, building activities on the Mississippi continued. After all, the French had been building dams and levees along large rivers such as the Loire for centuries.[23] Hence, they were going to deal with the fleuve St. Louis (the Mississippi River) in their customary manner, by sending engineers to the colony who would oversee the building of protective works. Levees and the excavation of a drainage canal that was to connect the Mississippi and Lake Pontchartrain had been planned from the start and were executed—out of necessity—on the basis of comparatively short knowledge of the local environmental conditions. In other words, what

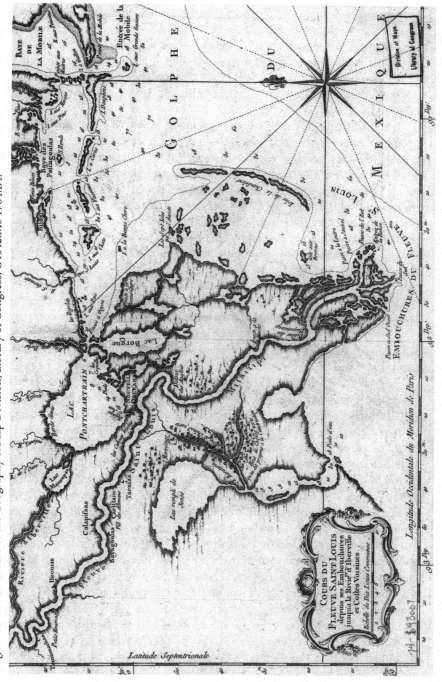

Map 2.1. "Cours du Fleuve St. Louis depuis ses Embouchures jusqu' à la Rivière d'Iberville et ses Costes Voisines" ("Course of the St. Louis River from its mouths to the Iberville River and its neighboring coasts), map by Jacques Nicolas Bellin, 1764. Reproduced from an original in the collections of the Geography & Map Division, Library of Congress, G4042.M5 1764.B4.

may appear as a matter of course—that the French colonizers would arrive in this new environment and import their technology as it had emerged from long-term experience in their homeland—was to become the root for a technological path dependence that has shaped the Mississippi Delta and flood protection policies of the present.[24] The French levees on the Mississippi had an immediate effect on the environment that was noted and discussed by contemporaries.

The realization of such major engineering works was not only a time and money-consuming matter, but also required a large workforce. From the engineers' correspondence with the directors of the Company of the West (after 1719 Company of the Indies) it appears, however, that the latter was unwilling to make large-scale investments in the public works of Louisiana, and that there were neither enough white indentured servants nor African slaves in the colony to carry them out. Chief engineer Pierre Le Blond de La Tour repeatedly complained in his letters that the colony was in dire need of African slaves, since "the whites cannot resist the climate," the assumption being at the time that Africans, by dint of their subtropical and tropical places of origin, were preadapted to Gulf Coast Louisiana's heat and humidity. "Here, everything is difficult for the lack of everything," the engineer wrote, expressing his frustration at this situation in a 1722 letter to the directors of the company.[25]

Apart from the river and New Orleans's city levees, another, rather large-scale, engineering project was envisioned while the future site of Louisiana's capital was still being cleared of the underbrush. It concerned the navigability of the river for large ships. During their explorations of the mouths of the Mississippi, Bienville and Iberville had found that only one of the three passes was navigable for large vessels with a certain draft. This was a supremely important issue since the question as to whether war or merchant ships loaded with cannons or goods could sail through the mouths and upriver was to decide whether it made sense to place a settlement (let alone the capital city) there in the first place. By sounding the pass that was deemed suitable for the passage of larger ships, the engineers established that it was blocked by a sandbar which reduced the water depth to only twelve feet.[26] Adrien de Pauger, second engineer, described this sandbar as a "shoal or deposit of mud [that is] hardened in some places" and that was formed by the "flux [of the low tide] and by the weakening of the current of the river in this place."[27] The French engineers clearly understood the hydrological problem they were facing at the mouths of the Mississippi and they also knew how to solve it.[28] As early as April 1718, the Company of the West had apparently sent six iron dredges and four grippers to Louisiana in order to excavate the sandbar and to open the pass for larger ships.[29] Yet the project was delayed, on the one hand for lack of workers, on the other hand, and more fatally, because the ship on which the dredges were stored was carried away by the 1722 hurricane. In January 1723 de La Tour wrote to the directors of the company that he was working on the model of a dredge which he intended to build on location. It was never achieved, however, because the necessary resources were missing from the colony.[30]

From a geological point of view, this sandbar, which would eventually have blocked the river's final outlet into the Gulf of Mexico, was part of the reason for the build-up of the alluvial soil New Orleans was built on. Without human dredging, the river would over time be diverted into a new, adjacent delta. The millennia-long repetition of this process had caused the deltaic plane to rise above sea level before the advent of French engineering.[31]

The 1722 Hurricane and Its Aftermath

Compared to the hurricanes that hit New Orleans in the later decades under French rule, the 1722 hurricane received a relatively wide publicity, probably precisely because it hit New Orleans so shortly after its foundation and at a time when John Law's propaganda to people the colony was still fresh in Europeans' minds.[32] Several different authors who had been eyewitnesses to the storm recorded the event. Among those who included their experience in a *History of Louisiana*, which was eventually disseminated to a wider audience by publication, were the Jesuit Father Pierre-François-Xavier de Charlevoix and the plantation owner Antoine-Simon Le Page du Pratz.[33] Apart from those authors, there is also the administrative correspondence between the colonial officials and the commissioners of the Company of the Indies. Bernard Diron d'Artaguiette, for example, had been appointed inspector-general of Louisiana in 1721 and was traveling the colony in this function when the hurricane hit.

On 10 September d'Artaguiette noted in his journal that a heavy wind had prevented the ship *L'Aventurier* to leave New Orleans. Yet, neither he nor any of the other authors who wrote about the Louisiana hurricane seem to have been able to read this as a sign for an approaching hurricane. Then, on 12 September d'Artaguiette noted that the hurricane had started at 10:00 in the evening and that it continued until noon the next day. In New Orleans the wind destroyed thirty-four houses, sheds, the church, the presbytery, and the hospital. A particularly grave loss was that of the ships, which were mostly thrown ashore by the wind and either damaged or broken to pieces. They were the only means of transport and were vital for the provisioning of the colony in case of scarcity when foodstuffs had to be sought at Veracruz, in the viceroyalty of New Spain, or at Saint-Domingue. According to d'Artaguiette, "Everything in port was lost," which in effect meant the total isolation of a colony deprived of its seafaring vessels.[34]

With regard to environmental knowledge, d'Artaguiette concluded his account of 12 September with a noteworthy remark regarding the flood risk caused by the hurricane. He wrote, "If the Mississipy had been high this hurricane would have put both banks of the river more than 15 feet under water, the Mississipy, although low, having risen 8 feet."[35] That is, although the French had experienced the 1715 hurricane at Mobile and very likely a number of tropical storms before, the 1722 hurricane was their first experience of the effects a storm surge could have on the Mississippi River and of its potential risk to inundate the city and its environs. Despite the heavily damaged houses and ships, there were apparently no casualties in New Orleans, as we learn from chief engineer Pierre Le Blond de La Tour's letter to the directors of the company. At the newly established German Coast upriver from New Orleans, however, several people drowned as a result of the sudden flooding of Lac des Allemands.[36]

The continuous rain that soaked the city for a month after the event completely spoiled what the hurricane had left of the crops so that no seeds remained for sowing in the next season.[37] This was especially daunting since expectations had been high for the 1722 harvest. At the end of August 1722, thirteen days before the hurricane hit, Le Blond de La Tour had written to the directors that the colony was beginning to establish itself and that everybody was claiming concessions and setting themselves up.[38] These modest blossoms of settlement activity were set back, at least momentarily, by the hurricane.

Apart from Le Page du Pratz's description of the hurricane as a frightening phenomenon, the accounts of the hurricane appear rather sober and matter-of-fact and neither disclosed the emotional effects the hurricane had on individuals nor made reference to religious interpretations of the event. However, some of the distress that prevailed in New Orleans after its near-destruction by the hurricane is conveyed by Le Blond de La Tour's same letter, in which he writes a few paragraphs farther below,

> We will have so many things to attend to that I hardly know where to begin. . . . The habitants . . . cannot give me any help since they are in the same situation as we are, the levees having been overturned, we must have patience. Most of all I ask God to sustain my health in order to bear the fatigues I am experiencing. I have not changed clothes nor slept since the beginning of these hurricanes [sic] and I do not even know where to retire to. I am alone here, Mr. de Bienville, being at his plantation and indisposed, is hardly in a state to attend to any detail, I am trying to remedy everything promptly and to act with the greatest economy possible.[39]

Even though an eighteenth-century and a twenty-first-century hurricane are in many ways difficult to parallel, the engineer's exclamation that he had neither slept nor changed clothes as a result of the hurricane sounds familiar to present-day contemporaries through the broadly mediatized accounts of

Hurricane Katrina (2005), Hurricane Sandy (2012), and the major hurricanes of the 2017 season (Harvey, Irma, and Maria).

While we have a clear conception of the material (and emotional) damage of these twenty-first-century disasters, it is more difficult to assess with some accuracy the destructiveness of the 1722 hurricane. Historical hurricane climatologist Mike Chenoweth classifies it as a major hurricane (i.e., Category 3 to 5), but with its center over Mobile (on the coast of present-day Alabama) rather than New Orleans.[40] In other words, the settlement was not hit full force, yet the impact was strong enough for all the ships and three-quarters of the buildings to be destroyed. Due to a lack of stones, houses in early French New Orleans were built from wood and covered with bark or wooden shingles.[41] This way of building and use of materials differed considerably, for example, from nearby and even more hurricane-prone Cuba, where the majority of houses were traditional wattle-and-daub, thatched roof *bohios*. This semi-permanent architectural style was a legacy of the indigenous Caribs, and, though more likely to be blown over by a hurricane, could be rebuilt quickly. In addition, its component parts were less dangerous when blown around by hurricane winds.[42] While the French in Louisiana did not adopt the architecture of the indigenous peoples they came in contact with, they did over time adopt architectural elements from different areas, as far apart as France, New France, and the French Caribbean islands. Likely one of the earliest adaptive architectural features was to build houses raised away from the frequently flooded and damp soil of the Mississippi Delta. The abundant availability of timber in this riverine environment made building in wood inexpensive, and so rebuilding after destruction could still be swift. However, a major problem to be considered with wood and its stability in high winds is the fact that it would rot quickly in the humid climate of the Gulf Coast, in particular when in contact with the soggy ground.[43] Furthermore, the wetlands at the mouths of the river were still in a process of natural growth and formed an effective buffer against hurricane winds and storm surge, which may have further diminished the strength of the hurricane and its impact on the infant city.[44]

Despite the general discouragement the effects of the hurricane had caused among the settlers, by January 1723 the more tenacious part of the population had started rebuilding and repairing the damage the storm had caused and was apparently gaining strength. According to engineer le Blond de La Tour, some settlers were even planning on planting indigo, the seed of which was to be shipped from Saint-Domingue.[45] The year 1723 thus saw the beginning of a Louisiana indigo boom that continued into the Spanish dominion of the colony when the trade with the dye plant was hampered by Spanish export regulations.[46] Hence, on the surface it appears as if the nascent society was returning to its frontier normal relatively swiftly. Considering the low social and material complexity of the colony it is likely that it did. Yet, on the other hand,

Louisiana's colonial officials may have had an interest in presenting things in a brighter light than they actually were in order to keep the directors and investors of the company in the belief that their profits would soon be forthcoming.

However, did the hurricane spur any adaptive measures, in particular regarding d'Artaguiette's observation of storm surge and rising flood levels of the Mississippi? Indeed, in 1724 second engineer de Pauger wrote to the directors of the company, urging that it was "indispensable to build a slipway or little port, between the city and the house of Mr. de Bienville, in order to protect the pirogues[47] and ships from hurricanes which damage and destroy them by shattering them on the coast." He contended that it was "the only proper place [for the port] because it is protected from the currents."[48] This suggestion is important. It implies that at least the engineers now regarded hurricanes as a possibly recurring risk against which certain preventative measures could be taken in order to protect valuable goods and infrastructure, such as ships, from damage—and the company from expenses.

Apparently, New Orleans's houses were rebuilt in brick or a mixture of brick and wood in the aftermath of the 1722 hurricane. Whether this change in building materials was a reaction to the storm or whether it belonged to de Pauger's general plan for improving the city must remain open, however.[49] Map 2.2 provides an impression of the outline of the city two years after the hurricane. Ultimately, de Pauger's port was the only concrete, proactive measure that was proposed in the administrative correspondence of the colony with regard to the 1722 hurricane. Even though d'Artaguiette had noted the rising river level caused by the hurricane, no levee building took place as a reaction to this observation. That is, levees in front of the city of New Orleans and along the Mississippi had been projected and built since the flood of 1719, yet they had been designed with the obvious and more frequent risk of annual river floods in mind and not with regard to flooding by storm surge.[50] With regard to the hurricane port, the directors of the company were neither as far-sighted as the engineers on location, nor was it part of the mercantilist philosophy to make lavish investments in the colony. In a memoir to the newly appointed governor Etienne Périer in September 1726, the directors wrote that they found such a project altogether "too considerable," not least because it was proposed together with the dredging of a canal that was to connect Bayou St. Jean and the Mississippi for easier communication.[51]

Hence, while the company's financial worries concerned the overall scale of the two projects, it did not take into account the long-term gain that could have protected the valuable ships and boats from hurricanes. Watercraft were the only viable means of transport in this aquatic environment. That is, trade with other French settlements farther upriver from New Orleans was operated by canoes and pirogues on the Mississippi, while ocean-going ships took the French along vital trade and supply routes over the waters of the Gulf of Mex-

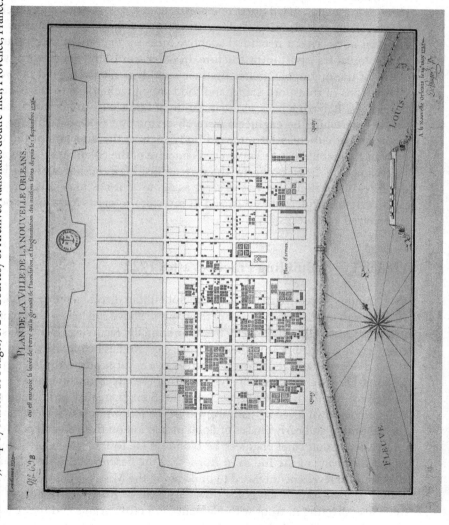

Map 2.2. "Plan de la Ville de la Nouvelle Orleans ou est marquée la levée de terre qui la garantit de l'inondation, et l'augmentation des maisons faites depuis le 1er Septembre 1723" (Map of the city of New Orleans showing the earthen levee that protects it from flooding, and showing the increase in houses since 1 September 1723), map by Adrien de Pauger, 1724. Courtesy of Archives Nationales d'outre-mer, Provence, France.

ico to the Spanish and French cities of Havana, Cap François, and Veracruz. If they were destroyed by a hurricane, it was not only costly to rebuild the ships for lack of workforce and know-how that persisted throughout the first three decades of the colony, but the complete destruction of all major ships also meant the temporary isolation of the colony from the surrounding settlements. De Pauger's failed hurricane port is therefore an instance in which the politico-economic decision-making structures of the French company government out-played a structural adaptive measure that might have protected vital colonial transport infrastructure. In other words, the financial considerations of the metropole, following their own dynamics, rendered the young city's means of transport, trade, and food supply vulnerable to the effects of hurricanes. Referring back to the question of knowledge about hurricanes, it seems that, while the engineers were observing and working with the local environment closely, a far-removed body such as the directors of the company in Paris could not assess or even conceive of the risk of hurricanes at the Louisiana Gulf Coast properly. The mercantilist logic did not allow for lavish expenses on a colony that was to serve as a source of raw materials. The company therefore protected its own and its investors' interests by saving expenses it perceived as unnecessary.

French Levee Building Practices after 1722

Even though protective structures were not built in direct response to the hurricane, work on the levee in front of the city and above and below it was continued to safeguard the nascent city from the annually recurring river floods. The river-levees will reappear in the hurricane case studies below when protective structures were damaged or overtopped by storm surge pushed upriver to New Orleans. Due to their centrality in protecting the city against the flood hazard as well as due to the path dependence the French created in implementing their homegrown levee system, we will in the following take a closer look at the beginning and early phases of flood protection on the Mississippi River.

In a letter that chief engineer Le Blond de La Tour wrote to the directors of the Company of the Indies in April 1722, he described in some detail the two kinds of levees he intended to build along the Mississippi below New Orleans: "The one on the left going downriver will be made of two lines of piles and close sheeting in front with filaments and cross beams and the space between them will be filled with fascines and well beaten soil all linked together. The one on the right side is simpler; there will be only one line of contiguous piles; and as trees descend the river they will be put behind [the line of piles] and could thereafter form a dam."[52] De La Tour added that he would choose the more successful and least costly of the two manners of levee described.

The levee in front of New Orleans was already being built and was to be an earthen dyke; it was, however, according to the engineer, neither high enough nor broad enough yet. It was projected to reach a breadth of twelve French feet (about 10.8 American feet or 3.2 meters) and to be protected from erosion by a "line of palisades made of carpentry."[53] De La Tour suggested that all ships traveling upriver to New Orleans should be ordered to bring sand for the levee; in turn, they could load and take with them New Orleans's native soil that was "so rich that whenever it rains one sinks in to one's knees."[54] Indeed, from the present-day perspective of historical geography, the French were about to build a city onto "thin layers of extremely finely textured alluvial soils, high in water and organic content, recent in their formation, and highly vulnerable to transformation through human activity."[55]

One year later, engineer de Pauger, who had been assigned by his superior Le Blond de La Tour to build New Orleans and oversee the works on the levees below the city, described to the directors of the company the kind of structures he envisioned to support the levee in front of the city. He wanted "to build a quay or dam structure . . . which continues along the front of New Orleans and which should be made of a line of contiguous well-embedded piles to serve as a . . . berm for a palisade covered with layers of fill, as I have seen them on the quays of Calais, Dieppe and Le Havre, for lack of masonry."[56]

The engineer thought this undertaking indispensable for flood protection and for preventing the river board from being eroded. In the same letter, de Pauger suggested that the "principal habitants" should send their African slaves in order to build the levee in front of the city. It seems, however, that the settlers did not follow the engineer's idea willingly so that in 1728 an ordinance was issued by the Superior Council of Louisiana, declaring that all habitants were to send their slaves for thirty days in a row to carry out public works at a time—not during sowing or harvest season—marked by the Council. The penalty for noncompliance with the ordinance was six *livres* per day on which the owner's slaves did not show up on the building site.[57]

Work progressed only slowly. Le Blond de La Tour wrote that almost all the (white) *ouvriers* (workers) who had come to the colony had been obliged to make their own tools on location.[58] In addition, "the excessive heat of the summer which lasts for a long time" made it "impossible to even work until nine in the morning and restart work at three [in the afternoon]" and it was "impossible to rest at night because of the midgets and mosquitoes."[59] The lack of workers to build those protective structures swiftly was a recurring theme in the colonial correspondence.[60] Apart from the missing manpower and a forbidding summer climate, French engineering traditions encountered an unforeseen problem in the geologically young alluvial plane: no stones were to be found, nor were there any quarries nearby, nor would there have been the infrastructure to transport stones over long distances.[61] As a consequence, it appears from de Pauger's account, the Mississippi levees were, at least initially, adapted to the local resources and built without masonry. However, even in France masonry had been in use for levee building only since the end of the era of Colbert (i.e., since the 1680s); before that time the slopes of levees had been fortified with wood.[62] In Lower Louisiana stones were obviously not only needed for levee building. In the same letter in which he had complained about the summer heat and the mosquitoes, Le Blond de La Tour exasperatedly demanded of the company to send stones from St. Leu in France.[63] It seems that the scarcity of stones suitable for building, on the one hand, laid the foundation for a particular local architectural style based on wood; on the other hand, it was precisely this dependence on the lightweight building material that augmented the settlers' vulnerability to the hazard of hurricanes.[64]

In May 1724 de Pauger wrote to the directors in Paris and told them that the river had risen higher than the year before and that it was necessary to start redoubling the levee to its projected breadth of twelve feet. The area where the hospital was located was apparently inundated at the time of de Pauger's writing since the lack of workers had hampered finishing the levee there.[65] The floods lasted until June and prevented the settlers as well as the Indian nations between New Orleans and Natchez (which the French called Fort Rosalie) from sowing anything. Exacerbating the situation, the floods were followed by six weeks of continuous rain, resulting in high crop prices and general food scarcity in the colony.[66]

A 1725 letter by the Superior Council provides more information on how the levees above and below the city levee of New Orleans were built. After the miserable year of 1724, the Council was hopeful that 1725 would be better, in particular because of "the universal precaution the settlers have taken against the inundation by building levees, more or less extensive, according to their ability, but all of them sufficient to prevent the overflow, until a levee of three feet will contain the stream."[67] In other words, as in the French and German levee-building tradition, the property owners themselves were responsible for the building and maintenance of levees on the riverfront of their terrain.[68] However, a significant departure from the European tradition in Louisiana was that with the increasing numbers of enslaved Africans brought to the colony, an enslaved workforce was doing the actual leveeing and not the habitants themselves.

An element of potential vulnerability emerges from the tacit assumption conveyed by the Council's description of sufficient height of the levees to prevent overflow. The phrase implies that the settlers had formed an image of the river's normal flood regime during the three decades the colony had existed and during the even shorter period of close coexistence with the river since the building of New Orleans in 1718.[69] In other words, while the colonists had included flood-level fluctuations they perceived as normal into their levee design, their experience with the environment had not been long enough to form an image of the scale of devastating aberrations from that perceived normalcy.

Yet, in June 1727 Governor Périer observed that the water in the Mississippi had risen "one and a half feet higher than normal" and that this was due to the levees that had to be built for the protection of the crops. He added that since only part of the settlers' levees were finished—"be it by weakness or by negligence"—he had ordered to have them built from the first to the last plantation above and below New Orleans, which would "result in twenty leagues of levees on both sides of the river." Although this undertaking could not be achieved during the current year, he stated optimistically that it would be very advanced by the next.[70]

Governor Périer's ordinance on how those levees on the riverfront were to be maintained appeared only in 1732, however. Even though the properties behind the river levees were owned privately, the road on their crest was open to the public and needed to be maintained for this purpose. The document ordered that every habitant who owned land adjacent to the river was obliged to clear the trees from the river board to a depth of three *arpents* and to provide moorings for ships in the form of large blocks of oak wood of a certain size embedded in the ground, at the distance of one *arpent*.[71] Furthermore, the habitants were to build "a levee of six feet's breadth by at least two feet's elevation for the comfort of the pedestrians and horsemen," and to leave "inside of the levee . . . a road of eight *toises* of breadth for the wheelbarrows [. . .]." The owners were obliged to maintain those levees and paths in their own and the community's interest.[72] These (and two later) ordinances resulted in the building of fifty miles of road along the river above and below New Orleans by the end of the French dominion in 1762.[73]

Apparently, it was difficult for the authorities to enforce their ordinances even with penalties in place, since a scribble in the margin of the order on building bridges noted that it had not been carried out uniformly. The 1732 ordinance on levees on private properties was re-issued in September 1735, it seems, because the habitants had not complied with the earlier one.[74] The new ordinance shows almost identical phrasing, yet it contains an interesting addition regarding the nexus of property ownership and levee building: "Terrain where no levees have been built by January first, next, are declared vacant and will be reunited with the domaine[75] by virtue of this ordinance, and without the necessity of issuing others, in order for the lands to be redistributed to the individuals who demand them."[76] This declaration is reminiscent of dyke laws dating back to medieval times and that were also in use in the German North-Sea communities and the Netherlands. Thus, the German *Spadelandsrecht* (literally spade-land-law) ordered that the dyke overseer (or dyke judge, *Deichrichter*) would plant a spade in the levee section of property owners who had been unwilling or unable to maintain their levee. By this symbolic ac-

tion, the property owners lost the claims to their land that then was offered—
including the obligation to build and maintain the levee—to their relatives,
neighbors, or the local parish.[77] While no archaic spade rituals were involved
in the New Orleanian case, the process of dispossession as a consequence of
noncompliance with an existing levee ordinance follows the same logic and
reappears during the Spanish dominion of Louisiana.

New Orleans's early levee-building practices stand in the context of a long
history of French levee building and the cultures of disaster that developed in
the cities and villages along the rivers of France since medieval times.[78] The
evolution of France's levees was meticulously researched by the French geographer Roger Dion in his doctoral thesis on the Loire Valley and in a separate
book on the Loire levees.[79] According to Dion, the stretch of the Loire between
Angers and Tours was the cradle of the levee in its shape of an earthen embankment crested by a road.[80] This is also the kind of levee that came to be
built along the Mississippi River in the early eighteenth century. Before the
mid-sixteenth century, dam structures built along the Loire were called *turcie* (from Latin *tursia*). They consisted of "mixed materials, consolidated by
a battery of piles," and were, by definition, submersible structures.[81] In other
words, the farmers who cultivated land behind those dams were used to receiving the benefits (fertile sediment) as well as the ravages (destroyed crops)
of occasional floods that overtopped their protection. By 1550 the word *levée*
had come into common usage to describe dams along the Loire and with it a
new way of building flood protection that replaced the old *trucies*. According
to Dion, the proper meaning of *levée* was earthen embankment. Devoid of
wooden piles, those structures were destined to be insubmersible. Overtopping would weaken or breach the earthen levees, so that the only measure to
ensure their long-term functionality was to elevate them above the level of the
highest known floods.[82]

The reasons for the sixteenth-century precedence of the *levée* over the *turcie*
were apparently—and not surprisingly—mainly commercial. The larger cities
along the Loire, such as Tours, Orléans, and Blois, were anxious to protect
their bridges from dangerous flood waters and to keep the river navigable for
trade even during the summer months when inundation usually spread the
waters into the Loire Valley. However, navigability could be ensured only by
insubmersible dams that kept the river from leaving its bed. Hence, it was the
interests of the influential merchants that dictated the change in dam technology. Yet, the rural population along the river did not oppose the better protection of their crops.[83] However, at the end of the sixteenth century it became
clear that the new *levées* could not contain the water of the largest floods and
that the effects of breaches of those insubmersible structures were much graver
than those of the annual floods of earlier decades.

It seems that during the seventeenth century and the beginning of the eighteenth century the floods of the Loire in France led to the same considerations as came to be known as "levee only" policy on the Mississippi in the United States at the turn of the twentieth century. In 1629, under the reign of Louis XIII, a royal order was issued demanding that every valley along the Loire introduce a *déchargeoir* (spillway) after such a partial lowering of the embankment for the water to spill into the flood plain had saved the levee from breaching at Blois. The king's council even envisioned destroying entirely some of the existing levees to secure settlements from further harm. The order was not executed, however, since the population between Ouzouer and Saumur on the Loire where it should have been implemented opposed the measure.[84] In 1680, under the supervision of Colbert, Louis XIV's comptroller general of finances who was also directing the public works of the kingdom, the levees were elevated to the height of 5.5 meters above low water levels. By 1711 levees were further elevated to 6.8 meters and spillways had been introduced only between Gien and Tours. After a harrowing 1733 Pentecost flood that overtopped even the recently elevated levees and that devastated fertile lands for decades with sandy deposits, the question whether the existing spillways should be maintained or closed was of the highest importance to the authorities.

With regard to the solution of the "spillway or not" question in eighteenth-century France, Dion remarks that the problem could no longer be reassessed at its basis since "the levee system was a fact that had to be accepted, and for a long time, the discussions which it was the subject of could only center around the choice of the best-suited correctives."[85] Dion thus essentially describes path dependence of this structural adaptation to a flood-prone environment.

Even though Dion provides descriptions of the construction of *turcies* and *levées,* juxtaposition with engineer de Pauger's account of the levees he was planning to build along the Mississippi does not allow for a clear classification according to either type. With regard to the institutional structures that had developed around levee building in France, Le Blond de La Tour and de Pauger's involvement with the Mississippi levees stood in the tradition of the engineers employed by Colbert along the Loire. It is important to underline, that building levees, in the shape of those uniform insubmersible embankments, was a monumental, centralized undertaking under the aegis of the French crown rather than the community enterprise that had been the *turcies.* Local *associations syndicales* (district councils) were formed, with annually elected *syndics* who oversaw public works such as roads and *turcies.*[86] Throughout the seventeenth century, in France as well as in Germany, the shift toward absolutism also brought levee building under more centralized governance structures.[87] Thus, in France after 1676 the comptroller of finances was directing those public works supported by the royal treasury.[88] Accordingly, colonial Louisiana's engineers were appointed to their posts by the French king and supervised the labor on the levees of New Orleans and the adjacent plantations up- and downriver from the city.

Returning to the question of the technology transfer from France to the Mississippi Delta, it may seem obvious that colonists would implant technologies of their homeland in newly settled territory—What else should they do? Yet for a history of adaptation and vulnerability to natural hazards it is important to magnify the starting point of such implantations. Not for the mere sake of searching for historical beginnings, but because the transfer of technologies from one environment to another creates material facts from which in turn may arise institutions, expectations, and/or oblivions that can be changed or reversed only by major efforts or disruptive events. I am, in short, referring to the path dependence mentioned above that will reappear throughout this book.

The "Pull of the Hinterlands" during Spanish Rule

Although the Spanish inherited the French levee system on the Mississippi, they initially intended not to involve their new city government—and by extension the royal treasury—in its maintenance. As we have seen, achieving a reliable line of flood defense with the customary system of levee maintenance by property owners was an issue from the earliest years of levee building on the Mississippi. The phrase that habitants were building levees "according to their ability" describes the fact that the different stretches of levees along the river were quite clearly of varying quality as early as the French period. Although records of noncompliance with levee ordinances are not as detailed during the first fifty years of New Orleans's existence as during the Spanish dominion, the marginal notes in the French records are telling enough. It is likely that the Mississippi levee system suffered from neglect in the years between 1731 and 1762. That year the French crown ceded Louisiana to Spain after the Seven Year's War, leaving the colony, which had never exactly been showered with royal attention, largely to its own devices.[89]

With the definite takeover of Louisiana by the Spanish in 1769, New Orleans received its first proper city government, the Cabildo. It was presided over by the governor who was responsible to the Captain General of Cuba, who, unlike many regional commanders of the Spanish Caribbean, communicated directly with King Charles III and the Council of the Indies.[90] New Orleans's levees start figuring in the Cabildo's records very soon after that institution's creation. For the most part it was not the levee in front of the city that was mentioned, however, but the levees of the plantation owners above the city. The original system of the landowners' responsibility for the upkeep of their own dam and stretch of road was maintained under Spanish rule. Increasingly, however, the city government became involved in building and repairing flood protection, despite the prohibition of spending city or royal funds on such public works.[91]

Four months after the Spanish takeover of Louisiana by Lieutenant General Alejandro O'Reilly in August 1769, and shortly after its creation in November of the same year, the New Orleans Cabildo decided to prohibit cart owners from driving across the city levee in order to protect the structure, although it made an exception for cart drivers that were receiving freight from ships anchored in front of the levee.[92] Apparently, this ordinance was not heeded by the cart owners; they continued using the road on the crest of the levee in its whole length, as did horse riders. In 1772 the Cabildo finally spent public funds to repair the further dilapidated levee in front of the city. Surprisingly, it exempted property owners fronting the river, who, according to the Code O'Reilly, would have been liable for the costs and upkeep.[93]

The 1772 repairs were not durable, however. In April 1774 high water in the river compelled the council to agree "to build a solid levee to protect the city from the current of said river" and to auction the repair works to an "honest resident" who would carry them out according to contract.[94] Two nonpermanent *comisarios anuales* (annually elected councilmen) of the Cabildo were responsible for overseeing public works in general and the levees in particular and for detecting breaches on both banks of the Mississippi.[95] Despite those measures, problems with breaches continued into the 1790s. In August 1779 and 1780 violent hurricanes caused the Mississippi to rise, while 1782 saw ordinary river floods, all of which affected New Orleans's levees adversely. In the early 1790s Governor Carondelet had floodgates installed near the city and repairs became less frequent.[96]

It seems reasonable enough that the Cabildo would be interested in the maintenance of the levee in front of the city. Yet the city government's involvement even extended to the privately owned and maintained levees, especially above New Orleans. Breaches in one levee not only affected the crops and property of its owner, but also those of his or her neighbor.[97] In particularly damaging cases, the water might even spread into New Orleans proper, so that the maintenance of the dam structures of the upriver plantations was of city-wide, public concern. It was difficult for the Cabildo, however, to force landowners to keep their levees in good condition. In several cases, owners abandoned their property after exhausting their financial means for repairing their levees. Consequently, as in the French and German dyke-laws described above, abandoned land was returned to the public domain and was redistributed together with the obligation to maintain the appendant levee.[98]

One such case of property abandonment was that of Mr. Saubadon's lands, situated four leagues above the city. The records of the Cabildo session of

8 November 1782 relate how the *regidores* (councilors) who were responsible for overseeing public works and the *alcalde ordinario* (judge), Don Francisco Maria de Reggio, presented the "complaints and clamor" of a group of inhabitants to the council.[99] The plaintiffs, neighbors of Mr. Saubadon, had lost their crops because the latter had abandoned his lands and because his levee had caved in, and the river had flooded their properties via the breach in Mr. Saubadon's dam. Apparently, the Council had had notice of the bad condition of the Saubadon levee on 12 October, when it appointed *alférez real* (royal standard bearer) Don Francisco Pascalis de la Barre with the task to oversee the immediate repairs of Mr. Saubadon's levee in order to prevent further damage.[100] However, efficient mending of the breach was thwarted by a government internal dispute over competencies. The "unsound and careless repairs" thus continued unsupervised and were carried out by a foreman with little engineering skill and at the wrong time. The shoddy workmanship was blamed for drowning the neighbors' crops and, as we learn toward the end of the document, for inundating the city's orchards. Adding insult to injury, the standing flood waters were "contributing to sickness and fever which has been spreading since September in this Capital" and was apparently still ongoing at the time of the November session.[101]

In February 1790 a further case of city intervention in the maintenance of privately owned levees appears in the Cabildo records. Don Juan Bautista McCarty (also spelled Macarty) and Don Leonardo Massange had abandoned their lands in the Tchoupitoulas district above New Orleans. Consequently, their levees had fallen into disrepair and had already been breached several times when the Cabildo got involved in 1790. Underlining in particular the aspect of public health, the councilors decided to take care of the situation despite the crown's prohibition of using city funds for such works and appropriated 3,480 pesos for the repair of the McCarty and Massange levees.[102] With this financial decision the Cabildo was in fact spending funds it did not have. Only two years earlier, on 21 March 1788, New Orleans had experienced a devastating city fire, and the treasury had not yet recovered.[103] As a consequence, the Cabildo had to incur a debt of 7,481 pesos in order to prevent further damage and a renewed health hazard due to inundation in 1790.[104]

In June 1792, the case of Don Francisco Bernoudy came before the Cabildo. This resident owned a plantation across the Mississippi River and had, according to his own account, tried since 1779 to build and maintain a good levee that had "deprived him of his earnings." Consequently, he saw himself forced to abandon these lands and to acquire property elsewhere. In his appeal to the Cabildo, Bernoudy remarked that his leaving his land would be very detrimental to all the inhabitants in his neighborhood and that their impossibility to stand such burdensome work, would compel them to take the same steps in order to remedy such inconveniences on the lands at Bonet Carre and on the lands of Don Santiago Contreele, Don Juan Bautista Macarty and Don Leonardo Mazange, and that therefore, the councilors of the Cabildo should be so kind as to lend him the considerable sum of 10,000 pesos in order for him to fix his levee.[105] The Cabildo verified Bernoudy's claims and found them to be true. If his dams were not repaired, crops on between twelve and fourteen leagues (thirty-five miles) of land would be flooded and destroyed. The councilor charged with Bernoudy's case, however, did not recommend the loan since the New Orleans treasury still lacked the funds at the time. Consequently, Francisco Bernoudy was referred to the royal treasury to apply for financial support.[106]

After the dams of the land adjacent to the McCarty and Massange properties broke again in 1792, the Cabildo sent for cartloads of earth to mend the breach while at the same time appealing to Governor Carondelet for help in the matter.[107] The latter issued a levee ordinance in June, a few days after Bernoudy's case had been considered by the Cabildo. The document presented clear regulations as to the manner of repairing levees as well as to who was to bear the financial responsibility for such repairs. In particular, the document strengthened the position of the syndics charged with overseeing the levees in particular districts.[108] Local knowledge of their district was mentioned as the primary motive for the biannual election of the particular syndics in office. Vested with this skill and their official position, their orders were to be obeyed by the inhabitants "punctually under penalty of fine of forty piastres [. . .]."[109] After careful inspection of the levees of their district, the overseers would tell the plantation owners what amendments they would have to make to their flood protection after the harvest season. As a general rule—and according to ancient practice—the ordinance decreed that all levees be elevated to the highest known flood levels of the respective year when the river had destroyed the protective works.

Owners of levees particularly prone to ruptures were held to have tools and materials for emergency repair at the ready under penalty of a fine of 100 piastres. If a break did occur, the syndics would order all landowners of their district to send their slaves for repair works at the owner's cost. Noncompliance with this order was to be punished with a fine of 200 piastres.

This last point was clearly an attempt to shift cost-bearing back to the landowners, while the obedience to the syndics called for at the beginning of the ordinance was directed against negligent and careless attitudes of plantation owners. While the levee ordinances of the French period laid out how dams should be built and that landowners were to maintain them, the Carondelet ordinance is the first detailed order concerning the levees of the lower Mississippi that included regulations on preparedness and—with the paragraph on raising the dams to the highest known flood level of the year—on adaptation. The common practice of raising flood protection to the highest known, rather than the highest imaginable, level of inundations is one of the most pertinent instances in which the future of the past comes to bear and reflects the human propensity to blank out so called Black Swan events.[110] That is, the historical orientation on the worst known past flood occurrence blocks the view of a possible, even larger-scale future event. As such, levee building is an example for an adaptive practice that simultaneously created vulnerability on a larger scale, as described in chapter 1. Even though none of the points in Carondelet's levee ordinance is in any sense new knowledge or groundbreaking, it is the first clear regulation of inhabitants' behavior regarding the flood risk in and around New Orleans. The points it aimed to enforce shed light on problems that had been ongoing for decades, judging from the three cases of property abandonment presented above.

The Saubadon, McCarty/Massange, and Bernoudy cases illustrate how much life in the Mississippi's aquatic environment was inherently based on solidarity. It was a community effort that required the equal attention and compliance of every landowner along the river front in order to ensure everyone's prosperity and well-being. The preamble of Carondelet's levee ordinance circumscribed the solidarity issue by stating, "The maintenance of the levees interests all the inhabitants where crevasses ruin in an instant the fruits of a year of labor of all the citizens, whose fortune and existence depends in a great part upon the success of the crops."[111] The negligence or incapability of one planter to maintain his levee not only threatened the livelihood of several neighbors, it could also afflict the whole city with food scarcity and fevers. When Louisiana changed hands from France to Spain in 1762, the colony experienced its first major wave of immigration since John Law's campaign between 1717 and 1719.[112] The increase in newcomers with diverse geographical origins is likely to have exacerbated the levee building and maintenance problem along the Mississippi, in particular above the city.

The three cases presented above illustrate the fact that property abandonment was a rather widespread solution for insolvency or for owners fatigued with annual river floods and the upkeep of their levees. The apparent ease with which owners left their lands behind in order to seek their fortune elsewhere increased the vulnerability of New Orleans to inundation, sickness, and food scarcity. This is only one of several *socio-cultural* factors connected with the technology of levee building, which acquired a specific shape in a multiethnic colonial immigration society such as New Orleans.

The fact that a vast open hinterland existed beyond the early settlements in the New World made coercion with regard to flood protection more difficult than in more densely populated and legally structured Europe.[113] Attractive alternatives to New Orleans could be found upriver in such locations as Natchez or the Illinois country. Two further aspects that rendered levee building solidarity precarious in New Orleans are time and social and ethnic diversity.

European riverine and coastal communities had developed their levee-building cultures—that is, an ensemble of technological structures interlaced with property ownership, legal rights, and institutions—in the same location since the Middle Ages or antiquity. German North Sea Coast communities, for example, developed distinct means of social control and legal obligations concerning dyke building that coevolved with communal self-organization of free farmers on the ground.[114] The French and Spanish authorities in the New World, on the other hand, had to transplant such traditions into a new environment and coerce them on societies that were a lot less homogenous and—featuring the institution of slavery—more forcefully patched together than any of their counterparts on the European continent. The social fabric and institutions that held together a community had to be reconstituted and adapted to the local conditions. In other words, even without levees generating a measure of solidarity in those new societies was a challenge. The diversity of people from different geographical backgrounds could have also made the development and continuity of levee building practices and local knowledge difficult.

Although the French and Spanish colonial powers imported their longstanding technological traditions and attached legal framework, they implanted them in natural and social environments whose combined dynamics confronted the Spanish government with unexpected difficulties. The New Orleans Cabildo had to break Castilian law in order to make up for the hazard that negligent landowners created for the whole city and who evaded enforcement by just moving away. Levee building thus increasingly became a centralized Cabildo concern that the Spanish crown had not initially planned for. This development followed its predecessors on the European continent, where a heightened influence of absolutist authorities over levee and dyke building is discernible from the mid-seventeenth century.[115] Clearly, problems of solidarity existed in European coastal and riverine communities, too, where the levee building technologies and institutions implanted in the New World had originated. I suggest, however, that the continuity of institutions, a relative homogeneity of societies, longstanding local traditions, and higher population densities made social control and rule enforcement less of a struggle in European levee-building cultures than in the comparatively mobile and highly diverse societies that were forming on the lower Mississippi.

"Levees Only"—A French Legacy

After the Louisiana Purchase in 1803, levee building in Louisiana remained a local municipal or private issue until the introduction of the Swamp Acts of 1849 and 1850. Legislation was spurred by the Sauvé Crevasse Flood of 1849, when a dam at Pierre Sauvé's plantation (in present-day River Ridge, Jefferson

Parish), upriver from New Orleans, broke. The consequent inundation spread out over seventeen miles (27.3 kilometers), affected two thousand structures, and rendered twelve thousand residents temporarily homeless. Due to its magnitude—it was considered the worst flood of New Orleans until Hurricane Katrina in 2005—the event gained national attention.[116] The acts passed in its wake offered the states of the Lower Mississippi valley unsold public lands that they were to sell to private interests. The revenues of those sales were to be used for levee construction and maintenance. At the same time, two survey studies of the Mississippi River were commissioned by the federal government—one by army engineer Andrew Humphreys, the other by civilian engineer Charles Ellet.[117]

Humphreys's report had taken eleven years to complete and attracted attention across the Atlantic; it suggested concentrating exclusively on levees, strongly supervised by the federal government. Ellet, on the other hand, promoted a mixed approach using levees as well as spillways and reservoirs—interlaced mechanisms that would require congressional action on a large scale. Neither of those approaches could gain the upper hand immediately since the Civil War (1861–65) devastated Louisiana's infrastructure and its levee system in particular. However, after the war Humphreys became chief of the Army Corps of Engineers and was able to use his position of power to discredit the civilian engineer Ellet and promote his levees-only approach until his resignation in 1879.[118] In that same year Congress founded the Mississippi River Commission. This body was created after engineer James Eads's federally funded jetties, located in the South Pass of the Mississippi, had proved a success and had thus made federal funding of flood control works feasible. Eads became a member of the commission and a further—if not the most—influential proponent of the "levees only" approach to flood control.

The iconic Great Mississippi Flood of 1927 became a sort of culmination point for the levees-only approach after floods in 1912, 1913, and 1922 had brought record high water marks on the gauges of the Mississippi River. Continuously rising flood levels showed that increasing levee height was not creating the desired effect of banning the flood hazard for good. Yet, in 1923 the Mississippi River Commission stubbornly maintained that "levees afford the only practicable means for flood control in the lower Mississippi Valley."[119] In the wake of these floods the coalition of advocates of a more mixed or spillway approach to the flood problem strengthened considerably.

Finally, in April 1927 heavy rainfall had swollen the Mississippi so much that the threat of inundation for New Orleans could no longer be ignored. The Citizens' Flood Relief Committee geared into action, deciding that the levee at Poydras, below the city, would have to be dynamited in order to release pressure on New Orleans. This decision essentially entailed saving New Orleans—the center of commerce—at the expense of the poor downriver parishes of St. Bernard and Plaquemines, which would be flooded by the water pouring through the artificial cut in the levee. While no public hearings or referenda were held on this far-ranging resolution, the Citizens' Flood Relief Committee conferred directly with the Mississippi River Commission, the War Department, and the state of Louisiana. Consequently, dynamiting the Poydras levee and flooding the downriver parishes in favor of saving New Orleans was set for 29 April 1927 at noon, after supposedly every inhabitant had been evacuated by local officials. The economic and environmental impact of the artificial breach of the Poydras levee on Plaquemines and St. Bernard were devastating and long lasting: 250 people died in the event and some 160,000 families were displaced from their homes. The region's oyster fishing and muskrat-trapping trades—the parish inhabitants' main sources of income—were affected for years by the flooding of the terrain.[120]

James Parkerson Kemper, a civil engineer who was born on a sugar plantation in the Bayou Teche Country in 1868, started studying hydraulics in earnest after heavy losses to his family's plantation in the flood of 1912. This experience and his subsequent studies made him a fierce critic of the Mississippi River Commission's "levees only" policy. Kemper stylized himself as the lone voice in the wilderness with regard to his opposition against the established opinion that levees alone would save the day: "The subject was debated in the Louisiana Engineering Society and the sentiment was 300 to one in favor of levees only. The writer [Kemper] was the one."[121]

After the 1927 flood, when resentment against the rigid flood control policy was growing, Kemper made known his version of the historiography of levees only, which he dated back to before the French period of Louisiana, in several publications. According to the engineer, the approach was originally based on a hydraulic theory the Italian scientist Gian-Domenico Guglielmini had set up in the seventeenth century. It held that levees increased the velocity of the flow of a river and consequently also of its sediment. The latter would thus scour out and deepen the river bed so that ultimately, through levees, the flood level of the river would go down.[122] "The fallacy of this theory was shown time and again, but the authorities would brook no opposition," Kemper exclaimed in an address that reviewed the 1927 flood ten years later. He continued that this erroneous theory had "worked for 210 years, first by the French Crown, then by the Spanish Crown, again by the French Crown and finally by the United States, beginning in 1803."[123] However, in Kemper's view the reason for the longevity of Guglielmini's theory was not only that levees had become a structural fact, which would take a lot of time and investment to change. Rather, he saw the fault with the *political* structures that had formed around levee building in the Lower Mississippi Valley: "In Louisiana, the Board of State Engineers and State Levee Boards are appointed by the governor and always are important factors in the scheme of campaign patronage. Very few levee board members are ever appointed with a view to their qualifications as river experts. The levee builders constitute a powerful political body and they are well organized. Many millions of dollars are dispensed each year by the Federal and State authorities in levee construction and practically everyone engaged in the work is a levees only man."[124]

With the recognition that political patronage and money interests had encrusted flood control in the Mississippi Valley during the nineteenth and early twentieth centuries, Kemper illustrates an important aspect that contributes to the emergence of new forms of vulnerability as a result of adaptive processes and practices. So far, it was Humphreys who has been credited with leaving the legacy that guided flood control on the Mississippi River for the next century.[125] However, as we have seen throughout this chapter, the levees-only approach as a practice is, in fact, a French legacy. The very existence of New Orleans is owed to the firm adherence of the French engineers to "levees only"—even if contemporaries obviously did not call their approach that. That is, the French—as later the Americans—adhered to an unshakeable optimism that such structures would solve the city's flood problem satisfactorily and permanently. Kemper's slightly simplistic localization of the roots of the "levees only" approach in Guglielmini's theory necessarily overlooked what we are able to see with historic hindsight: the French had experimented with spillways on the Loire during the 1620s because of the problem of mounting flood levels and increased levee heights. However, since the public opposed the introduction of spillways, which were implemented only haltingly, no alternative solution to the constant raising of levees had been found by the time Louisiana became a French colony. As a consequence, Louisiana's engineers imported the French levee-building tradition as it was in 1718 and perpetuated its path dependence in the levee system on the Mississippi. After the Spanish, the Americans became the second heirs to the established fact of the French's rigid approach to the flood problem.

Charles Ellet, Andrew Humphrey's opponent, has been credited with the "recognition that humans had exacerbated the Mississippi's inundations by confining flood waters behind levees thus presage[ing] the work of George Perkins Marsh, who . . . is hailed as one of the first modern environmentalists, because he recognized that humans had an impact on processes previously labeled natural."[126] As we have seen throughout this chapter, the "levees only" approach (albeit not under this term), as well as the realization that levee building altered flood levels, were already current among the French engineers of the seventeenth and eighteenth centuries. In 1727 Governor Périer wrote to the company: "The waters of the river St. Louis [Mississippi] have risen one and a half feet above normal which comes from the levees which we were obliged to build and of which we cannot dispense without running the risk of losing the harvest and the plantations."[127] The problem of changing flood levels through human agency is described even more clearly in an anonymous "memoir to serve for the establishment of Louisiana" written after 1750. Among other environmental factors, this memoir considered the increased sedimentation that had been occurring at the river mouth since the French had built a post on La Balize at the outer edge of the East Pass (see map 2.3 below). The memoir suggested, "The deposits have only become thus considerable since we have stopped the overflow of the [Mississippi] river with the levees which force it to take a great volume of water to its mouth, which before was discharged into the lakes of the east and west."[128]

Charles Ellet and George Perkins Marsh might be the first Americans to recognize human influence on the rising flood levels of a river—a process that the French clearly recognized as caused by human agency. Similarly, army engineer Andrew Humphreys thus, without knowing, perpetuated a policy that had existed for more than two centuries. The fact that Ellet's and Marsh's realization came more than a hundred years after the remarks of Louisiana's French colonial personnel underlines the difficulty of transmitting environmental (and engineering) knowledge from one environment to another, as well as across time and different political and educational regimes. This apparent untranslatability of knowledge together with the structural path dependence of an existing levee system that relied on insubmersible earthen dams magnified the adaptive practice's flipside—vulnerability—throughout the nineteenth and early twentieth centuries.

Adaptation and Environmental Learning at La Balize

While levee building as an imported practice quickly started showing similar effects along the Mississippi River as levees in France, what did the early settlers learn about hurricane impacts and their effects on the alluvial soil of the delta environment? The 1722 hurricane not only made clear that hurricanes were a risk to be reckoned with along the Gulf Coast, but also introduced the French engineers to the malleability of the soil at the mouths of the Mississippi. De Pauger, who was in charge of planning and building New Orleans as well as fortifying the river mouth, was planning to build a fort and store house on the island he called La Balize, located at the easternmost mouth of the Mississippi River.[129] The strategic and economic importance of this place was recognized early. Since the journey from the Gulf upriver to New Orleans could take weeks for larger ships due to contrary winds, the island was ideally situated as an easily accessible point to unload goods and control the river traffic. It was particularly well-suited as a stopover from the point of view of the greater Caribbean, since the high point of the Spanish sailing route between Veracruz and Havana lay just below the Mississippi River mouth. Although mercantilist policy forbade Spanish ships to trade goods with foreign nations, Bienville expressly highlighted La Balize's advantages in terms of the interco-lonial contraband trade.[130]

A year after the 1722 hurricane, on 23 September 1723, de Pauger wrote to the company directors that "this island was eaten by the hurricane, to the point where it was cut and there was left no more than a peninsula of little elevated ground, covered with underbrush and sources of salty water. Some long-standing colonists have ascertained this, and I pale at seeing it so dimin-ished."[131] Of course, the engineers had observed changes in the river mouths before, and were, in addition, familiar with deltaic landscapes and the protec-tive structures they required, from France. Already in a letter of 23 April 1722, chief engineer Le Blond de La Tour had thus observed that "the grounds at the [Mississippi's] mouths are very extensive and very low which causes the wa-ters to overflow them and to bring trees with them which get stuck there and form several islands and several passes which lessen the force of the [river's] current."[132] In August 1722, just days before the hurricane, Le Blond de La Tour had had the opportunity to sound the passes at the mouths of the Mississippi. While paddling along in his canoe, he noted that the environment had much changed compared to the previous year. Apparently, the little islands he had mentioned to the directors had grown considerably.[133]

Despite observing the fast-changing alluvial environment and despite see-ing the damage the 1722 hurricane had wrought at La Balize, second engineer de Pauger was determined to develop this strategically and economically de-sirable island into a grand place, even a city.[134] However, apparently, there had also been voices that discouraged the establishment of La Balize, foreseeing its eventual abandonment. De Pauger, in turn, fervently defended his project to the directors of the company. He wrote that the river mouth and La Balize were of such an advantageous situation that, if they were located in France, and, had the king bestowed on him the honor of developing them, he would "employ what was dearest to him" to build in a short space of time a magnificent port and to make La Balize a "considerable place."[135] In the same letter, written nine months after his observations on the erosion of the island by the hurricane, and only shortly after remarking in another letter to the company that the is-land was partly inundated, he insisted that "the terrain is solid and not subject to inundation, as one has falsely tried to inform you [. . .]." The problem of ero-sion was, according to this new account by de Pauger, also under control since the island was to "be fully protected from ever being damaged or diminished, as it will be lined by piles towards the channel in order to be safe from heavy seas." In addition to this protection, the island was to be elevated by transport-ing soil and mud there with dredges and boats.[136]

De Pauger's vision for La Balize was compelling. In 1723, when the clear-ing of the island began, the French engineer described it as being 112 *toises* long and, behind the first row of buildings that was facing a quay, fifteen *toises* in breadth.[137] This space could be used "for creating gardens which would make everybody look upon this island with envy and to come and breathe the good air that reigns there."[138] Apart from this recreational idea, de Pauger was planning to build a store house for the (contraband) trade with the Spanish, batteries to defend the entrance of the Mississippi, and a chapel that was to have a double-life as a beacon in order for the ships to navigate safely through the shallow waters. All buildings were elevated to three feet above the (then-observed) highest tides. Also, de Pauger had apparently finished building the outdoor oven of the bakery as well as the forge of the smithy.[139]

Keeping in mind hurricanes and the fast-changing delta environment, perhaps the most intriguing and daring feature from today's perspective is the bridge connecting La Balize with its small neighboring island (see map 2.3). On the latter, slaves were lodged in wooden barracks. That the bridge did in fact exist and was not just an imagined edifice, as for example the city wall projected for New Orleans, we learn from a report almost twenty years after ground was broken at La Balize. In 1740 two hurricanes affected New Orleans and the Gulf Coast in short succession, on 11 and 18 September. *Lieutenant de Roi* Louboey wrote that the island had been hard hit and that the battery and the bridge had been swept away by the hurricane.[140] While the 11 September hurricane submerged La Balize under two feet of water, neither the island nor New Orleans had been at the center of the storm.[141] Dauphin Island, on the other hand had been eroded by half—Governor Bienville reported that three leagues of soil had disappeared from its center—by the first of the two hurricanes and Mobile was badly damaged by the wind and storm surge that had risen to ten feet.[142]

Ten years later, La Balize again figured prominently in the colonial correspondence. The storm surge of the 1750 hurricane[143] had inundated all the buildings on the island and caused damage to the stored goods. In addition, the East Pass, the main shipping route, had been silted up by the sands that the hurricane had transported there, reducing its depth from sixteen to twelve feet.[144] One year later, Michel, commander at La Balize, reported that the post was now perpetually flooded by about one foot of water and that the inundation would rise to three feet during hurricanes. With this situation at hand, Michel concluded that the island could no longer sustain the garrison and that the fort should be abandoned.[145] What de Pauger had argued against almost thirty years earlier had finally happened and had proven the—unidentified—doubters of the Balize project to be correct.

With regard to adaptation/vulnerability and environmental knowledge, it is clear that the contemporaries were by no means ignorant of the risks that might be involved in building on La Balize. For example, flood levels were closely monitored by the royal engineers, who were experts of hydrology and

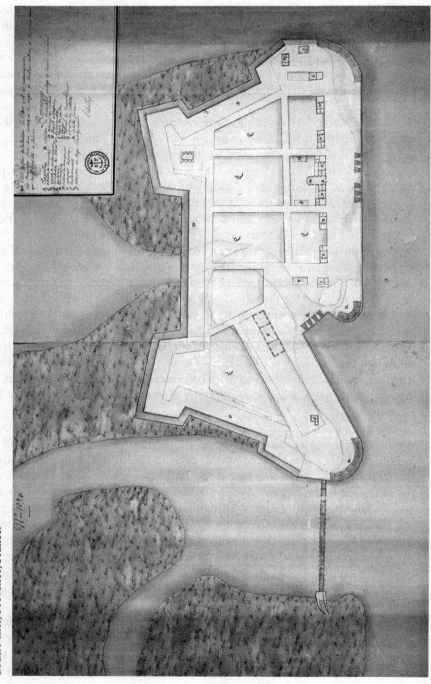

Map 2.3. "Plan du Fort de La Balise en l'Etat qu'il est presentement; les ouvrages faits sont marques en Rouge et couleur de bois, et en jaune ceux qui sont projettés a faire" (Map of the Fort La Balize in its current state, Nutimez fils, 1729. Courtesy of Archives Nationales d'outre-mer, Provence, France.

fortification. Clearly, erosion by wave action or by the current of the river was a known problem for which the engineers had time-tested technological solutions (building palisades of wooden piles in front of levees, river boards, and embankments). However, although de Pauger had witnessed in person the erosion of the island after the 1722 hurricane, it seems that the scope of erosion by hurricanes and the possibility of recurrence of this risk were not understood (and/or not heeded) until later.[146] As related above, according to de Pauger's account, there were even voices that cautioned against the establishment of the post, for fear of inundation. The option of building the fort elsewhere was discussed but was not chosen. It seems that de Pauger's personal ambition as the developer of this commercial and strategical node point drove its realization and, ultimately, the demise of the project after a mere thirty years of existence. The existing knowledge had either not sufficed or was impeded from being used to prevent this Louisianan mini-Atlantis.

In the engineer's letters, the hazard of inundation and erosion appears manageable by implementing the proper technologies, such as surrounding the islands with wooden piles and elevating their grounds to three feet above the highest (known) tides. The impression of technological feasibility, transmitted so nonchalantly from Louisiana to Paris, was partly owed to the need to maintain the image of a well-functioning colony, in order to keep the company satisfied and investors investing. The French colonial records this chapter is based on witness the enviro-technological path-dependence of decision-making processes taking place under such circumstances.

Interestingly, the submersion of the French settlement did not prevent Louisiana's first Spanish governor, Antonio de Ulloa, from making another attempt at fortifying the entrance of the river close to old La Balize on an island he called Real Católica in 1767.[147] Clearly, control of the ship traffic and commerce to and from New Orleans and farther upriver was as crucial for the Spanish as it had been for the French rulers. It was furthermore important to have a beacon and pilots at the river mouth to prevent the frequent shipwrecks that occurred in the shallow deltaic waters. It is, however, quite surprising that there was apparently no learning effect from the French experience. This is true, in particular, in the light of the reported contact that had existed between Governor Ulloa and the French engineer Hyppolite Amelot. The engineer had come to Louisiana in 1750, around the time when La Balize became uninhabitable; he succeeded Bernard de Vergès as chief engineer of Louisiana after the latter's death.[148] At the time of planning Fort Real Católica, the abandonment of La Balize had taken place only some fifteen years before; the inscription *ancient Fort noyé* (old submerged fort) could be found on a map depicting the "Mouths of the River St. Louis" dated 1764.[149] The changes wrought in the pass of La Balize over twenty years can be seen on two maps by Jacques Nicolas Bellin from 1744 and 1763 (maps 2.4 and 2.5). Lieutenant Philip Pittman, a

Map 2.4. "Carte des Embouchures du Mississippi, sur les Manuscrits du Dépôt des Cartes et Plans de la Marine" (Map of the mouths of the Mississippi, in the manuscripts of the Depot for Maps and Plans of the Marine), map by Jacques Nicolaos Bellin, 1744, showing the "Embouchure par ou les vaisseaux entrent" (River mouth through which the ships enter) in the right-hand corner, and the fort of La Balize below the entrance. Courtesy of Bibliothèque nationale de France, gallica.bnf.fr/.

Map 2.5. "Embouchures du Fleuve St. Louis ou Mississipi" (Mouths of the Saint Louis or Mississippi River), map by Jacques Nicolas Bellin, 1763, showing the changes in the mouths of the Mississippi since 1744: the "Entrée de la Balise qui n'est plus practicable" (Passage of La Balize that can no longer be used) on the right and the "Passe de l'Est dont on se sert aujourd'hui" (East pass that is in use today [i.e., in 1763]), at the top. Reproduced from an original in the collections of the Geography & Map Division, Library of Congress, G4042.M5 1763.B4.

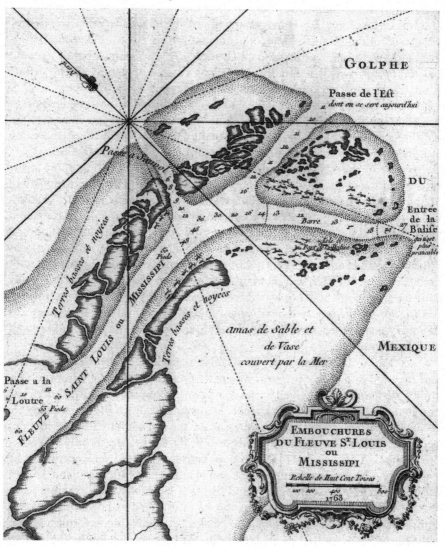

British army engineer who traveled up the Mississippi in the mid-1760s, noted that the remains of old La Balize were still visible in the swampy marshes.[150]

It is hardly conceivable that Ulloa was not aware of the fate of the French fort. The Spanish governor had received excellent training as an engineer at the Naval Academy of Cádiz and had drawn the plans for Real Católica himself.[151]

The strategic importance of a post at the river mouth apparently overrode considerations of longevity—the building of Fort Real Católica went ahead and was finished in 1767. However, the island's terrain was too marshy to support the foundation of the fort and thus, no full garrison—including the pilot's station, church, barracks, hospital, surgeon's house, and a bakery—could be supported by it. It seems that in Ulloa's case the volatility of the deltaic soil became apparent much quicker than in French La Balize, since in 1770 a group of engineers inspected Real Católica and reported on the erosion of the island by river and wave action. Consequently, the post was moved to the old French site, not least because Lieutenant General O'Reilly deemed enemy attacks more likely to come through Lakes Borgne and Pontchartrain.[152]

Because of the key importance of a pilot station and trading point at the river mouth, La Balize continued its existence at the East Pass after the death of Real Católica. The settlement was mentioned, lightly anglicized into The Balize, in newspaper reports after the Great Barbados Hurricane of 1831, when it apparently did not sustain much damage and sustained only minor flooding to its buildings.[153] In 1853 La Balize, by then also known as Pilotstown, was relocated to the Southwest Pass because the shipping channel it had been built on by de Pauger in 1723 had silted up.[154] Seven years later, La Balize's era finally came to an end in 1860, not by submersion or sinking soil, but again through devastation by the repeated hurricanes of the 1860 season. The settlement was definitely abandoned, and its last traces disappeared throughout subsequent hurricane impacts.[155]

The case of the French post La Balize has underscored path dependence and the temporal aspect in environmental knowledge and adaptation/vulnerability. De Pauger had arrived in the colony only one year before the hurricane and had no experience of this specific environment. Even the "long-standing colonists" he mentioned as his witnesses for the erosion of La Balize had not been in Louisiana longer than twenty-two years, during which only one other hurricane had occurred (1715) that could have served as a precedent. On La Balize, the trial-and-error approach came to a first halt with the abandonment of the permanently submerged island in 1751. Ultimately, the example of La Balize, Real Cátolica, or Pilotstown can be interpreted as both a case of untranslatability of environmental knowledge between different cultures and political regimes, as well as an illustration of human tenacity in the face of environmental hazards if a location is deemed strategically and/or commercially valuable.

Notes

1. Mathé Allain, *Not Worth a Straw: French Colonial Policy and the Early Years of Louisiana* (Lafayette: Center for Louisiana Studies, University of Southwestern Louisiana, 1988), 30.

2. Ibid., 49; Marcel Giraud, "The Official Initiative," in *The French Experience in Louisiana,* ed. Glenn R. Conrad, The Louisiana Purchase Bicentennial Series in Louisiana History (Lafayette: Center for Louisiana Studies, University of Southwestern Louisiana, 1995), 59. Jérôme Phélipeaux *compte* of Pontchartrain, had just succeeded his father Louis as the minister of marine and finances in 1699.

3. Vidal and Havard, *Amérique Française,* 82.

4. As a motive for Iberville's perseverance in pointing out the importance of a Gulf Coast colony, Mathé Allain suggests that "the letters and memoirs he addressed to Pontchartrain . . . leave little doubt that the Canadian visualized Louisiana as a new New France and himself as another Jean Talon." Mathé Allain, "French Emigration Policies. Louisiana, 1699–1715," in Conrad, *French Experience,* 107.

5. Allain, *Straw,* 50.

6. Allain, "Emigration," 106. According to Marcel Giraud, Louisiana never quite overcame this, in a way, programmed weakness of the beginnings. Marcel Giraud, *Histoire de la Louisiane Française. Le Règne de Louis XIV,* 1st ed., 4 vols., vol. 1 (Paris: Presses Universitaires de France, 1953), 1, 22.

7. Allain, *Straw,* 61.

8. Giraud, *Règne,* 1, 102–3, 272–73.

9. Marcel Giraud, *Histoire de la Louisiane Française. L'Époque de John Law (1717–1720),* 1st ed., 4 vols., vol. 3 (Paris: Presses Universitaires de France, 1953), 317.

10. Thomas Falconer, Robert Cavelier La Salle, and Henri de Tonti, *On the Discovery of the Mississippi, and on the South-western, Oregon, and North-Western Boundary of the United States* (London: S. Clarke, 1844), appndx., 26–27.

11. Instruction pour M. Perrier, 14 Avril 1718, Pierre Margry, *Découvertes et établissements des Français dans l'ouest et dans le sud de l'Amérique septentrionale (1614–1754). Mémoires et documents originaux. Première formation d'une chaine de postes entre le fleuve Saint Laurent et le Golfe du Méxique (1683–1724)* (hereafter *Découvertes*), 6 vols., vol. 5 (Paris: Maisonneuve, 1887), 605.

12. Richard Campanella, *Time and Place in New Orleans. Past Geographies in the Present Day* (Gretna, LA: Pelican, 2002), 21, 23; Mémoire de M. Hubert, 11 Avril 1723; Margry, *Première Formation,* 5, 642.

13. Bienville to Pontchartrain, 25 February 1708, in Dunbar Rowland and Albert G. Sanders, eds., *Mississippi Provincial Archives (1701–1763): French Dominion,* 3 vols., vol. 2 (New York: AMS Press, 1973), 122.

14. *Feluques* (feluccas) were small, fast-sailing ships that could also be propelled by oars. They ran under lateen sails and were built so that the helm could be used at either end of the vessel. Nancy M. Miller Surrey, "The Commerce of Louisiana During the French Regime, 1699–1763" (Ph.D. thesis, Columbia University, New York, 1916), 63.

15. Margry, *Découvertes,* vol. 4, 399. The *lieue* (league) of the Île-de-France (Paris) measured 4.18 kilometers, or 2.5 miles. Paul Delsalle, *Vocabulaire Historique de la France Moderne. XVIe—XVIIe—XVIIIe Siècles,* 2nd ed. (Paris: Armand Colin, 2007), 74.

16. Giraud, *Règne*, 1, 35.
17. Campanella, *Dilemma*, 109–10.
18. Giraud, *Époque*, 3, 318–19.
19. Claude C. Sturgill and Charles L. Price, "On the Present State of the Province of Louisiana in the Year 1720, by Jean-Baptiste Bernard de La Harpe," *Louisiana Historical Quarterly* 54, no. 3 (1971), 45. In the early years the river was not used for transport since the depth of the mouths of the Mississippi had yet to be established in order to allow for the passing of large vessels up to the new city. Giraud, *Époque*, 3, 319–20.
20. On rice as a Louisiana staple, see Morris, *Big Muddy*, 48, 52.
21. Valdeterre to Directors, n.d. [ca 1720], *Instruction sommaire*, HTML, ANOM, Colonies, C13A 6, fol. 357v, fol. 358v.
22. Margry, *Découverte*, vol. 4, 449ff.
23. "Three quarters of the 40 leagues of terrain reserved by the Company, from the English Turn, which is on the board of the sea, to the canal of Manchac and around New Orleans were inundated in 1719." Memoire concernant la colonie de la Louisiane 1664 à 1731, n.d., ANF, ANOM, Colonies, C13 C 1, fol. 28r. Forty leagues correspond to 167.2 kilometers (103.8 miles). Delsalle, *Vocabulaire*, 74; Roger Dion, *Histoire des levées de la Loire* (Paris 1961).
24. The concept of path dependence describes the process of increasing (economic and social) costs that develop over time when switching from one policy alternative to another. In addition, path dependence includes the understanding that there are distinctive formative moments or conjunctures that shape and reinforce divergent paths practice or decision-making. See Paul A. David, "Clio and the Economics of QWERTY," *American Economic Review* 75, no. 2 (1985); Paul Pierson, "Increasing Returns, Path Dependence, and the Study of Politics," *American Political Science Review* 94 (2000).
25. Le Blond de La Tour to Directors, 23 April 1722, ANF, ANOM, Colonies, C13 A 6, fol. 308r; on preadaptation see William B. Meyer, "Appendix A: Climate and Migration," in *The Role of Migration in the History of the Eurasian Steppe: Sedentary Civilization vs. "Barbarian" and Nomad*, ed. Andrew Bell-Fialkoff (New York: St. Martin's Press, 2000), 291.
26. About 12.8 American feet or 3.9 meters.
27. Adrien de Pauger to Directors, 23 September 1723, ANF, ANOM, Colonies, C13 A 7, fol. 259r. See also Margry, *Première Formation*, 5, 660.
28. Walter M. Lowrey, "The Engineers and the Mississippi," *Louisiana History: Journal of the Louisiana Historical Association* 5, no. 3 (1964), 235.
29. Margry, *Première Formation*, 5, 602–3. An English translation of this document by the directors of the company exists. See Sally Dart, "French Incertitude in 1718 as to a Site for New Orleans," *Louisiana Historical Quarterly* 15 (1932).
30. Le Blond de La Tour to Directors, 15 January 1723, ANF, ANOM, Colonies, C13 A 7, fol. 195r; de Pauger to Directors, 29 May 1724, ANF, ANOM, Colonies, C13 A 8, fol. 50v.
31. Richard Campanella, *Geographies of New Orleans. Urban Fabrics Before the Storm* (Lafayette: Center for Louisiana Studies, 2006), 77.
32. Cécile Vidal, "Les Autorités et les Colons Face aux Catastrophes Naturelles (Inondations et Ouragans) en Basse-Louisiane sous le Régime Français" (unpublished paper

presented at the Conference: La Louisiane à la Dérive. Louisiana Adrift, EHESS Paris, 2005), 6.

33. The discoverer Jean-Baptiste Bénard de La Harpe as well as the officer Jean François Benjamin Dumont de Montigny included accounts of the 1722 hurricane in their respective *Journal Historique* and *Mémoires historiques* of Louisiana. Jean Baptiste Bénard de La Harpe, *Journal historique de l'établissement des Français à la Louisiane* (New Orleans, LA: A.-L. Boimare, 1831), 339–42; Jean-François-Benjamin Dumont de Montigny, *Mémoires historiques sur la Louisiane*, 2 vols. (Paris: Cl. J. G. Bauche, 1753), vol. 2, 48–49.

34. Journal de Diron D'Artaguiette, ANF, ANOM, Colonies, C13 C 2, fol. 198v. (English translation from Newton Dennison Mereness, *Travels in the American Colonies*, ed. National Society of the Colonial Dames of America (New York: The Macmillan Company, 1916), 24.

35. Journal de Diron D'Artaguiette, ANF, ANOM, Colonies, C13 C 2, fol. 198v. One *pied de Paris* measured 32.48 cm (1.06 feet); Delsalle, *Vocabulaire*, 93. Hence, the Mississippi rose by about 2.6 meters (8.48 American feet) and the banks would have been overflowed by 5.1 meters (16.7 American feet).

36. Le Blond de La Tour to Directors, 30 September 1722, ANF, ANOM, Colonies, C13A 6, fol. 339r; Conte and Conrad, "Germans," 79.

37. Le Blond de La Tour to Directors, 15 January 1723, ANF, ANOM, Colonies, C13 A 7, fol. 193r.

38. Le Blond de La Tour to Directors, 30 August 1723, ANF, ANOM, Colonies, C13 A 6, fol. 328v.

39. Le Blond de La Tour, 30 September 1722, HNOC, ANOM, Colonies, C13A 6, fol. 340r–340v.

40. Chenoweth, "Reassessment," Table IV.

41. Salmon to Minister, 3 February 1733, HNOC, ANOM, Colonies, C13A 17, fol. 29.

42. Johnson, *Climate*, 16.

43. In a letter to the minister of the marine, Bienville wrote, "The barracks . . . are made of piles in the ground covered by bad bark . . . , the wood of the beds and the straw mattresses rot within very little time, the weapons and uniforms are exposed to the injuries of the weather." Bienville to Minister, 5 August 1733, HNOC, ANOM, Colonies, C13 A 16, fol. 134r. See also Miller Surrey, "Commerce," 94. On creole architecture see Richard Campanella, "The Evolution of Creole Architecture," *Times Picayune*, Friday, 8 April 2016.

44. Campanella, *Dilemma*, 317, 324.

45. Le Blond de La Tour, 15 January 1723, ANF, ANOM, Colonies, C13 A 7, fol. 197v. Le Blond de La Tour writes, "The hurricane having occurred at a time when we had occasion to expect an abundant harvest did not fail to discourage most of the habitants, however they are starting to regain strength, having almost mended the damage it [the hurricane] had caused to their buildings."

46. Jack D. L. Holmes, "Indigo in Colonial Louisiana and the Floridas," *Louisiana History: Journal of the Louisiana Historical Association* 8, no. 4 (1967), 331, 339.

47. A pirogue was a larger sized boat (forty to fifty feet long with a carrying capacity of between one and fifty tons); it was also sometimes called canoe (*canot*). The pirogue had seats for rowers, with an oar at the stern for navigation; it could also set a sail if

winds prevailed. They were easy to build and often replaced boats provided by the government; they were the principal means of transport between Lower Louisiana and Illinois. Miller Surrey, "Commerce," 57–58.

48. De Pauger to Directors, 15 September 1724, ANF, ANOM, Colonies, C13 A 8, fol. 80v.

49. Campanella, *Dilemma*, 304.

50. On the 1719 flood and levee building, see Mémoire concernant la colonie de la Louisiane, fol. 25; Bienville to Directors, 6 June 1719, ANF, ANOM, Colonies, C13 C 2, fol. 14r.

51. Company to Périer, "Mémoire de la Compagnie," ANF, ANOM, Colonies, C13 B 1, fol. 88v–89r. "Mr. de Pauger heretofore proposed to make an opening to the board of the river below New Orleans in order to build a little port there which the Brigantines, scallops and canoes could enter in order to be safe from the flooding of the river as well as from hurricanes. He also proposed to push this canal to Bayou St. Jean so as to communicate from Lake Pontchartrain to the river and to establish mills along this canal, but the Company found the undertaking of such a project too considerable."

52. Le Blond de La Tour to Directors, 23 April 1722, ANF, ANOM, Colonies, C13 A 6, fol. 308r.

53. Twelve French feet correspond to 10.8 American feet. Campanella, *Time*, 19, 85. De Pauger to Directors, 9 February 1724, ANF, ANOM, Colonies, C13 A 8, fol. 24v. For the conversion of French feet in to meters see Delsalle, *Vocabulaire*.

54. Le Blond de La Tour to Directors, 23 April 1722, ANF, ANOM, Colonies, C13 A 6, fol. 310r.

55. Campanella, *Dilemma*, 83.

56. De Pauger to Directors, 23 September 1723, ANF, ANOM, Colonies, C13 A 7, fol. 260r. This document is also transcribed in Margry, *Première Formation*, 5, 655–67.

57. The Superior Council was created by royal decree in 1712 and developed into Louisiana's central administrative body. See Jerry A. Micelle, "From Law Court to Local Government. Metamorphosis of the Superior Council of French Louisiana," *Louisiana History: Journal of the Louisiana Historical Association* 9, no. 2 (1968). On noncompliance see Superior Council, Arrest du Conseil, 8 June 1723, ANF, ANOM, Colonies, A 23, fol. 41v. For the ordinance see Superior Council, Arrest du Conseil, 28 February 1728, ANF, ANOM, Colonies, A 23, fol. 87v.

58. This was apparently no easy task, since in some places neither coal nor charcoal could be found to forge nails and screws. See de Pauger to Directors, 29 May 1724, ANF, ANOM, Colonies, C13 A 8, fol. 51r.

59. Le Blond de La Tour to Directors, 9 December 1721, ANF, ANOM, Colonies, C13 A 6, fol. 131v.

60. On the missing workforce, see Le Blond de La Tour to Directors, 15 January 1723, ANF, ANOM, Colonies, C13 A 7, fol. 197v; de la Chaise to Directors, 6 September 1723, ANF, ANOM, Colonies, C13 A 7, fol. 16v; de Pauger to Directors, 3 January 1724, ANF, ANOM, Colonies, C13 A 8, fol. 18r; De Pauger to Directors, 29 May 1724, ANF, ANOM, Colonies, C13 A 8, fol. 54v. On the hot climate, see Le Blond de La Tour to Directors, 23 April 1722, ANF, ANOM, Colonies, C13 A 6, fol. 309r; Le Blond de La Tour to Directors, 30 August 1722, ANF, ANOM, Colonies, C13 A 6, fol. 325r–325v; Superior Council, Arrest du Conseil, 8 June 1723, ANF, ANOM, Colonies, A 23, fol. 41v.

61. Le Blond de La Tour to Directors, 9 December 1721, ANF, ANOM, Colonies, C13 A 6, fol. 132r.
62. Dion, *Levées*, 172.
63. Le Blond de La Tour to Directors, 9 December 1721, ANF, ANOM, Colonies, C13 A 6, fol. 132r. "In a memoir, I have demanded that stones be brought from France instead of the east; and there was a Director of the Company who said that this was unnecessary, that there were enough stones in this country [Louisiana] as beautiful as those of St. Leu—I haven't seen them yet. If there are quarries, which I do not doubt, they must be very far away."
64. On the scarcity of stones and the adaptation of building materials, see also Campanella, *Dilemma*, 83–84.
65. According to de Pauger, the "Gentlemen of the [Superior] Council" had "borrowed" fifteen of the fifty African slaves who had been assigned to the task of building the levee near the hospital and had them work for their own purposes. De Pauger to Directors, 29 May 1724, ANF, ANOM, Colonies, C13 A 8, fol. 54r.
66. Superior Council to Directors, 27 February 1725, HNOC, ANOM, Colonies, C13 A 9, fol. 56v., fol. 57r., and fol. 57v.
67. Ibid., fol. 54v.
68. Hans Joachim Kühn, *Die Anfänge des Deichbaus in Schleswig-Holstein* (Heide, Germany: Boyens, 1992), 83ff; Marie Luisa Allemeyer, *"Kein Land ohne Deich!" Lebenswelten einer Küstengesellschaft in der Frühen Neuzeit*, Veröffentlichungen des Max-Planck-Instituts für Geschichte 222 (Göttingen, Germany: Vandenhoeck & Ruprecht, 2006), 85–87.
69. Again, I refer to Rockman's and Fuchs and Wenzel's notions of knowledge of natural cycles and disaster memory taking roughly a generation to accumulate or dissolve, respectively.
70. Périer to Directors, 4 June 1727, HTML, ANOM, Colonies, C13 A 10, fol. 228v.
71. The *arpent*'s measure varied according to whether the *arpent de Paris* or the *arpent du roi* was used. The former measured 34.19 ares (36.8 square feet), the latter measured 51.07 ares (54.9 square feet). Delsalle, *Vocabulaire*, 9.
72. Périer and Salmon, Ordonnance de M. Périer et Salmon, 4 November 1732, ANF, ANOM, Colonies, A 23, fol. 110v. A *toise* in general measured a little less than two meters (6.5 feet). The *toise* of Parisian masons measured 1.94 meters (6.3 feet). Delsalle, *Vocabulaire*, 115.
73. De Vaudreuil and Salmon, Ordonnance de M. de Vaudreuil et Salmon, 13 October 1743, ANF, ANOM, Colonies, A 23, fol. 138v; Miller Surrey, "Commerce," 93.
74. The 1732 ordinance also has a marginal note reading "was not executed for the mooring, the clearing, nor for the maintenance of the roads and bridges." Périer et Salmon, Ordonnance de M. Périer et Salmon, 4 November 1732, ANF, ANOM, Colonies, A 23, fol. 110v.
75. The *domaine* (manor) was part of the seigneurial system, the socioeconomic structure of old regime France. While New France was administered according to the model of French provinces with only a few modifications, in Louisiana, lands were not granted *en seigneurie*, as a seignorial estate, but *en roture*, that is, as a commoner's freehold. William Beik, *A Social and Cultural History of Early Modern France* (Cambridge, UK: Cambridge University Press, 2009), 57; Vidal and Havard, *Amérique Française*, 103.

76. Bienville and Salmon, Ordonnance de M. de Bienville et Salmon, 15 September 1735, ANF, ANOM, Colonies, A 23, fol. 121r.

77. Kühn, *Deichbau*, 87. The essence of this law is expressed in a German proverb: "Wer nicht will deichen, muss weichen"—Those who do not build levees must leave. Marie Luisa Allemeyer, ". . . dass man dem grausam Toben des Meeres nicht etwa kann Widerstand thun mit Gewalt," Kontroversen um den Küstenschutz im 17. und 18. Jahrhundert," in *Inszenierungen der Küste*, ed. Norbert Fischer, Susan Müller-Wusterwitz, and Brigitta Schmidt-Lauber (Berlin: Reimer, 2007), 87.

78. On cultural aspects of France's flood history (such as religious explanations of disasters, disaster memory, and the implementation of early disaster response systems) see René Favier, "Bordelais et Aquitains Face aux Inondations à la Fin du XVIIIe Siècle," in *Les Passions d'un Historien. Mélanges en l'Honneur de J.-P. Poussou*, (Paris: Presses de l'Université Paris-Sorbonne, 2010); René Favier and Anne-Marie Granet-Abisset, "Society and Natural Risks in France, 1500–2000. Changing Historical Perspectives," in Mauch and Pfister, *Natural Disasters*. The French original to this article is René Favier, "Sociétés Urbaines et Culture du Risque. Les Inondations Dans la France d'Ancien Régime," in *Les Cultures du Risque (XVIe–XXIe siècle)*, ed. François Walter, B. Fantini, and Paul Delvaux (Geneva: Presses d'Histoire Suisse, 2006); René Favier and Christian Pfister, *Solidarité et Assurance. Les Sociétés Européennes Face aux Catastrophes (17e–21e Siècles)* (Grenoble CNRS MSH-Alpes, 2008).

79. Roger Dion, *Le Val de Loire. Étude de Géographie Régionale* (Tours, France: Arrault et Cie, 1933); Dion, *Levées*.

80. Dion, *Val*, 325.

81. Dion, *Levées*, 140–41.

82. Ibid., 141; Dion, *Val*, 380.

83. Dion, *Levées*, 145–48, 155.

84. Ibid., 164–65.

85. Dion, *Val*, 178–79.

86. Ibid., 119; Beik, *France*, 57.

87. Allemeyer, *Deich*, 154.

88. Dion, *Val*, 378.

89. John Preston Moore, *Revolt in Louisiana: The Spanish Occupation, 1766–1770* (Baton Rouge: Louisiana State University Press, 1976), 31–33.

90. Gilbert Din and John E. Harkins, *The New Orleans Cabildo: Colonial Louisiana's First City Government 1769–1803* (Baton Rouge: Louisiana State University Press, 1996), 57, 100; Light Townsend Cummins, *Spanish Observers and the American Revolution, 1775–1783* (Baton Rouge: Louisiana State University Press, 1991), 6.

91. The Spanish Law of the Indies as well as the Code O'Reilly that applied to New Orleans since 1769 prohibited the spending of city funds on public works. Din and Harkins, *Cabildo*, 235, 238. The Code O'Reilly was a digest of Spanish law drawn up by Lieutenant General Alejandro O'Reilly who had been appointed by Spanish king Charles III to quell the Louisiana revolt of October 1768. On the Code O'Reilly see ibid., 50; on the revolt of 1768, see Moore, *Revolt*.

92. The Spanish Cabildo replaced the French Superior Council in 1769. The two institutions are hardly comparable, however, since the Superior Council was not designed as a city government and came to administer the whole province of Louisiana, whereas

the New Orleans Cabildo was a governing body concerned with the city proper. Din and Harkins, *Cabildo*, 101. On the evolution of the Louisiana Superior Council see Micelle, "Law Court"; Juan Bautista Garic, 9 December 1769, NOPL, Acts and Deliberations of the Cabildo, 18 August 1769–27 August 1779, AB 301, Reel 91-14, Book 1, fol. 8.

93. Din and Harkins, *Cabildo*, 236.

94. Juan Bautista Garic, 22 April 1772, NOPL, Acts and Deliberations of the Cabildo,18 August 1769–August 27, 1779, AB 301, Reel 91-14, Book 1, fol. 182-3.

95. Din and Harkins, *Cabildo*, 66.

96. Ibid., 242. The Cabildo minutes of October 1781 and November 1782 report the levees being in disrepair and crop losses due to breaches. On hurricanes and floods see Leonardo Mazange, October 12, 1781, NOPL, Acts and Deliberations of the Cabildo, 8 September 1779–25 June 1784, AB 301, vol. 2, Book 2, fol. 77–78; Leonardo Mazange, 8 November 1782, NOPL, Acts and Deliberations of the Cabildo, 8 September 1779–25 June 1784, AB 301, vol. 2, Book 2, fol. 144-45.

97. The Cabildo minutes of 8 November 1782, for example, reveal that the levee at Mr. Saubadon's property was breached because he had abandoned his land and the flood protection had not been maintained. The minutes state that the neighbors of Mr. Saubadon feared that their crops would be destroyed by this breach and consequent inundation. Leonardo Mazange, November 8, 1782, NOPL, Acts and Deliberations of the Cabildo, 8 September 1779–25 June 1784, AB 301, vol. 2, Book 2, fol. 144.

98. Din and Harkins, *Cabildo*, 237.

99. Leonardo Mazange, 8 November 1782, NOPL, Acts and Deliberations of the Cabildo. 8 September 1779–25 June 1784, AB 301, vol. 2, Book 2, fol. 145.

100. The royal standard bearer belonged to the voting members of the Cabildo and belonged to the group of *regidores perpetuos* (permanent councilors). Din and Harkins, *Cabildo*, 57.

101. Leonardo Mazange, 8 November 1782, NOPL, Acts and Deliberations of the Cabildo. 8 September 1779–25 June 1784, AB 301, vol. 2, Book 2, fol. 144, fol. 146.

102. Pedro Pedesclaux, 19 February 1790, NOPL, Acts and Deliberations of the Cabildo. 1 January 1788–18 May 1792, AB 301, vol. 3, Book 2, fol. 95; Din and Harkins, *Cabildo*, 238.

103. Father de Sedella, auxiliary vicar at New Orleans wrote to the Bishop of Santiago de Cuba that the fire, fueled by a strong wind, laid waste to three quarters of the city on Good Friday 1788. Sedella to Hechavarria y Elguezua, 28 March 1788, AANO, Correspondence, IV-4-c, A.L.S., 8 vo.

104. Pedro Pedesclaux, 9 April 1790, NOPL, Acts and Deliberations of the Cabildo. 1 January 1788–18 May 1792, AB 301, vol. 3, Book 2, fol. 102; Din and Harkins, *Cabildo*, 239.

105. Pedro Pedesclaux, 22 June 1792, NOPL, Acts and Deliberations of the Cabildo. 25 May 1792–17 April 1795, AB 301, vol. 3, Book 3, fol. 7.

106. Din and Harkins, *Cabildo*, 241.

107. Ibid., 239.

108. Laura L. Porteous, "Governor Carondelet's Levee Ordinance of 1792," *Louisiana Historical Quarterly* 10, no. 4 (1927). The levee ordinance transcribed and translated by Laura Porteous in 1927 was apparently a French-language copy of a Spanish original.

The French transcript has several spelling mistakes and the translation from French to English has some semantic mistakes in it (p. 513). Porteous's French transcript and English translation both use the term *syndic* (syndic) for the office of the levee overseer. Porteous's French transcript and English translation both use the term *syndic* for the office of the levee overseer. In old regime France the syndic (or *grand voyer*) was indeed responsible for overseeing public works and this office seems very similar to the *comisario anual* described by Gilbert Din in that syndics were elected on an annual or biannual basis and both were responsible for public infrastructure. Beik, *France*, 57; Vidal and Havard, *Amérique Française*, 161. In fn. 11 (p. 239) Din states that syndics already existed and "were present under the French, and the older rural districts probably continued their use." This seems plausible, yet a French/Spanish continuity of the office of syndic remains questionable in the light of Din's own statement that the French Superior Council did not concern itself greatly with public works. Cf. Din and Harkins, *Cabildo*, 101.

109.   Porteous, "Levee Ordinance," 513.

110.   Nassim Nicholas Taleb, *The Black Swan: The Impact of the Highly Improbable*, 1st ed. (New York: Random House, 2007), xvii–xviii.

111.   Porteous, "Levee Ordinance," 513.

112.   Din notes that there were about three thousand inhabitants in New Orleans in the 1760s and that in 1785 the population had increased by two thirds to 4980. This may not least be because of the immigration of a group of Acadians expelled from Canada in 1762 after British takeover and by the influx of people from the Canary Islands in 1777. Din and Harkins, *Cabildo*, 5–6; Gilbert C. Din, "The Canary Islander Settlements of Spanish Louisiana. An Overview," *Louisiana History: Journal of the Louisiana Historical Association* 27, no. 4 (1986), 354; Carl A. Brasseaux, "A New Acadia. The Acadian Migrations to South Louisiana, 1764–1803," *Acadiensis* 15, no. 1 (1985), 126.

113.   John G. Clark in his article on the role of the New Orleans Cabildo in the economic development of the city speaks of the "disintegrative pull of the hinterland on the city." The latter apparently increased during the 1780s when rising numbers of Americans started settling in the upper and lower Mississippi Valley. John G. Clark, "The Role of the City Government in the Economic Development of New Orleans. Cabildo and City Council, 1783–1812," in *The Spanish in the Mississippi Valley, 1762–1804*, ed. John Francis McDermott (1974), 134, 137.

114.   Allemeyer, *Deich*, 83, 91–94.

115.   Ibid., 154; Dion, *Levées*, 168.

116.   Campanella, *Dilemma*, 310; Ari Kelman, *A River and Its City: The Nature of Landscape in New Orleans* (Berkeley: University of California Press, 2003), 162.

117.   Kelman, *River*, 162; Morris, *Big Muddy*, 141.

118.   Kelman, *River*, 163–64. On the postbellum conditions of the Mississippi levees see Morris, *Big Muddy*, 147–60; John M. Barry, *Rising Tide: The Great Mississippi Flood of 1927 and How it Changed America* (New York: Simon & Schuster, 1997), 21–22.

119.   U.S. Army Chief of Engineers, *Annual Report of the Mississippi River Commission for the Fiscal Year Ending June 30, 1924* (Washington DC: Government Printing Office, 1924) as quoted in Kelman, *River*, 170. See also Susan Scott Parrish, *The Flood Year 1927: A Cultural History* (Princeton, NJ: Princeton University Press, 2016), 28.

120. Kelman, *River,* 169, 173–74, 178, 186–87.

121. Henry E. Chambers, *History of Louisiana,* vol. 3 (Chicago: American Historical Society, 1925), 327; James Parkerson Kemper, *A.B.C. of the Flood Problem: A Discussion By J.P. Kemper, C.E. Consulting Engineer of the National Flood Prevention and River Regulation Commission* (New Orleans: National Flood Prevention and River Regulation Commission, 1927), LSM, James Parkerson Kemper Papers, RG 52, Folder 6, 6–7.

122. Kemper, *Flood Problem,* 2; James Parkerson Kemper, *Address before the Round Table Club of New Orleans: Subject: Flood Control or Prevention in the Mississippi Valley,* 8 April 1937, LSM, James Parkerson Kemper Papers, RG 52, Folder 17, 2–3; Todd Shallat, *Structures in the Stream. Water, Science, and the Rise of the U.S. Army Corps of Engineers* (Austin: University of Texas Press, 1994), 20–21.

123. Kemper, *Address before the Round Table Club,* 3.

124. Kemper, *Flood Problem,* 7.

125. Morris, *Big Muddy,* 162.

126. Kelman, *River,* 163.

127. Périer to Directors, 4 June 1727, HTML, ANOM, Colonies, C13 A 10, fol. 228v.

128. Anon., Memoire pour sevir à l'établissement de la Louisianne, n.d. [after 1750], ANF, ANOM, Colonies, C13 C 1, fol. 93v.

129. De Pauger to Directors, 23 September 1723, ANF, ANOM, Colonies, C13 A 7, fol. 257r.

130. Dawdy, *Empire,* 111–12; see esp. en 25, 275.

131. De Pauger to Directors, 23 September 1723, ANF, ANOM, Colonies, C13 A 7, fol. 258r. This letter is also transcribed in Margry, *Première Formation,* 5, 655–67.

132. Le Blond de La Tour to Directors, 23 April 1722, ANF, ANOM, Colonies, C13 A 6, fol. 307v.

133. Le Blond de La Tour to Directors, 30 August 1722, ANF, ANOM, Colonies, C13 A 6, fol. 324r.

134. De Pauger to Directors, 3 January 1724, ANF, ANOM, Colonies, C13 A 8, fol. 10v.

135. De Pauger to Directors, 29 May 1724, ANF, ANOM, Colonies, C13 A 8, fol. 50v.

136. Ibid., fol. 51v.; de Pauger to Directors, 3 January 1724, fol. 10v.

137. American Gulf Coast historian Robert S. Weddle mistakenly sets the date of the establishment of La Balize at 1734. Robert S. Weddle, *Changing Tides: Twilight and Dawn in the Spanish Sea, 1763–1803* (College Station: Texas A&M University Press, 1995), 43; with the *toise* of Parisian masons measuring 1.94 m (6.3 feet), this would amount to 217.3 meters (705.6 feet) in length and 29.1 meters (94.5 feet) in breadth. Delsalle, *Vocabulaire,* 115.

138. De Pauger to Directors, 23 September 1723, ANF, ANOM, Colonies, C13 A 7, fol. 258r–259r.

139. De Pauger to Directors, 23 September 1723, ANF, ANOM, Colonies, C13 A 7, fol. 258r–259r; Anon., *Memoir pour servir à l'établissement de la Louisianne,* n.d. [after 1750], ANF, ANOM, Colonies, C13 C 1, fol. 93r.

140. Louboey to Minister, 7 March 1741, HNOC, ANOM, Colonies, C13 A 26, fol. 175r.

141. Two French feet correspond to 64.9 cm and 2.1 American feet. Delsalle, *Vocabulaire,* 93.

142. Ten feet is equal to 3.3 meters or 10.5 American feet. Three leagues correspond to 12.54 kilometers or 7.8 miles. See Bienville to Minister, 8 March 1741, HNOC,

ANOM, Colonies, C13 A 26, fol. 66r–67r; and de Beauchamp to Minister, 25 January 1741, ANF, ANOM, Colonies, C13 A 26, fol. 202rff.

143. The storm hit New Orleans and the surrounding area on 3 September 1750. See Vaudreuil-Cavignal to Minister, 24 September 1750, HTML, ANOM, Colonies, C13 A 34, fol. 276r–276v.

144. From about 17.02 American feet, or 5.1 meters, to 12.78 American feet, or 3.89 meters, respectively.

145. Michel to Minister, 28 May 1751, HTML, ANOM, Colonies, C13 A 35, fol. 260v.

146. For example, when the September hurricane of 1740 eroded half of Dauphin Island.

147. Moore, *Revolt*, 70–71.

148. Weddle, *Tides*, 13, fn 9.

149. Moore, *Revolt*, 74.

150. Philip Pittman, *The Present State of the European Settlements on the Mississippi* (London: J. Nourse, 1770), 8.

151. Moore, *Revolt*, 3, 70.

152. Weddle, *Tides*, 15, 23–24.

153. "The Late Storm," *National Gazette*, Philadelphia, 8 September 1831, 3.

154. Élisée Reclus, "Fragment d'un Voyage à la Nouvelle Orléans," *Le Tour du Monde* 1, no. 12 (1860), 186.

155. The 1860 hurricanes made landfall on the Louisiana Gulf Coast on 12 August, 15 September, and 2 October. Ludlum, *Hurricanes*, 171–77. The second hurricane completely destroyed recently relocated La Balize. "The Late Gale in the Gulf," *New York Herald*, 25 September 1860, iss. 8783, 4.

CHAPTER 3

Moving out of Harm's Way

"In order to protect themselves against this tempest, some of them abandon their houses for fear of being buried under the ruins and save themselves by hiding in caves and crevices. Or they even throw themselves prostrate in the middle of the fields where they remain throughout the whole storm," reported Charles de Rochefort, a Protestant minister, of the inhabitants of Tobago in his *Histoire Naturelle et Morale des Iles Antilles* published in 1658. To this de Rochefort added that other islanders would seek shelter in a sturdily built house in their neighborhood. Yet, he continued, "there were even some who retired to little huts which the slaves had built after the model of the Caribs since it was recognized by experience that these small and roundly shaped cottages with no other opening than a door and rafters that touch the ground were usually spared." The "more elevated houses," presumably those built by the colonists, on the other hand, were moved in their entirety from one place to another, if they were not totally destroyed by the wind.[1]

De Rochefort's report is probably one of the earliest to describe the practice of evacuation in case of a hurricane, though similar accounts of the more-hurricane-resistant architecture of slave and indigenous dwellings exist for St. Kitts and Jamaica from the early eighteenth century.[2] While from a present-day perspective (at least in the United States) the term "evacuation" might evoke the image of highways clogged with thousands of cars, in disaster research evacuation is rather neutrally defined as "a social process where agents relocate from one area threatened by exceptional social and structural disruption to an area perceived as less threatening." Horizontal or site evacuation—the most common form of protection from natural hazards—is the process of moving to private or public areas, including emergency shelters intended for short-term protection.[3] Historically, hurricane evacuation meant relocating to hurricane huts or other sturdy buildings, such as the local schoolhouse that could accommodate a large number of people. The practice of evacuating outside a hurricane's zone of impact by car became feasible on a large scale only after the convergence of automobiles as a means of mass transportation and improved hurricane forecasting technology in the mid-twentieth century, as we will see toward the end of this chapter.

Having such an early documentation of evacuation practices is significant because such accounts appear less frequently in historical sources. Evacuation, as a practice geared toward remaining in, or returning to, the place of settlement did not disrupt, or only temporarily disrupted, that place's economic and social fabric. Disaster migration, on the other hand—the other manner of moving out of harm's way—was historically much more noteworthy. The permanent departure of a part of a colonial settlement's population was usually registered by the authorities and deemed detrimental to the colony's development, as we will see below.

Furthermore, the French minister's account is noteworthy for the subject of adaptation to hurricanes since it allows a glimpse of the indigenous architecture of the Caribbean, which was evidently much better suited to resist the caprices of tropical weather than were the buildings of the French colonists. Second, it shows that proponents of both immigrant groups (forced as well as free) recognized this superiority of local knowledge and adaptation to the environment. Yet, it was the African slaves who actually built the shelters according to the indigenous model; the colonizers, on the other hand, continued building houses that were prone to being blown away in a hurricane and seem to have looked down on those "little huts" with some disdain, at least initially. De Rochefort's account illustrates an important paradox: although the French colonists fully recognized the advantages of the indigenous way of building houses, they did not adopt it to develop their own Creole architecture right away. The reasons for this initial rejection were mostly cultural. Building European-style houses was a way to distinguish "civilized" colonials from the *sauvages* ("savages", as eighteenth-century French colonists used to call native Americans). European ideas of climate and health also played a role in placing Caribbean plantation mansions on deforested hillocks where they could catch even the lightest summer breeze to ease the heat for their inhabitants. However, this choice of site also exposed them to the violence of hurricane winds, while the slave huts were built on lower-lying ground, which protected them from the full force of tropical cyclones.[4]

Matthew Mulcahy in his study on hurricanes in the British Caribbean notes, however, that by 1706 the (British) residents of Saint Christopher and Nevis had adopted the practice of building hurricane houses. According to the author, those structures also appeared in Jamaica and South Carolina, yet apparently they were not widespread, nor is there a clear cause for their decline.[5] The early colonial correspondence between the Louisiana engineers and Paris does not mention the adoption of hurricane huts from the French Caribbean nor any comparable structures being built on the plantations above or below New Orleans. Judging from the initial focus of the engineers on continental French building practices, it seems that the Caribbean influences that we can identify in the architecture of New Orleans today started emerging only toward the mid-1700s when New Orleans had firmly established its place in the local, (Circum-) Caribbean trade network.[6] These examples of early Caribbean architectural (non-) adaptation illustrate how cultural factors played a decisive role in enhancing or reducing European colonials' vulnerability in new and unfamiliar environments. Only over time, and with the empirical proof of African slave huts surviving what European plantation mansions did not, did colonial settlers start adopting indigenous architectural features.[7]

"The Chapter of Accidents Is Infinite in This Country"

Maybe if hurricane huts or sturdier buildings for people to evacuate to had been available in four-year-old New Orleans during the 1722 hurricane, historical accounts would have been different. In the absence of such resistant architecture, however, colonial official Delorme noted one month after the cyclone that soldiers, mariners and settlers were deserting the colony continuously. They were demanding to return to France as a consequence of the hurricane and of the dire situation in its aftermath. The only solution Delorme saw to this problem was to grant them the passage back home on the ships of the Company of the Indies.[8] Lest this may seem like an overreaction on the part of the settlers, it is important to recall the prehistory of the hurricane, with several changes of the colony's capital and, in the case of New Orleans, the relocation of part of the habitants to Natchez after the flood of 1719.[9] In other words, many of New Orleans's settlers already had a history of reestablishing themselves in the colony and for some the destruction by the hurricane was apparently the proverbial last straw. So, for the 1722 event, there is a clear reference between the hurricane and the wish of part of the population to migrate. It is thus a first instance of French New Orleanian post-hurricane disaster migration, or opting out or nonadaptation to New Orleans and its environs.

It has to be underlined however, that back-migration to France—even under normal (i.e., nondisaster) circumstances—was nothing unusual and did not only happen in Louisiana but also in New France and the French Caribbean.[10] For those who had come to Louisiana with very little and who had not been able to establish a proper subsistence in the colony yet—mostly due to royal or company government short-sightedness and the frequent moving of cities—it was likely a more favorable prospect to restart their existence in their known home country rather than trying again in Louisiana. Comparatively weak governmental and social structures as well as the relative lack of material wealth thus rendered the decision to return to France conceivable. For the respective government of the colony—be it royal or by company—the desertion of settlers was disastrous, however, since manpower mattered crucially in reaping the hoped-for profits from the colony.

The next hurricane recorded in the French colonial sources that affected New Orleans occurred on 29 August 1732. Besides being a decade of levee building and heightened engineering activity along the lower Mississippi, the ten years between New Orleans's first and second hurricane experiences was also one of increased French–Indian conflict. Initial French relations with the Indian nations of the Lower Mississippi Valley had been amicable enough and were characterized by a high dependence of the French on indigenous foodstuffs and strategic alliance. However, John Law's 1717 to 1720 settlement scheme for Louisiana increased pressure on some of the Indian villages, in particular at Fort Rosalie (present-day Natchez). The elevated soil of this area was not as prone to floods as the New Orleans site had been; it was fertile and apparently well-suited for growing tobacco, which was the Company of the Indies' new plan for making Louisiana a profitable colony at last.[11] Increasing encroachment of French settlers on the villages of the Natchez throughout the decade between 1722 and 1732 led to heightened tensions and skirmishes between the newcomers and the Natchez.[12] This phase culminated in the so-called Natchez Uprising (also known as the Natchez Massacre) of 1729, during which about 145 French men, 36 women, and 56 children were killed.[13] This escalation of violence was a reaction to a previous, provocative announcement by the French commander, De Chepard (also spelled Détcheparre), at Fort Rosalie, that the colonists were going to take possession of the land of the largest Natchez village, and that the indigenous population was to leave the territory and to move elsewhere.[14]

The Natchez Uprising spread the fear of further Indian attacks among the French colonists at New Orleans. The killing of the settlers at Fort Rosalie effectively marked a turning point in the French–Indian relations in the Lower Mississippi Valley. After the massacre, the French together with their ally, the Choctaw, started intimidating the Chickasaw who were allied to the English and provided refuge to the Natchez. The latter had abandoned their villages after the French had launched a revenge coup against them in 1730–31. To make matters worse, as a consequence of the Indian revolt the Company of the Indies saw itself unable to maintain the Louisiana colony any longer and ceded it back to the French crown.[15]

It was during this atmosphere of heightened tensions and anxiety that the hurricane of 29 August 1732 occurred. Lieutenant Louboey sent the following account of events to the minister of the marine (Jean-Frédéric Phélipeaux, count of Maurepas) in Paris who had become the addressee of such reports after the resignation of the company:

> I have had the honor to inform your Eminence of the most interesting events that have passed in this colony until 19 July 1732 and I have taken the liberty of presenting to his Eminence the need it [the colony] has for prompt

succor in order to take a more advantageous form than the one it has had until present. We all hope for one which would put us into a state of acting in favor of its establishment and security but unfortunately fate has decided differently, and we see ourselves set back more than ever by the accidents that have happened and which were impossible to foresee. The hurricane of August 29, last, ravaged the whole harvest, overthrew the houses and destroyed three quarters of the foodstuffs, tobacco, cotton and other crops which put the settlers in the saddest situation of the world and three quarters would have perished of hunger had there not been some three or four thousand quarts of rice in the stores of the Company, the distribution of which saved the population from a famine. And to make matters worse in the time in which we were awaiting with great impatience the arrival of the king's ship to diminish our suffering, we learned with pain, Milord, that it had parted from Cap François on the 5th of the same month without anyone having had the slightest news, which made us fear with great reason that an accident had happened to it . . . , the storm lasting for a long time on the sea with extreme violence, according to what we were able to learn from the people of a small Spanish cargo boat which came to New Orleans.[16]

In Louboey's account the hurricane appears as a major setback to the colony's development, not only with regard to the built environment (overturned houses) but especially with regard to the food situation. It is thus important to put Louboey's description of the barely avoided famine into the wider context of early Louisiana's food economy. Initial experiments with planting wheat at Biloxi and Mobile had failed disastrously so that the French on the Gulf Coast—apart from depending on the irregular food shipments from France—soon relied on Indian crops (maize, in particular) for their subsistence. A lively food trade—what Daniel Usner called a "frontier exchange economy"—developed between the indigenous population and the French newcomers throughout the first two decades of the colony. The colonists preferred the easier option of buying foodstuffs from the Indian nations to tilling their own soil, and thus a mutual dependence on each other's exchange products developed, with European tools and blankets traded for Indian maize.[17]

As early as 1708 wheat had reentered the menus of Louisianans by way of trade with the French settlers at Illinois, where the crop grew abundantly. Yet the Illinois wheat supply varied greatly from year to year, owing to climatic factors in Illinois on the one hand and to the arduous and dangerous transport route that was the Mississippi, running through the territory of various Indian nations who were not all allies of the French colonists, on the other. Thus, despite the fact that by 1730 the important Illinois trade was well-established, the company had not been able to stop food shipments from France as it had sought to.[18]

In other words, two of the main local food sources, wheat from Illinois and maize from the local Indian nations, were inherently dependent on stable social relations, while shipments from France were usually dependent on favorable sailing conditions as well as the French government's willingness or ability to send them. It seems likely that the tense diplomatic situation with some of the Indian nations after the Natchez Uprising and the French retribution rendered trade relations more volatile. The addition of a hurricane that destroyed the colonists' own crops as well as, possibly, the ship with provisions from France, laid bare the vulnerable situation of the Louisiana colony with regard to food availability. According to Lieutenant Louboey's account, the French population would have experienced a famine had it not been for the rice stored in the warehouse. The crop had begun to be planted along the banks of the Mississippi after the first slave shipment to Louisiana in 1719 and had become a staple for the African population as well as for the French colonists. Yet, even good rice yields were incapable of fully relieving the hardship that frequently arose from delayed supplies from France as well as from the Illinois country.[19]

The colony was granted no break from its subsistence difficulties—a fact that Governor Bienville laconically commented on, writing that he was "aware of the fact that the chapter of accidents is infinite in this country." According to reports by Bienville and *commissaire-ordonnateur* Salmon, a drought occurred during the months of April and May 1733 that "dried out the earth in such a way that it was hardly possible to work the soil." This was followed by extreme rainfall that lasted for more than two months and that apparently persisted at the time of Bienville's writing his letter. More severely, "these two extremities caused the delay of sowing, [so] that the early tobacco crop was flattened to the ground and some of the settlers were obliged to cut it at its foot so that it was only a little higher than the rice and all of this will make a very mediocre harvest." From Bienville we also learn that the habitants, in order to overcome the previous year's hardship, had to sell their cattle. While this provided the colony's soldiers with a long-hoped-for source of fresh meat, it added to the settlers' situation of extreme dearth.[20]

As if the events of early 1733 had not been bleak enough, a hurricane ravaged New Orleans and the surrounding region on 17 July from La Balize to Natchez. The storm lasted for thirty hours and was apparently "almost as strong as the one of last year." It overturned some buildings and Bienville estimated that half of the maize crop, which was almost ripe, was lost.[21] The rice, on the other hand, had hardly been affected and the reserves that had been made of this crop, that were still in the warehouse, were "the salvation of the Colony."[22] According to Governor Bienville's letter the desertion of the colony would have been complete had it not been for the officials' ability to distribute the rice among the population.[23] *Commissaire-ordonnateur* Salmon wrote that the events of 1732 were still fresh in people's minds and that the renewed loss of almost all the crops

> distressed the settlers in such a way that some resorted to asking for their passage to France and others sold their property in order to move to Illinois. I had the honor of pointing out to Your Highness in my letter of 19 January 1732, that there had been a great number of workers employed by the Company and which were not employed on account of the King, who demanded to return to France. I suggested retaining them by the means of paying them out of the state expenditures so that the colony would not be totally deserted. ... The settler, absorbed in his misery, fell even more into consternation when he learned that specie had neither been sent with the *Gironde,* nor with the *Saint Anne.* He does not even think about merchandise which is sent off or stored in the warehouses, he imagines this colony to be abandoned and without security, which tightens the purse for the little there is to be had here. . . . We live here from day to day, it is not the same as in one of the old Colonies where you find resources.[24]

Even though it is not mentioned in the colonial official's letters reporting on the hurricanes, this second hurricane impact still occurred in the context of the ongoing aftermath of the Natchez Uprising and the heightened tensions within the French-Indian alliance of Louisiana.[25] Anxiety with regard to the social environment coupled with the almost complete lack of resources for subsistence and trade caused by the two hurricanes and the climatic extremes thus drove habitants either to migrate back to France or to the more prosperous Illinois settlement to the north. Salmon's account illustrates the vulnerability of an underpopulated colony. It might have been able to absorb the impact of one hurricane and the consequent destruction of its subsistence and export basis, but the recurrence of climatic extremes (drought and extreme precipitation) in the crucial months of sowing and a back-to-back hurricane impact overstretched the settlers' capacity for shock absorption. "The settler for his own part who had difficulty to support his family, could hardly give employment to the worker who has no other resource than his arms, so he remained idle."[26] With the cattle sold as a consequence of the hardship of the previous year, neither planters nor workers had a basis for subsistence. Although there are no numbers available, the migration of settlers caused by the combination of climatic and social factors apparently called into question the existence of the colony that counted merely about eight thousand individuals in the 1730s, three thousand of which lived in New Orleans and its vicinity.[27] Judging from the *commissaire-ordonnateur's* report, a substantial number of colonists was bent on leaving the colony. This decision was especially daunting considering the general French unwillingness to populate the New World colonies, even more so in the face of the specific dearth of immigrants to Louisiana due to its bad reputation in Europe.[28] Reverse migration of a part of the population ultimately rendered those who remained more vulnerable to intercolonial conflict as well as to further subsistence crises. In the colonial frontier exchange economy a certain level of food security as well as produce for colonial trade could be attained only if a large enough population was present to cultivate the soil.

Although it appears from Salmon's account as if the hurricanes and their impacts had been the sole cause for the desertion of the colony, the tense diplomatic relations with the local Indian alliance and the change from company government back to administration from Versailles, resulting in the appointment of new colonial personnel in 1731, probably added to the settlers' frustration. Salmon's patronizing description of the settler as being "distressed" and "absorbed in his misery" is, in fact, the closest the colonial correspondence gets to conveying the situation of the actual settler on the ground. At the same time, Salmon described the very real economic crisis that resulted from the aftermath of the two hurricanes and the settler's losing faith in the viability of the colony. The—real and imagined—lack of produce as well as of specie for exchange and trade "tightened the purse" and dried up the local economy.

The exodus of the settlers in reaction to the 1732–33 hurricanes can be assessed as an instance of disaster migration and hence as nonadaptation to the local environs since, apparently, part of the population in and around New Orleans decided that it would not continue to live with the hurricane risk and its consequences. Clearly, the combined impacts of the hurricanes, drought, and heavy rainfall did not destroy New Orleans and the surrounding plantation complex so irrevocably that the population was forced to leave en masse. A large enough number of habitants clung to their existence in and around New Orleans and stayed. Disaster migration was hence self-administered and—disregarding force of circumstance—voluntary. Yet, the disaster migration from New Orleans and its environs at least temporarily jeopardized the existence of the colony.

Paul Lachance in his demographic study on Louisiana, in fact, notes a population decline for Upper and Lower Louisiana between 1732 and 1737, with figures at 6,072 and 5,659 inhabitants, respectively.[29] Lachance mentions the Natchez Uprising in 1729 and the curtailment of the slave trade of the 1730s as reasons for the decline.[30] It is plausible however, that some of the diminishing of the population is also related to the hurricane and drought events of the early 1730s.

Did the colonial government introduce new measures with regard to building codes and food security as a consequence of the hurricanes? The ordinances concerning the built environment that were issued between November 1732 and October 1743 all pertained to levee building and maintaining, rather than to the houses of the city and the material they should be constructed with.

It seems that either building with more storm-safe material was not conceived of yet, or that it was deemed impossible with the lack of stone quarries in the vicinity of New Orleans. However, with regard to the food situation of the colony, Bienville, at the end of his report to the minister of the marine urged, "It is an essential policy always to keep 2,000 or 3,000 quarts of rice in the warehouse which could be renewed annually or biannually, according to the events, be it by selling it or be it by having it renewed."[31] He thus drew an immediate lesson from the experience of having rice in the city's stores that helped prevent the famine that would have been caused by the coupled climatic impacts. Again, it is impossible to tell whether his suggestion was heeded and if rice did become a sort of emergency or hurricane staple. Taking into account present-day New Orleanian Creole Cuisine, rice certainly remained an integral part of Lower Louisiana's food culture.

An accumulation of climatic extremes and diplomatic tensions similar to those of 1732–33 occurred again only six years later, in 1739–40. In September 1739 Governor Bienville launched the second campaign against the Chickasaw. Twelve hundred French soldiers and 1,500 of France's Indian allies were on their way to a site near present-day Memphis, Tennessee, whence they intended to start their campaign, when an unusually late 11 October hurricane hit the Gulf Coast.[32] Although a connection with the hurricane is not explicitly made in the sources, a January 1740 letter from Lieutenant Louboey that followed his account of the hurricane in October stated that the colony had experienced three months of continuous rain.[33] It is likely that this extreme precipitation was a result of the hurricane. The unfavorable weather conditions—resulting in impassable roads and sickness among the soldiers—had a decisive effect on the campaign being a disastrous failure. In addition, the rainfall caused the Mississippi to rise and to inundate the lower Mississippi area "against ordinary" in January 1740.[34]

In September of the same year, the Gulf Coast was hit by two hurricanes within eight days.[35] Although New Orleans was not greatly affected, it was involved in providing disaster relief in the form of foodstuffs to Mobile and Dauphin Island, both of which were badly damaged. The first hurricane washed away half of Dauphin Island, destroyed all the ships on the coast, and drowned three hundred cattle. Apparently the effects of the second hurricane were felt in an area including Biloxi, the Pascagoula River in present-day Mississippi; and Mobile, the Alibamons, and Tombigbee River in present-day Alabama.[36] The torrential rainfall caused by the hurricane—this time the connection is made clear by the commander of Mobile, de Beauchamp—overflowed all the rivers and destroyed crops from Carolina to Mobile.[37] This extensive devastation of Lower Louisiana's food sources—Indian as well as French—resulted in extreme food scarcity and an inflation that doubled the price for rice and almost tripled it for maize.[38]

Louboey and de Beauchamp in their letters to the minister of the marine, the count of Maurepas, do not mention whether the three hurricanes and the consequent subsistence crisis caused another wave of disaster migration among the settlers; it is, however, conceivable that they did. Furthermore, it is likely that the combined effects of those two back-to-back hurricane events in a time period of six years did not allow for a thorough recovery of the French Louisiana Gulf Coast area.

For the next decade the French sources are quiet with regard to hurricane impacts on the French settlements. It is important to keep in mind, however, that in the meantime the population of New Orleans and its environs had to grapple with the annual floods of the Mississippi and with the shifting climatic patterns from phases of extreme rainfall to extreme drought. On 3 September 1750 the last reported hurricane of the French period of Louisiana swept over the Gulf Coast leaving in its wake destroyed crops and houses and changing the mouths of the Mississippi, a vital node of ship traffic to and from New Orleans. Apparently, the area had experienced a drought in spring and continuous thunderstorms, "storm upon storm" in the months preceding the hurricane.[39] Despite the inclement weather the harvest would have been abundant, according to Governor Vaudreuil-Cavagnial, had it not been for the cyclone that destroyed it all and caused the by-now familiar pattern of postdisaster price inflation in the colony.[40]

The fact that "the economy of Louisiana proved a grave disappointment" to the French crown between the colony's retrocession in 1731 and its passing over to Spain toward the end of the Seven Years War (1756–63) in 1762 was the result of a mixture of political, social, and environmental factors.[41] Prominent among those factors were the double-headed structure of the French Louisiana government, which generated conflict and factionalism and prevented coherent policies from being implemented;[42] the wars with the Chickasaw that consumed considerable human, financial, and material resources; and the propensity of the settlers to engage in trade with the native nations of the region and to smuggle within local illicit trade networks in order to provision themselves, which worked against the mercantilist goals the colony was supposed to fulfill.[43] Hurricanes could affect staple and cash crops in vast areas, disrupting local and regional food markets and supply networks, even more so if the storms occurred in consecutive years. Ensuring a more or less regular shipment of the crops the mother country desired from the colony was difficult to maintain even without the sociocultural factors coming into play. As a result, Louisiana depended on the royal treasury and provisions from France without providing meaningful returns as late as the 1750s. In other words, throughout the French period the colony never became self-sustaining and disaster migration in the aftermath of hurricane impacts continued to be a problem, as we will see below.

Revolutionary Wars and Hurricanes

The September 1750 hurricane occurred at the beginning of a phase of virtual isolation of Louisiana from France, increasing particularly during the Seven Years War. Left to their own devices, the second generation of Louisiana Creoles developed their own modes of survival and increasingly relied on the established, illicit trade economy for provisioning and making a living. The period hence "encouraged self-assertiveness and disregard for authority."[44] When Louisiana's new Spanish governor Antonio de Ulloa took over the colony in March 1766 after its cession to Spanish king Charles III in 1762, the commercial and local political power structures that had developed largely out of necessity on the ground clashed with the rigid Spanish mercantilist policy that was to replace the laissez-faire French Louisiana regime.

With Spanish rule, new linguistic, commercial, and (in particular) geopolitical realities imposed themselves on New Orleans and Louisiana. As part of the Spanish colonial system, formerly French Louisiana found itself under the jurisdiction of the captain general of Cuba—at the time of the cession Antonio María Bucareli—who was directly responsible to the Council of the Indies and Charles III.[45] In other words, the royal subsidy appropriated to Louisiana as well as the governmental correspondence now reached Louisiana through Havana or Santo Domingo, rather than from Paris, across the Atlantic. Santo Domingo was the larger Caribbean captaincy general overseeing that of Cuba. After 1763 the Cuban capital became the most important military command in Spanish America, in particular after 1775 when the Spanish secretary of state, the marquis of Grimaldi and the minister of the Indies José de Gálvez, decided to make Cuba (and Louisiana) the bases for the observation of the American Revolution.[46] Havana as an economic and political center was, however, inherently vulnerable to hurricane strikes and thus to the interruption of the flows of finances, information, and goods to its new territorial possession.

Despite the new Spanish rule and the imposition of Spanish as the new official language, Louisiana remained largely culturally French, however, not least because of the immigration of Acadian refugees who had been expelled by the British from their northern homelands after the Treaty of Paris in 1763. Between 1764 and 1770 1,020 Acadians (a term that later linguistically morphed into Cajuns) settled west of New Orleans on Bayou Lafourche and on Bayou Teche, and above New Orleans on the Mississippi. However, the newcomers who arrived after 1766 were not allowed to choose their own place of settlement but instead were dispersed with strategic intent by Spanish Governor Ulloa, earning him the resentment of the Acadian community.[47] Even a larger-scale Spanish settlement scheme of bringing settlers from the Canary Islands to the Lower Mississippi Valley between 1779 and 1783 did not change the fact that the majority of Louisiana's inhabitants were francophone and culturally French.[48]

Louisiana's economic realities changed crucially under the new regime.[49] The French, British, and Spanish Caribbean had been an integral part of Louisiana's (illicit) trade network from the beginning, and under the laissez-faire attitude of the French crown toward its stepchild colony, it had evolved into a local economy striving for free trade.[50] The imposition of Spanish mercantilist policies threatened Louisiana Creole power relations that had co-evolved with the contraband commercial system and jeopardized emergency provisioning in case of hurricane events. Important French port cities such as Cap Français (today Cap Haitien) in Saint-Domingue, suddenly turned into forbidden destinations due to the new trade regulations. In other words, where before Louisiana's governor had called on nearby French as well as Spanish settlements (Mobile, Pensacola, Veracruz, and Cap Français) for the acquisition of foodstuffs after a hurricane or in cases of shortage, *legal* options of obtaining produce were now limited to Spanish destinations. Yet if those destinations happened to be affected by the same (or another) hurricane, Spain's commercial policy exacerbated the subsequent food shortage for all affected parties.[51]

The first two hurricanes to impact Louisiana during the Spanish Dominion coincided with Antonio de Ulloa's arrival in the French colony in 1766. The first, a September cyclone, did not affect New Orleans and its environs directly; the second, which lasted from 11 to 14 October, sank the Spanish convoy ships that were headed to Louisiana with the royal subsidy. It took more than a year for replacement funds to arrive and to relieve the hardship in Spain's newly acquired territory, despite Ulloa's urgent pleas. Since the whole Caribbean was devastated by the 1766 hurricane season the illicit supply network had broken down entirely so that neither legal nor illegal trade could provide the stricken colonies with the basic necessities. Sherry Johnson, in her study on hurricane disasters in the Spanish Caribbean sees Louisiana's revolt against the new Spanish regime in 1768 in connection with the 1766 hurricanes and the restrictive Spanish commercial regulations that prevented recovery and deteriorated basic living conditions in the colony.[52] However, the attempt of Louisiana's merchant revolutionaries at becoming a semi-independent French republic failed, the revolt was quelled, and Louisiana was definitely brought under Spanish jurisdiction by Irish-born lieutenant general Alejandro O'Reilly in 1769.[53]

Additional hurricanes affected New Orleans and the Louisiana Gulf Coast in 1772, 1776, 1779, 1780, 1793, and 1794. Of those six years the last four are of particular interest with regard to adaptation, subsistence crises, and migration because they occurred in two consecutive years, respectively, and coincided with the social disaster of war. Between 1775 and 1779 Spain had maintained its neutrality in the conflict between the thirteen rebellious American colonies and their British mother country.[54] Yet Spain was potentially hostile toward the British for taking Florida as a prize after the Seven Years War and the Treaty of Paris in 1763. What is more, Cuba had started relying on the flour shipments the American cities of Philadelphia and Boston provided to the British Caribbean islands in the aftermath of the 1772 hurricane season, which was felt more strongly on the islands than on the shores of the Louisiana Gulf Coast and in the Mississippi Delta.[55] In other words, although Spain declared neutrality in the British–American conflict that escalated in 1775, it continued trading with the North American cities in order to provision its Caribbean colonies with necessary foodstuffs that were still faltering throughout Spain's own grain belt.[56] With the situation thus preconfigured, Spain entered the Revolutionary War (or the American War of Independence) on the side of the rebellious colonies against Britain in May 1779.[57]

For Spain, important events were to unfold in Louisiana during the American Revolution that involved New Orleans prominently. Preparations toward an active role in the British–American conflict had taken place throughout 1777; in that same year Charles III authorized the augmentation of Louisiana's battalion by seven hundred recruits from the Canary Islands. Bachelors as well as married men were to go to Louisiana and settle there permanently. Apart from the need for military reinforcements, the minister of the Indies also deemed Louisiana was still underpopulated with Spaniards.[58] In this new conflict, Louisiana and New Orleans were once again thought strategically important for information gathering, for which the city's far-ranging merchant networks could be used, and because its port could receive news from inland via the Mississippi, as well as via the Caribbean Sea.[59]

The new soldiers and inhabitants of the colony were brought to New Orleans between 1778 and 1780 and, like the Acadians a decade before, were located in sites selected primarily to safeguard New Orleans against an enemy invasion coming via the Mississippi River. The Isleños' new homes had been chosen by Louisiana's governor Berndardo de Gálvez who had arrived in the colony in 1777 and who had, consequently, no long-term experience with the Mississippi Delta environment.[60] Two sites were chosen upriver from New Orleans: on Bayou Lafourche and on Bayou Manchac. Below the capital Gálvez chose Barataria to the west of the Mississippi and San Bernardo (later to become St. Bernard), across the river, close to the east bank.[61] Both of the last locations were inherently vulnerable to flooding through storm surge; that vulnerability became painfully apparent throughout the first two years of the settlement scheme that coincided with the 1779 and 1780 hurricanes.

Just as Governor Gálvez was preparing his campaign to move up the Mississippi in order to wrest Fort Bute at Manchac, Fort Panmure at Natchez and Baton Rouge back from the British, the 1779 hurricane hit New Orleans in the early morning hours of 17 August.[62] The winds continued for seven hours until 10:00 in the morning, destroying all the small transport vessels in the river, as well as the larger seagoing ships. Governor Gálvez reported that the city was "the most deplorable spectacle ever seen. There is hardly a house which wasn't destroyed, and many are ruined and damaged, the fields razed, the surrounding plantations, which were the only ones from which I could get notice until now, are all flattened; in one word: harvest, livestock and stores are all lost."[63] The governor had to temporarily suspend his plans of attacking the English settlements upriver because of the lack of transportation, provisions, and, above all, because his soldiers—many of whom were Canary Islanders who had arrived barely a month before the hurricane in July—were in no state to go to war.[64] "I think they would rather allow themselves to be killed than be separated from their unfortunate parents, wives, children and sisters, abandoned to pain and inclemency in the middle of the fields."[65] Apparently strong leadership and Gálvez's charismatic personality managed to change the soldiers' minds and on 27 August the governor marched up the Mississippi with a multiethnic army of 649 men from the Canary Islands, Ireland, the British colonies in North America, Louisiana, Mexico, Puerto Rico, Cuba, and Santo Domingo to win back the upriver settlements.[66]

On the heels of the 1779 cyclone and the successful campaign in the Lower Mississippi Valley came the August 1780 hurricane. It preceded three strong October hurricanes that wreaked havoc throughout the Spanish Caribbean and thwarted Gálvez's first attempt at regaining Pensacola.[67] Louisiana's intendant, Martín Navarro—not to be confused with his relative and Captain General of Cuba, Diego José Navarro—wrote to José de Gálvez, the minister of the Indies, that another hurricane had hit the Louisiana Gulf Coast on 24 August. According to the intendant's report, the day before the hurricane "the horizon turned to a color of pale fire the reverberation of which reflected on the surfaces making them appear yellow which foretold what was to follow." The storm was felt from 11:30 in the morning of 24 August until 3:00 in the morning of 25 August. Its violent winds destroyed the wooden houses of New Orleans entirely and sent debris flying so that "the air was obscured by fragments of houses." Again, the ships in the river were broken to pieces and ten people died during the storm, among them "a pregnant woman, three children and two slaves." Intendant Navarro surmised that 600,000 pesos would not be enough to repair the damage wrought by this slow-moving hurricane, and he feared that "the slowdown which this disaster occasioned . . . and the lingering suspicion that it could be repeated during the current year is a great obstruction to [the colony's] development."[68] In particular with regard to the newly arrived soldiers and families from the Canary Islands, who were not only supposed to support the war effort, but also to advance Louisiana's agriculture, Navarro was worried.

For, seeing these settlers taking the plague of the hurricane as periodical and thinking in nothing less than absenting themselves, as soon as they experienced this new loss, all unanimously voiced the intention of selling the little they have left—provided there are buyers—in order to establish themselves in another place. This fermentation of emigration in their minds obliges me to write the circular which I am including to you. In particular I offer them all the help they need. With justice, I made them understand that nothing is missing, that much has remained in the warehouses of the King, that if the shortage requires that I will send to Campeche for foodstuffs or to wherever they can be found, with the aim to calm [them], and that I will execute it with the least difficulty before exposing the province to a general famine.[69]

Navarro's account shows that the Canary Islander new arrivals did not have a long attention span when it came to dealing with loss from consecutive hurricane disasters. In the two years the settlers had been in the colony, a portion of the male population was involved in the war activities in Louisiana and all of the Isleños had experienced the two back-to-back hurricanes of 1779 and 1780 in their exposed deltaic homes. Seeing the few possessions they had destroyed twice in short succession led to the "fermentation of emigration in their minds."

The Canary Islanders were first uprooted by their migration to Louisiana from their homelands. In addition, during their first two years in the colony, some of them had to relocate locally due to the faulty site selection made by Governor Gálvez or because of the hurricanes.[70] Since the settlers were to form new communities mostly from scratch, there were no previous communal structures: cultural, social, or economic factors that could have exerted a strong pull for the Isleños to stay. Consequently, disaster migration to a safer and more prosperous environment was an obvious option to consider. Navarro's account of the new settlers' notion of migrating underlines the argument made in chapter 2, on how solidarity in levee building is undermined if migration is an easy way out of existential problems of property owners. Disaster migration as nonadaptation was hence detrimental for the entire community that stayed behind. Unfortunately, the 1779–80 sources provide no information on whether longer-standing inhabitants of New Orleans and its surroundings were also thinking about moving elsewhere in response to the hurricanes.

The problems of this new group of settlers—and by extension of all new groups of settlers—are in many ways reminiscent of those of the first French colonists who arrived in Louisiana in the first decades of the eighteenth century: having to relocate frequently because of bad site selection and threatening to set back the colonial enterprise by a group decision to migrate internally or travel back home. That the specter of this threat still existed becomes evident from Navarro's advice that "if His Majesty wants to suppress the emigration of those peoples, if a barrier should be made of this country and if it is to flourish in armament as well as cultivation," it was necessary for Charles III to grant free trade "to whichever nation wanting to undertake it."[71] In other words, a large work force was needed to make the colony flourish economically as well as to defend it against enemies. However, its subsistence—frequently jeopardized by hurricanes, river floods, and extreme drought and rainfall cycles—could not only be guaranteed by the labor of many hands but also by the liberalization of trade regulations. It is possible, therefore, that the threat of depopulation was also used as a means of pressure to attain more liberal conditions for intercolonial trade.[72] The latter point becomes more plausible when examining Spanish Louisiana's population figures, which were in fact rising rapidly between 1766 and 1788, from 11,034 to 37,200 people; most of the increase was due to the slave trade.[73] It is difficult to assess clearly the gravity of Navarro's statement. A population growth rate of 5.7 percent per annum may contradict the perception of large-scale population loss, particularly in the absence of exact figures for actual migrants. Yet, from the perspective of contemporary colonial administrators, the departure of white settlers who were supposed to contribute to the prosperity of the colony may have seemed more threatening than mere statistics suggest.

Ten years before the end of the Spanish reign in Louisiana, the worst climatic decade for the Caribbean had set in and affected the Lower Mississippi Valley adversely, too.[74] The three hurricanes that hit the Louisiana Gulf Coast and devastated New Orleans in 1793 and 1794 coincided with the repercussions the French Revolution was having in the Caribbean. Unlike twenty-five years earlier, this time Louisiana took no active part in the revolutionary movement that reverberated through Europe and French Saint-Domingue, in particular. However, New Orleans was affected by the Saint-Domingue Slave Revolt through the immigration of refugees from the Caribbean island. As in 1779–80, the first wave of refugees was concurrent with the back-to-back hurricane impacts. The addition of new members to an existing society, as well as war and natural disasters, are potentially disrupting events. The last straw was added to New Orleans's troubles in December 1794 when a city fire burned down what had been left by the two August hurricanes of the same year.

At the same time, the French Revolution was unfolding across the Atlantic. The declaration of the Déclaration des droits de l'homme et du citoyen (Declaration of the Rights of Man and of the Citizen) in metropolitan France in 1789 had important consequences for France's most cherished Caribbean colony Saint-Domingue and consequently led to the onset of the Haitian Revolution.[75] With regard to the motives of Saint-Domingue's slaves for rising in 1791, David Geggus presents a mix of factors that might have influenced the violent outbreak. Apart from aspects such as population increase through immigration, increasing workloads on sugar plantations, and the harsh treatment of slaves creating an atmosphere of deprivation, he also briefly mentions environmental decline and natural disasters. Geggus adds that the drought of 1790 was apparently "the worst in living memory." This observation coincides with Johnson's assessment of the 1790s as the worst climatic decade the Caribbean had ever seen.[76] Johnson's evaluation of the Caribbean, in turn, adds to earlier studies by Richard Grove and Joelle Gergis, Don Garden, and Claire Fenby, which find an extended El Niño Event to have prevailed across large regions of the world between 1791 and 1793.[77] Given Johnson's description of the dire climatic conditions on neighboring Cuba throughout the decades from 1760 to 1790, closer scrutiny of climate cycles and hurricane impacts on Saint-Domingue might strengthen the argument that subsistence crises had a part in the slave uprising on the island.

As a response to the ongoing revolt in Saint-Domingue, the Directory, the new metropolitan government that replaced the Jacobins in Paris, declared the abolition of slavery in all French territory and the extension of full citizenship to African-born slaves on 4 February 1794. This legislation, together with the rise of the slave leader Toussaint Louverture to power, caused first waves of white people and people of color to start leaving the island for France, Spanish Cuba, British Jamaica, the east coast of the United States, and Spanish Louisiana. Larger and more controversially received migration movements from Saint-Domingue to New Orleans and Louisiana occurred again in a period of increased Americanization in 1803–4, at the time of the Louisiana Purchase, and in 1809–10, as we will see in more detail in chapter 4.[78]

Of the 1793 hurricane, Louisiana's then-governor Carondelet wrote to Charles IV's secretary of state, Count Aranda, that it had occurred on 18 August, on "the same day on which fourteen years before the violent one of 1779 occurred." It wrought destruction in an area of seventy-seven leagues "from the mouth of the Mississippi upwards." As in all previous examples, the cyclone destroyed the boats in the river.[79] While this hurricane put strain on the inhabitants of New Orleans and its environs, worse was to follow in August of the next year. The double disaster of two consecutive hurricanes is comparable to the two September cyclones of 1740; in 1794, though, New Orleans was not grazed by the hurricanes but instead was struck directly.

According to Governor Carondelet the effects of the hurricane of 10 August 1794, were even worse than those of the hurricane in 1793. He could give an account only of this first hurricane, since the second August cyclone was approaching New Orleans as he was writing, his letter dating from the same day as the second storm hit, 31 August 1794. The 10 August hurricane lasted for nine hours and was felt from the mouths of the river to Baton Rouge. At the time of writing, the governor had no news yet as to whether effects had been felt as far as Fort Rosalie. At Plaquemines on the Mississippi below New Orleans, the storm surge rose to six feet and eroded the glacis of the fort. Torn-up trees piled up in the area, while entangled in their branches were the bodies of animals whose odor of decay—together with that of the dying fish that had been swept into the marshes—was "infecting the atmosphere." In New Orleans the water also rose to six feet and inundated the city from the back, via Lake Pontchartrain. It "covered the whole ground and came with terrible velocity to mix with [the waters] of the Mississippi, sweeping up trees, houses, cattle—alas, everything they encountered."[80] The flooding postponed work on the drainage canal Carondelet had planned to build for the notoriously soggy capital.

With regard to New Orleans's nutrition and economic infrastructure, the governor reported that the inhabitants of the coastal marshes had fled and left this formerly productive area where high quality rice had been cultivated deserted to an extension of ten leagues inland. Carondelet saw this as a great loss to a province for which rice was a primary subsistence crop. He estimated that the material loss caused by the hurricane would cost the royal treasury as much as 12,000 pesos to which he added another 3,000 pesos of disaster relief, in order to help those rice-growing families to return to their devastated coastal properties.[81] Yet, not only the rice had suffered but also the maize and indigo harvest, so that New Orleans and the plantations that fed the city and its market were deprived of all subsistence as well as cash crops. However, after the two hurricanes had destroyed all boats, the New Orleans merchants had no means to travel to neighboring ports in order to obtain emergency provisions for Lower Louisiana. Predictably, the cycle of price inflation due to food scarcity set in, which exacerbated the situation of the colony's inhabitants. Intendant Rendon described the hardship experienced after three consecutive hurricanes concurrent with a period of armed conflict as "augment[ing] the pain of those unhappy . . . victims of such disasters even more deplorably, since the war is another obstacle to draw on means to mitigate the common loss." Many farmers were so destitute and deprived of their means of subsistence in the aftermath of the hurricanes that Rendon distributed alms in the name of the king in order for them to survive.[82]

New Orleans's ordeal was not over yet, however. On 8 December the second fire in six years broke out and burned down a third of the city within three hours, including the royal and merchants' storehouses and provisions. All that could be salvaged from the flames was enough flour to last the capital for a month. Although the governor and intendant had sent to Havana, Veracruz, and Charlestown for foodstuffs, they saw the city in imminent danger of a famine and—because of the widespread devastation after four consecutive disasters—of an enemy surprise attack. Three hundred families had lost their homes due to the conflagration and had "fled to the fields or to the houses of friends and relatives."[83]

In a Cabildo session eleven days after the conflagration, a letter by attorney general Juan Bautista Labatut was read aloud before the congregation. The petition on behalf of the citizens graphically describes the effects of the series of disasters between 1779 and 1794 on New Orleans from the perspective of the contemporary authorities. Its central theme was the fact that at the end of the eighteenth century, if not a sizable at least still an economically important part of the capital's citizenry was ready to turn its back on New Orleans and move to a less catastrophe-ridden place. Labatut explained that the five hurricanes, many floods, two great fires, and the ongoing war with France, all having afflicted the city within fifteen years, had discouraged the inhabitants of New Orleans:

> [. . .] Besides having all resources exhausted by so many calamities, the fear of other similar misfortunes depresses the strongest spirits in starting anew to develop enterprises exposed to certain ruin. If this way of thinking (solely based on our misfortunes) is propagated, the emigration of several useful residents must be expected, who will go to work in other countries less exposed to so detrimental risks now desolating our own, and these same misfortunes will keep away others from coming to establish themselves here, the population will decrease instead of increasing, which is needed for the development of the agriculture, commerce and all other productive enterprises, the products of which will drop in proportion with the decrease in population.[84]

In order to reestablish the colony's economy and in order to "incite with the necessary reviving action [the] spirits" of the inhabitants, Labatut suggested that "the powerful hand of our august, kind Monarch" loan Louisiana 1 million pesos. The relief funds would be distributed among the owners of the houses that had burned down, in proportion to the buildings' size, so they could rebuild them. The attorney general further proposed that the new houses were to be built with fire-safe materials such as brick and with flat tile roofs.[85]

With regard to structural adaptation, this difference in the treatment of hurricane (wind) and fire disasters in New Orleans is interesting. In the petition, Labatut presents clear directives regarding a change of building materials in order to reduce fire risk; however, none of the hurricane events evoked a similar reaction. Presumably, wind was not seen as an element under human control, whereas fire, as a human tool, has always been part of settlements, and means of fire risk–reduction had coevolved with them.[86] This difference in perception of the two hazards is reflected in present-day categorizations where fire is seen as a "human-made" disaster, rather than as a "natural" one.[87]

Returning to disaster migration and Labatut's urgent appeal that the continuous chain of disasters could stimulate emigration and inhibit immigration, was there a real basis to this concern of depopulation? In historical hindsight the 1790s were indeed a decade when population growth stalled. According to Paul Lachance's study on Louisiana's demographics on the eve of the Louisiana Purchase, this was to a large part due to the decline in slave population: Between 1766 and 1788 Lower Louisiana's population grew at an annual rate of 5.7 percent. This rate dropped rather dramatically to between 0.7 and 1.8 percent from 1788 to 1803 because Spain curtailed the slave trade as a result of the Haitian Revolution during the last decade of its reign. Contemporaries feared nothing more than importing rebellion into their countries via enslaved Africans who had come in contact with Haitian rebels.[88]

As mentioned above, the first wave of refugees from Saint-Domingue arrived in New Orleans between 1791 and 1797. However, at this early stage they amounted to only some hundred people; the larger waves with several thousands of people reached the city only in 1803 and 1809.[89] In the eighteen years between 1785 and 1803 New Orleans's population grew from 5,020 to 8,056 people. Lachance estimates the total population of Upper and Lower Louisiana at fifty thousand in 1803.[90] Hence, from the perspective of local colonial government, the concern of depopulation and economic setback was in no way unfounded and apparently exacerbated after the chain of floods, hurricanes, fires, and wars the colony had experienced over two decades. At the same time, the argument of depopulation may again have been used in order to signal urgency to Charles IV of Spain, who was, after all, to send the sizeable sum of 1 million pesos of relief funds to Louisiana and to reduce import duties to 6 percent, according to Labatut's report.[91] Conclusively, the document shows that even after eighty years of its existence, the colonial capital New Orleans, and along with it the whole colony of Louisiana, rested on a relatively delicate demographic and, by consequence, economic balance. The fear that a part of the population would move away in the aftermath of a disaster, that new immigrants could be scared off, and that thus economic development would be hampered, lived on in Louisiana and elsewhere in the United States.[92] It reappears for example as late as the 1893 Cheniere Caminada Hurricane, which will figure prominently in chapter 5.

The documents of the French and Spanish colonial correspondence have illustrated how hurricane events, in particular if they occurred in two consecutive seasons or consecutively in the same season, could make living conditions in New Orleans and on the lower Mississippi difficult in an existential way. Subsistence crises and consequent inflation cycles in the aftermath of disasters, familiar from early modern European disaster history, drove part of the settlers to return to Europe or to move inland.[93] The fact that Lower Louisiana was comparatively only sparsely populated until the late eighteenth century made disaster migration as a form of nonadaptation in the aftermath of hurricanes problematic for the development of the colony, pointing to the vulnerability of the French as well as the Spanish colonial governments of Louisiana.

With regard to environmental knowledge and adaptation/vulnerability to hurricane disasters, the frequent turnover of colonial personnel was a problem, as illustrated by the case of Governor Bernardo de Gálvez and the Canary Islanders in the 1779–80 hurricanes. Gálvez, with only three years of experience of the Mississippi Delta environment, placed the new settlers chiefly with regard to strategic considerations, apparently not taking into account or not knowing about the region's risk of inundation through storm surge. This trial-and-error approach is reminiscent of the first French settlements that had to be relocated several times before a suitable place was found for the subsistence of their population. It is also reminiscent of the first Spanish Louisiana governor Ulloa's attempt at establishing another post at the mouths of the Mississippi, after La Balize had been permanently flooded a decade or so before. Strategic interests were hence often blind to local environmental realities and created new vulnerabilities for settlers who were part of a military or commercial scheme. Fatalities and storm damage in the exposed settlements founded by Bernardo de Gálvez downriver from New Orleans were usually high after hurricanes, while the city often had few casualties to deplore. A certain city/countryside divide had evolved as early as the French period along the lines of regional economic infrastructure. However, the unequal balance between city and countryside regarding vulnerability to hurricane impacts started to become more pronounced with Gálvez's settlement scheme.

From the American Storm Controversy to Hurricane-Predicting Jesuits

No doubt, the practices of disaster migration as well as of on-site evacuation continued individually or simultaneously on some scale in New Orleans and the downriver parishes during and after the hurricane events of the following decades (see figure 1.2). With regard to the evolution of hurricane science, however, political events such as the American Revolution (1775–83) and the ratification of the Constitution (1788) were crucial and provided the basis for expanding meteorological networks through the unification of a large part of the North American landmass. Thomas Jefferson's meteorological correspondence network and the later, regular data collection under his presidency (1801–9) are examples of this process. Interest in systematic measurements was expanding. Several journals in the United States at the beginning of the nineteenth century began to publish observations of barometric pressure, temperature, and precipitation, albeit in a still rather nonstandardized manner. Although the study of storms and hurricanes was not yet systematized, the combined efforts of individual actors from different fields—academia, medicine, and the press, as well as the federal government—amassed data covering a large part of the country throughout the first three decades of the nineteenth century.[94]

These activities were the basis for the unfolding American storm controversy and for the real takeoff of hurricane science, starting in 1831. This development now clearly unfolded as a discourse in the scientific setting of universities and academic journals, rather than as discrete accounts of local (indigenous) knowledge in *Histoires des Indes* (Histories of the Indies), the chronicles and travel accounts of the seventeenth and eighteenth centuries. The results of this increased scientific attention to hurricanes was ultimately going to benefit adaptation—in the form of evacuation—on the ground.

The controversy arose from the attempt at finding a solution to one of the most prominent problems in meteorology during the 1830s, the puzzle of the nature of the wind field in storms. For navigation, this was a practical problem, the solution of which became an increasingly pressing matter in the first few decades of the nineteenth century.[95] In 1831 meteorologist William C. Redfield, whom we met briefly in chapter 1, published an article on tropical cyclones' rotating winds and forward motion in the *American Journal of Science and Arts*.[96] Redfield, a marine engineer and self-taught meteorologist who had studied storm data for ten years prior to his first publication, had closely observed the damage wrought by a hurricane that affected his native Connecticut in early September 1821. From changing wind directions and the varying strength of gusts as well as the direction in which trees had been blown over, Redfield concluded in his first article that "the storm was exhibited in the form of a great whirlwind." In Redfield's perception, such whirlwinds were caused by the deflection of the trade winds by the Caribbean islands. The obstruction of the landmasses caused the moving atmosphere to form gyrating eddies that continued to move northward along the coastline of North America. By analogy with the formation of eddies or vortexes in water, he concluded that the whirls formed by the atmosphere functioned basically in the same centrifugal manner. Yet, Redfield supposed that those vortexes were quite shallow, "occupy[ing] a horizontal position at a considerable height in the atmosphere."[97] In his following articles, he continued to build on his moving vortex theory that he based on gravitation as the primary cause for all wind phenomena. Drawing on diverse sources, he brought together local reports of the 1821 hurricane as well as ship log data to prove the forward motion of this hurricane. In comparing meteorological observations and reconstructing hurricane tracks, he followed Benjamin Franklin who had pondered on the motion of storms in the 1740s. However, Redfield was able to do so on a vastly expanded basis of data.[98] Only through the connection of various sets of observations made on land as well as at sea was it possible for scientists to conclude empirically that they were dealing with the same storm system through time and not with several separate and stationary systems.[99]

Redfield's principal opponent in the controversy was James Pollard Espy, a teacher of classical languages and mathematics at the Franklin Institute in Philadelphia. The two scholars engaged in a lively and sometimes heated scientific discourse that left its traces mainly in the *American Journal of Science* and the *Journal of the Franklin Institute*. Espy associated the generation of storms with vertical thermal convection and as such became the forerunner to the polar front theory of cyclones that was developed by the Norwegian Vilhelm F. Bjerknes at the beginning of the twentieth century. From his observations of vertical motion during the formation of rain clouds, Espy concluded that adiabatic cooling was taking place in the process of vertical convection.[100] This explanation for cloud formation and for the generation of precipitation he then brought to bear on the study of the nature of storms. As opposed to Redfield, Espy maintained that whirlwinds or hurricanes were shaped in an "upward vortex" that touched the earth's surface rather than forming a "horizontal whirlwind."[101] That upward vortex was created by the continuous radial inflow of winds from all directions that needed to occur, according to Espy, in order to maintain the storm cloud. He thus formulated the law that "*in all very great and widely extended rains or snows, the wind will blow towards the centre of the storm.*"[102] In other words, Redfield's theory of the wind field in storms was centrifugal and rested firmly on the mechanical principles that were in general use at the beginning of the nineteenth century. Espy's theory, on the other hand, was centripetal and used thermal factors that had been explored in relation with the compression and expansion of gases by a number of scientists throughout the previous fifty years or so.[103]

Apart from the different outlook behind the formation of their theories, the two meteorologists came to such different results regarding the wind field of storms because they investigated different kinds of storms. It is important to point out that while the vocabulary for different wind phenomena was well-developed in the 1830s, in the case of synoptic scale phenomena such as mid-latitude cyclones and hurricanes, which did not readily lend themselves to naked-eye observation, it was still difficult for contemporaries to determine what they were actually observing. In fact, until the mid-nineteenth century, the term "storm" was still often used indiscriminately to describe such different phenomena as hurricanes, tornadoes, or large cyclones.[104]

James P. Espy's theory experienced a revival in the 1860s and 1870s after the storm debate had temporarily quieted down after 1840. The first law of thermodynamics, which was formulated in the 1860s, proved very compatible with Espy's thermal theory of cyclones (as well as with other meteorological phenomena), whereas Redfield's kinematic theory was discredited. In the first two decades of the twentieth century, the Norwegian meteorologist Vilhelm Bjerknes and his son Jacob Bjerknes were able to develop the polar front theory of cyclones on the basis of the nineteenth-century thermal theory of cyclones. That theory is still valid and is an integral part of meteorology today.

While the understanding of the formation of storm systems was a pressing issue in the emerging scientific field of meteorology, this body of new theoretical knowledge only slowly found its way into practical application for mitigating the impact of hurricanes. It took the coincidence of exceptional theoretical knowledge with the ability for hours of patient observation in one person for the first hurricane forecasts to be issued in the late nineteenth century.

This leap forward in hurricane science enabled a new kind of disaster preparedness and provided time for—still vertical or on-site—evacuation, and thus reduced harm to life and property. As we have seen in chapter 1, Europeans in the Caribbean initially relied on indigenous knowledge to give themselves advance notice of hurricanes. Over time, and as the indigenous populations of the Caribbean islands were reduced by European diseases and violence, the knowledge of the signs of an approaching hurricane became part of the newly amalgamated colonial societies' culture of disaster. This was also the case for the Louisiana Gulf Coast, as indicated previously in intendant Navarro's report in the aftermath of the 1780 hurricane, which mentioned the sky's color of "pale fire" that, according to Navarro, foretold what was going to happen.[105] However, in the absence of fast means of communication and transport, the use of such recognition of the signs of a coming hurricane, based on environmental observation, remained very limited and localized.

In the following account about Benito Viñes, a Jesuit priest who revolutionized hurricane forecasting and thus brought substantial change to evacuation as an adaptive practice, the geographical focus is, again, extended from the Gulf Coast to include the Caribbean. The Jesuit's empirical and scientific findings have to be seen in the larger context of an increase in population density on the Gulf Coast, the industrialization and economic development of the United States, and the development and differentiation of the sciences that accelerated after the mid-nineteenth century.

After a series of devastating hurricanes that had cost many lives in the island of Cuba, Father Viñes started setting up a hurricane warning system in Havana. In a one-man effort, the director of the observatory of the Real Colegio de Belén (Royal College of Belen) started forecasting hurricanes based on the observations that he and his brethren had made at the college since 1854. The College of Belen housed one of eleven Jesuit observatories dispersed over North and South America and was the most important one of the Latin American colleges. The Jesuit order had been a prominent actor in the acquisition of natural scientific knowledge of the French and Spanish colonial empires during the previous centuries. It was prohibited in 1773 but was restored in 1814, and its members were able to resume their religious, scientific, and educational work. Jesuits' astronomical and meteorological observatories were spread all over the globe according to their missionary activities. The most notable places for hurricane meteorology were located in or on the Pacific and the Indian Ocean, in Manila (Philippines), Zikawei (China), and Tananarive (Madagascar).[106]

As opposed to Redfield and Espy fifty years earlier, Benito Viñes concluded from his meticulous observation of cloud formation and wind currents that hurricane vortexes were not shallow but instead reached the altitudes of cirrus clouds that are generated in the frigid conditions of the higher atmosphere.[107] What is more, he was convinced that the high-altitude air currents were responsible for the steering of the hurricane and hence for the path it was going to take. The observation of wind directions with respect to his own position, barometric readings and consequent mathematical calculations allowed the Jesuit to predict hurricane tracks several days in advance. In his *Apuntes*, Viñes stressed that only sufficient observational data *together* with the application of the relevant physical laws could lead to precise projections of hurricane tracks.[108] Viñes's forecasts quickly became famous for their accuracy and were disseminated to the public via the press. Yet, the priest had more in mind than just a warning system confined to Cuba. In 1876 he started organizing a meteorological network that, by 1888, included twenty stations on different Caribbean islands. The Havana Chamber of Commerce as well as proponents of the private economy recognized the importance of Viñes's forecasts in preventing economic loss and loss of life, and, therefore, willingly granted his network telegraphic service free of charge. Thus, armed with a means of communication faster than the speed of a hurricane, the network could function efficiently in warning the inhabitants of the islands of approaching storms.[109] However, Viñes's first recorded hurricane forecast—the first known official hurricane forecast—was made before the network had grown into a fully fledged warning system, on 11 September 1875 for a hurricane that passed Havana on 13 September.[110]

The meteorological service, assigned to the U.S. Army Signal Corps, which also started working in 1870, immediately recognized the importance of hurricane forecasts for the American Gulf Coast states. From 1873 until the beginning of the Spanish–American War in 1898, the Signal Corps interacted with Viñes's observation network transmitted hurricane warnings via telegraph from the Belen observatory to the Signal Corps' central bureau in Washington. That bureau then issued warnings to local stations in the United States.[111] The high esteem in which the Jesuit meteorologist was held by the Signal Corps is illustrated by the fact that the U.S. Hydrographic Office in 1886 and the Weather Bureau in 1898 published partial translations of Viñes's works on hurricane observation in the Antilles.[112] The *Times-Democrat*, a New Orleanian newspaper, in a September 1890 issue praised the Jesuit priest, almost echoing du Tertre's (two centuries earlier) account of the hurricane-forecasting Caribbean Indians: "During the hurricane season, his opinion is anxiously sought after. . . . It has been a general custom for years for the Padre to inform the agents of various [ship] lines of the condition of the weather just prior to the departure of the vessels." However, as a consequence of the outbreak of the Spanish–American War, those amicable relations ended, and the Weather Bureau started training its own observers and setting up its own stations in the Caribbean. At the same time, the observations of the College of Belen were complicated by the downfall of Spanish supremacy and the following transfer of its privileges to new governmental institutions.[113] After the end of the American occupation in 1902, U.S. hurricane forecasting activities were transferred from Havana to Washington, DC, from where the Weather Bureau continued sending hurricane warnings until 1935. In that year the Weather Bureau decided that issuing warnings from "nearer to the scene of action" would make sense and it opened three hurricane warning centers: in San Juan, in New Orleans, and in Jacksonville.[114]

The disconnection between the Jesuit forecasting network and the U.S. Weather Bureau rather tragically exposed the deficiency of the American observers and their network during the Galveston hurricane of 8 September 1900. Fatefully, the then director of the Weather Bureau had put a ban on telegraphed forecasts from Cuba in order to eliminate competition with the U.S. weather service. On 6 September the Jesuits at Belen issued a statement in the local press that a hurricane that had passed Cuba was in the Gulf of Mexico, west-southwest of Tampa, Florida. On 7 September they issued further warning and on 8 September the Jesuits published a statement that the hurricane had reached the Texas coast—which, in fact, it had, killing about eight thousand unsuspecting people in its track over Galveston Island.[115] Isaac Cline, the Weather Bureau meteorologist at Galveston at the time, failed to forecast the hurricane and lost his wife in the storm surge that swept the island.[116] On 10 September, before the harrowing news of the destroyed Gulf Coast resort had spread, the U.S. Weather Bureau in Washington issued the—retrospectively ironic—statement that it had "noted slight indications that in the W N W is forming an atmospheric disturbance scarcely worth mentioning."[117]

While some of the Caribbean islanders were likely able to tell the signs of an approaching hurricane, clearly, hosting an institution with the unique dedication to observe weather phenomena on an hourly basis, and with the ability to forecast the track of an impending hurricane was quite an advantage. Even though by Viñes's time it was not news that hurricanes were moving on a trajectory, to forecast this track with some accuracy as much as one or two days in advance was groundbreaking with regard to adaptation. In the 1830s William Redfield had reconstructed the path of hurricanes after the fact. Viñes, however, with a skillful combination of empirical facts, physical theory, and mathematical calculation, from 1870 until his death in 1893, was able to predict those trajectories. Yet, his forecasts would have been of a much more limited impact without their dissemination via telegraph—a significant change in the knowledge infrastructure of meteorology. Already in 1849 the telegraph was used in the United States for simultaneous weather observations by the Smithsonian Institution.[118] The fact that Viñes had managed to secure telegraphic services for his forecasting network significantly changed the disaster risk for Cuba, as well as the surrounding islands and the North American Gulf Coast after 1870.

The importance of the longevity of an institution such as the Belen observatory, the frequency and regularity of its observations, and the experience with which records were made becomes evident from a comparison with the early forecasting attempts of the Signal Corps' hurricane warning service. At the Belen observatory, atmospheric phenomena were recorded hourly from 4:00 A.M. until 10:00 P.M., in times of special need observations were made hourly, day and night.[119] In his *Apuntes,* Viñes stated that he rode out on horseback countless times after a hurricane in order to measure precisely in which direction the uprooted trees were pointing, since "there is no weather vane that could mark with more precision or firmness the direction and succession of the most violent gusts."[120]

By comparison, the observers of the U.S. Army Signal Corps (which after 1891 became known as the U.S. Weather Bureau) took only three observations per day at times that did not represent average meteorological conditions but rather avoidance of the busy hours on the telegraph lines.[121] In other words, observations were wired from the stations to the central office in Washington, DC, which issued warnings and advisories until the reorganization of the hurricane warning service in 1935.[122] Predictably, the population in the hurricane-prone Gulf Coast states found it difficult to trust forecasts sent from remote Washington, DC.[123] The Cuban Jesuits, on the other hand, carried out their calculations literally in the eye of the storm in Havana. As an order devoted to proselytizing, education, and science, the Jesuits had a religious vocation to fully devote their waking hours to scientific study. The U.S. Army Signal Corps, on the other hand, besides having to train its military members, was faced with the difficulty of finding civilian "observers . . . engaged in occupations which admit to some extent their being present at the place of observation at the required hours of the day all the year round."[124] The organizational advantage of the Christian order over the secular weather service is evident—outmoded as it may seem—and apparently made a decisive difference for the possibility and accuracy of hurricane forecasts in the Caribbean and on the coast of the Gulf of Mexico.

The break between the U.S. Weather Bureau and the Belen observatory was a setback for North American hurricane warnings, a fact the weather service after 1900 tried to smooth over by decrying the Cuban forecasts as alarmist and overemotional.[125] On the local level, Weather Bureau meteorologist Isaac Monroe Cline introduced observation procedures oriented on Viñes methods when he was transferred from Galveston to New Orleans in 1901. However, he lacked the authority to make forecasting decisions by himself. Only in 1935 did the Weather Bureau decide to set up three regional hurricane warning centers with the mandate to issue warnings and advisories. Radio reports about wind conditions from ships had been instrumental for hurricane observations since 1905; however, apparently only in 1934 was a special system of direct calls introduced. According to this plan, commercial radio stations in different locations along the North American Gulf Coast would be informed of the areas from which ship reports were required. The operators at those stations would then contact the ship captains, forward them the specific observations that were desired, and tell them which Weather Bureau forecast center the data should be sent to. Funding of and attention for meteorological research remained marginal until 1936, at which time the Weather Bureau established its own research division.[126]

While Viñes's forecasting ability was widely admired and his two major Spanish publications were soon (at least in part) translated into English, his calculating methods only slowly and fragmentarily found their way into the daily practice of the American hurricane warning service. The reasons for the government agency's stolidness when it came to adopting new plans and procedures were—apart from a downright colonial attitude toward the natives of Cuba—apparently political. Institutional and procedural change was prevented by what Rappaport and Simpson in their article on hurricane forecasting technologies called Congress's "proclivity for *administration by crisis*." In other words, the funding of public programs was delayed until a crisis or disaster occurred that caused enough public outcry for Congress to allocate the finances. Clearly, this dependence of the Weather Bureau on the fitful political process hampered the development of institutional flexibility and innovation. It is obvious that part of the Weather Bureau's problem was also one of scale. Compared to the Belen observatory it had to cover a vast geographic and climatic area. Also, its mission was not a humanitarian one with the side effect of benefiting transport and economy as in the Jesuits' case; its task was, rather, to protect agriculture and transportation, the two main revenue-generating branches of the U.S. economy at the time.[127]

This short glance into the organizational structure of those two very different weather and storm warning services underline the fact that the internal (institutional) and external (political) conditions of institutions greatly influence the actual adaptation options of people to natural hazards on the ground. Institutions started playing an increasingly important role in the knowledge infrastructure of tropical meteorology and storm research from the beginning of the nineteenth century onward. In the United States the Army—besides providing the basis for the formation of the Weather Bureau—had been in-strumental in advancing meteorological observation. As we will see below, it was the war technology of the twentieth century that enabled hurricane science to reach its present state.

War Technology and Mass-Evacuation

Almost all important scientific findings and technological advances that tropical meteorologists take for granted today have been made after World War II. They are, in other words, of a very recent nature compared with the earlier centuries throughout which recognition of important phenomena that generate and drive hurricanes moved at a much slower pace. The most important technological devices that helped the gaining of a deeper understanding of the inner workings of tropical cyclones throughout the twentieth century were the airplane, radio, and rawinsondes, radar, satellites and the computer. The first upper air soundings that enabled meteorologists to locate hurricanes before landfall were conducted after World War I. Measurements of atmospheric pressure, temperature, wind speed, and humidity were taken by an aerosonde that was fixed to an airplane and recorded atmospheric changes. In short succession aerosonde technology was developed further and instead of planes, weather balloons came into use as a carrying device for the more advanced radiosondes. In 1944 those radiosonde data, for the first time since the last Cuban (Jesuit) hurricane warnings issued at the end of the nineteenth century, made it possible for the Miami Hurricane Forecast Office to order hurricane warnings for a clearly designated stretch of the Florida coast twenty-four hours in advance of landfall.[128]

The first hurricane reconnaissance flights were undertaken in 1943 and provided information about the atmospheric pressure and wind speeds in the eye and at the top of the storm. Importantly, they also produced the first visual images of what the eye and eye wall of a hurricane looked like. Finally, at the end of the 1940s radar images for the first time showed the characteristic shape of the spiral rain bands and the eye of a hurricane that most people today think of when speaking about tropical cyclones. Radar images also proved that hurricanes are warm core systems that reach from the surface of the earth through the entire troposphere and into the lower stratosphere. Radar imagery thus put an end to the idea of hurricanes as shallow vortexes which, according to hurricane specialist Kerry Emanuel, had survived tenaciously since the early nineteenth century.[129] In the late 1940s the rapidly expanding and improving network of surface and upper air stations provided further crucial insight into hurricane formation, such as easterly waves as breeding grounds for tropical cyclone development.[130] Around the same time, the works of two influential tropical meteorologists, Erik Palmén and Herbert Riehl, found that for their formation, hurricanes needed warm sea surface temperatures (about 26–27° Celsius) and a distance of about 5° latitude to the equator on the one hand, and that the interaction of lower tropospheric disturbances with upper tropospheric troughs favored hurricane generation, on the other hand.[131] Riehl, who is today considered to be the founder of the field of tropical meteorology, in his book *Tropical Meteorology,* coined the term of the hurricane as a heat engine that converted the warm sea surface temperatures into mechanical work, lifting up warm air and transporting it into regions of cold air through evaporation and condensation.[132]

By the mid-1950s the appreciation of the usefulness of radar technology to track tornadoes had led to the establishment of a radar network in the state of Texas that was to become the forerunner for a later national network that also detected hurricanes.[133] However, despite advanced technology, both tornado and hurricane warnings had to deal with issues of precision that had concerned the Weather Bureau already at the turn of the century. Apart from causing substantial economic loss, warnings disseminated to too large an area or to the wrong area could undermine the credibility of the meteorological service, attracting accusations of crying wolf. This became a particularly pressing problem at the beginning of the 1960s, when large-scale, pre-landfall evacuation became feasible to deal with the threat of an impending hurricane.

Significantly, in the United States the advancement of hurricane forecasting technologies and the use of the automobile as a widespread means of transport had to converge to enable mass (self-) evacuations of urban areas to safety.[134] Zelinsky and Kosinski found that Hurricane Carla, which made landfall between Galveston and Corpus Christi on 11 September 1961, was the first U.S. hurricane with a reasonable historical record of large-scale evacuation by car. As many as five hundred thousand residents left their homes on the Gulf Coast in advance of Carla's landfall on the Texas coast.[135] Until Hurricane Katrina such temporary mass exoduses seemed to be the only way to prevent the large-scale death tolls known in the late nineteenth and early twentieth centuries such as in the Cheniere Caminada Hurricane in 1893 (two thousand victims) and the Galveston Hurricane in 1900 (eight thousand victims); these warnings did not (and obviously still do not), however, prevent the loss of property. The local railway system in and around New Orleans at the turn of the twentieth century could not have performed the evacuation service that private cars did in the 1960s since the network was not dense enough.[136] At the same time, hurricane forecasting techniques were still in their infancy and warnings could not be issued accurately or early enough to allow for the mass movement of people, as in the case of Galveston in 1900. In other words, only the mid-twentieth century temporal coincidence of the spread of the car, the advanced airplane reconnaissance, and radar data (and thus improved forecasting of hurricanes) and television as a mass medium to disseminate warnings brought about a significant change for the people on the ground.[137] Interestingly, and somewhat in contrast to Zelinsky and Kosinski, for New Orleans Richard Campanella sees a shift from the traditional way of evacuating to sturdier buildings within the city to using cars for external evacuation occurring only in the 1990s. According to the Geographer, the change in attitude was driven by soil subsidence, rising sea levels, an increase in active hurricane seasons, and the consequent official urgings for evacuation by private vehicle.

However, Hurricane Katrina showed again, that technological development and the coincidence of the relevant technologies do not necessarily ensure successful adaptation with regard to hurricane evacuation by car. In many instances income levels and, partially connected with the former, race and ethnicity decided who owned a car and could afford to move out of the city on relatively short notice. For others who did own a car, having to care for elderly relatives, owning a pet, or feeling the need to guard their property took precedence over removing themselves from Hurricane Katrina's trajectory. In other words, socioeconomic factors ultimately decided how adaptive the practice of migrating temporarily by car was going to be.[138]

Notes

1. Rochefort, *Histoire Naturelle*, 246.
2. Louis P. Nelson, *Architecture and Empire in Jamaica* (New Haven, CT: Yale University Press, 2016), 76–77.
3. John Barnshaw, "Evacuation, Types of," in *Encyclopedia of Disaster Relief*, ed. K. Bradley Penuel and Matt Statler (Los Angeles: SAGE, 2011), 186 (quote), 187.
4. Nelson, *Architecture*, 77.
5. Matthew Mulcahy, *Hurricanes and Society in the British Greater Caribbean, 1624–1783*, Early America (Baltimore: Johns Hopkins University Press, 2006), 127–29. On "Storm Towers" of the Santee Delta in North Carolina that were made of brick and apparently only came into use in the nineteenth century see Elias B. Bull, "Storm Towers of the Santee Delta," *South Carolina Historical Magazine* 81, no. 2 (1980).
6. Richard Campanella in his article identifies three major influences on New Orleans's architecture: New French/Canadian, continental French, and French Caribbean. C.f. Campanella, "Creole Architecture," H7. On generational change in New Orleans see Dawdy, *Empire*, chap. 4, "From Colonal Experiment to Creole Society," 139–88.
7. In this context, Marcy Rockman speaks of barriers to environmental learning and, thus, adaptation. Rockman, "Knowledge," 15.
8. Delorme to Directors, 30 October 1722, HNOC, ANOM., Colonies, C13 A 6, fol. 403r.
9. Bienville, Legat, de Villardeau and Hubert to Directors, 28 October 1719, ANF, ANOM, Colonies, C13 C 4, fol. 14r.
10. Vidal and Havard, *Amérique Française*, 206; and James Pritchard, "Population in French America, 1670–1730: The Demographic Context of Colonial Louisiana," in *French Colonial Louisiana and the Atlantic World*, ed. Bradley G. Bond (Baton Rouge:

Louisiana State University Press, 2005), 198; see also Jean-Francois Mouhot, *Les Réfugiés Acadiens en France, 1758–1785. L'Impossible Réintegration?* (Paris, France: Septentrion, 2010).

11. Tobacco and cotton (as well as indigo) were planted for export. At the time of the hurricane, tobacco was an important crop since the Company of the Indies had promoted its planting with regard to the company's monopoly in the French kingdom. The aim was to make Louisiana the tobacco provider for France and thus to reduce dependence on the English tobacco-producing colonies of Virginia and Maryland. Cécile Vidal, "French Louisiana in the Age of the Companies, 1712–1731," in *Constructing Early Modern Empires: Proprietary Ventures in the Atlantic World, 1500–1750,* ed. Lou H. Roper and Bertrand van Ruymbeke (Leyde: Brill, 2006), 156.

12. Andrew C. Albrecht, "Indian–French Relations at Natchez," *American Anthropologist* 48, no. 3 (1946), 336. The Indian nation the French called Natchez apparently called themselves Thelöel. They came to be called Natchez by the colonists because the latter conflated the name of one of the nation's villages, Naches, with its inhabitants. Ibid., 321.

13. A list of the French killed in the Natchez Uprising is provided in Maduell, *Census Tables,* 104.

14. Usner, *Indians,* 67–72. For detailed accounts of the Natchez Uprising see also Patricia D. Woods, "The French and the Natchez Indians in Louisiana. 1700–1731," in Conrad, *French Experience,* 286–91; Patricia D. Woods, *French-Indian Relations on the Southern Frontier, 1699–1762* (Ann Arbor: UMI Research, 1980) and Albrecht, "Natchez."

15. Usner, *Indians,* 72, 81–82.

16. Louboey to Minister, 28 January 1733, HNOC, ANOM, Colonies, C13 A 17, fol. 218v–219r.

17. Usner, *Indians,* 192–96. See also Sauvole's journal on early (1699–1700) crop planting in Louisiana: Margry, *Découverte,* 4, 449ff.

18. Cécile Vidal, "Antoine Bienvenu, Illinois Planter and Mississippi Trader: The Structure of Exchange between Lower and Upper Louisiana Under French Rule," in *Colonial Louisiana and the Atlantic World,* ed. Bradley G. Bond (Baton Rouge: Louisiana State University Press, 2005), 111, 118, 128; and Vidal, "Age of the Companies," 158.

19. Usner, *Indians,* 207; John G. Clark, *New Orleans, 1718–1812: An Economic History* (Baton Rouge: Louisiana State University Press, 1970), 28.

20. Bienville to Minister, 5 August 1733, HNOC, ANOM, Colonies, C13 A 16, fol. 139v., fol. 136r. The *commissaire-ordonnateur* was the next official below the governor who was the highest-ranking colonial offical. Essentially, the *commissaire-ordonnateur* shared the administration with the governor and functioned as minister in charge of finances, while the governor was in charge of general administration and the military. The *commissaire-ordonnateur* also held certain judicial rights. Both men were meant to act as a check upon each other. However, the shared administration led to almost constant disunity and political factionalism in Louisiana. Donald Lemieux stresses that the office of the *commissaire-ordonnateur* is not identical (or terminologically interchangeable) with the *intendant* in New France. Donald J. Lemieux, "Some Legal and Practical Aspects of The Office of *Commissaire-Ordonnateur* of French Louisiana," *The French Experience in Louisiana,* ed. Glenn R. Conrad (Lafayette, LA: Center for Louisiana Studies, University of Southwestern Louisiana, 1995), 395–6.

21. Bienville to Minister, 5 August 1733, HNOC, ANOM, Colonies, C13 A 16, fol. 140r.
22. Salmon to Minister, 1 August 1733, HTML, ANOM, Colonies, C13 A 17, fol. 183r.
23. Bienville to Minister, 5 August 1733, HNOC, ANOM, Colonies, C13 A 16, fol. 142r. "[. . .] And if we had not still had 3000 quarts of rice in the warehouses of the Company which Sieur Salmon distributed with the greatest economy possible we would have had a complete desertion."
24. Salmon to Minister, 1 August 1733, HTML, ANOM, Colonies, C13 A 17, fol. 182r–183r, 185r.
25. Woods, *French–Indian Relations,* chap. 10, "The Return of Bienville: The First Chickasaw Campaign, 1733–1736," 111ff.
26. Bienville to Minister, 5 August 5, 1733, HNOC, ANOM, Colonies, C13 A 16, fol. 141r.
27. Vidal, "Exchange," 129. The 1727 census for New Orleans and its environs (not including Biloxi and Mobile, but including New Orleans proper, the settlements along the Mississippi from its mouth to Pointe Coupee, Gentilly [or Chantilly], and Bayou St. John) counts 1,327 habitants (French and German settlers), 133 *engagés* (indentured servants), 1,561 enslaved Africans, and 75 enslaved Indians, or 3,096 individuals in all. See Maduell, *Census Tables,* 81. The Indian population of French colonial Louisiana and Illinois in 1730 was estimated at 59,000. Pritchard, *Empire,* Appendix I., 423.
28. Carl A. Brasseaux, "The Image of Louisiana and the Failure of Voluntary French Emigration, 1683–1731," in *Proceedings of the Fourth Meeting of the French Colonial Historical Society, April 6–8, 1978,* ed. Alf Andrew Heggoy and James J. Cooke (Washington, DC: University Press of America, 1979).
29. French colonial *haute et basse Louisiane* (Upper and Lower Louisiana) comprise the region from the mouths of the Mississippi River up to what was known to the French as the Illinois Country, today parts of the states of Missouri, Illinois, and Indiana.
30. Paul Lachance, "The Louisiana Purchase in the Demographic Perspective of its Time," in *Empires of the Imagination. Transatlantic Histories of the Louisiana Purchase,* ed. Peter J. Kastor and François Weil (Charlottesville: University of Virginia Press, 2009), 150.
31. Bienville to Minister, 5 August 1733, HNOC, ANOM, Colonies, C13 A 16, fol. 142r.
32. Michael J. Foret, "The Failure of Administration: The Chickasaw Campaign of 1739–1740," in Conrad, *French Experience,* 314; Louboey to Minister, 20 October 1739, HNOC, ANOM, Colonies, C13 A 24, fol. 221r.
33. Louboey to Minister, 29 January 1740, HNOC, ANOM, Colonies, C13 A 25, fol. 215v.
34. Foret, "Failure," 314; and Louboey to Minister, 29 January 1740, HNOC, ANOM, Colonies, C13 A 25, fol. 215v.
35. They occurred on 11 and 18 September 1740. The first lasted for twelve hours and the second for eighteen hours. De Beauchamp to Minister, 25 January 1741, ANF, ANOM, Colonies, C13 A 26, fol. 203r.
36. After company takeover in 1718 the administration of Louisiana was reorganized and the territory was divided into nine districts: New Orleans, Biloxi, Mobile, Alibamons, Natchez, Yazoo, Arkansas, Natchitoches, and Illinois. See Moore, *Revolt.*
37. De Beauchamp to Minister, 25 January 1741, ANF, ANOM, Colonies, C13 A 26, fol. 203r. provides an elaborate account of both hurricanes and their effects at Dauphin Island and Mobile. See also Louboey to Minister, 7 March 1741, HNOC, ANOM, Colonies, C13 A 26, fol. 175v.

38. Before the hurricanes rice was sold at six *livres tournois* per quart, afterwards it was sold at twelve. Maize rose from six *l.t.* to fifteen or sixteen *l.t.* Salmon to Minister, 8 March 1741, HNOC, ANOM, Colonies, C13 A 26, fol. 129v.

39. Michel to Minister, 29 September 1750, HTML, ANOM, Colonies, C13 A 34, fol. 347r.

40. Vaudreuil-Cavagnial to Minister, 24 September 1750, HTML, ANOM, Colonies, C13 A 34, fol. 276v.

41. Moore, *Revolt*, 31.

42. Vidal and Havard, *Amérique Française*, 155–57.

43. On the French–Indian trade in the lower Mississippi valley see Usner, *Indians*, 192–96; on French smuggling see Dawdy, *Empire*, chap. 3, 107ff; and Moore, *Revolt*, 104. With regard to illicit trade, Johnson remarks for the Cuban situation that "when faced with crisis, time and again local residents took matters into their own hands and resorted to the contraband trade with regions that could provide life-saving provisions to ensure the community's survival." The same is true for French Louisiana. Johnson, *Climate*, 195.

44. Moore, *Revolt*, 29.

45. Din and Harkins, *Cabildo*, 101.

46. Cummins, *Spanish Observers*, 7, 34.

47. Brasseaux, "A New Acadia," 127–29.

48. Nathalie Dessens, *From Saint-Domingue to New Orleans: Migration and Influences* (Gainesville: University Press of Florida, 2007); ibid., 246.

49. For a detailed study, see Clark, *New Orleans*, chap. 9, 158–80.

50. In a food shortage in 1707 Bienville reported to Minister de Pontchartrain that he had sent a ship to Veracruz in order to ask for food there. Apparently the colony (then with headquarters on the Mobile River in Mobile Bay) had suffered from a scarcity of foodstuffs for two months. Bienville wrote that he had tried to delay the dispatch to Veracruz as long as he could, but since the French had already helped out the Spanish at Pensacola, he could no longer delay in seeking help for his own people. Bienville to Minister, 20 February 1707, HTML, ANOM, Colonies, C13 A 2, fol. 5r. On Louisiana's dream to become a port of free trade see Vidal and Havard, *Amérique Française*, 696. The push for free trade was the essence of the Louisiana revolt of 1768; see Moore, *Revolt*, 155.

51. Johnson, *Climate*, 104–7.

52. Ibid., 71–72; Moore, *Revolt*, 124, 129.

53. The most detailed account of the Louisiana revolt is by John Preston Moore, in particular Moore, *Revolt*, chap. 10, 185–215; a short summary is presented by Vidal and Havard, *Amérique Française*, 692–98. Weddle, *Tides*, chap. 2, 10–24 offers an alternative perspective concentrating on explorers. Although Sherry Johnson does not focus on Louisiana and provides only a short paragraph on the revolt, her book is an invaluable source for putting Louisiana's history into the enviropolitical context of the Spanish Caribbean.

54. Cummins, *Spanish Observers*, 4–5.

55. After legislation had been passed in 1773 that allowed the Spanish monopoly company to trade with foreign nations in cases of emergency, Spanish ships sailed from Cuba to the ports of Jamaica and Barbados to buy urgently needed foodstuffs. According to Spanish mercantilist rule, regular flour shipments to the Spanish Caribbean normally had to come from Mexico. However, this breadbasket failed disastrously between 1770

and 1773 when the El Niño/La Niña climatic pattern held Mesoamerica in a tight grip with a large-scale drought spreading throughout Mexico and the north coast of South America. Consequently, Charles III authorized emergency trade with the Americans. Johnson, *Climate,* 97–98, 114.

56. The Continental Congress enacted an embargo on shipping flour and other foodstuffs to the British West Indies in 1774; this ban on trade started to take effect in fall 1775. Spain was hence faced with the interruption of its new supply network on the American east coast. As a consequence, Charles III decided to increase the trade volume between North America and the Spanish peninsular ports, thus bypassing the British West Indies and reshipping the North American flour from Europe to the Spanish Caribbean colonies. Johnson, *Climate,* 126–27.

57. Cummins, *Spanish Observers,* 113.

58. Din, "Canary Islanders," 354. "Isleño" ("Islander") is a term the Canary Islanders used for themselves and that their descendants still use today. See ibid., 353.

59. Cummins, *Spanish Observers,* 200.

60. José de la Pena y Camara et al., eds., *Catálogo de Documentos. Archivo General de Indias, Sección V, Audiencia de Santo Domingo* (New Orleans, LA: Loyola University, 1968), appdx. 2, 429.

61. Din, "Canary Islanders," 356–58.

62. Thomas E. Chávez, *Spain and the Independence of the United States: An Intrinsic Gift* (Albuquerque: University of New Mexico Press, 2002), 170.

63. Gálvez to Navarro, 19 August 1779, HNOC, AGI, Papeles de Cuba, Leg. 1232, Ed. 145, Reel 6, doc. 202, fol. 659v.

64. A status report of the Canary Islander immigration by Governor Gálvez stated that by July 1779 1,582 people had arrived from the Spanish islands. Din, "Canary Islanders," 355.

65. Gálvez to Navarro, 19 August 1779, HNOC, AGI, Papeles de Cuba, Leg. 1232, Ed. 145, Reel 6, doc. 202, fol. 659v.

66. Chávez, *Independence,* 170; Gálvez to Navarro, 21 August 1779, HNOC, AGI, Papeles de Cuba, Leg. 1232, Ed. 145, Reel 6, doc. 203, [fol. 2].

67. Chenoweth, "Reassessment," tab. 1; Chávez, *Independence,* 182.

68. Navarro to Gálvez, 29 August 1780, HNOC, AGI, Papeles de Cuba, Leg. 593, Ed. 87, Reel 107, fol. 53r ("the horizon"), fol. 53v ("the air was"), fol. 54v ("a pregnant woman"), fol. 55v ("the slowdown which").

69. Ibid., fol. 58r–58v ("For, seeing these").

70. Din, "Canary Islanders," 357–58.

71. Navarro to Gálvez, 29 August 1780, HNOC, AGI, Papeles de Cuba, Leg. 593, Ed. 87, Reel 107, fol. 56r.

72. How the (climatically) difficult provisioning situation in the Spanish Caribbean influenced Spain's mercantilist policies is discussed in Johnson, *Climate;* see esp. chaps. 3 and 5, 74–76, 126–29.

73. Lachance, "Demographic Perspective," 151.

74. Johnson, *Climate,* 154.

75. Dessens, *Saint Domingue;* Nathalie Dessens, "From Saint Domingue to Louisiana: West Indian Refugees in the Lower Mississippi Region," in Bond, *French Colonial Louisiana,* 247.

76. David Patrick Geggus, "Saint-Domingue on the Eve of the Haitian Revolution," in *The World of the Haitian Revolution*, ed. David Patrick Geggus and Norman Fiering (Bloomington: Indiana University Press, 2009), 12; Johnson, *Climate*, 154.

77. Johnson apparently did not use Grove's or Gergis, Garden, and Fenby's articles for her conclusion. Richard Grove found an El Niño event to have extended over South Asia between 1788 and 1795, affecting large groups of people with severe drought. Richard Grove, "The Great El Niño of 1789–93 and Its Global Consequences: Reconstructing an Extreme Climate Event in World Environmental History," *Medieval History Journal* 10 (2007), 80. Gergis, Garden, and Fenby's research studied the same period in Australia, during which British colonialists attempted the first settlement and met with climatic difficulties such as drought, storms, and excessive rainfall. Gergis, Garden, and Fenby criticize Grove for his use of natural proxy data, which they deem too one-sided (he only uses a coral reef record from Galapagos) for his claim of the 1788 to 1795 El Niño. Based on new evidence from a number of different natural proxies, Gergis, Garden, and Fenby in turn, suggest an El Niño event to have occurred between 1791 and 1793. Joelle L. Gergis, Don Garden, and Claire Fenby, "The Influence of Climate on the First European Settlement of Australia. A Comparison of Weather Journals, Documentary Data, and Paleoclimate Records, 1788–1793," *Environmental History* 15, no. July (2010), 488.

78. Dessens, "Saint Domingue," 249.

79. Carondelet to Aranda, n.d. [1793], HNOC, AGI, Papeles de Cuba, Leg. 178, Ed. 144, Reel 166, doc. 92.

80. De las Casas to Campo de Alange, 15 September 1794, [copy of: Carondelet to de las Casas, 31 August 1794], HNOC, AGI, Audiencia de Santo Domingo, Leg. 2643, ind. 845, fol. [599r].

81. De las Casas to Campo de Alange, 15 September 1794, [copy of: Carondelet to de las Casas, 31 August 1794], HNOC, AGI, Audiencia de Santo Domingo, Leg. 2643, ind. 845, fol. [599v].

82. Rendon to Alcudia, n.d. [December 1794], HNOC, AGI, Papeles de Cuba, Leg. 638, Ed. 141, Reel 6, doc. 1 ("augmenting the pain"), doc. 3.

83. Ibid., doc. 3.

84. Pedro Pedesclaux, 19 December 1794, NOPL, Acts and Deliberations of the Cabildo. 25 May 1792–10 April 1795, AB 301 1779–1795, vol. 3 No. 3, fol. 180.

85. Ibid.

86. On fire and human society, see Stephen J. Pyne, *Fire in America: A Cultural History of Wildland and Rural Fire* (Princeton, NJ: Princeton University Press, 1982).

87. On the ambivalence of fire as a natural or human-made hazard see Eleonora Rohland, *Sharing the Risk: Fire, Climate and Disaster: Swiss Re, 1864–1906* (Lancaster, UK: Crucible Books, 2011), 56–59.

88. Lachance, "Demographic Perspective," 154. Governor Carondelet stopped the importation of slaves from the French islands in 1792 for fear of the spread of revolutionary ideas. Jack D. L. Holmes, "The Abortive Slave Revolt at Pointe Coupée, Louisiana, 1795," *Louisiana History: Journal of the Louisiana Historical Association* 11, no. 4 (1970), 357.

89. Gabriel Debien and René LeGardeur, "Les Colons de Saint-Domingue Réfugiés à la Louisiane (1792–1804)," *Revue de Louisiane/Louisiana Review* X (1981), 119, 132, as quoted in Paul Lachance, "The 1809 Immigration of Saint Domingue Refugees to New Orleans: Reception, Integration and Impact," *Louisiana History* 29 (1988), 110 fn. 5.

90. M. ***, *Mémoires sur la Louisiane et la Nouvelle Orléans* (Paris: Ballard, 1804), 135, 138. The anonymous author emphasizes that all censuses are incorrect and too low in their counts. The 1785 census partitions New Orleans's population into 2,826 whites, 563 free people of color, and 1,631 slaves. For 1803 the count is 3,248 whites, 1335 free people of color, 2773 slaves, and 700 "non-residents" listed under "whites." Sailors and the garrison were not included. Also, ostensibly absent are any Indian nations. On the Louisiana censuses of the eighteenth and nineteenth century see also Lachance, "Demographic Perspective," 144 and 171, fns. 4 and 5. An in-depth demographic study of the Spanish period is provided by Antonio Acosta Rodríguez, *La Población de Luisiana española, 1763–1803* (Madrid, Spain: Ministerio de Asuntos Exteriores, 1979), but Lachance criticizes it for using ahistoric categories. Lachance, "Demographic Perspective," 144, 152.

91. Pedro Pedesclaux, 19 December 1794, NOPL, Acts and Deliberations of the Cabildo, 25 May 1792–10 April 1795, AB 301 1779–1795, vol. 3 No. 3, fol. 182.

92. See, for example, the earthquake and fire of San Francisco in 1906, when city officials tried to suppress news about the earthquake and styled the disaster as a city fire, explicitly in order not to scare off immigrants. Carl-Henry Geschwind, *California Earthquakes: Science, Risk, and the Politics of Hazard Mitigation* (Baltimore: Johns Hopkins University Press, 2001), 21. See also Eleonora Rohland, "Earthquake versus Fire: The Struggle over Insurance in the Aftermath of the 1906 San Francisco Disaster," in Janku, Schenk, and Mauelshagen, *Historical Disasters in Context*, 188.

93. The classic study on subsistence crises in Europe is still Wilhelm Abel, *Massenarmut und Hungerkrisen im vorindustriellen Europa. Versuch einer Synopsis* (Hamburg, Germany: Parey, 1974).; See also Christian Pfister and Rudolf Brázdil, "Social Vulnerability to Climate in the 'Little Ice Age': An Example from Central Europe in the Early 1770s," *Climate of the Past Discussions* 2 (2006); Emmanuel Le Roy Ladurie, *Histoire Humaine et Comparée du Climat. Canicules et Glaciers, XIIIe–XVIIIe Siècles* (Paris, France: Fayard, 2004), passim; Emmanuel Le Roy Ladurie, *Histoire Humaine et Comparée du Climat. Disettes et Révolutions, 1740–1860* (Paris, France: Fayard, 2004), passim; Steven Engler et al., "The Irish Famine of 1740–1741: Famine Vulnerability and 'Climate Migration,'" *Climate of the Past* 9 (2013); Mauelshagen, *Klimageschichte der Neuzeit 1500—1900*, 92–96.

94. Fleming, *Meteorology*, 9–10, 21.

95. Kutzbach, *Thermal Theory*, 10.

96. For a detailed study about the American storm controversy, including a table with the most important publications that contributed to it, see Fleming, *Meteorology*, chap. 2, 23–54; Kutzbach, *Thermal Theory*, 10–18.

97. Redfield, "Remarks," ("the storm was . . ."), 21; ("occupying a horizontal . . ."), 23, 28; paragraph between quotes, 24, 30–32.

98. Fleming, *Meteorology*, 7, 25. According to his own statement, Redfield used information from more than seventy locations for his 1821 reconstruction. Redfield, "Remarks," 37. On Franklin as a weather observer and an observer of Atlantic storms see Joyce E. Chaplin, *The First Scientific American: Benjamin Franklin and the Pursuit of Genius* (New York: Basic Books, 2006), chaps. 4 and 5, on Atlantic storms esp. 122–23.

99. Redfield, "Hurricane," 191.

100. Adiabatic cooling (or heating) is the process that occurs when an enclosed gas is expanded (or compressed) so rapidly or in such a well-insulated vessel that no heat is transferred between the gas and its environment. Before the formulation of the laws of thermodynamics in the 1860s, the conservation of heat was explained by the caloric theory. The caloric was thought to be a gas or fluid that contained heat and was aggregated around all other gas molecules. Removing gas (and therefore caloric) from a given volume would therefore also reduce the remaining gas's temperature. Thomas S. Kuhn, "The Caloric Theory of Adiabatic Compression," *Isis* 49, no. 2 (1958), 132, 139.

101. James P. Espy, "Essays on Meteorology. Examination of Hutton's, Redfield's and Olmsted's theories," *Journal of the Franklin Institute of the State of Pennsylvania* 18, no. Aug (1836), 106; Fleming, *Meteorology*, 25.

102. James P. Espy, *The Philosophy of Storms* (Boston: Little and Brown, 1841), 8 (original italics).

103. Kutzbach, *Thermal Theory*, 25.

104. Ibid., 16.

105. Navarro to Gálvez, 29 August 1780, HNOC, AGI, Papeles de Cuba, Leg. 593, Ed. 87, Reel 107, fol. 53r.

106. Agustín Udías, "Jesuits' Contribution to Meteorology," *Bulletin of the American Meteorological Society* 77, no. 10 (1996), 2309.

107. Benito Viñes, *Investigaciones Relativas a la Circulación y Traslación Cyclónica en las Huracanes de las Antillas* (Havana: de Pulido y Diaz, 1895), 18; Emanuel, *Wind*, 7.

108. Benito Viñes, *Apuntes Relativos a los Huracanes de las Antillas en Setiembre y Octubre de 1875 y 76* (Havana: Tipografía y Papeleria El Iris, 1878), 37. In addition to, and as a result of his observations, Viñes invented an apparatus, the cyclonoscope, that helped locate the hurricane vortex with respect to the observer. See Mariano Gutiérrez-Lanza, *Apuntes Historicos Acerca del Observatorio del Colegio de Belén* (Havana: Avisador Comercial, 1904), 9..

109. Observers were stationed in Trinidad, Barbados, Antigua, Martinique, Puerto Rico, Jamaica, and Santiago de Cuba. Walter Mary Drum, *The Pioneer Forecasters of Hurricanes* (Havana: Stormont & Jackson, 1905), 19.

110. Udías, "Contribution," 2312

111. Edgar B. Calvert, "The Hurricane Warning Service and Its Reorganization," *Monthly Weather Review* March (1935), 86.

112. See the respective forewords of Benito Viñes, *Practical Hints in Regard to West Indian Hurricanes* (Washington, DC: Government Printing Office, 1886); and Benito Viñes, *Investigation of the Cyclonic Circulation and the Translatory Movement of West Indian Hurricanes* (Washington, DC: Weather Bureau, 1898).

113. *Times-Democrat*, September 1890, as cited in Drum, *Forecasters*, 20–21 ("During the hurricane"), 21.

114. Calvert, "Warning Service," 86.

115. Drum, *Forecasters*, 26; Raymond Arsenault, "The Public Storm: Hurricanes and the State in Twentieth Century America," in *American Public Life and the Historical Imagination*, ed. Wendy Gamber, Michael Grossberg, and Hendrik Hartog (Notre Dame, IN: University of Notre Dame Press, 2003), 269–70..

116. Isaac Monroe Cline, *Storms, Floods and Sunshine* (New Orleans: Pelican Publishing Company, 1945), 98.

117. U.S. Weather Bureau as cited in Drum, *Forecasters,* 27.

118. Gustavus A. Weber, *The Weather Bureau: Its History, Activities and Organization,* vol. 9 (New York: Appleton, 1922), 2.

119. Drum, *Forecasters,* 7.

120. Viñes, *Apuntes,* 25.

121. Fleming, *Meteorology,* 158.

122. Calvert, "Warning Service," 86.

123. Edward N. Rappaport and Robert H. Simpson, "Impact of Technologies from two World Wars," in Simpson et al., *Coping with Disaster,* 47.

124. Fleming, *Meteorology,* 88.

125. The Belen observatory continued its weather observations and hurricanes forecasts after Viñes's death in 1893. Udías, "Contribution," 2313. On the possessive behavior of the Weather Bureau toward Cuban hurricane forecasts under Willis Moore, see Erik Larson, *Isaac's Storm: A Man, A Time, and the Deadliest Hurricane in History,* 1st ed. (New York: Crown, 1999), 93–97.

126. Rappaport and Simpson, "Impact," 44, 47.

127. Ibid., 45 ("proclivity for *administration*"; original emphasis); 46.

128. Ibid., 48–9.

129. Kerry Emanuel, "A Century of Scientific Progress. An Evaluation," in Simpson et al., *Coping with Disaster,* 180; and Riehl, *Tropical Meteorology,* 300.

130. Emanuel, "Progress," 182; Jamie D. Mitchem, "Hurricanes/Typhoons," in Penuel and Statler, *Encyclopedia of Disaster Relief,* 327.

131. Emanuel, "Progress," 182; Erik Palmén, "On the Formation and Structure of Tropical Hurricanes," *Geophysica* 3, no. 1 (1948), 31; Riehl, *Tropical Meteorology,* 332.

132. Chris Mooney, *Storm World: Hurricanes, Politics, and the Battle over Global Warming* (Orlando, FL: Harcourt, 2007), 29.

133. Rappaport and Simpson, "Impact," 51–52.

134. In 1950 motor vehicle registration in the U.S. stood at 49.2 million. That number had doubled to 108.4 million by 1970, which left only 17 percent of American households without a car. James Flink, *The Automobile Age* (Cambridge, MA: MIT Press, 1988), 359.

135. Wilbur Zelinsky and Leszek A. Kosinski, *The Emergency Evacuation of Cities: A Cross-National Historical and Geographical Study* (Savage, MD: Rowman & Little-field, 1991), 43; Stephen Lichtblau, "Preliminary Report—Hurricane Carla," Weather Bureau, http://www.nhc.noaa.gov/archive/storm_wallets/atlantic/atl1961/carla/pre loc/new03.gif, 2.

136. On the development of New Orleans's railways, see Kelman, *River,* 117.

137. In 1960 87.3 percent of Americans owned a television set. See G. Calvin Mackenzie and Robert Weisbrot, *The Liberal Hour: Washington and the Politics of Change in the 1960s* (New York: The Penguin Press, 2008), 35; Campanella, *Dilemma,* 61, 321.

138. Alan Berube and Steven Raphael, "Access to Cars in New Orleans," *The Brookings Institution* (2005), www.brookings.edu/metro/20050915_katrinacarstables.pdf.; Rachel Weinberger, "Rebuilding Transportation," in *Rebuilding Urban Places after Disaster: Lessons from Hurricane Katrina,* ed. Eugenie Birch and Susan M. Watcher (Philadelphia: University of Pennsylvania Press, 2006), 129.

CHAPTER 4

Disaster and Social Order

Historian Donald R. Hickey called the War of 1812 a "forgotten conflict" because its memory has faded in the face of the memory of the American Civil War. Similarly, the 1812 hurricane became a forgotten hurricane since its memory has apparently faded in the face of the War of 1812.[1] At least the hurricane is mentioned nowhere in the relevant War of 1812 literature, despite the fact that it affected U.S. and British war ships patrolling the Gulf in the summer of 1812. A recent historical climatological reconstruction even suggests that the Great Louisiana Hurricane of 1812 was the "closest major hurricane that ever passed by [New Orleans]."[2] By the measure of nineteenth-century contemporaries, the 1812 hurricane was so impressive that it was remembered and used for comparison with the Great Barbados Hurricane that hit New Orleans in August 1831. Even forty years later the 1812 hurricane was still compared to the Last Island Hurricane of August 1856 (see figure 1.2) that completely destroyed the summer resort of the same name.[3] Yet, the omission of the 1812 hurricane from historical memory is not surprising only because of its strong physical impact: it is also peculiar because of the social disaster—for the white ruling elite—of a slave revolt that apparently almost broke out while the elements were raging around New Orleans. The 1812 attempt was not a singular event, however. Only a year before the largest slave revolt on U.S. territory had swept the plantations above New Orleans and had almost reached the city. While the Deslondes Slave Revolt in 1811 and earlier slave revolts of New Orleans's upriver plantations have been fairly well researched, the attempted uprising of 1812, together with the hurricane, have gone unnoticed by historians so far.[4]

Of course, the Great Hurricane of 1812 did not by itself cause social disorder, but rather, the cyclone occurred at a time when the young United States, Louisiana and New Orleans went through a phase of intense social transformation. In 1812 four processes had been under way that unsettled—or at least questioned—the existing social order on the local level, as well as internal security on the national level in the United States.

Turbulent Times

After Saint-Domingue's first slave uprising in 1791, Governor Carondelet had stopped slave imports from that and other French Caribbean islands in 1792 as a precaution to prevent revolutionary ideas from spreading among the slaves of Louisiana. However, it was difficult to maintain this measure strictly because slaves from Saint-Domingue had been smuggled to the Gulf Coast since the French dominion of Louisiana. In addition, the first few refugees from the French Island, mostly whites and free people of color with their slaves, arrived in New Orleans in 1793.[5] While French and Spanish Louisiana had a record of small-scale slave resistance and *marronage* (slaves running away from their masters) the situation was changed by the ongoing large-scale uprising on the nearby island with which Louisiana shared the three-caste social structure: whites, free people of color, and slaves.[6] Even though the ratio of whites to slaves was still in favor of the whites in Louisiana during the 1790s, the revolutionary example of the French island posed a potential threat to the Spanish colony's social order. However, not only rebellious slaves but also rebellious whites who adhered to the French Revolution's principles troubled Spanish authority during the 1790s, in particular after the outbreak of war between France and Spain in 1795.[7]

The two decades between the outbreak of the revolution in Saint-Domingue and the War of 1812 were crucial with regard to New Orleans's social vulnerability as well as the young Union's internal security, however. Together, the overthrow of the white planter elite on the Caribbean island and the third regime change in Louisiana's one hundred–year history set in motion a far-ranging process of social change in the new U.S. territory. Both events pushed white Louisianans to redefine their so far rather fluid identities in a more fixed manner and reshaped the state's social order in accord with the Anglo American structure of society.[8] In Louisiana differences in French and Spanish racial policies had enabled interactions among Europeans, Africans, and Native Americans that were culturally inconceivable for Anglo American contemporaries.[9] Hence, belonging to the United States as a territory and attaining rights of American citizenship bore potential for social conflict not only between Louisianans and Americans but also within Louisianan society. Different visions of nationhood—a concept in its infancy—had the different racial groups scramble to be on what they perceived the right side of the newly emerging power structures. According to the Haitian example, slaves in Louisiana repeatedly tried to revolt against whites and free people of color. White Louisianans and free people of color strove to acquire equality with and to become American citizens. Yet the American notion of equality—that whites could become citizens while Indians and blacks remained fixed in their identities—had created new ways of oppression in the United States that, so far, had no parallel in Louisiana.[10]

During the first twenty years of the Spanish reign Lower Louisiana's social dynamics changed, with the suddenly booming slave trade that had stagnated during the 1740s and 1750s under the French. At the beginning of the 1790s the explosive political potential of the French and Saint-Domingue Revolutions started influencing the increasingly checkered ethnic mix of Louisiana's population: slaves of African and Caribbean descent, free people of color of Louisianan and Caribbean descent, white French Louisianans, French newcomers, Spanish newcomers, Canary Islanders, Acadians, some Anglo Americans, members of various Indian nations, Germans, Irish, and some British people. And indeed, white as well as black rebelliousness, directed against the Spanish colonial regime, was manifested in and around New Orleans after 1791.[11] After France's abolition of slavery in all its territories in 1794, slave revolts became a particular threat for the internal security of West Indian and Gulf Coast plantation economies that were built on the institution entirely. In Pointe Coupee, about 150 miles upriver from New Orleans, slave conspiracies were discovered and crushed before they could become revolts in 1791 and 1795. These subversive activities confirmed the Spanish authorities' fear of the spread of revolutionary thought among the slave population. Two more incidents involving slave resistance occurred throughout 1796 but ultimately turned out to be false alarms.[12] Nevertheless, these early attempts of Louisiana slaves to revolt against the white planters show the dynamism that swept from the Caribbean to the Gulf Coast.

In 1800 Spain secretly traded Louisiana back to France in the Treaty of San Ildefonso, in exchange for Tuscany. Napoleon Bonaparte's plan was nothing less than to recreate a French empire in the Americas. He would crush the revolution in Saint-Domingue, reestablish prerevolutionary conditions on the island, and make Louisiana the supply base for Saint-Domingue, which was to continue producing sugar and revenues for France as a plantation economy. However, the French regent's scheme for western expansion did not work out. Napoleon's army was defeated by the Saint-Domingue rebels and the yellow fever pathogen. When in 1803 it was clear that the Caribbean island was lost to France, maintaining Louisiana by itself became fruitless. Napoleon abandoned his grand idea and sold Louisiana to the United States.[13] Neither the Treaty of San Ildefonso nor the agreement of the Louisiana Purchase clearly delimited the borders of Louisiana, however. This ambiguity was to remain a source of conflict with Spain, who still held Texas, California, and New Mexico to the south and west of Louisiana. Also, it remained a threat to U.S. national security well into the first decade of the nineteenth century.[14]

The four years immediately preceding the Louisiana Purchase have become known as the Retrocession Crisis, since the rumor of renewed French interest in the North American colony threatened the young Union under President Thomas Jefferson.[15] If France were to control the Mississippi River and become the other power on the North American continent, the Jefferson administration feared conflicts over commerce and borders that were certain to result in war. Hence, as early as 1801 Jefferson played with the thought of purchasing the strategically most important parts of Louisiana from the French. That is, it was initially not the intention of the U.S. government to buy the whole territory of Louisiana but rather just the Island of Orleans—from the river mouth to the city—and the provinces of East and West Florida. The American diplomats in Paris were thus all the more surprised when they were suddenly offered the whole colony in 1803, after not making any progress in their negotiations during 1802, when Napoleon was still intent on keeping Louisiana for his western scheme.[16] So, on 30 April 1803 the United States had not only acquired a large territory they had yet to wholly familiarize themselves with, but also a new, foreign, and much larger population than they had originally planned for.

From the American perspective, the proximity to revolutionary Saint-Domingue and the unpredictability of a population that did not share the United States' largely Anglo Protestant cultural background made Louisiana, and in particular New Orleans, a gateway for an enemy invasion on the one hand and a site for slave insurrection on the other.[17] The first decade of territorial Louisiana hence became a test of the loyalty particularly of white Louisianans, who now found themselves subsumed under the label "Frenchmen" and who had to find out what this actually meant in their new context.[18]

At the same time, dynamic and profoundly unsettling changes occurred within Louisiana's slave population. During the 1790s Spanish Louisiana had already started evolving from a society with slaves to a slave society.[19] This process became even more pronounced when between 1803 and 1812 about twelve thousand slaves were brought to Louisiana—now under American authority—after the slave trade was freed from Spanish trade regulations. In the course of this development, New Orleans became the busiest slave market in the South. By 1806 slaves together with free people of color made up the majority of the population of territorial Louisiana.[20] While Creole Louisiana slaves spoke French, Spanish, Creole, or Creole French, one-half to two-thirds of the newcomers spoke none of these languages, making communication difficult. In addition, the expansion of many plantations from small- into large-scale enterprises required new modes of slave control and coercion that fueled resistance and restlessness among the slave population of the Lower Mississippi Valley.[21]

In 1804 the Governance Act separated Louisiana into two parts: the Territory of Orleans from the mouths of the Mississippi to the 33rd parallel, and the District of Louisiana north of that line. The western border of those new lands remained under conflictive negotiation with the Spanish. Thomas Jefferson appointed William C. C. Claiborne as the first governor of the Territory of Orleans. Claiborne arrived in New Orleans with a large detachment of the U.S. Army, making clear how much the new territory and its peoples were perceived as potential threats to the United States' security. The Army was intended to defend Louisiana against foreign invasion and slave insurrections, as well as against Native American or white rebels threatening American authority. While the governor represented the executive power of the new territory, a thirteen-member council held the legislative authority, and the judiciary lay with the three-member superior court.[22] The Governance Act provided for the filling of these governmental positions by appointment through U.S. authorities rather than by election through Louisianans. This provision obviously differed from full statehood (and citizenship), which Louisianans expected to acquire with their incorporation into the United States. They perceived not being able to elect their own territorial government as quasi-colonial rule that contradicted the very Declaration of Independence. In a Remonstrance, white Louisianans argued that they would not be citizens of the United States according to the Government Act of 1804 and presented their own understanding of citizenship.[23]

Meanwhile, apart from being apprehensive of a French or Spanish challenge to American authority, Governor Claiborne was worried about the influx of refugees and slaves from the West Indian islands, in particular from Saint-Domingue. In addition, in October 1804 Claiborne received disturbing news of a slave conspiracy at Natchitoches, about 250 miles northwest of New Orleans, and it was not to be the last such news.[24] Synchronously with the expansion of the plantation economy and the growth of the enslaved part of the population, the fear of slave uprisings became a constant companion of the American government as well as the white planter elite in and around New Orleans. Indeed, in 1806, a plot was discovered in the capital city itself, yet it was again quelled before a violent outbreak.[25] Despite the militia that had come to New Orleans with the American governor, a paramilitary city guard was created in 1809 in order to enforce the new Black Code, suppress further slave revolts, and hunt for maroons. Thus, New Orleans's first urban police force was created by the Anglo American authorities in a context of mounting racial tensions, as a tool of racial supremacy during a period in which social order and national security was perceived to be vulnerable. Free people of color, who had been an important part of the militia before, were no longer admitted.[26]

Finally, one year before the 1812 hurricane, in January 1811, what had been conspiracies so far broke into open violence in the Deslondes Slave Revolt, the largest slave uprising in United States history.[27] It started on the German Coast plantations, upriver to the west of New Orleans, where more than 60 percent of the population were slaves. On 8 January 1811 the slaves of the Andry (also spelled André) Plantation injured their master, Colonel Manuel Andry, killed his son, and started marching toward New Orleans, burning down plantations on their way. Contradictive eyewitness reports estimated the slave army to be between 150 and 500 men strong. The owners of the neighboring plantations were warned by slaves who did not take part in the uprising and struggled to flee ahead of the rebels to the city, where their accounts quickly spread rumors, panic, and chaos. General Wade Hampton marched against the rebel slaves with his white army detachment and the planters who were far better armed than the slaves. On 11 January the army and planters killed sixty-six slaves, and captured twenty-nine, bringing them to trial on 13 January. Twenty-one of the accused were found guilty by the white five-man special court headed by the local parish judge. They were shot and decapitated, and their heads were stuck on poles that were put up along the German Coast as a warning to imitators.[28]

Despite attempts at downplaying the real extent of the rebellion, the uprising left a deep imprint in the collective psyche of the white planters in and around New Orleans. Within the same year, yet another flare-up of panic occurred, this time on Christmas Eve. That day Claiborne wrote to the same Colonel Manuel Andry whose son had been killed by his own slaves in the uprising of January, that news had reached him "of a spirit of insurrection having been manifested among the Negroes of the German Coast." Hence, Claiborne appointed Adlard Fortier to "cause patroles [*sic*] service to be regularly performed, & all the Police regulations especially such as relate to Slaves to be strictly observed."[29] In the end, the incident turned out to be no more than a scare yet, clearly, anxieties about the overthrow of white supremacy were running high.

The lines that demarcated those anxieties are closely connected with the process of Louisiana's incorporation into the United States and they deepened throughout the decade between the Louisiana Purchase and 1812, when white Louisianans worked their way toward statehood. Statehood promised to white Louisianans freedom and equality, ideals that had propelled American independence in the first place. The nemesis of this white aspiration of course had to be the slave population's model for freedom and equality, the successful Haitian Revolution—to whites it was the world turned upside down. Free people of color, on the other hand, had to fight for their own place in the newly emerging order, striving for the same rights as whites, who, in turn, sought to widen the racial gap and exclude them whenever possible.

Between the first angry reaction of Louisianans against the Governance Act in 1804 and the year 1812 the local, francophone planter elite and Anglo American officials had had ample opportunity to interact and to clarify the question of loyalty that had yet been open at the time of the Purchase.[30] Hence, in 1812 Washington officials permitted Louisianans to draft their own state constitution. This decision spelled the end of the territorial system and collapsed the Territory of Orleans and District of Louisiana into the State of Louisiana. Statehood brought with it the new political organs of the Louisiana Supreme Court and the state's bicameral legislature, the general assembly.

Only two months after Louisiana's admission to the Union in April 1812 the young state and the loyalties of its population were put to the test again when it had to mobilize for the war the United States had declared on Great Britain in June 1812.[31] Two months later, during the night of 19 to 20 August, a strong hurricane hit the Gulf Coast and New Orleans and reawakened the specter of slave rebellion.

Hurricane and Slave Revolt?

On Wednesday 19 August around 11:00 in the morning privateer Dominic Youx (also spelled You) left his ship *Pandoure* at Plaquemines and started out for New Orleans in a smaller boat in order to hand his *lettre de marque* (letter of marque) and the muster roll of his ship to the French consul, Anne-Louis de Tousard.[32] Youx must have come to New Orleans in expectation of the ship captures he was going to make in the Gulf after the United States had declared war on the British in June 1812. Around 3:00 in the afternoon the wind had picked up so strongly, however, that he was forced to tie his boat down at the house of Charles Jacob, about sixteen leagues (forty miles) below New Orleans. Youx sought refuge with the Jacob family and during the next hours saw floodwaters rise to almost ten feet (three meters) above the ground floor of Charles Jacob's house. The captain ended up on the roof of the house together with the family where they all clung and waited for the howling storm to abate, fearing for their lives.[33]

Meanwhile, in the city itself things looked no less grim. When the citizens dared to set foot in front of their doors on Thursday morning 20 August, "the streets [were] lined with all kinds of ruins—trees—tops of houses" and people were standing "looking up with uplifted hands and eyes."[34] Several letter writers, whose accounts were circulated in the local as well as in the national newspapers, described the damage wrought by the hurricane winds in vivid colors. The meat market building, which had been built only four years before, completely collapsed. Its rebuilding, and in particular its new site, was debated at considerable length in New Orleans's Conseil de Ville (City Council) in the aftermath of the hurricane.[35] The wind had damaged almost all the houses in the city, blown off the roof of the Ursuline's convent church, and uprooted large trees.[36] The loss of ships was particularly distressing for a nation that had just declared war on another nation. Almost all of those moored in front of New Orleans had been damaged or sunk by the storm surge that tore them away and first swept them upriver, against the normal current of the Mississippi. The reversal of the flow to normal brought them back down again, crashing them into each other.[37] The storm surge had also "considerably damaged" the city levee and those of the Faubourg St. Marie and Faubourg Marigny (map 4.1).[38]

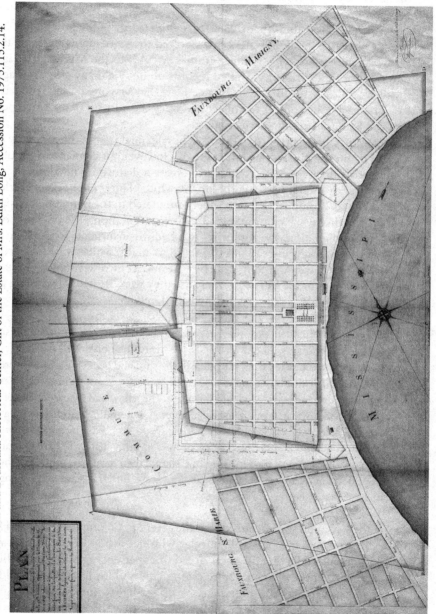

Map 4.1. "Plan dressé en éxécution de l'arrêt du Conseil de Ville de la Nouvelle Orleans, approuvé par le Maire le 15 Juin 1807" (Map drawn in execution of the resolution made by the City Council of New Orleans, approved by the mayor on 15 June 1807), map by James Tanesse, 1807, showing the Faubourg St. Marie and the Faubourg Marigny. Courtesy of the Louisiana State Museum and Louisiana Historical Center, Gift of the Estate of Mrs. Edith Long, Accession No. 1975.115.2.14.

Consequently, a committee of councilmen was formed that was to accompany the levee *voyer* (overseer) on a tour of inspection in order to report on the necessary repairs.[39]

While the newspapers reported no casualties from the city proper, vast numbers perished in the floodwaters that covered the settlements in the marshes below New Orleans, with "whole families swept into the Mississippi," as one newspaper put it.[40] The city council records do not yield any clearer image on the death toll, apart from the dryly stated fact that Mayor Charles Trudeau was to "appoint a police officer to collect and bury the corpses of drowned people that can be found along the river board."[41]

So far, the damage record of the 1812 hurricane does not differ greatly from the hurricanes of the eighteenth century. However, an element so far absent from hurricane accounts was added to create a disturbing new mix of social and natural disasters, particularly for the white planter elite of New Orleans. A letter dated 22 August that was widely circulated in the national newspapers told of "the discovery of an intended insurrection among the negroes" of the city. With indignation, the author reproached the insurgents for "tak[ing] advantage of that night instead of waiting till to-night, which was their original plan." The writer went on to narrate how he and a coworker stayed in his shop during the night of the hurricane, because they were "fearful of sleeping alone that night."[42] While the hurricane intensified outside

> our minds were filled with the images of negroes and assassins, each noise we heard startled us. About 11 o'clock, we heard the noise of a crow bar [at the] window which led from the office to the yard and believing that we were about to be assailed by a band of blacks, we both took arms, with which I was well provided and proceeded into the office. The fellow had succeeded in getting the window partly open just as we entered, but finding it iron gated, was obliged to leave it. We were now at a loss how to proceed. The great fear we had of its being a band of blacks determined us immediately to knock upon the door. If they continued to assault we should then have time to unlock the front door, and through that, to make our escape into the street after giving them as many shots as we could.[43]

Yet the two men soon realized that they were not being "assailed by a band of blacks" but rather by a single burglar who fled when he became aware of the shop owners' alarm. Still, their dread of experiencing a slave rebellion at a moment when the elements were raging and undermining their building's and the city's security did not wane. "A bright light" they saw "through the upper part of the front door . . . convinced us that the city was on fire and the blacks out." After continuing to relate how the chimney of the neighbor's house had crashed into their shop's office and a description of the destruction they saw on the morning after the storm, the author added, "The negroes are completely frustrated in their intentions. Some white men at their head are in prison."[44]

The slave uprising of January 1811 and the subsequent Christmas Eve scare of a new attempt were apparently very fresh in white New Orleanian's minds for fears to be running so high during the 1812 hurricane. The circulation of this letter in national newspapers also made it an ideal medium to raise apprehensions about slave revolts elsewhere in the country and to spread rumors. However, did the account of the anonymous shopkeeper have any foundation? According to the meeting minutes of the city council, attempts had been made "during several consecutive nights to lay fire to the city and to disturb public peace."[45] The meeting minutes relate further that on 20 August, after the wind had calmed down and the damage had been inspected, Mayor Charles Trudeau had procured a city guard in support of the militia that was to patrol the city during the night in order to guarantee public peace.[46] According to Mayor Trudeau,

> Since 20 August, we have not stopped having the most vivid fears that criminals are trying to set fire to the city despite the exactitude of the militia and city guard patrols. The day before yesterday a Negro was found hidden in a store house for ship tar and other combustible materials; unfortunately, the negligence of the man who was appointed to guard him allowed for the escape [of the detainee]. Last night an extremely bold attempt at burning down the house of Mr. Rillieux, Rue Toulouse, was made. Workers who were appointed to make some reparations there found the fire lit in four places of the store house rented to Messrs. Hugh Morro et Cie. It seems that the criminals had double keys because all the doors were exactly closed. . . . it seems that the villains were of cold blood and it is probably not irrational to presume that the men who directed the coup were of superior intelligence than the negroes, which requires us to redouble the vigilance in our patrols and other measures of public security.[47]

Those further measures of public security were to close the "cabarets of the city and the faubourgs [suburbs]" at nightfall, and to order a curfew for slaves starting at 7:00 P.M. If slaves were found in the streets after that time, they would be put into prison. The mayor's city guard was furnished with arms and six hundred ball-cartridges were placed in the city hall, to be distributed to the watchmen whenever needed.[48] Such measures had been ordered after the 1811 revolt to maintain peace and quiet in the city. Significantly, since then the territorial militia had been reorganized thoroughly in order to be able to respond more rapidly to incidents of slave rebellion.[49] Those precautions helped to prevent the success of "three projects of insurrection of the negroes," which, according to consul de Tousard's colorful letter to a lady friend "threatened to have the scenes of S[ain]te Domingue renew themselves here."[50]

It appears that the anonymous shopkeeper's published letter thus vented a widespread fear, which is mirrored in the city council's and mayor's communication. Furthermore, the anonymous writer's claim that "white men" were at the head of the attempted insurrection(s) is supported by Mayor Trudeau's racist statement about the "men of superior intelligence" who he supposed led the initiative. The fact that whites are claimed to have been involved in the actions during and after the 1812 hurricane shows that the spirit of the French Revolution was still very much alive in francophone New Orleans and that slave insurrections were not fought only along the lines of race but also of social class.

More importantly, however, the 1812 hurricane is the first instance where, in New Orleans, fears of a slave rebellion coincide with this disruptive natural hazard. Neither the French nor the Spanish eighteenth-century sources mention actual or rumored slave rebellions or unruliness in the aftermath of hurricanes affecting the city. As mentioned above, slave resistance against planters had certainly existed since the French era of Louisiana, mostly in the form of *marronage* and runaway slave communities in the swamps. Never had revolutionary dynamics reached a scale such as during the 1790s and 1800s, however. Nowhere else on the North American continent did the transition from a society with slaves to a slave society, and thus to a full plantation economy, coincide with the Age of Revolution.[51] Louisiana was an economic latecomer in this respect. Added to those two concurrent processes was the third—the incorporation of Louisiana into the United States. All three factors required a redefinition of the various ethnic groups' identities along deepening lines of racial segregation and ultimately resulted in the reshaping of New Orleans's social order according to the Anglo American model.

In the mature plantation economies of the West Indies, the fear of African slaves using hurricane disasters as an opportunity to overthrow white supremacy had a tradition dating back to the seventeenth century.[52] This fear was a function of the skewed ratio of slaves to whites that characterized slave societies and made them politically vulnerable, especially in times of war or during hurricane season. The large-scale destruction of infrastructure during tropical cyclones, including military defense structures and arms, increased the white minority's apprehensions of losing control over the slave population. Although looting by African slaves as well as whites became common in the aftermath of hurricanes, the Caribbean planter elite's fear of revolt during or after hurricanes was never realized.[53] The recognition that New Orleans shared many cultural traits with the Caribbean Islands is not a new one; the co-occurrence of a hurricane and an actual attempt of African slaves at rising against the authorities is further proof for the similarity and entanglement of the two region's socioeconomic structures. Yet, as opposed to the Caribbean islands, in New Orleans, the (white) fear of a slave revolt during the chaotic situation occasioned by a hurricane was apparently realized.

However, given the fact that no hurricane forecasts could yet be made, the co-occurrence of both events in 1812 was by chance. That is, since "slave rebellions were usually carefully planned affairs," the rebellious slaves and whites of New Orleans must have decided spontaneously to advance their planned rebellion to the night of the hurricane while the storm was raging.[54] Clearly, the hurricane did not cause the vulnerability of political institutions, rather its destructive force laid bare the already volatile structures of everyday life—embodied by the newly formed, supremacist police force—to reveal this vulnerability inherent in a society built on inequality. For adaptation to hurricanes in New Orleans, this political and social vulnerability became an impediment for disaster relief and rebuilding in the aftermath of the hurricane, as fear of a slave revolt led to a high military presence in the city. The 1812 hurricane hence acts as what Tony Oliver-Smith called a *crise revelatrice* (revelatory crisis) through which we see an emerging slave society acting out its endemic mistrust of the enslaved black population concerning security.[55] Consequently, the hurricane of 1812 shows how internal societal factors unrelated to hurricanes may complicate adaptation to this hazard. In other words, natural disasters may play different roles in processes of adaptation. A classic of sorts is the role of disasters as trigger for adaptive processes, a perspective that has been popularized by simplistic models of human behavior. However, depending on circumstances, the opposite is the case, and disasters, by exposing and aggravating social inequality, may lower resilience and hamper adaptation.

The fact that that in 1812 Louisiana statehood coincided with a war and a natural disaster is interesting with regard to the process of nation building. Both types of events have been described as establishing identity, solidarity, and feelings of unity among the affected populations in the face of a common external threat and through the mobilization of disaster relief. Environmental historian Christian Pfister found that in nineteenth-century Switzerland, in the absence of wars after 1847, natural disasters became the events that helped shape a feeling of nationality and belonging through supra-regional fundraising for disaster victims.[56] Regarding war as a unifying event, Peter Kastor highlights the role of the War of 1812 as a case of Louisianan's loyalty proven after the defeat of the British in the Battle of New Orleans in 1815. White Louisianans as well as free people of color and a few Indian nations had come together to fight the foreign invasion. After the end of the war the doubts about the seriousness of Louisianans' attachment to the United States had been dissolved, culminating in the moment when the U.S. Congress thanked Louisiana's people for their courageous action to defeat the British.[57] It would be wrong, however, to presume that fighting a common aggressor had leveled the widening disparities between the ethnic groups, especially in New Orleans. If at all, the war as well as the Hurricane of 1812 created unity among the white elite who, in both instances, was fighting against an external as well as an internal enemy in order to prove their identity as worthy citizens of the United States. In other words, war and natural disaster might have had a unifying effect temporarily, but only along the lines marked by the institution of slavery and by racial segregation, with those fault lines in fact becoming more pronounced in the process.[58]

Americanization, War, Depression, and Yellow Fever Epidemics

In New Orleans the struggle for a new social order, and ethnic and cultural hegemony of the French Creoles over the Anglo American newcomers (or vice versa) was by no means over after the War of 1812. This scramble for power found expression in a prominent conflict in which aspects of ethnicity, differing understandings of property rights, and land-use intersected; this power struggle was fought in the city's court between 1805 and the mid-1830s. In the batture case (also known as *John Gravier v. Mayor, Aldermen, and Inhabitants of the City of New Orleans*), John Gravier, who owned property in New Orleans's Faubourg St. Marie, intended to make use of the batture on the riverside of the suburb's levee.[59] The batture was a stretch of river sediment that was inundated during the high-water season of the Mississippi. During the time it was dry, it was considered public space and was used by New Orleanians to store goods or, as the road on the levee, for promenading.[60] Even though Gravier's property did no longer abut the levee directly—he had divided up part of his property and sold it off—he laid claim to the batture by first building a levee around it so as to secure it from flood waters. When he decided to prohibit people from using the batture, public protest arose. The batture case became a drawn-out affair that was finally settled in favor of the public in 1820. The question whether the batture was a public space or whether it could be developed by a private property owner was at the core of the conflict, with two legal traditions, French civil law and Anglo American common law, clashing violently.[61] Finally, after its first fifteen years as an American city, New Orleans's white Creole-dominated Conseil de Ville gained the upper hand over the American upstarts. The Conseil de Ville and the court hence not only signaled the dominant legal tradition but also the dominant culture and identity of the city.

The French Creole ethnic and cultural hegemony over New Orleans was not to last for long, however. In 1835 the batture in front of the Faubourg St. Mary—by now almost exclusively settled by Anglo Americans—became once more a bone of contention.[62] This time the ensuing conflict over land use at the waterfront led to the city's splitting into three separate municipalities along established ethnic fault lines.[63] The First Municipality was what today is the French Quarter with a predominantly French Creole population; the Second Municipality, the Faubourg St. Mary, was overwhelmingly inhabited by Americans; and the Third Municipality, the suburbs downriver from the French Quarter, was home to New Orleans's latest immigrants and poorer classes. Each municipality had its own council, which was subordinate to a general council and mayor who had mandates limited to common interests. This system was maintained until 1852 when it was abandoned, and the city reunited, this time with an American-dominated city council.[64]

Simultaneous with its Americanization the decades between 1812 and the Civil War also saw the rapid industrialization and urbanization of New Orleans. Throughout the American South those two processes were perceived with suspicion since, in the eyes of pro-slavery Southerners, they undermined democracy and the very economic and social culture the Southern states were built on. Urbanization as it was occurring in the North was seen to concentrate large numbers of unskilled and underpaid workers who would use their right to vote to revenge themselves out of jealousy on the "ruling class, known as the citizens by the Constitution." Against this Northern "specter of mob rule," stood the South's paternalist order of slave society where "the lowest and most ignorant and degraded class . . . are not, as in the North, citizens and voters, but are negro slaves, who have no political rights." Hence, the fact that in the South no whites had to "degrade themselves" by doing menial labor was perceived as ensuring equality among whites and to prevent riots and strikes as they were known from Northern cities. As opposed to the North's free wage-labor society, where workers were at the mercy of employers, in the South's slave society slave-owners perceived themselves as governing their households as benevolent fathers caring for the welfare of their dependents.[65] Growing cities in the South such as New Orleans, Baltimore, and St. Louis, as centers of commerce took a similar demographic and industrial development as those of the North and thus became embodiments of what pro-slavery politicians rejected as un-Southern. As a consequence, secessionist politics in the 1850s were influenced and complicated by this city—country-side dichotomy.[66] Yet ultimately an idealized image of rural life tuned to the city—urban paternalism—managed to unite planters and non-slaveholding whites in their rejection of Northern free wage-labor society and to vote for secession in 1861.[67] The Civil War broke out in the same year, but in 1862 New Orleans capitulated before the federal troops that consequently occupied the city.

During Reconstruction Louisiana became the epicenter of exceptional violence. Between 1865 and 1877 the Confederate veterans' counterrevolution against Northern abolitionists took the form of terrorist acts against freedmen and their families, and of paramilitary action in order to disrupt elections. The

Confederate backlash was fought with standing (volunteer) troops in order to overthrow the new state government.[68] In New Orleans six street battles were fought in this context between the end of the Civil War and the withdrawal of federal troops in 1877. In addition to the violent sociopolitical postbellum upheavals, Louisiana's economy was prostrated by the war. After surrender to the Union, deflation struck the South because the Confederate currency lost its value; this, in turn, led to a drop in land values. Returning planters found that their farm animals had died, their tools had deteriorated, and that their former coerced workforce, now free, had migrated to the cities. Many freedmen refused to work on plantations for wages so that agricultural labor was scarce, and the production of food crops became a serious concern.[69]

The wartime destruction and neglect of infrastructure further hampered Louisiana's economic recovery, since transport and communication were interrupted by impassable roads, bridges that had been swept away, and railroads that were damaged or had fallen into disrepair. Railroads had started to be built in New Orleans in the mid-1850s, when the railroad boom was at its height in the North. At the beginning of the Civil War, Louisiana boasted 386 miles (621.2 kilometers) of railroad that were largely damaged as a consequence of war action. It was not until the 1870s that an integrated Southern rail system had developed with New Orleans at its center.[70] Louisiana's telegraph lines, which were to become central for the first hurricane forecasts transmitted from Cuba to the U.S. Gulf Coast in the 1870s, were affected by the war, too. The first wire had been set up in 1847 to connect New Orleans with Washington. After the war telegraph lines were rebuilt relatively quickly and extended to Galveston, Opelousas, Natchitoches, and Thibodaux.[71]

The worst and longest-lasting damage was sustained to the Mississippi Delta's levee system. After 1865 it was practically nonexistent. As we have seen in chapter 2, before the war it was the property owner's responsibility to maintain the levees outside of New Orleans proper. They were held by the levee ordinances to send slaves for repair works. This system had a checkered history of success in preventing *crevasses* (breaks) from happening. With the abolition of slavery, the coerced workforce that had hitherto taken care of the vital infrastructure of the Lower Mississippi Valley was gone and damage went unattended. Consequently, large stretches of Lower Louisiana's earthen levees were simply washed away. What is more, under the new labor system—that is, in the absence of slaves—the state proved incapable of repairing old damage as fast as new breaches occurred. Only after the federal government took over the issue of flood control in 1879 did Louisiana's levee system regain some semblance of effectiveness.[72]

On the heels of postwar violence and desolation came the first of two economic depressions that were to affect the United States as a whole and New Orleans as Louisiana's commercial center in particular. The economic crisis of the 1870s started with the failure of New York businesses and the Panic of 1873, and lasted until 1879. New Orleans banks suspended currency payments and business slowed gradually into 1874. In addition, many Northern merchants who had made considerable gains in the immediate postwar years in the South left with their savings, so that no new investments were made. There are no reliable estimations for the numbers of unemployed; however, a contemporary estimated that as many as five thousand New Orleanian families were starving in 1874 and 1875. According to an 1874 newspaper report, the seriousness of the situation was also expressed in a "mania for self-destruction"—that is, a surge in suicide numbers. Yet small signs of hope prevailed in the form of Lower Louisiana's growing lumber industry as well as in the building of James B. Eads' jetties in the Mississippi's South Pass to deepen the shipping channel and thus to improve river commerce.[73]

Apart from destructive hurricanes, repeated yellow fever outbreaks claimed thousands of New Orleanians' lives throughout the nineteenth century. In terms of death toll, yellow fever was by far the deadliest natural disaster other than Mississippi floods and hurricanes. Starting on a smaller scale in 1796, 1811, 1817, 1819, and 1822, devastating epidemics swept through the city in 1847, 1853, 1858, 1878, and 1905, killing about forty thousand New Orleanians in their course (figure 1.2).[74] The fact that these epidemics became virulent only at the beginning of and during the nineteenth century is a result of the changing economy in and around New Orleans. Starting in the 1790s sugar increasingly replaced indigo as an export crop on Lower Louisiana's plantations. The vessels used for sugar-making on sugar plantations were ideal breeding grounds for the *aedes aegypti* mosquito, the vector that spread the virus among New Orleans's population.[75]

Yellow fever outbreaks often caused mass panics since they spelled the total disruption of everyday-life. Commerce and communication were interrupted due to quarantine regulations and missing personnel, sometimes for as much as three to four months; communities blockaded themselves from the outside world so as to prevent the disease from reaching them. Those citizens who had the means regularly left New Orleans during what was perceived as the Yellow Fever Season.[76] Apart from this seasonal migration, the excess mortality severely disrupted the city's social fabric. For example, in the 1853 epidemic between eight thousand and twelve thousand inhabitants (one tenth of the population) succumbed to the disease.[77] Because of the perceived immunity of blacks against yellow fever, and because few white, able-bodied men remained alive in 1853, enslaved Africans were forced to dig graves for whites. Predictably, this raised racial tensions, with rumors of a slave rebellion running as wild as after the hurricane of 1812.[78]

Even though the real etiology of yellow fever finally was discovered in 1900, the disease—much like fire and floods, but unlike hurricanes—was always perceived as a disaster that could be prevented by the proper means of sanitation. Those means as well as the question as to who was to administer them—the state or the federal government—remained a hotly discussed political topic. The recurring yellow fever epidemics with their severe social and economic impacts thus significantly shaped the South's debate about public health and its institutions well into the twentieth century.[79] Yellow fever is hence an example of how the repetition of a disaster drove institutional development and adaptation. This suggests that the repeated occurrence of hurricane impacts during the same period may have led to a similar—or possibly connected—development with regard to local disaster relief.

Notes

1. On the memory of the war of 1812, see J. C. A. Stagg, *The War of 1812: Conflict for a Continent* (New York: Cambridge University Press, 2012), 1–12, esp. 1–4. Donald R. Hickey, *The War of 1812: A Forgotten Conflict* (Urbana: University of Illinois Press, 1989).

2. For the name of the 1812 hurricane see Ludlum, *Hurricanes,* 75; Mock et al.'s study of the 1812 hurricane uses a wide variety of primary sources ranging from newspapers, to ship log books, to diaries and ship protests. They did not use the French City Council records of New Orleans, however which provide important insight into the "disaster management" from the perspective of the city authorities. Mock et al.'s reconstruction of the 1812 hurricane is the earliest complete historical reconstruction for a hurricane path that closely affected New Orleans. It is possible that some of the eighteenth-century hurricanes came close, or in the case of the 1779 hurricane even hit New Orleans directly, however, their historical tracks are yet awaiting further research. Cf. Mock et al., "Louisiana Hurricane."

3. On September 8, 1831, the *National Gazette* of Philadelphia quoted an article by the *New Orleans Argus* of August 18, 1831: "The [Great Barbados] hurricane was the greatest gale we have experienced since the great hurricane of 1812." *National Gazette,* Philadelphia, 8 September 1831, 3. After the devastating Last Island Hurricane of 1856, New Orleans's *Daily Crescent* wrote that the 1812 hurricane had been "the most destructive storm during the present century so far as property [is] concerned." As cited in Walter Pritchard, "The Last Island Disaster of August 10, 1856: Personal Narrative of his Experiences by one of the Survivors," *Louisiana Historical Quarterly* 20, no. 3 (1937), 698.

4. James H. Dormon, "The Persistent Specter: Slave Rebellion in Territorial Louisiana," *Louisiana History: Journal of the Louisiana Historical Association* 18, no. 4 (1977); Holmes, "Slave Revolt"; Thomas Marshall Thompson, "National Newspaper and Legislative Reactions to Louisiana's Deslondes Slave Revolt of 1811," *Louisiana History: Journal of the Louisiana Historical Association* 33, no. 1 (1992); Albert Thrasher, *On to New Orleans! Louisiana's Heroic 1811 Slave Revolt,* 2nd ed. (New Orleans: Cypress Press, 1996); Daniel Rasmussen, *American Uprising: The Untold Story of America's Largest Slave Revolt* (Harper Collins Publishers: New York, 2011).

5. Holmes, "Slave Revolt," 357; Robert L. Paquette, "Revolutionary Saint Domingue in the Making of Territorial Louisiana," in *A Turbulent Time: The French Revolution and*

the Greater Caribbean, ed. David Barry Gaspar and David Patrick Geggus (Blooming-ton: Indiana University Press, 1997), 213

6. Daniel C. Littlefield, "Colonial and Revolutionary United States," in *The Oxford Handbook of Slavery in the Americas,* ed. Robert L. Paquette and Mark M. Smith (Oxford: Oxford University Press, 2010), 220–21; Holmes, "Slave Revolt," 341; and Daniel H. Usner, Jr., "From African Captivity to American Slavery: The Introduction of Black Laborers to Colonial Louisiana," *Louisiana History: Journal of the Louisiana Historical Association* 20, no. 1 (1979), 42.

7. Hall, *Africans,* 317.

8. Peter J. Kastor, "'They Are All Frenchmen': Background and Nation in an Age of Transformation," in Kastor and Weil, *Empires of the Imagination,* 240.

9. Littlefield, "United States," 219.

10. Peter J. Kastor, *The Nation's Crucible: The Louisiana Purchase and the Creation of America* (New Haven, CT: Yale University Press, 2004), 30–31.

11. Short-lived Jacobin clubs distributed revolutionary literature among the people and revolutionary songs were sung in the streets. Hall, *Africans,* 316.

12. Holmes, "Slave Revolt," 343; Gilbert Din, *Spaniards, Planters, and Slaves: The Spanish Regulation of Slavery in Louisiana, 1763–1803* (College Station: Texas A&M University Press, 1999); Gilbert C. Din, "Carondelet, the Cabildo, and Slaves. Louisiana in 1795," *Louisiana History: Journal of the Louisiana Historical Association* 38, no. 1 (1997), 24.

13. Paquette, "Territorial Louisiana," 206–7, 210; Kastor, *Crucible,* 40; see also John R. McNeill, *Mosquito Empires: Ecology and War in the Greater Caribbean, 1620–1914* (Cambridge, UK: Cambridge University Press, 2010), 236–66.

14. David J. Weber, *The Spanish Frontier in North America,* Yale Western Americana Series (New Haven, CT: Yale University Press, 1992), 291–92.

15. James E. Lewis, "A Tornado on the Horizon: The Jeffersonian Administration, the Retrocession Crisis, and the Louisiana Purchase," in Kastor and Weil, *Empires of the Imagination,* 117.

16. Kastor, *Crucible,* 39–41; Lewis, "Louisiana Purchase," 118–19.

17. Emily Clark rejects the notion of religion "as a monolithic stumbling block to [New Orleans's] 'Americanization.'" For a differentiated account on religion and identity after the Louisiana Purchase see Emily Clark, "Refracted Reformations and the Making of Republicans," in Kastor and Weil, *Empires of the Imagination,* 180–203.

18. Kastor, "Frenchmen," 241.

19. Ira Berlin, *Many Thousands Gone: The First Two Centuries of Slavery in North America* (Cambridge, MA: Belknap Press, 1998), 325. Berlin defines a society with slaves as one where "slavery was just one form of labor among many" while a slave society was one where "slavery stood at the center of economic production, and the master-slave relationship provided the model for all social relations." Ibid., 8.

20. New Orleans's community of free people of color experienced a dramatic increase with the expulsion of Saint-Domingue refugees from Spanish Cuba in 1809–10. An estimated ten thousand new residents were added to the city with this wave of refugees, 3,102 of which were free people of color compared to 2,731 whites. See Paul Lachance, "Repercussions of the Haitian Revolution in Louisiana," in *The Impact of the Haitian Revolution in the Atlantic World,* ed. David Patrick Geggus (Columbia: University of South Carolina Press, 2001), 216. On the reception of those refugees in New Orleans

see Lachance, "Immigration." On their sociocultural impact on New Orleans see Nathalie Dessens, "The Saint-Domingue Refugees and the Preservation of Gallic Culture in Early American New Orleans," *French Colonial History* 8 (2007).

21. Jean-Pierre Le Glaunec, "Slave Migrations in Spanish and Early American Louisiana: New Sources and New Estimates," *Louisiana History: Journal of the Louisiana Historical Association* 46, no. 2 (2005), 214–15, 218.

22. Paquette, "Territorial Louisiana," 212; Kastor, *Crucible*, 55, 89.

23. Kastor, *Crucible*, 57–58, 136; see also Pierre Sauvé, Jean-Noel Destrehan, and Pierre Derbigny, "Remonstrance of the People of Louisiana," *Annals of Congress* 8th Congress, 2nd sess. (1804); for a German translation of part of the "Remonstrance" see Eleonora Rohland, "Beschwerde der Bürger von Louisiana: Der 'Louisiana Purchase' 1803 und die lokale Opposition gegen die amerikanische Territorialregierung," in Büschges, *Das Ende des alten Kolonialsystems.*

24. On apprehensions of French or Spanish coups see Claiborne to Madison, 17 January 1804, in Dunbar Rowland, ed. *The Letter Books of William C.C. Claiborne, 1801–1816,* 6 vols., vol. 1 (Jackson: Mississippi State Library Archive, 1917), 339–40; Claiborne to Madison, 6 February 1804, in ibid., 363–64. On the influx of West Indian slaves and refugees see Claiborne to Madison, 8 May 1804, in ibid., 2, 134; Extract Claiborne to Boré, 8 February 1804 in ibid., 360–61; on the slave conspiracy at Natchitoches see Turner to Claiborne, 16 October 1804, in ibid., 386–87.

25. Dormon, "Slave Rebellion," 393.

26. Kastor, *Crucible,* 91.

27. Ibid., 127–29. For a short but detailed analysis of the revolt see Dormon, "Slave Rebellion." The most recent and one of the few monographs on the 1811 uprising lists only edited/printed source materials and no archival records as primary sources. The author furthermore quotes a (nonaccessible) database he compiled on the basis of two monographs that are printed editions of archival records: Glenn R. Conrad, *The German Coast: Abstracts of the Civil Records of St. Charles and St. John the Baptist Parishes, 1804–1812* (Lafayette: Center for Louisiana Studies, University of Southwestern Louisiana, 1981); Thrasher, *Slave Revolt*; Rasmussen, *Uprising.*

28. Kastor, *Crucible*, 127–29; Dormon, "Slave Rebellion," 397–98.

29. Claiborne to Andry, 24 December 1811, in Dunbar Rowland, ed. *The Letter Books of William C.C. Claiborne, 1801–1816,* 6 vols., vol. 6 (Jackson: Mississippi State Library Archive, 1917) 18; Claiborne to Fortier, 24 December 1811, in ibid., 17; Claiborne to Hamilton, 26 December 1811, in ibid., 20. Not only slaves were feared to revolt: Indian nations such as the Choctaw were also perceived as threatening white supremacy with their resistance against increasing encroachment of their hunting grounds. Claiborne to Hampton, 30 December 1811, in ibid., 22.

30. Governor William Claiborne's marrying a francophone Creole from New Orleans is only one example. See Jane Lucas DeGrummond, "Cayetana Susana Bosque y Fanqui: 'A Notable Woman," *Louisiana History* 22 (1982); Sarah Russell, "Ethnicity, Commerce, and Community on Lower Louisiana's Plantation Frontier, 1803–1828," *Louisiana History* 40 (1999).

31. Kastor, *Crucible*, 136, 149, 151–53. On the War of 1812, particularly in New Orleans and Lower Louisiana and with regard to the incorporation of Louisiana into the U.S., see ibid., 153–80. On U.S. diplomacy and the War of 1812, focusing more on the

Canadian and Atlantic Coast war theaters see J. C. A. Stagg, *Mr. Madison's War: Politics, Diplomacy, and Warfare in the Early American Republic 1783–1830* (Princeton, NJ: Princeton University Press, 1983); and Stagg, *War of 1812*. On Andrew Jackson's declaring New Orleans under Martial law and the conflict this decision generated between him, the francophone citizenry he mistrusted, and American politicians, see Matthew Warshauer, *Andrew Jackson and the Politics of Martial Law: Nationalism, Civil Liberties and Partisanship* (Knoxville: University of Tennessee Press, 2006), 29–45.

32. A letter of marque was a government commission that made a privateer a regular combatant who was subject to martial law. "Lettre de Marque," *Grand Dictionnaire Encyclopédique Larousse 6* (1984): 6245.

33. La Porte [Affidavit describing Dominic Youx's shipwreck], 23 August 1812, HNOC, Dominique You Papers, 1812–1813, Mss 55, Folder 13, [doc. 1].

34. "Extract of a Letter," 25 September 1812, *Lancaster Journal* 19 (21), [3].

35. New Orleans's Cabildo became the Conseil de Ville in 1805, consisting of the mayor, a recorder, a treasurer, and fourteen aldermen. The Conseil's minutes and correspondence were held in French until well into the nineteenth century. Kastor, *Crucible,* 89. A detailed damage report is also provided in Mayor Charles Trudeau's letter to the Conseil; see Trudeau to Conseil, 22 August 1812, NOPL, New Orleans Conseil de Ville. Messages from the mayor, AB 505, 1805–1836, vol. 5: 11 January 1812—30 December 1813, fol. 99–102.

36. "Dreadful Hurricane," 24 September 1812, *Boston Gazette,* vol. 37 (26), [2]; on placing the meat market see Conseil de Ville de la Nouvelle Orléans, Meeting of 22 August 1812, NOPL, Official Proceedings, AB 300, 1803–1836, vol. 2: 6 July 1807–31 May 1817, [fol. 2]; Conseil de Ville de la Nouvelle Orléans, Meeting of 25 August 1812, NOPL, Official Proceedings, AB 300, 1803–1836, vol. 2: 6 July 1807–31 May 1817, [fol. 1]; Conseil de Ville de la Nouvelle Orléans, Meeting of 5 September 1812, NOPL, Official Proceedings, AB 300, 1803–1836, vol. 2: 6 July 1807–31 May 1817, [fol. 1].

37. "Extract of a letter from Gen. Wilkinson," 28 September 1812, *American and Commercial Daily Advertiser,* [1]; Mock et al., "Louisiana Hurricane," 1659.

38. Faubourg Sainte Marie (later St. Mary) is located upriver adjacent to what today is called the French Quarter, the Old Town, and Faubourg Marigny is located downriver adjacent to the French Quarter (see map 4.1).

39. Conseil de Ville de la Nouvelle Orléans, Meeting of 25 August 1812, NOPL, Official Proceedings, AB 300, 1803–1836, vol. 2: 6 July 1807–31 May 1817 [fol. 1].

40. "Dreadful Hurricane," 24 September 1812, *Boston Gazette* 37 (26), [2]; "Extract of a Letter," 25 September 1812, *Lancaster Journal* 19 (21), [3].

41. Conseil de Ville de la Nouvelle Orléans, Meeting of 25 August 1812, NOPL, Official Proceedings, AB 300, 1803–1836, vol. 2: 6 July 1807–31 May 1817, [fol. 1]. If not stated otherwise, all translations from French to English are by the author.

42. "Extract of a letter," 21 September 1812, *Commercial Advertiser* [New York] 15 (6290), [3].

43. Ibid.

44. Ibid.

45. Conseil de Ville de la Nouvelle Orléans, Extraordinary Meeting of 2 September 1812, NOPL, Official Proceedings, AB 300, 1803–1836, vol. 2: 6 July 1807–31 May 1817, [fol. 1].

46. Conseil de Ville de la Nouvelle Orléans, Extraordinary Meeting of 29 August 1812, NOPL, Official Proceedings, AB 300, 1803–1836, vol. 2: 6 July 1807–31 May 1817, [fol. 19].

47. Trudeau to Conseil, 2 September 1812, NOPL, New Orleans Conseil de Ville. Messages from the Mayor, AB 505, 1805–1836, vol. 5: 11 January 1812—30 December 1813, fol. 107–8.

48. Conseil de Ville de la Nouvelle Orléans, Extraordinary Meeting of 2 September 1812, NOPL, Official Proceedings, AB 300, 1803–1836, vol. 2: 6 July 1807–31 May 1817, [fol. 1]; Conseil de Ville de la Nouvelle Orléans]; Extraordinary Meeting, evening of 2 September 1812, NOPL, Official Proceedings, AB 300, 1803–1836, vol. 2: 6 July 1807–31 May 1817, [fol. 1]. The adoption of the English term "watchmen" in the French report is interesting with regard to incorporation and identity that seem to have been shaped, among other factors, by questions of (white) security.

49. Dormon, "Slave Rebellion," 400.

50. De Tousard to Pourrat, 31 September 1812, HNOC, Late Colonial and Early Territorial Louisiana Collection, Mss. 579, Box, 2, Folder 34.

51. This process was set in motion by the Louisiana planters' shift from cultivating tobacco and indigo to planting cotton and sugar. The (comparatively late) success of sugar in the Lower Mississippi Valley was brought about by the know-how of Saint-Domingue immigrants. Berlin, *Slavery*, 325–26; Lachance, "Immigration," 131.

52. Mulcahy, *Hurricanes*, 97–98; S. D. Smith, "Storm Hazard and Slavery: The Impact of the 1831 Great Caribbean Hurricane on St. Vincent," *Environment and History* 18, no. 1 (2012).

53. Mulcahy, *Hurricanes*, 95, 99.

54. Ibid., 100.

55. Anthony Oliver-Smith, "Anthropological Research on Hazards and Disasters," *Annual Review of Anthropology* 25 (1996), 303–28, 304.

56. Christian Pfister, "Von Goldau nach Gondo. Naturkatastrophen als identitätsstiftende Ereignisse in der Schweiz des 19. Jahrhunderts," in *Katastrophen und ihre Bewältigung. Perspektiven und Positionen,* ed. Christian Pfister and Stephanie Summermatter (Bern, Switzerland: Haupt, 2003), 78. For an English version see Christian Pfister, "Disasters, Interregional Solidarity and Nation-Building. Reflections on the Case of Switzerland, 1806–1914," in *Solidarité et Assurance. Les Sociétés Européennes Face aux Catastrophes (17e–21e Siècles),* ed. René Favier and Christian Pfister (Grenoble, France: CNRS MSH-Alpes, 2008). The subject of disasters and their shaping of state power has most recently been explored by Franz Mauelshagen, "Natural Disasters and Legal Solutions in the History of State Power," *Solutions* 4, no. 2 (2013).

57. Kastor, *Crucible*, 165–68, 179.

58. On African Americans as a nation within a nation, the evolution of African American organizations and the gradual formation of a community, see the recent study of John Ernest, *A Nation within a Nation: Organizing African American Communities Before the Civil War,* The American Ways Series (Lanham: Rowman & Littlefield, 2011), 5–12, and chap. 2. That solidarity existed within but not across the racial divide is mentioned by Paul Lachance in his analysis of the reception of Saint-Domingue refugees in New Orleans. Lachance, "Immigration," 113–14.

59. Kelman, *River*, 19, 23.

60. Campanella, *Dilemma*, 26; Kelman, *River*, 20–21.

61. Kelman, *River*, 24, 47.

62. Campanella, *Dilemma*, 171, on New Orleans's antebellum ethnic geography see pages 170–75; see also Joseph G. Tregle, "Creoles and Americans," in *Creole New Orleans: Race and Americanization,* ed. Arnold Hirsch and Joseph Logsdon (Baton Rouge: Louisiana State University Press, 1992), 135.

63. Kelman, *River*, 71, 75.

64. Campanella, *Dilemma*, 32, 163.

65. Virginia secessionist Edmund Ruffin as quoted in Frank Towers, *The Urban South and the Coming of the Civil War* (Charlottesville: University of Virginia Press, 2004), ("ruling class"), 17, ("the lowest and"), 15–16.

66. Most votes against secession came from New Orleans. Ibid., 199.

67. Ibid., 30, 37.

68. James K. Hogue, *Uncivil War: Five New Orleans Street Battles and the Rise and Fall of Radical Reconstruction* (Baton Rouge: Louisiana State University Press, 2006), 11–12.

69. Joe Gray Taylor, *Louisiana Reconstructed, 1863–1877* (Baton Rouge: Louisiana State University Press, 1974), 314, 317, 325.

70. Kelman, *River*, 117–18; Taylor, *Louisiana*, 318; Peirce F. Lewis, *New Orleans: The Making of an Urban Landscape* (Santa Fe, NM: Center for American Places, 2003), 48–49.

71. Taylor, *Louisiana*, 339; Eleanor Beatrice Carleton, "The Establishment of the Electric Telegraph in Louisiana and Mississippi," *Louisiana Historical Quarterly* 31, no. 2 (1948), 430–31.

72. Taylor, *Louisiana*, 317–19, 360.

73. Ibid., 358–60; ("mania for self-destruction") *Daily Picayune*, September 1, 1874, as quoted in ibid., 362.

74. Campanella, *Dilemma*, 26, 34–36, 40, 44; and Urmi Engineer Willoughby, *Yellow Fever, Race, and Ecology in Nineteenth-Century New Orleans,* The natural world of the Gulf South (Baton Rouge: Louisiana State University Press, 2017), 44–45.

75. McNeill, *Empires*, 47–58; Willoughby, *Yellow Fever*, 42–62.

76. Margaret Humphreys, *Yellow Fever and the South* (Baltimore: Johns Hopkins University Press, 1992), 2, 8–10.

77. Campanella, *Dilemma*, 35.

78. Kelman, *River*, 106–8. African American slaves and free people of color's perceived immunity to yellow fever was often used as a justification for slavery. Humphreys, *Yellow Fever*, 7.

79. Humphreys, *Yellow Fever*, 13.

CHAPTER 5

Hurricanes vs. "Mass Idleness"

By 1893, the year of our next close-up of a hurricane that affected New Orleans and its environs, the practice of granting federal disaster relief was well established throughout the United States. As Michele Landis Dauber showed in her publications, granting disaster relief had been an integral part of American political culture from the very beginning of United States history in 1776.[1] The concept of disaster used by Congress in deciding whether relief should be provided to victims did not differentiate between "human-made" or "natural disasters," however. Rather, the victim's inability to control or prevent loss, as well as his or her moral innocence, were criteria for eligibility. This focus on sudden deprivation and the question of blameworthiness had its roots in the intellectual and spiritual traditions of Lockean philosophy, the British Common Law, and Puritanism. If the claimant was found blameless of the misery that had befallen him or her, funds were usually granted liberally.[2] As a consequence of Congress's focus on sudden loss and the blameworthiness of victims, rather than on a categorical distinction between "natural" and "human-made," relief for loss was granted in a broad variety of disaster cases. The range stretched from riot victims who lost property in the 1794 Whisky Rebellion to citizens affected by flood or fire.[3]

Dauber traces the development of a disaster narrative in claims for federal disaster relief, which evolved from appropriations for individuals to appropriations for communities, cities, or regions, toward the beginning of the nineteenth century. The disaster narrative's "plot structure . . . is fixed, but the set of plausible occupants for the roles of 'disaster' and 'victim' have expanded and contracted over the last two centuries," writes Dauber. War, unemployment, and even old age came to be narrated in this way, using previous disaster relief cases as a precedent to justify present claims.[4] However, the disaster relief precedent was not only paramount in enabling and expanding the scope of cases in which funds were appropriated, but it was also an element of denial of relief. Congress would abstain from appropriations in order not to create a precedent that would serve as an analog to future claimants who would, it was apprehended, request similar treatment.[5] Appropriations were made under the taxing and spending power vested in Congress and under the General Welfare

Clause in particular. Both legal powers had been the site of hot debate when it came to congressional disaster relief appropriations.[6]

Along with the practice of considering disaster relief claims, a bureaucracy for the distribution of appropriations had developed. In the aftermath of the War of 1812 when Congress granted charitable relief for war losses, it established a prototype of a national relief distribution organization with a relief commissioner who was to review applications and assign funds. Reaching into the twentieth century the disaster relief precedent became the argumentative basis for the New Deal welfare programs that included health and unemployment insurance.[7]

In 1881 a new element was added to the existing disaster relief practice when the United States ratified the Treaty of Geneva and Clara Barton founded the American Red Cross. The organization relied exclusively on funds and items from charitable donations and did not receive money from the federal treasury, even though it worked in close collaboration with federal agencies. While the sole task of federal disaster relief institutions at the end of the nineteenth century was to distribute financial appropriations in the aftermath of calamities, the American Red Cross was the United States' first (non-governmental) supranational emergency management system that provided medical and material aid to disaster victims on location. On the federal level, an emergency management apparatus developed only from the late 1950s onward.[8] The distinction between the local and federal levels and the different requirements of the institutions, all running under the term "disaster relief," is important with regard to the local structures that evolved in New Orleans after 1893. Originally, the Red Cross Society as it emerged from Europe was intended to grant aid only in the aftermath of wars. However, at a congress in Geneva in 1863 Barton argued that the United States was remote from other countries and consequently the probability of war was rather low. However, Barton found that "great overmastering calamities" of various kinds were widespread and frequent and that, therefore, relief of sufferings from storms, earthquakes, floods and other disasters should be added to the duties of the American Red Cross. This addition became known as the American Amendment.[9] After the Ohio and Mississippi Floods of 1882, during which the National Red Cross provided relief to several Southern cities, associate state- or regional-level Red Cross societies were formed. Apparently, the work of Barton's national society had left such an impression that New Orleans organized a Red Cross Society for the entire state of Louisiana.[10]

Thus, in 1893 federal disaster relief as well as the national- and state-level American Red Cross were institutions available to relieve hardship in the aftermath of severe hurricane impacts in New Orleans. More than a century of political and judicial practice had established federal relief appropriations in the aftermath of disasters. The national Red Cross, by comparison still a young organization, had had ample opportunity to test its ability at home and abroad in the decade preceding the 1893 hurricane in New Orleans.[11] However, before we focus on the shape of disaster relief on the city-level, it is important to consider the national context in which the events of the 1893 Cheniere Caminada Hurricane unfolded, since it considerably influenced the debates about disaster relief appropriations on the federal level.

In the fall of 1892 members of the U.S. business community were still optimistic about their country's economic development. After all, the past two years had proven prosperous, the economy had expanded. Yet, there were small signs to worry about, such as the continuous outflow of gold, a drop in cotton output, and a decline in railroad construction and petroleum production. Then on 20 February 1893 a first tremor occurred, when the Philadelphia and Reading Railway Company went into bankruptcy. A second tremor followed on 22 April, when the federal treasury's gold reserve went below the $100 million minimum mark. With the failure of the National Cordage Company on 4 May began the Panic of 1893, which led to a large number of bank failures, especially in the South and West, to the hoarding of capital, to price declines, and eventually to workers being laid off. By July and August unemployment was widespread throughout the country.[12] In anticipation of the fall and winter months, local governments throughout the United States saw the growing numbers of jobless with great concern and tried to alleviate some of the hardship by organizing public works programs. Yet relief was very limited and, generally, the newly inaugurated President Grover Cleveland's credo was adhered to: "In America people support the government," and it was "not in the province of the government to support the people."[13] This may be surprising, after learning about the broad scope of Congress' perception of disaster. If victims of riots could benefit from federal disaster relief, could not unemployment have figured as a disaster, too? According to Dauber, poverty and unemployment—the term used before the 1890s was "idleness"—were treated differently from other calamities that befell people. Again, the question of who was at fault was as important as causation. With work and industry as prerequisites of God's grace, the Puritan worldview perceived poverty or pauperism as a condition of the able-bodied who refused to work, hence poverty was morally debased and likely self-inflicted.[14] Therefore, "idleness," even if it was inflicted by disastrous forces beyond the individual's control, such as the workings of national and international markets, did not come under consideration for disaster relief. During the height of the depression in 1893, attempts were made in Congress to frame "mass idleness" as a national catastrophe rather than as an individual failing. Yet, the advance in favor of the depression-stricken population came to nothing, among other reasons for the "difficulty in representing wide-spread suffering that was not due to calamitous natural events as a 'disaster.'" Only modern data-gathering and presentation techniques such as statistics, documentary photography, radio, and film made it possible to broaden the scope of federal disaster relief to unemployment in the 1930s.[15]

While the country was thus experiencing the unabated first throes of the economic depression of the 1890s, on 27 August 1893 a Category 3 hurricane and storm surge swept over the Sea Islands, a low-lying archipelago off the coast of South Carolina. It killed between three thousand and five thousand of the free black farmers who had settled there after the Civil War.[16] The storm rendered approximately thirty thousand people homeless and without any means of self-preservation, since all their possessions had been washed away by the tidal wave occasioned by the hurricane. News about the disaster made it into the newspapers only haltingly over the next few days due to the interruption of communication lines. When the magnitude of the event became clear, Clara Barton, president of the American Red Cross, was asked whether this was not a case for her organization to relieve. She declined, arguing that it was beyond the Red Cross to deal with such a calamity. During the first week of September 1893 Barton heard "pitiful paragraphs from various Southern sources," in particular from the governor of South Carolina. After conferring with her neighbor General Matthew C. Butler who was a senator for South Carolina, Clara Barton changed her mind and decided to set out for Beaufort, South Carolina, where she set up the headquarters of her ten-month relief mission to the Sea Islanders. The relief work of the National Red Cross for the storm sufferers started in earnest on 1 October 1893, more than a month after the hurricane had made landfall on the archipelago.[17]

The Cheniere Caminada Hurricane of 1893

While Clara Barton traveled to South Carolina and reorganized the local Beaufort Relief Commission to become part of the Red Cross effort, another hurricane had formed over the northwest Caribbean Sea, crossed the Yucatan peninsula and, on 1 October, was churning as a rapidly intensifying Category 4 hurricane toward the coast of Louisiana.[18] As in South Carolina, a group of rather densely settled, low-lying barrier islands skirted the Louisiana coast west and east of the mouths of the Mississippi. The people who lived on Cheniere Caminada, off Barataria Bay, west of the mouths of the Mississippi, were mostly fishermen and their families who engaged in the local fishing trade. They were the descendants of the various settlement schemes the Mississippi Delta had seen in its almost two hundred-year history of colonial settlement. A motley collection of nationalities and ethnicities could be found on the islands and in the marshlands west of the Mississippi before it flowed into the

Gulf. Apart from French Creoles, Anglo Americans, free people of color, and descendants of freed African slaves, there were the descendants of Bernardo de Gálvez's Canary Islander community, Germans, Austrians, Chinese, and Malayans. Grand Isle, the neighboring island, on the other hand, had become a popular summer resort for New Orleans's business elite and for the plantation owners' families of the region.

At Cheniere Caminada,[19] the effects of the approaching hurricane were felt starting between 7:00 and 8:00 P.M. on the evening of Sunday 1 October 1893. Strong waves rapidly rose from six to eight feet, and, together with the increasing wind, they started claiming the first of the only lightly built houses. Père Grimaud, the island's Catholic priest, noted that the wind blew from the southeast for several hours and then, at around 11:00 P.M., "a sudden ominous lull" occurred, indicating that the hurricane's center was passing directly over the island.[20] The west winds that burst after the passing of the storm's eye destroyed what the southeast wind before had not claimed. "Soon the Cheniere ceased to exist. Out of 450 houses only four remained, and these were filled with crowds of trembling, despairing people."[21] According to the priest, on Sunday morning, 1 October 1893, 1,471 people had lived on Cheniere Caminada. On Monday morning, 2 October, when the storm abated, only 696 of them were still alive: 779 men, women, and children had been swept away by the storm surge that washed over the islands or had been crushed to death amid the floating debris of their own houses.[22] The survivors, left only with rags of clothing, emerged from the ruins to find the corpses of four hundred of their neighbors, families, and friends, whom they started burying hurriedly all day Monday and Tuesday. However, soon they realized that the hurricane had also swallowed their food stores and their fresh water cisterns, as well as their boats, their only means of transport and communication, so that they were now facing death by starvation if timely help did not come from New Orleans.

As on Cheniere Caminada, the same scenes of destruction and desolation played out on the two islands at the mouth of Barataria Bay, Grand Terre and Grand Isle, as well as in the marshes along the Mississippi below New Orleans. However, Grand Isle naturally made headlines because of its fame as a summer resort with three grand hotels, and because some of the storm victims on that island were members of wealthy New Orleanian families.[23] Severe effects were also felt along the coast of Mississippi and southwestern Alabama, raising the total death toll from all three states to two thousand people.[24] Meanwhile, in New Orleans on Monday morning, 2 October, the collapse of the Soraparu market hall, on Soraparu and Tchopitoulas Streets, featured prominently in the *Daily Picayune*. Droves of citizens had gathered around the building that had been blown down by the storm, afraid that people were buried under the ruins. The *Picayune* reporter stated that he "waded about in the water which has flooded the whole neighborhood" of the Soraparu market. On Jackson and

St. Charles Avenues the water had flooded the sidewalks and "in some places was nearly knee-deep."[25]

On Tuesday 3 October, while the survivors on the barrier islands and in the marshes tried burying their dead relatives and feared for their own rescue, the *Picayune* wrote about the damage the hurricane had caused to the Queen and Crescent Railway Bridge that crossed Lake Pontchartrain. In a second article on the damage to boats and barges, the newspaper remarked that property in the city had suffered less than might have been expected. Furthermore, the interruption of train and telegraph lines and the city's only then known fatality were mentioned.

On Tuesday evening "the first faint intimation was received in New Orleans of the frightful catastrophe that had transpired."[26] It was likely carried to the city by the boat that had set out from Cheniere to New Orleans before the hurricane made landfall to get ice for the fishermen of the islands to preserve their catch. The ice boat happened on the scene of desolation on its return journey to the island, just as the survivors realized their lack of provisions. It left its cargo for the islanders to quench their thirst and returned to the city for help.[27] "That the destruction had been so unparalleled was beyond the bounds of reasonable belief."[28] Therefore, the *Picayune* itself chartered a small steamboat that was sent to explore the situation at the islands of Barataria Bay. Another reporter was sent downriver by train to take note of the destruction on the plantations along the Mississippi. Slowly, news of the extent of the damage started reaching New Orleans over the next two days. The *Picayune* front-page headline on 5 October counted "over a thousand lives lost," and the next few pages were filled with harrowing eyewitness accounts of survivors of the storm collected by the reporters on the *Picayune* and other relief boats that had set out from New Orleans for Bayou Cook, Barataria Bay, and the islands of Grand Isle and Cheniere Caminada. On their mission, the relief boats happened on luggers filled with storm survivors rendered homeless, without means of subsistence and often barely with clothes to cover them. They were on their way to search for help in the city.[29]

"Impromptu" Local Storm Relief

New Orleans's citizens started their disaster relief efforts on Wednesday afternoon, and on Thursday 5 October, when the first news of the large number of fatalities and destitute people spread through the city. While Clara Barton had just started relieving the South Carolina storm victims, General Vinet, president of the Red Cross of Louisiana, sent out a call to the public to aid the Louisiana storm survivors. However, in the case of the Louisiana hurricane it was not the Louisiana Red Cross Society that took the relief activity under its wing. Rather, the Red Cross was only one of several operations that were under way in New Orleans to help the washed-out people. Apparently, "an impromptu movement" of citizens organized two relief expeditions by calling on "all citizens of New Orleans who feel the imperative necessity to come to the immediate help of the hundreds of unfortunate people who have been victims of the recent storm," inviting them "earnestly . . . to meet at the Truck Farmers' Hall, No. 269 Decatur Street . . . this Thursday at 2 p.m."[30] Businessmen working around the French market held an informal meeting at which they collected clothes and foodstuffs to be shipped out to the devastated areas immediately. Two further appeals for donations went out to "charitably disposed fellow-citizens," one by a group of men who called themselves "Relief Committee" and another by the Commercial Club of New Orleans, one of the leading social clubs at the time.[31]

For the next five days the civic Louisiana Red Cross Society, the French Market Protective Association, the Citizens' Central Storm Relief Committee (CCSRC), the ecclesiastical Sisters of Charity and the Methodist ministers operated independently, collecting money from the public and purchasing food and clothes to send to the devastated areas below New Orleans.[32] The New Orleans Board of Trade sent out a call for contributions to the boards of trade of other cities. The latter measure bore fruit quickly, and two days later the *Picayune* was able to report "aid from abroad," meaning Pittsburgh and Galveston. Chicago, New York, Boston, and St. Louis had promised help but had not sent anything yet.[33] In addition, Mayor Fitzpatrick called a special meeting of the city council to ask for the appropriation of funds to relieve the people affected by the hurricane. The city council promptly passed legislation to appropriate $2,500 (the equivalent of $68,800 in 2016) from the accounts of Public Charities and Public Health.[34]

Two days later the CCSRC, chaired by Robert Bleakley, president of the Commercial Club, met in the New Orleans Chamber of Commerce where first steps to a tighter organization of the relief work were made. After Theodore Wilkinson, in charge of relief for Plaquemines Parish, had presented a list of damages in his district, one of the members of the committee suggested that a subcommittee of three should be formed to confer with "prominent people of the parishes," in order to determine the real needs of the people. New Orleans's mayor, also a member of the CCSRC, put forward the suggestion that since the Plaquemines police jury had appointed a relief committee, all applications from this parish should be submitted to its police jury and that a member of the Plaquemines police jury should be elected into the CCSRC in order to systematize relief in the parishes below the city.[35] The same organizational process was repeated with the Jefferson and St. Bernard Parish police juries, the other two parishes severely affected by the hurricane.[36] Duties soon became assigned to different subcommittees. The CCSRC's final report lists six of the latter: one for finances, one for requisitions, a Lugger Relief Committee, one for relief in the parishes, a Committee on Collections, and a Committee on Purchases.[37] In order to centralize local and national donations, a central relief fund was set up under the auspices of Mayor John Fitzpatrick. Meanwhile, at the meeting of the French Market Protective Association, disagreement arose over the distribution of funds and over the quickly exhausted treasury. The French Market Protective Association agreed to appeal to the CCSRC for cooperation and for "the formulation of some systematized method of distributing necessary provisions." They were promptly invited to attend the CCSRC's next meeting.[38]

On 12 October the total collections counted at the meeting of the now consolidated CCSRC amounted to $11,188 (the equivalent of $308,000 in 2016). In an official address that the newspapers were asked to circulate as widely as possible, the committee thanked donors for their generous contributions. Curtailing their statement in the next paragraph, however, the committee remarked that "the donations so far received are not adequate to the appalling calamity existing in the storm-stricken districts, and even the money collected by all the different exchanges and this committee, together, is not sufficient to carry out the alms and objects for which we have been organized."[39] The pressing question for the CCSRC was not only the satisfaction of storm sufferers' immediate needs, but also how to support them throughout the approaching winter months. Clearly, charity could be stretched only so far, in particular in a year of economic depression.

Clara Barton, still operating her Red Cross relief from Beaufort, South Carolina, expressed the difficulty in "housing, feeding, clothing and nursing 30,000 for eight months with no aid from the Government and no fund but direct charity from the American people" in a published letter. The appropriations and provisions she was able to obtain would not last for even a month.[40] While the numbers of sufferers were not quite as daunting for New Orleans's CCSRC, it also met with tight purses due to the general crisis of that year. Answering the call of the New Orleans Board of Trade, the chairman of the Cincinnati Board of Trade sent the $502 (the equivalent of $12,900 in 2016) collected by its members along with a letter. It stated that the board found it "very hard times to make collections for relief work away from home, as we have so many unemployed requiring active relief in our midst and our people are being severely called upon."[41]

The difficulty of the city and state authorities in going beyond local and national charitable donations in disaster relief in 1893 is illustrated by the invitation of Louisiana's governor Murphy J. Foster to the CCSRC's meeting of 15 October. After thanking the people of the state and the country for their generous donation, Foster stated regretfully that "as chief executive of the state the governor's powers are limited by law. The state has no funds for purposes of this character [. . .]."[42] New legislation for emergency appropriations by the state could not be made since the Louisiana legislature was not in session at the time of the hurricane so no financial support could be obtained from the state authorities.[43] Consequently, the committee members asked Governor Foster whether he would issue a personal appeal to the Louisiana public, his voice promising to be influential and possibly eliciting further, much-needed donations. Foster's appeal was published in the *Daily Picayune* three days later.[44] Three weeks after the storm, the committee had collected and distributed $40,000 (about $1 million in 2016) of relief funds in the form of clothing, provisions, and building materials.[45] As we will see below, it was barely enough.

Disaster Migration Revisited

Throughout the relief work, it had become clear that "an entire industry has been pretty nearly wiped out" on the coast of Louisiana. According to the *Picayune,* the governor's call to the general public of the state of Louisiana came so late—eighteen days after the hurricane's landfall—because none of the charitable committees had been able to really fathom the extent of the damage and, accordingly, the full costs of it.[46] However, due to the well-organized and soon systematized relief efforts, the CCSRC together with the parish police juries and the Louisiana Red Cross had soon shifted from providing food and clothing to helping the storm sufferers rebuild their houses and boats in an attempt to make them self-sufficient fishermen again.[47]

Rebuilding? Indeed, the CCSRC's efforts to provide lumber for the storm sufferers' new houses in the same area recasts the question of disaster migration and adaptation from the eighteenth century to the end of the nineteenth. According to New Orleans's *Daily Picayune,* the remnants of the population of Barataria Bay were "disheartened" by the destruction of their families and livelihoods and thought of moving away from the scene of desolation. While the *Picayune* was not inclined to criticize "the feelings of individuals," it could see "no good reason for the abandonment of the Barataria Bay settlements."[48] The article—entitled imperatively "A Region Not to Be Abandoned"—argued that the 1893 hurricane was the only storm of a serious nature that had crossed the islands of Cheniere and Grand Isle since 1793.[49] Besides, the article continued, Last Island, to the west of Cheniere Caminada, which had been swept by a destructive hurricane in 1856, had not been affected by any storm before or since either. This was taken as evidence for the fact that neither of these barrier islands lay "in the customary track of hurricanes" and that there was "no legitimate ground for believing that such another storm will visit there in another century."[50]

Why was the presence of fishermen—who had invariably been described as poor, simple, and, with most of them originating from different nations, as barely able to speak English—so important?[51] In its last two paragraphs, the *Picayune* article laid out why the people of Grand Isle and Cheniere Caminada needed to stay there despite the hurricane's effects, clearly speaking the language of New Orleans's leading class. The "famous fishing grounds" and "celebrated oyster beds" were "situated most advantageously with respect to New Orleans, which furnishes an unlimited market for the product of the fisheries. These interests must constantly grow, and it is plain that the Barataria waters must be in the future more extensively than ever resorted to for the supply of the fish and oyster consumption of a great city, and its facilities for distributing such products. This renders it necessary that people should live in that region, and they will do so." The article continued that even if some people were now afraid to live on the islands, this could have no influence on the public at large; that neither California nor Charleston had been abandoned just because those places had repeatedly experienced earthquakes throughout their history. Even though the phrasing of this last argument is affirmative, it reveals the authorities' by-now-familiar fear of depopulation and of the consequent decline of trade in the city proper. Conclusively, the article remarked that all there needed to be done at the islands was to rebuild more strongly so that houses could withstand a hurricane. It was positive that such resilient buildings could be created simply by leaving galleries and balconies out of future architectural plans.[52] Such optimism was unfounded, however. Four days later the *Picayune* published a report of a mass exodus at Cheniere Caminada that described the storm survivors as being in a "state bordering on demoralization" and as being "terrified" of staying any longer on the island. The New Orleans newspaper belittled these feelings as "superstitious dread" and lamented condescendingly that it was "in vain that the more valorous cajole and reason with them and point out that such a supernatural visitation might not be witnessed again for a century to come." Clearly, the "more valorous" business elite of New Orleans thought it knew better than the "unfortunate residents of the island" what was good for them. All the reasoning was to no avail, however. The remainder of Cheniere's population left the island and either moved to the city, to the lower section of Bayou Lafourche, or to other less-exposed areas. The report ended with the insight that Cheniere Caminada would never recover from the 1893 hurricane, which proved to be correct. The island was abandoned after the storm and never regained its reputation as a tourist destination.[53]

Ad Hoc or Not?

Returning to the CCSRC and our premise that disaster-related practices and organizations do not arise from a singular extreme event, the question arises how spontaneous and impromptu the organization of disaster relief in fact could have been in New Orleans after the hurricane. Clearly, acting in the name of charity was nothing new to the citizens.[54] Yet statements, such as that the CCSRC had "been organized for the very purpose of relieving the distress of the survivors of the storm," suggest that at least the CCSRC, if not the other associations, too, did form particularly with regard to relieve the storm sufferers of 1893.[55] The hypothesis that the CCSRC was an ad hoc committee is substantiated by its own final report. The latter quotes president Robert Bleakley's message to the CCSRC of 5 December, when the relief efforts came to an end: "We have arrived at a period in the history of this Relief Committee, when I think it best to wind it up." Bleakley suggested distributing any remaining funds among the widows and orphans of the storm sufferers who had come to the city. He concluded, "We have done the best we could with the funds placed at our disposal; we have not been able to do everything that we would have liked to have done for the sufferers, but we have relieved their temporary necessities, and placed many of them in a position where they could earn their own livelihood."[56] Clearly, Bleakley meant to dissolve the CCSRC. However, if it had formed spontaneously in 1893, could it be possible that a hurricane relief organization had formed in a similar way before? And did it become a permanent institution after the 1893 hurricane?

On 17 August 1831 a destructive hurricane affected New Orleans, as well as the plantations and bayou country inhabitants below the city. It became known as the Great Barbados Hurricane since it claimed some 1,500 lives on that island. This was also the storm that William Redfield reconstructed the track of in 1831 (see chapter 1).[57] In New Orleans, wind damage was sustained to houses and fences, and to the ships in port. The levee at Macarty's Plantation above the city was breached and New Orleans was inundated from the back up to Rampart Street. Of the "farms belonging to a long settled and industrious class of agriculturists" at Terre aux Boeufs (St. Bernard Parish), the newspaper report only had to say that the area was completely inundated and that the farmers and their families thus had "no other prospect . . . but that of being reduced, without the aid of their more wealthy neighbors, to poverty and ruin."[58] In an address to the city council, Mayor Denis Prieur did mention the "rather considerable part of our [New Orleans's] population that has suffered considerable losses and inconveniences from which it has not yet been relieved."[59] However, in none of Prieur's further addresses was there an indication of concerted relief efforts on behalf of the people below New Orleans or of spending funds from the city treasury.[60]

The next severe hurricane that caused New Orleans to flood from the back of the city was the Last Island Hurricane of 1856. Similar to the Cheniere Caminada Hurricane, this hurricane wrought its greatest destruction on the barrier islands west of the mouths of the Mississippi. Last Island (also called Isle Dernière) is the western-most island of the same archipelago to which Grand

Isle and Cheniere Caminada belong. In 1856 it was, like Grand Isle in 1893, a popular summer resort for planter and merchant families.[61] It was swept by a Category 4 hurricane on 10 August 1856.[62] While New Orleans again escaped lightly, the island's houses were blown or swept away entirely and about 140 of the resort guests died. Search parties were sent down to the coast in order to search for survivors, however, no relief effort comparable to that in 1893 was undertaken.[63] Rather, in a New Orleans *Daily Picayune* article of 17 August, the fear was expressed that survivors of the storm could still be found stranded on one of the smaller barrier islands or in places where they could not be readily found by those ships that had ventured out to search for them. The article suggested that a boat should be sent out for the purpose of collecting those dispersed survivors, and that "we are sure that the expenses would be cheerfully subscribed at once by citizens." The *Picayune* article continued:

> It should be the function of the Government officers to do this [the organization of rescue efforts], as it is done at the North, on similar occasions of inquiry, in sending out Government vessels to search for shipping and sailors supposed to be in danger. We believe there is no Government vessel on this station; but in looking round for the proper agency to take the lead in this matter, the [Tax] Collector or his chief officers—in his absence—appear to be the natural leaders in a measure, even if it be only to summon citizens together, to take counsel and make voluntary arrangements for these objects.[64]

The newspaper report suggests that in 1856, New Orleans—as opposed to cities in the antebellum North—had neither an organized governmental nor a civic (or voluntary) body in charge of disaster relief or rescue operations comparable to the one formed in 1893. This lack of concerted disaster relief activities was likely also a consequence of New Orleans's tripartite city government between 1836 and 1852, which did not allow for coordinated relief action as we see it emerge during the postbellum era. Clearly, in none of the previous cases did the papers mention associations such as the CCSRC or the French Market Protective Association. The United States ratified the Convention of Geneva (The International Red Cross Treaty) in 1881, so before that time no local Red Cross branch was available to provide help to the people either.[65]

In the light of New Orleans's underdeveloped general poor relief, the absence of specific *disaster* relief may not be surprising. In addition, Louisiana's French and Spanish past had left the state with the legacy of Roman law, and, in the absence of English Poor Laws, until 1880 without any regulation for the destitute. However, during the 1850s and the Civil War, the city council as well as military authorities started giving subsidies to the private (sectarian and racially segregated) charities in order to provide for the poor.[66] The social disaster of the Civil War spurred the creation of veterans' benevolent associations, which, after 1865, also could have provided aid in the aftermath of natural disasters.[67] After 1880, the number of private charities in New Orleans increased and, following the lead of the North, became more organized. The shift to systematization and streamlining of charities occurred through the rise of the charity organization movement, or what has been called scientific charity. [68] This change in the realm of charitable institutions in general together with relief practices that had emerged in the aftermath of other more-frequent natural and biological disasters such as floods and yellow fever epidemics seem to have paved the way for the disaster relief in the 1893 hurricane.

Interestingly, in her recent book on yellow fever in New Orleans, Urmi Engineer Willoughby counts forty benevolent organizations that formed relief committees during the epidemic of 1878, among them also the "Orleans Central Relief Committee."[69] Hence, the evidence presented so far points to the development of organized (hurricane) disaster relief in New Orleans between the Last Island Hurricane in 1856 and the Cheniere Caminada hurricane in 1893. And from the *Picayune*'s account, it seems that decisive lessons in the systematization of relief were learned in 1893.

With regard to the permanence of the CCSRC, it is interesting to see this organization appear under different but similar names during several disastrous events that affected New Orleans, such as the yellow fever epidemic of 1878, the Cheniere Caminada Hurricane of 1893, and again in 1915 when a Category 4 hurricane made landfall at Grand Isle on 29 September.[70] In this last case, New Orleans's mayor Martin Behrman proudly declined help offered by other states, and, together with the "New Orleans Relief Committee and public-spirited citizens of the city," had started relief and rescue activities on 2 October for the storm stricken areas on the coast below the city and along Lake Pontchartrain. In a further parallel to the events of 1893, Louisiana's governor Hall came to New Orleans. In 1915, however, the official arrived early, only three days after the hurricane, to confer directly with the inhabitants of the affected parishes (St. Bernard and Plaquemines) and to issue a state-wide appeal for donations.[71]

Clearly, the Citizens' Relief Committee had reassembled—albeit with a different cast of actors—in 1878 as well as in 1915. The omission of the word "storm" in its name may point to the fact of a broader use of the committee not only in hurricanes but also in other disasters or cases of hardship.[72] In 1893 the governor was expressly invited to the CCSRC's meeting and a member of the committee suggested that the governor issue an appeal to the public. In 1915, on the other hand, the governor's visit and the publishing of a state-wide call for help seem to have become a routine act. It remains unclear, however, whether the Citizens' Central Storm Relief Committee was and remained an ad hoc congregation that formed when the need for it arose.

The appearance of a Citizen's Relief Committee after the Great Galveston Hurricane of 1900 begs the conclusion that this form of organizing local relief for a variety of disasters had become quite common by the turn of the nineteenth century, at least in the Gulf South. In Galveston, the Relief Committee ultimately replaced the city government in the aftermath of the storm and became the permanent, new form of government after the state had granted the city a new charter. According to John Edward Weems's book on the Galveston Hurricane, in this way "the city commission form of government was born" that spread quickly throughout the United States.[73] So, with regard to hurricane adaptation, apparently, institutional change within or of city governments occurred in the aftermath of two hurricane events in Louisiana and Texas at the turn of the nineteenth century. At least in the case of Galveston those changes became a permanent and new form of government that was then adopted by other cities that had not experienced a disaster but found the leaner organization more suitable.[74] The cases of New Orleans's and Galveston's Storm Relief Committees and the following process of institutional change throughout the United States are thus examples of the change of political culture and institutional adaptation in the aftermath of (hurricane) disasters.

Spending "Public Money for Private Uses"

In 1893 a change in the provision of hurricane disaster relief was not only discernible on the local level in New Orleans, but was also discussed in Congress for the first time. Disaster relief for other Louisianan calamities, such as Mississippi floods, had been the subject of debate before, however.[75]

On 6 October 1893, two months before the CCSRC held its closing session in New Orleans, a joint resolution (H. Res. 69) was introduced to the House of Representatives by Louisiana's democrat House member Robert C. Davey.[76] It authorized the secretary of war to issue rations and medical supplies for the people affected by the 1893 Cheniere Caminada Hurricane. The resolution explained that "the State of Louisiana was visited by a terrific storm" and that "on the Gulf Coast and in the Parishes of Plaquemines and Jefferson there is great danger of starvation." Therefore, the Resolution resolved for the appropriation of $25,000 (equivalent to $688,000 in 2016) that was to be administered by the secretary of war to benefit the storm sufferers along the Louisiana Gulf Coast.[77] House Resolution 69 was referred to the Committee on Appropriations after its introduction to the House.

One month after the introduction of Davey's joint resolution for Louisiana, Clara Barton's neighborly connections were finally going to pay off, or so it seemed. On 2 November the U.S. Senate met for its morning session to discuss disaster relief for the South Carolina Sea Islands hurricane. The day before, in the afternoon session, a bill "to relieve the sufferers from the recent cyclone on and near the sea islands by the coast of South Carolina and Georgia" (S. 1149) had been introduced. Subsequently, Barton's neighbor, General Matthew C. Butler, who had advised her to set up the relief operation in Beaufort, had reinforced her appeal that the South Carolina hurricane required aid from the federal government.[78] In the morning session debate first ensued over the question whether the bill should even be reintroduced for discussion. This was followed by a motion for the bill to be referred to the Committee on Appropriations. Clearly, part of the Senate carefully sought to avoid debating the subject of disaster relief at a time when the country was gripped by the economic depression and unemployment was soaring.[79] Republican senator George Hoar (Massachusetts), who had introduced the bill, was in favor of the Senate deciding on the bill there and then, so pressing did he see the need for its enactment. The senator stated that the delay to another session of Congress or, worse, the referral to a Committee involved "starvation on a huge scale, a case like that of the famine in Ireland." He argued that the appeal by Barton and the Red Cross and Senator Butler's own first-hand account of the scene of desolation should be testimony enough for the Senate to act at once and appropriate public funds for the relief of the thirty thousand homeless and starving (mostly African American) Sea Islanders.[80]

Democrat Senator Arthur P. Gorman (Maryland), who had motioned for the referral to the Committee on Appropriations, expressed his sympathy with Hoar's intention; however, he remained firm in his opinion that the case should be considered by a body that would take into consideration the total amount of the appropriations by Congress, which was "becoming a matter of great concern to the people."[81] He was opposed by Democrat senator Wilkinson Call (Florida) who argued that the money requested by the bill was limited and that such expenses had been made before, in the case of the Ohio and Mississippi River floods. According to his opinion, it was the duty of the government to act in cases where private charity did not suffice. Diverging from the subject of the hurricane victims of South Carolina, Call brought to the Senate's mind the great numbers of unemployed who would have a difficult time getting through the winter of 1893.

Call's statement was followed by that of the republican William Stewart (Nevada) who cautioned of causing a costly precedent with the South Carolina bill. Like Call, he suggested the government had better spend its funds on the unemployed who had come into this dire situation "not on account of cyclones of nature but on account of cyclones of legislation, . . . by reason of an inadequate supply of money to keep enterprise in progress." Senator William Peffer (Kansas) of the Populist Party, on the other hand, opined that this was not a case of mere charity but that they would be spending "other men's money," since the U.S. Treasury consisted of the money of all U.S. citizens. Therefore, he argued, the Senate had no right to "appropriate public funds for private uses" (i.e., paying for the disaster relief of South Carolina or Louisiana). John R.

McPherson, democrat Senator for New Jersey, argued that two thousand people had died in South Carolina and another two thousand in Louisiana, "by reason of the same cyclone" and that the disaster had caused "greater mortality ... than has been caused by any battle in modern times"—both obvious misconceptions. McPherson argued for a direct consideration of the bill by the Senate, not least because he suspected that such cases would be brought before Congress again in the future.[82]

Finally, Democrat senator Donelson Caffery of Louisiana took the floor to speak in support of Senator Hoar and the South Carolina bill. Caffery stated that he was in favor of a consideration of the South Carolina relief bill without the time-consuming intervention of a committee. Obviously, his suggestion was not without self-interest. Introducing Louisiana's situation, he explained, "My own state has lately been visited by a hurricane of unprecedented severity. Two thousand and eight persons actually lost their lives by that calamity, and the survivors in the stricken district are absolutely bereft of the means of livelihood. Whilst my State has not made any demand upon the General Government for aid, it is appropriately and properly a case where governmental aid should be extended." By stating that Louisiana had so far not made any claims to the federal government, Caffery pointed to the self-sufficiency and independence of his Southern state. Yet, by implicitly referring to disaster relief precedents, the Democrat senator in fact requested federal support for the Louisiana storm sufferers. Unlike the unemployed, mentioned by Senators Call and Peffer, the people of Louisiana fit well into the disaster narrative, having experienced sudden loss through no fault of their own.

Caffery added that his colleague, Senator Edward D. White of Louisiana, would in time prepare an amendment to the South Carolina bill so it would also apply to the storm-stricken areas of Louisiana. Senator Hoar assured Caffery that, if the motion to refer the bill to the Committee of Appropriations were voted down, he would gladly accept the Louisiana senator's amendment to the South Carolina relief bill, particularly since Caffery had personal knowledge of the affected area along the Gulf Coast. Senator Caffery replied by providing more detail about the affected population, stating that it was made up of mostly poor fishermen and that the death toll went into the thousands. His statement continued with information that the New Orleans newspapers— glorifying the city's relief effort—obviously had sought to avoid publishing: "Although in that State there has been organized charity in behalf of these sufferers, yet there remains a great deal of distress. The Legislature is not in session, and, therefore, no appropriation can be made by that body. Though the acutest suffering has been assuaged by the gratuities and gifts of benevolent individuals through organized charities, yet a great deal remains to be done and a great deal of suffering appeals to the common humanity of the whole United States for relief."[83]

Evidently, the "gifts of benevolent individuals" could only relieve the immediate needs of the inhabitants of Cheniere Caminada, Grand Isle and the river parishes below New Orleans. However, sustaining the storm sufferers over the long-term and helping them rebuild their livelihoods went beyond the reach of charity.

Neither Representative Davey's Joint Resolution (H. Res. 69) to appropriate $25,000 for the relief of the Louisiana Gulf Coast, nor Senators Hoar and Caffery's bill for the Sea Islanders of South Carolina (S. 1149) with an amendment in favor of Louisiana were enacted into law. The Cleveland administration remained true to its motto that it was "not in the province of the government to support the people." Clara Barton wrote that "for some reason which we never knew, no response was given" to her appeal for governmental aid. With the advantage of insight into the Senate's debate of November 1893, it becomes clear that inhibitions regarding the legitimacy of using the federal treasury for "private uses" at a time when economic depression was weighing hard on the whole country was the likely cause that prevented both bills from going any farther. In 1893 the fear of creating a precedent in the face of widespread want won over the disaster narrative. That is, the coincidence of the two kinds of differently judged disasters—supposedly self-inflicted "mass idleness" as well as no-fault-of-their-own hurricane impacts—paralyzed the existing institution of federal disaster relief. With this legal and political constellation at hand, the unifying role natural disasters have played elsewhere (and as briefly mentioned in chapter 4) could not be achieved in 1893.

Thus, back in New Orleans, only two months after the hurricane impact and without the support of the federal government, Robert Bleakley closed the CCSRC down on 5 December 1893, remarking that they had done the best they could with the donated money at their disposal and that they had managed to put many of the storm sufferers "in a position where they could earn their own livelihood."[84] It remains an open question, however, how many people actually profited from the relief measures, and whose fate really turned to the worse after the Cheniere Caminada Hurricane of 1893.

Clearly, the national economy was an important factor for the overall relief performance of the CCSRC as well as for the possibility to claim federal disaster relief appropriations. The effects of the economic depression of 1893 made it difficult for other chambers of commerce to collect money for out-of-state disaster relief. Similarly, on the federal level the suffering of the unemployed was weighed argumentatively against the suffering of the hurricane victims, and ultimately a relief appropriation was denied for fear of creating the precedent that would open the gates to requests for unemployment relief. In other words, the national economic situation clearly influenced the capacity of New Orleans and its environs to recover from the Cheniere Caminada Hurricane. The state of the national economy as a central factor for the development of disaster relief institutions will recur in a different guise in the next chapter on Hurricane Betsy in 1965.

Notes

1. Michele Lenore Landis Dauber, "Helping Ourselves. Disaster Relief and the Origins of the American Welfare State" (PhD thesis, Northwestern University, Chicago, 2003); Michele Lenore Landis Dauber, *The Sympathetic State: Disaster Relief and the Origins of the American Welfare State* (Chicago: University of Chicago Press, 2013).
2. Dauber, *Sympathetic State*, 14; Dauber, "Helping Ourselves," 31–32, 35, 39–40. With convincing evidence from congressional appropriation debates throughout the nineteenth century, Dauber argues against the established historical opinion that the late nineteenth-century U.S. had an underdeveloped welfare state and was solely governed under the augury of a rugged individualism and the free play of market forces. See Dauber, *Sympathetic State*, 33.
3. Dauber, "Helping Ourselves," 29; Dauber, *Sympathetic State*, 24.
4. Dauber, *Sympathetic State*, 6–7.
5. Dauber, "Helping Ourselves," 58.
6. Dauber, *Sympathetic State*, 19–20.
7. Ibid., 174.
8. Keith Bea, "The Formative Years. 1950–1978," in *Emergency Management: The American Experience, 1900–2010*, ed. Claire B. Rubin (Boca Raton: CRC Press, 2012), 83.
9. Red Cross, A Bill Making Appropriation to Enable the American Association of the Red Cross to Extend its Organization, 1882; LoC, Clara Barton Papers, [5]. Foster Rhea Dulles, *The American Red Cross: A History* (New York: Harper & Brothers, 1950), 16. On the early history of the American Red Cross see also Julia F. Irwin, *Making the World Safe: The American Red Cross and a Nation's Humanitarian Awakening* (Oxford, UK: Oxford University Press, 2013), esp. 13–34.
10. Clara Barton, *The Red Cross: A History of This Remarkable International Movement in the Interest of Humanity* (Washington, DC: J. B. Lyon, 1898), 108.
11. For American Red Cross operations in different locations around the world see ibid. and Clara Barton, *The Red Cross in Peace and War* (Washington, DC: American Historical Press, 1910).
12. Charles Hoffmann, *The Depression of the Nineties: An Economic History* (Westport, CT: Greenwood, 1970), 53–55, 57, 67.
13. Samuel T. McSeveney, *The Politics of Depression: Political Behavior in the Northeast, 1893–1896* (New York: Oxford University Press, 1972), 34.
14. Dauber, *Sympathetic State*, 49; Dauber, "Helping Ourselves," 33.
15. Dauber, *Sympathetic State*, ("Difficulty in representing"), 51.
16. Barton, *Red Cross*, 197, 203.
17. Ibid., ("pitiful paragraphs"), 201, 203.
18. Keim and Muller, *Hurricanes*, 76.
19. The French word *chénier* was used as a field name along the Gulf Coast to describe groves of water oak. A man named Caminada was one of the first property owners on

the island; hence the name Cheniere Caminada for the island. Dale P. Rogers, *Cheniere Caminada Buried at Sea* (Thibodaux, LA: D.P. Rogers, 1981), 2, 6.

20. Rose C. Falls, *Cheniere Caminada, or, The Wind of Death: The Story of the Storm in Louisiana* (New Orleans: Hopkins' Printing Office, 1893), 8; Keim and Muller, *Hurricanes*, 76.

21. Falls, *Cheniere Caminada*, 10.

22. Keim and Muller set the number of inhabitants of Cheniere Caminada at 1,500 and the death toll at 800. Keim and Muller, *Hurricanes*, 76.

23. Falls, *Cheniere Caminada*, 11. According to Dale P. Rogers, Grand Isle began to be developed into a fashionable holiday resort at the beginning of the 1860s. Rogers, *Cheniere Caminada*, 4.

24. Keim and Muller, *Hurricanes*, 76.

25. "City Struck by a Storm," *Daily Picayune*, 2 October 1893, 58 (251), 1.

26. "The Full Story of the Storm," *Daily Picayune*, 6 October 1893, 57 (255), 1.

27. In 1868, an enterprise on Delachaise Street in New Orleans successfully began to manufacture ice, furnishing grocers (and fishermen) with the means to preserve perishables. Campanella, *Dilemma*, 37; Falls, *Cheniere Caminada*, 12.

28. "The Full Story of the Storm," 1.

29. "Over a Thousand Lives Lost," *Daily Picayune*, 5 October 1893, 57 (254), 1.

30. Final Report CCSRC, AANO, Folder "Hurricanes," 3; "Relief Readily Volunteered by All," *Daily Picayune*, 5 October 1893, 57 (254), 6.

31. "Relief Readily Volunteered by All"; Falls, *Cheniere Caminada*, 63.

32. "Systematizing the Relief Work," *Daily Picayune*, 10 October 1893, 57 (259), 3.

33. "Aid from Abroad," *Daily Picayune*, 8 October 1893, 57 (257), 4.

34. Final Report CCSRC, AANO, Folder "Hurricanes," 10.; For the monetary value conversion see Lawrence H. Officer and Samuel H. Williamson, "Measuring Worth," retrieved 14 February 2018 from http://www.measuringworth.com/index.html. I used the real price index for this and all following conversions. As of February 2018 the converter was able to provide values only as far back as 2016.

35. "Systematizing the Relief Work"; Final Report CCSRC, AANO, Folder "Hurricanes," 9 ("prominent people").

36. "The Relief Work in Good Shape," *Daily Picayune*, 24 October 1893, 57 (273), 6. See list of committee members in Final Report CCSRC, AANO, Folder "Hurricanes," 1–2. This list also shows that the citizens on the committee were all leading businessmen of the city, including the president of the chamber of commerce, and the presidents of the stock exchange, the cotton exchange, and the maritime exchange, to mention just a few.

37. Final Report CCSRC, AANO, Folder "Hurricanes," 2–3.

38. "French Market Society Votes," *Daily Picayune*, 11 October 1893, 57 (260), 2.

39. Final Report CCSRC, AANO, Folder "Hurricanes," 12–13 ("the donations"); "Relief Work in Good Shape," *Daily Picayune*, 11 October 1893, 57 (261), 1.

40. "Red Cross Society's Southern Relief," *Daily Picayune*, 19 October 1893, 57 (268), 8.

41. "Relief Work Still in Progress," *Daily Picayune*, 22 October 1893, 57 (271), 10.

42. Final Report CCSRC, AANO, Folder "Hurricanes," 15; "Gov. Foster Proud of the People," *Daily Picayune*, 15 October 1893, 57 (264), 2 ("as chief executive").

43. Congressional Record, Senate, 53rd Cong., 1st. sess. 2 November 1893, 3078.

44. "An Appeal to the Public," *Daily Picayune*, 18 October 1893, vol. 57 (264), 4.

45. "The Relief Work in Good Shape."

46. "The Governor's Appeal for Relief," *Daily Picayune*, 18 October 1893, 57 (264), 4.

47. "The Relief Work in Good Shape.".

48. "A Region Not to Be Abandoned," *Daily Picayune*, 14 October 1893, 57 (263), 4.

49. This is clearly wrong. New Orleans was affected by hurricanes in 1812, 1831, 1837, 1856, 1860, and 1888. While the storm center may not have crossed the islands in those cases, at least in the first three hurricanes, people were reported drowned in the settlements below New Orleans. "A Region Not to Be Abandoned."

50. "A Region Not to Be Abandoned."

51. "They are a simple and credulous people, without artifice and can be easily imposed upon. . . . They all speak French and have a kind of patois of Spanish and other languages. Few of them understand 'American.'" "Best Plans of Relief," *Daily Picayune*, 11 October 1893, 57 (260), 2.

52. "A Region Not to Be Abandoned."

53. "Grand Isle and Cheniere," *Daily Picayune*, 18 October 1893, 57 (267), 12.

54. At the first meeting of the Citizens' Storm Relief Committee on 5 October, chairman Robert Bleakley stated that "as in all previous calls in the name of charity" he expected the people of New Orleans to "respond appropriately." Final Report CCSRC, AANO, Folder "Hurricanes," 5.

55. "Relief in Good Shape," *Daily Picayune*, 12 October 1893, Vol. LVII, No. 261, 1.

56. Final Report CCSRC, AANO, Folder "Hurricanes," 16 ("We have arrived," "We have done").

57. Ludlum, *Hurricanes*, 136–37.

58. "New Orleans, Aug. 22," *Salem Gazette*, 13 September 1831, 9 (73), 2 ("farms belonging to," "no other prospect")

59. Prieur to Conseil, 24 August 1831, NOPL, New Orleans Conseil de Ville. Messages from the Mayor, AB 505, 1805–1836, vol. 14: 9 January 1830–31 December 1831, fol. 187.

60. Prieur to Conseil, 31 August 1831, NOPL, New Orleans Conseil de Ville. Messages from the Mayor, AB 505, 1805–1836, vol. 14: 9 January 1830–31 December 1831, fol. 190; Prieur to Conseil, September 7, 1831, NOPL, New Orleans Conseil de Ville. Messages from the Mayor, AB 505, 1805–1836, vol. 14: 9 January 1830–31 December 1831, fol. 194.

61. "Last Island Inundated," *Daily Picayune*, 14 August 1856, 1; Ludlum, *Hurricanes*, 168–69.

62. Keim and Muller, *Hurricanes*, 70.

63. "The City," *Daily Picayune*, 12 August 1856, 1; Ludlum, *Hurricanes*, 169.

64. "Relief for the Wrecked," *Daily Picayune*, 17 August 1856, 2.

65. Barton, *Red Cross*, 57, 59.

66. On the social clubs and mutual aid societies founded by free blacks in New Orleans see John W. Blassingame, *Black New Orleans, 1860–1880* (Chicago: University of Chicago, 1973), 13, 147–48.

67. White Confederate veterans formed benevolent associations in New Orleans such as the Hays's Brigade Benevolent Association, offering help to sick and wounded veterans. Hogue, *Uncivil War*, 34.

68. Elna Green, "National Trends, Regional Differences, Local Circumstances. Social Welfare in New Orleans, 1870s–1920s," in *Before the New Deal: Social Welfare in the South, 1830–1930*, ed. Elna Green (Athens: University of Georgia Press, 1999), 82–85. The term "scientific charity" is also known as "scientific philanthropy." See Judith Sealander, "Curing the Evils at their Source: The Arrival of Scientific Giving," in *Charity, Philanthropy, and Civility in American History*, ed. Lawrence J. Friedman and Mark D. McGarvie (Cambridge, UK: Cambridge University Press, 2003), 219–22.

69. Willoughby, *Yellow Fever*, 123–25.

70. The first time after the Cheniere Caminada Hurricane was in 1909. Keim and Muller, *Hurricanes*, 70.

71. "Relief Measures," *Times Picayune*, 3 October 1915, vol. 79 (249), 1A ("New Orleans Relief").

72. In the Great Mississippi Flood of 1927 a Citizens' Flood Relief Committee had formed according to Ari Kelman's account. Kelman, *River*, 171–79.

73. John Edward Weems, *A Weekend in September* (College Station: Texas A&M University Press, 1957), 161–62; Erik Larson, *Isaac's Storm: Isaacs Sturm*, Swiss Re Special ed. (Zurich: Swiss Re, 1999), 200.

74. After the storm Galveston's city commission had five members instead of the thirteen of the old City Council. C.f. Weems, *September*, 162.

75. The Congressional Globe, the repository of congressional debates before the Congressional Record shows no listing of the 1831 hurricane and the Last Island Hurricane (1856) in the Register of Debates. However, on several occasions in congressional debates, members presented lists of disaster relief precedents, among which usually figured a number of Mississippi floods. Dauber, *Sympathetic State*, 46, 60.

76. Congressional Record, House, 53rd Cong., 1st sess., October 6, 1893, 2258. For short biographies of U.S. Senate and House members (including their party affiliation and state) see "Biographical Directory of the United States Congress, 1774 to Present," http://bioguide.congress.gov/biosearch/biosearch.asp.

77. H. Res. 69, NARA, RG 233, Records of the U.S. House of Representatives, 53rd Cong., 1st sess., 6 October 1893, [1].

78. Congressional Record, Senate, 53rd Cong., 1st sess., 2 November 1893, 3075–76.

79. Unemployment estimates for the months of September and October 1893 were as high as 2 to 3 million. See Hoffmann, *Depression*, 67–68, 97, 106–7.

80. Congressional Record, Senate, 53rd Cong., 1st sess., 2 November 1893, 3076.

81. Ibid.

82. Ibid., 3076–77 ("not on account"); ibid., 3077–8 ("other men's money," "appropriate public funds"); ibid., 3078 ("by reason of," "greater mortality").

83. Ibid. ("Although in that").

84. Final Report CCSRC, AANO, Folder "Hurricanes," 16.

CHAPTER 6

To Mandate or Not to Mandate . . .

Between 1890 and 1960 the population of New Orleans increased almost threefold from 242,039 to its all-time peak of 627,525.[1] This population growth and the following urban expansion were not least a consequence of the municipal drainage system that started being built in 1893 and that enabled the development of previous swamplands into habitable quarters of the city. Between 1910 and 1950 the New Orleans lakefront grew in popularity for the affluent white population. The latter, at the same time, kept black New Orleanians from this new land with segregationist deed covenants. The hazard of storm surge coming through Lake Pontchartrain that might overflow this low-lying area was seemingly eradicated by building earthen embankments along the lake shore between 1926 and 1934. This neutralization of New Orleans's risk topography together with Jim Crow laws set in motion a process of disaggregation of the city's erstwhile racially mixed social geography. This process increased between 1960 and 1980 due to the flight of parts of the white population to the suburbs.[2]

By 1960 New Orleans had become "one of the most impoverished, most unequal, most violent, and least educated places in the United States." That is, three out of four black New Orleanians lived near the poverty line, while half of them lived below it. In addition, the national homicide rate of the city was twice that of the national average, and the physical infrastructure of the city was underdeveloped and dilapidated.[3]

Since Hurricane Katrina, the Lower Ninth Ward has become a symbol for the connection between black poverty and environmental injustice. However, it had been flooded forty years earlier by Hurricane Betsy in 1965. President Lyndon B. Johnson, less hesitant than George W. Bush in 2005, visited New Orleans and the Lower Ninth Ward the day after Betsy had struck the city to form his own impression of the situation on the ground. Soon afterward, Johnson started receiving letters from Lower Ninth Ward residents who were struggling with the federal disaster relief system to get back on their feet, as the following sections will show. The Lower Ninth Ward was originally a mixed neighborhood with descendants of Irish, German, Sicilian, French, or Latino immigrants living close to the Mississippi's water front, while those living at the back-of-town, toward the back-swamps, were usually poor or working-class

African Americans. During the early 1960s, when Lyndon B. Johnson's Great Society legislation abolished school segregation, the white population of the Lower Ninth Ward followed the familiar pattern and moved downriver into suburban St. Bernard Parish. While its geographical location at the downriver bottom of the city had historically predestined the Lower Ninth Ward to be the site of trades and activities that were polluting and/or noisy, engineering interests almost rendered the Lower Ninth Ward a peninsula—and therefore more flood-prone—between 1918 and 1960. In 1918 the Industrial Canal was excavated, splitting the former Ninth Ward in two, hence the *Lower* Ninth Ward. Discharging into the Industrial Canal, the Intracoastal Waterway was built along the back of the Lower Ninth Ward in 1940, in order to enable east-to-west barge traffic. Finally, in the early 1960s, just before Hurricane Betsy hit New Orleans and storm waters were funneled through it into the Lower Ninth Ward, the Mississippi River–Gulf Outlet Canal was excavated to connect the other two waterways with the Gulf of Mexico.[4] All three projects were built with economic concerns in mind and had apparently not (sufficiently) considered the risk of flooding through storm-driven waters.

On the local New Orleans level as well as on the national level, the early to mid-1960s were a time of great change regarding legislation aimed at decreasing aspects of social vulnerability such as poverty, racial inequality, and public health. One of the strongest engines of social and political change in the late 1950s and early 1960s United States was television. While only 7 percent of Americans owned a television set in 1950, this number had grown to 87.3 percent in 1960. In an unprecedented way, the medium made formerly local problems like poverty or the civil rights movement issues of national concern. Television was a powerful force in shaping a national identity that started replacing regional identities in the early 1960s.[5] Apart from bringing Americans together over social and political issues, television also made local or regional natural disasters national events.[6] As mentioned in chapter 3, the dissemination of Hurricane warnings—improved by radar imagery together with the advent of cars as a means of mass-transport—enabled the first large-scale evacuation of parts of the Gulf Coast (Texas and Louisiana) in 1961, when Hurricane Carla hit Matagorda Island, Texas.[7]

Television also played a significant role in bringing to power the President who brought about the liberal hour in the politics of the United States in the mid-1960s, right around the time when Hurricane Betsy made landfall in New Orleans.[8] Lyndon B. Johnson succeeded John F. Kennedy after the latter's assassination in 1963 and vowed to continue pursuing Kennedy's course on civil rights. Johnson remained true to his word and in June 1964 signed into law the Civil Rights Act, which strengthened black voting rights, outlawed discrimination in public facilities and in the workplace, and banned school segregation. At the same time, Johnson began developing his vision of the Great Society and his War on Poverty. Both programs were aimed at no less than "elevat[ing] national life" and at "advanc[ing] the quality of American civilization."[9] In particular, between 1964 and 1965 Johnson signed legislation such as the federal health insurance programs Medicare and Medicaid and the Voting Rights Act, which changed the face of American politics.[10] Under Johnson the federal government extended its authority over such a range of tasks as it had never before attempted. In 1964 Ronald Reagan criticized the Johnson administration by warning of the "full power of centralized government." Only four years later the preliminary end of the liberal hour and centralized government came with the election of Richard Nixon in 1968; Nixon's presidential campaign accused Johnson's Great Society of overextending its powers, enlarging bureaucracy, and spending too much tax money. Despite the short period of liberalist policymaking, historians Mackenzie and Weisbrot conclude their analysis of the 1960s by calling those years the "durable decade" for the changes in social relationships, values, and—most centrally—in the law that were brought about during this period.[11]

This is, in brief, the context of federal politics within which the debate about disaster relief and disaster and flood insurance unfolded in the aftermath of Hurricane Betsy, between 1965 and 1968. On the city level in New Orleans, the effects of the War on Poverty and Great Society programs were not yet felt at the time of Hurricane Betsy since most of them only really blossomed in the later 1960s. White politicians' concern with poverty in New Orleans was specifically directed at the African American community, since poverty was largely associated with African Americans who were perceived as an obstacle in the South's way to economic development.

While those vulnerability-reducing programs targeting public health and poverty eradication had been implemented and were slowly starting to unfold their effects, private or federal programs of hazard insurance had not yet materialized. However, insurance against natural hazards is an important aspect of adaptation to natural hazards in that it moderates harm to property and (ideally) reduces hardship in the aftermath of disasters.[12] By making them calculable, insurance transforms natural hazards into risks, and those risks are then socialized by insurance.[13] That is, the "natural" becomes "social" through the application of the law of large numbers. That law spreads the risk of an individual's property loss caused by a natural hazard over as many insured units or policy holders as possible so as not to incur catastrophic loss.[14] What is more, insurers can spread this risk even farther by *re*insuring part of the risks they are taking on from policy holders. Similar to hurricane knowledge and science, insurance has passed through a process of historical evolution that has not been uniform across different countries. Legal, political, and economic traditions significantly contributed to the shape national insurance industries acquired throughout the nineteenth and twentieth centuries, in particular.

As we will see, these seemingly purely economic details about the development of different insurance markets—that is, a country's regulatory bodies, whether its businesses are in their majority mutual or joint stock companies, whether they are private or state enterprises, the openness of markets for (foreign) reinsurance companies as well as the fact that charitable institutions exist alongside with the insurance industry as in the United States—are important aspects for the role insurance is able to play in alleviating hardship and vulnerability in the aftermath of disasters and thus for adaptation to natural hazards. These factors together form specific business environments that determine the insurance companies' own business risk, which, in turn, determines the risks these companies are ready to underwrite for individuals. Legal traditions and rather elusive cultural concepts such as the secure society[15] in the German-speaking countries of Europe, or freedom and independence in the United States, influence, for example, whether mandatory (compulsory) insurance seems feasible—or necessary, for that matter. All of these systemic and usually rather invisible factors are at the background of this chapter.

"Billion Dollar Betsy" Makes Landfall in New Orleans

On 26 August 1965 a tropical depression formed in an area of disturbed weather in the North Atlantic, some five hundred miles north of Suriname and French Guyana. The National Hurricane Center called it Betsy a few days after it had developed into a tropical storm.[16] This meteorological anthropomorphism was still a fairly recent development in an evolving hurricane culture. The practice of giving female names to tropical cyclones in alphabetical order was introduced in 1953 under Grady Norton, then the director of the Miami Hurricane Warning Office, the forerunner of the National Hurricane Center.[17] Television, radio, and the new satellite technology enabled New Orleanians to follow the progress of Betsy across the Bahamas when it was still only a tropical storm.

On Wednesday 8 September 1965, Betsy—now a hurricane—had entered the Gulf of Mexico after "an amazing turnabout" and continued to steer toward the coast on a west-northwest course. This made New Orleanians "feel a little uneasy" and they "listened intently to the hurricane bulletins and followed its course with increasing anxiety." On Thursday morning 9 September the wind had risen, the sky was overcast, and white foam crested the waves on the Mississippi River, a phenomenon deemed rare by a New Orleans eyewitness.[18]

Still, citizens hoped that the storm would pass them by as late as Thursday afternoon. At 6:00 P.M. this hope was shattered when the news was broadcast that the hurricane's center was heading directly toward the city: "TV and radio stations devoted much of their time to hurricane advisories and bulletins, advice relative to precautionary measures to be taken and the names and locations of areas in and around the city which should be evacuated."[19] However, in New Orleans evacuation at the time of Hurricane Betsy did not mean large-scale temporary migration to other places by car, as we would think of today, but more commonly what Richard Campanella has called "micro-scale, intra-urban movement to sturdier structures."[20] While some citizens were feeling increasingly apprehensive at Betsy's approach, others apparently felt no fear and "stopped for cocktails at one of our favorite spots in the *Vieux Carré*, the Absinthe House. Our banter was filled with witticism as we sipped a Martini and watched a telecast of Betsy's approach. What wonderful weather to be caught under a bar!"[21] Earlier in the day, New Orleans Mayor Schiro had broadcast a speech on TV and radio, informing people about "this very dangerous hurricane" and what was being done to assure New Orleans the best possible protection under the circumstances.[22]

By 10:00 P.M. on Thursday 9 September the winds had increased greatly, and shortly afterward electricity was interrupted and telephone lines went dead. The hurricane had made landfall at Grand Isle, just as had happened in 1893, with wind speeds between 100 and 160 miles per hour (160 to 257 kilometers per hour). The tidal wave caused by the storm was at sixteen feet (4.9 meters) above sea level when the hurricane came ashore and had decreased to eleven feet (3.3 meters) when it arrived in New Orleans, overtopping levees and protective works.[23] The storm surge inundated the lower part of the Mississippi Delta, except the natural levees of the Mississippi River and Bayou Lafourche, as well as the western half of the city of New Orleans in the small morning hours of Friday 10 September. As in previous hurricanes, the parishes of St. Bernard, Jefferson, and Plaquemines were swept by saltwater and experienced high levels of property destruction. A combination of levee breaches of the Industrial Canal and overtopping of levees by the storm tide led to the inundation of the seventh, eighth, and ninth wards, and to a partial flooding of Gentilly.[24] Unlike the parishes below New Orleans, where the water of the storm surge is able to flow back into the sea, the bowl-shaped topography of the city prevents the tidal water from retreating. That is, houses, cars, infrastructure, and industry is submerged at varying depths in standing saltwater, until the latter is pumped out of the bowl eventually. In 1965 it took the authorities two weeks to drain the floodwaters from the inundated parts of New Orleans.[25] The hardest hit area of the city was the poor, largely African American Lower Ninth Ward. Only the streets closest to the Mississippi River, a lower-income white area in 1965, remained dry.[26]

The president of the United States, Lyndon B. Johnson, was convinced by Louisiana senator Russell Long to visit devastated New Orleans immediately, with the argument that this action would win him back the state of Louisiana in the next elections.[27] The phone conversation between Long and Johnson took place at 2:26 P.M. on 10 September, when New Orleanians were just beginning to assess the damage to their city. Five hours later, the president was on his way to New Orleans, which he toured on foot and by boat to form an impression of the magnitude of the disaster.[28] As the night fell over New Orleans, the president visited George Washington Elementary School in the Lower Ninth Ward, where three thousand storm sufferers had found shelter. Almost reminiscent of saints' legends, one federal disaster report had the president walking among the flood victims unrecognized in the dark, listening to their woes and sorrows.[29]

Apparently, not only the vision of winning back Louisiana in the next election but also the experience on the ground made a deep impression on Johnson. Upon his departure, he stated that all the red tape that might prevent the local, state, and federal levels from working smoothly to bring relief to the stricken people of New Orleans and the Louisiana Gulf Coast needed to be cut. He repeated this conviction in a telephone call with Robert Phillips, head of the disaster program of the Office of Emergency Planning (OEP),[30] on 14 September 1965, expressing his hope that "all the government people can put their shoulder to the wheel without regard to hours, without regard to red tape." Louisiana Senator Long, who joined the phone call, took the president's request one step further, asking Phillips not to "violate the law, but insofar as you can find a way, to make the law bend to the problem" and thus free the way for all levels of government to help hurricane Betsy victims back on their feet.[31]

Significantly, federal (natural) disaster management had developed parallel to Civil Defense since the Kennedy administration in 1961. The Cuban Missile Crisis in 1962 only served to reinforce the ties between "natural" and "human-made" disaster management. As a result, federal and regional response to Hurricane Betsy was significantly swifter than after Hurricane Katrina in 2005.[32] While the federal emergency management machinery was churning into action on 10 September, New Orleanians took stock of their devastated urban environment. Bennett M. Augustin, a resident of a non-flooded area of the city wrote that in Carolyn Park, a residential subdivision of St. Bernard Parish, people emerged into the streets after the storm in the early morning hours of 10 September. They were in a state of elation at apparently having survived the hurricane rather unscathed, when suddenly a wall of water—the storm surge that had swept Grand Isle and the places below New Orleans—rushed in from the marshlands behind Carolyn Park. People living nearest the swamps barely had time to climb into boats or onto their attics and roofs the water rose with such rapidity in the streets. "Within a few minutes all their household possessions had been ruined and lost, their houses gutted by the floodwater and some had barely escaped death by drowning."[33] Presaging Hurricane Katrina, albeit on a much smaller scale, the destruction the stagnant, salty floodwater wrought on houses and furniture after it had settled in the city often required the total rebuilding of homes and the replacement of furniture.

Hurricane Betsy ended up claiming the lives of 81 people, most of them in New Orleans, St. Bernard, and Plaquemines; 17,600 people were injured, 175,000 families lost property because of Betsy, and more than 120,000 people temporarily crowded into emergency shelters. Approximately 4,760 square miles (some 12,328.3 square kilometers) of land in Louisiana were covered by the salty floodwater, resulting in $275 million damage, while hurricane winds claimed "only" $77 million of the $352 million total damage (approximately $2.7 billion in 2016).[34] Including insured losses ($897 million in 1965) the total amounted to more than $1 billion ($6.7 billion in 2016 values), which made "Billion Dollar Betsy" the costliest disaster in U.S. history at the time.[35]

Dear Mr. President

On 10 September, the day of the president's visit to New Orleans, Louisiana's governor McKeithen transmitted a telephone message to Johnson, requesting that his state be declared a disaster area.[36] McKeithen reported thirty-five parishes in his state "extensive[ly] damage[d]" by Betsy and at the time estimated that losses of property and agriculture were in excess of $100 million. The governor asked President Johnson for an initial emergency allocation of $2 million, an amount that was to multiply over the following months of recovering and rebuilding.[37] The practice of issuing a disaster declaration followed the protocol of the Federal Disaster Assistance Act of 1950 (PL 81–875), which was enacted after devastating floods in Missouri. It constituted the United States' first comprehensive disaster relief law.[38] After PL 81–875 was passed, the decision to grant disaster relief was in the hands of the president who could act without the consent of Congress. From the point of view of disaster victims, the declaration of an area as a disaster area had the beneficial effects that, first, the president could subsequently allocate relief funds to that area, and second, that the Small Business Administration (SBA) was able to issue low-interest disaster loans to businesses and property owners in order for them to get back on their feet.[39] Regarding adaptation and vulnerability, the existing disaster legislation contained some serious drawbacks, however.

As mentioned above, the most costly and extensive damage in Hurricane Betsy resulted from the floodwater that had submerged part of New Orleans and the towns downriver, and only a minor portion from wind. In 1965 only a small handful of private insurers underwrote flood insurance in the United States since the insurance industry's general understanding was that a comprehensive program was not feasible because repetitive and large-scale loss from hazard-prone properties was certain, and companies underwriting flood insurance were thus ultimately doomed to bankruptcy.[40] While the Homeowners Insurance program covered windstorm, fire, and hail damage, property owners were not able to buy insurance against flood damage.[41] In other words, in the 1960s U.S. citizens could not take the precautionary measure of buying flood insurance to compensate for their losses, the only disaster aid available to them was after the fact, through SBA disaster loans. This disaster relief program clearly favored people who could afford to buy their own house or who owned a business and who could prove to the administration that they had stable jobs that would enable them to repay the loan.[42] People who did not own property or who owned property but had no permanent employment, on the other hand, were rendered even more socially vulnerable by the impact of the hurricane. That is, especially elderly people, single mothers, and other people with low incomes often did not qualify for a loan and thus had only charity—the Red Cross—or public welfare programs to fall back on. However, dependence on social welfare bore a social stigma that was a source of embarrassment and emotional stress for many, in particular if people found themselves forced into it by no apparent fault of their own.[43]

It is not that flood insurance had not been a subject of discussion before Hurricane Betsy. Flood insurance was granted by private insurance companies as early as 1890. Yet, after experiencing devastating losses in the Great Mississippi Flood of 1927, most of them withdrew from covering flood damage for the next forty years.[44] Next, the Federal Flood Insurance Act (PL 84-1016)— the United States' first legislation on flood insurance—was passed in 1956 as a reaction to mounting flood losses throughout the country.[45] The program involved the federal state initially as both insurer and reinsurer (i.e., insurer of insurers), in order to encourage private underwriting companies to enter this risky market. However, besides highlighting the problem of adverse selection, the U.S. insurance industry particularly disliked the entry of the federal state into the insurance market, which it deemed the domain of the private economy.[46] Ultimately, the insurance industry's skepticism and Congress finding the allocation of finances for the program impracticable prevented the legislation from being enacted.[47] It is important to note, that the U.S. private insurance industry had only considered the form of so called single peril flood insurance, according to the industry's tradition of insuring single lines of risk only and not providing coverage for multiple risks in one package.[48] The debate on insurance triggered by the Alaska earthquake in 1964 and by Hurricane Betsy in 1965 showed, however, that alternative forms of disaster insurance were conceivable. Conspicuously, they were not introduced into the discussion by proponents of the private insurance industry.

Soon after the storm had swept over New Orleans, President Johnson started receiving letters from Hurricane Betsy victims. The overwhelming majority of these victims wrote about having problems receiving an SBA disaster loan, about inadequate help by the Red Cross, or for direct help from the president because they were desperate to recover their livelihoods. Whether letter writers were African American can only be known with certainty in those cases where the authors stated this fact explicitly, which was the minority. Despite the fact that the Lower Ninth Ward is a historically African American–owned and –inhabited part of the city, it would be scientifically unsound to infer that those who did not self-identify as being black were African American, merely based on their address. I will therefore refrain from assigning authors to racial groups.

Corelia Thomas, for example, a single mother of four "lost everything I had clothes and all which was equal to about 29 hundred dollars [. . .]" (equivalent to $22,100 in 2016). She applied for an SBA loan of $2,500 (equivalent to $19,000 in 2016) since she felt she could buy less-expensive clothes and furniture than before, but was refused because she rented the house she lived in. However, her landlord had repaired her house, "but I have nothing to go in it yet. It is getting cold and me and my children are not together, we are not in the same places, the cost is very high. Would you please help me get a loan."[49] Corelia Thomas's letter was forwarded to Robert Phillips, director of the Government Readiness Office, who was entrusted with answering such requests. Phillips forwarded her letter to the Red Cross headquarters for the Betsy relief at the New Orleans Army Base. The Red Cross reported back on 17 November 1965 that the Thomas family had received food, clothing, and financial support of $900 (about $6,840 in 2016) for household supplies.[50]

Marion Hill, a Lower Ninth Ward resident and single mother of six children, wrote to the president that she lost all clothes in Hurricane Betsy and that five of her children needed new clothes to go to school. She got $92 from the Red Cross to buy clothes, which, in her opinion, was not enough to provide warm winter garments for her kids. At the end of her letter she stated with pride that despite the fact that she did not have a husband, she was "not on the welfare. I support myself and my children on my salary. I was doing very good for myself and family before the flood." From the Red Cross report attached to the letter we learn that Marion Hill and her children lived with two other related families at North Roman Street in the Lower Ninth Ward. Together they amounted to a seventeen-member family unit who ultimately received $1,668 (equivalent to $12,700 in 2016) for food, clothing, household appliances, and repairs on their home. The report states that the family unit was "pleased with [the] Red Cross."[51] Unfortunately, we do not know whether the donation sufficed to bring the Hills back on their feet.

Apart from those letters dealing with failed SBA applications and Red Cross donations, a small number of writers asked the president to initiate a flood or disaster insurance program. For example, on 22 October 1965, one and a half months after Hurricane Betsy, the Gentilly Terrace and Gardens Improvement Association sent the president two resolutions: one requesting the president and Congress to improve structural flood protection measures, and the other to provide "insurance for those perils for which the insurance industry cannot provide protection to policyholders." According to the association, those measures "could have been of substantial help in reducing the loss of life and property caused by Hurricane Betsy."[52] W. J. Finnin, a resident from Metairie, Jefferson Parish (part of metropolitan New Orleans) struck a more personal note on 21 September:

> We here in the New Orleans area are beaten, just as surely as a nation is beaten at war. It was kind and compassionate of you to visit us after Hurricane Betsy's devastating trail left us bankrupt of what it took many people a whole life time to accumulate in the way of down payments on houses, furniture, etc. All of this is hopelessly gone, with no recourse to insurance companies because flood insurance is not a fact. . . . Would it not be better for the people to pay monthly premiums for flood damage insurance backed by the government if necessary, than to have them prostrate at one time or another, such as many are now begging for loans to repair their homes and replace furniture, and feed and clothe their children? . . . We, particularly in the coastal areas, desperately need tidal insurance, so that we may feel secure when disaster strikes in the form of a hurricane. In Metairie, a suburb of New Orleans where I now live, there were ten feet of water in the 1947 hurricane, and we were plagued by that memory two weeks ago when we knew Betsy was coming and we had no flood insurance.[53]

Finnin's letter shows that at least part of the population wanted to be able to contribute to their own safety and ability to recover by buying flood insurance, rather than relying purely on the bailout by federal disaster loans. His description of people "begging for loans"—in Finnin's account the alternative to flood insurance—mirrors the subject of many desperate letters to the president. Interestingly, at the end of his letter, Finnin invoked disaster memory in order to strengthen his argument for flood insurance. On the level of personal and emotional appeal the reference to a previous disaster experience makes perfect sense. Yet, for the private insurance industry, this precedent in almost the same area was precisely the argument *against* underwriting flood insurance, because, in their eyes, it was proof that catastrophic loss was certain.

Federal Disaster Relief, Moral Hazard, and the U.S. Insurance Market

Clearly, considerations of a flood insurance program were warranted at this point in time. However, working out a viable program that could bring all parties to the table would require time and would not help the acute need of New

Orleanians in the aftermath of Hurricane Betsy. Some immediate financial support exceeding that of previous disaster legislation was needed. Thus, on the basis of public hearings held in New Orleans and Baton Rouge on 25 September 1965, Congress began to draft the Southeast Hurricane Disaster Relief Bill (H.R. 11539), also known as the Betsy Bill. Its most important short-term feature was a modification of the Small Business Act (PL 85–536) for the three states affected by Hurricane Betsy. As a longer-term measure for dealing with large-scale disasters, the bill authorized a feasibility study of different modes of disaster insurance and a review of the Federal Flood Insurance Act of 1956 (PL 84-1016).[54] The Louisiana delegation to Congress urged their Washington-based colleagues to sign the bill into law as quickly as possible, since the congressional session was nearing its end and people on the ground in Louisiana were in need of all the assistance they could get. Congressional support for the bill was apparently widespread since, two months after Hurricane Betsy had flooded the Mississippi Delta, on 8 November 1965, the bill became Public Law 89-339.[55] For those Louisianans who had been deemed eligible for an SBA disaster loan, this meant two things. After 8 November they could—if their loan exceeded $500—cancel a maximum of $1,800 of the loan exceeding the $500. Alternatively, interest on their loan could be waived up to an amount of $1,800 over a period of three years. Despite the fact that, at the time, the federal government was not authorized to give outright grants to disaster victims, this legislation allowed for making them—up to the amount of $1,800 per borrower—through the back door of the SBA disaster loans. Yet, people who had loans below $500 did not benefit from the Betsy Bill, and neither did people who had not been deemed eligible for a loan by the SBA that had set up a field office on St. Charles Avenue in New Orleans.[56] People with small or no disaster loans continued to be referred to the Red Cross for assistance.[57]

Evidently, the Betsy Bill was another step toward the deeper involvement of the federal state in granting disaster relief after the fact in all those cases of risk the private insurance industry deemed uninsurable, namely floods, earthquakes, and landslides. During the 1950s the perception was reinforced that floods (by overflow or storm-driven waters) were by far the most frequent and costliest natural disaster in the United States. The consequent extended involvement of the federal state to help affected businesses and private individuals weighed heavily on the national treasury.[58] What is more, due to the United States' tradition of legislating by precedent, it was to be expected that future disasters would bring even more engagement of the federal state in disaster relief efforts. In fact, this had been the trajectory of disaster relief in the United States since the Federal Disaster Relief Act of 1950, which had created the Disaster Fund and had given the president far-ranging authority to administer the latter.[59] While a part of the population clearly wished for the implementation of flood or disaster insurance as a precautionary measure, the fact that the federal government granted financial aid for rebuilding after a natural disaster created a moral hazard.[60] After all, why should one take precautions and pay (in a risk zone possibly very high) monthly insurance premiums, if the federal state continued to provide low-interest money for re-erecting destroyed houses in the same place, disaster after disaster?

This moral hazard problem had paradoxically evolved, on the one hand, from increased structural flood protection, authorized by the federal government and built by the Army Corps of Engineers starting in the 1930s.[61] The promise of technological protection had had the adverse effect of attracting an increasing number of people to flood-prone areas who had to be saved by charity or the federal government in the absence of an insurance program if those structures failed. In other words, the moral hazard also largely resulted from the abstinence of the private insurance industry from insuring a risk it found impossible, or unprofitable, to bear. In a marked difference to the United States, European insurance markets since the nineteenth century had developed in such a way that specialized reinsurance companies could reinsure large-scale risk that exceeded the financial capacity of direct insurance companies. Private reinsurers were (and are) global agents, servicing insurance companies only, remaining invisible for the public. This system of risk-spreading diminishes the loss borne by individual insurance companies by transferring part of it to one or several reinsurance companies with the result that direct insurers were able to acquire larger-scale risks and thus to insure more people in flood-prone areas.[62] However, the smooth functioning of this system was (and is) dependent on the structure of the respective country's insurance market and on the ability of reinsurers to spread their (usually high-level) risks over as wide a geographical area as possible.[63] As opposed to Europe, in the United States specialized reinsurance companies are subject to the same single-state regulatory laws as direct insurance companies. That is, insurance regulation is the state's authority, and each of the fifty states has its own regulatory framework.[64] Insurers as well as reinsurers have to get licensed state by state in order to become players in the respective insurance markets. Specialized reinsurers, seeking to spread their risk widely, are hence faced with fifty separate markets they have to gain access to in order to achieve a measure of operative security for themselves. In general, therefore, reinsurance in the United States was understood as a reciprocal relationship between private insurance companies or as the task of the federal government, rather than as a relationship between an insurer and a specialized private reinsurance firm.[65] Apart from the fractured domestic market, insurers in the United States had been faced with restrictions as to the lines of risks they were able to underwrite until 1949, when the practice was disbanded. In other words, until 1949, insurers could only insure either fire or life but could not underwrite both.[66] This restrictive policy was known as the American system and had been the subject of debate much more frequently than the fifty-fold insurance regulation and market access. Even without the restriction on the lines of risk, the (constitutionally based) fragmentation remained and proved an obstacle in the development of a domestic U.S. market for specialized reinsurance, which is expressed by the fact that in the 1950s and 1960s U.S. reinsurance rates were no higher than 2.6 to 2.9 percent.[67]

Furthermore, in the absence of a market for flood or disaster insurance, it did not make sense for domestic or foreign reinsurance companies to cover this risk in the first place. However, the existence of a well-functioning reinsurance market could have provided an incentive for the direct insurers to enter such risky (but, with the backing of private industry reinsurance, potentially profitable) business. With no private reinsurance companies to cover flood or disaster loss in general, paradoxically the U.S. private insurers at first also resented the federal government taking on this role. As mentioned earlier, it was the insurer's conviction that the federal state should "stay out of competition with private business."[68] The vacuum thus created by the insurance industry needed to be filled and, hence, pushed the federal state deeper into its role of granting disaster relief after the fact. As explained above, this role was subsequently enforced each time by post-disaster relief politics.

This detailed outline of the U.S. insurance market's intricacies and its (non-) interaction with federal disaster relief is crucial to understanding New Orleans citizens' situation on the ground in the aftermath of Hurricane Betsy. The systemic and seemingly far-removed workings of economic policy, insurance regulation, and market structures had (and have) a direct influence on people's vulnerability to natural hazards, which is clearly visible in the letters to President Johnson. On the other hand, these structural preconfigurations form the background for the unfolding of the congressional debate on disaster/flood insurance before and after the enactment of the Southeast Hurricane Disaster Relief Bill of 1965. This debate led to the signing into law of the National Flood Insurance Program (NFIP) in 1968 (PL 91-79), the United States' first operative flood insurance program and landmark legislation with regard to adaptation (and vulnerability) to natural disasters.

"Single Peril" Flood Insurance or "All-Risk" Disaster Insurance?

Politicians in Washington had been watching the extension of federal responsibility in disaster relief with concern for a while before Hurricane Betsy and the enactment of the Southeast Hurricane Disaster Relief Act. It was felt that natural disasters had increased throughout the United States since the late 1950s and early 1960s. Indeed, in 1964 alone eighteen presidential disaster declarations were issued, and federal disaster funds by the OEP in excess of

$44.7 million (amounting to $340 million in 2016) had been allocated.[69] In July 1965 Governor Buford Ellington, director of the OEP, wrote in a memorandum to President Johnson that because of this increase in disasters and because of the recognition that these calamities were a federal responsibility, the role of the federal government had increased accordingly.[70] A later memorandum by Ellington's assistant director, Charles Brewton, from August 1965 explained the implications of this perceived change in extreme events for the federal government and treasury:

> The Federal Government is caught up in a situation wherein it has become the nation's underwriter for most losses sustained in disasters from risks not now covered by commercial insurance. . . . The impact of major disasters upon the United States Treasury and Federal revenues has gone beyond the point of even being measurable. This is to say nothing of the disruption of the Federal budgeting process and the impact to the disaster region from a host of causes including settlement time lags greater than is the case where there is private insurance protection.[71]

Brewton continued that many members of Congress were seeking a way out of this vicious circle of spending federal revenues. Raising the issue of fairness, he explained how members of Congress from less disaster-prone areas found themselves impotent "to hold in check proposals that correct one set of inequities while creating new ones" because there was no alternative source of disaster relief they could refer to.[72] Hence, the reasons in favor of establishing an insurance program were "almost without number." Citizens should be given the opportunity to take care of their own security. With regard to the hazards, the insurance industry had "neither concluded to cover nor challenge[d] seriously on an experimental basis," the United States remained "a nation of mendicants," the OEP assistant director concluded. With regard to the insurance program he had in mind, he informed Ellington about his belief that

> the insurance industry might be induced to produce an all-risk policy. The Government could stimulate blanket coverage by having Federal lending and insuring agencies require insurance coverage for disaster-type risks as is already required for standard risks. Private bankers and lenders would unquestionably institute similar requirements. Persons familiar with the Government life, health and medical insurance programs are of the opinion that an offer by the Government to exact such a requirement of federal lending and insuring agencies would probably be sufficient to produce the desired response by the insurance industry. If such an all-risk policy were produced, policy holders (i.e. the public) would pay a premium calculated to create a fund sufficient to cover disaster losses.[73]

After the Alaska earthquake in 1964, that state's senator Anderson had recommended to study the insurance of earthquakes, floods, and other disasters.[74] In the context of this recent disaster experience, OEP officials were not thinking about a single-risk flood insurance program, but rather about multi-peril, or all-risk, disaster insurance that was to include all the so far uninsured disaster risks. Outlining the details of this idea to Ellington, Brewton described the solution to the problem of how to achieve blanket coverage, because this was one of the major obstacles the private insurance industry saw in realizing a flood or disaster insurance program. In order to reflect the actual flood risk, policies in flood zones would have to be very highly priced, while those in less-flood-prone areas would be less expensive. It was contended that people on high ground or away from flood plains would not bother to buy even lower-rate flood insurance, so insurers would be left with high-risk policies only (adverse selection). Brewton's all-risk approach and the possibility of convincing federal as well as private insurance and lending institutions to make such all-risk insurance a condition for their services showed one way of evading adverse selection and, hence, a solution to this dilemma. Everyone who obtained a mortgage would automatically become insured against all kinds of natural disasters (i.e., windstorm, fire, hail, flood, landslide, and earthquakes) regardless of whether she lived in a zone at risk of these hazards. Applying the law of large numbers by broadening the policyholder base and by bundling risks drastically reduced the probability of "catastrophic loss," and the incurrence of large-scale loss at the same time by the same event. Taking this "single package, broad-coverage approach" would also solve the problem of equity that existed under the current federal disaster loan program, as Ellington suggested in a 30 July memorandum to President Johnson.[75]

The ongoing discussion of the OEP's idea of all-risk disaster insurance received new momentum through Hurricane Betsy one year after the Alaska earthquake in 1964. In section 5, the Southeast Hurricane Disaster Relief Act of 1965 provided for the secretary of the U.S. Department of Housing and Urban Development (HUD) to "undertake an immediate study of alternative programs which could be established to help provide financial assistance to those suffering property losses in flood and other natural disasters, including alternative methods of Federal disaster insurance, as well as the existing flood insurance program."[76] The study was to be finished and presented to President Johnson and Congress by August 1966.

While in November 1965 citizens were struggling to recover from Hurricane Betsy in New Orleans, HUD in Washington, DC, set to work on the requested insurance study. In the meantime, the OEP continued ventilating its idea of all-risk disaster insurance. As in the months immediately after Betsy, citizens' impulses regarding disaster insurance were processed through the governmental machinery. On 22 March 1966 Franklin B. Dryden, acting director of the OEP at the time, answered a letter from a member of Congress that included an interesting document regarding disaster insurance. It was an essay from a Seattle business owner written in April 1964. Under the impression of the Alaska earthquake in 1964, Palmer C. Lewis lamented that besides all the government agencies, which helped produce the United States' high standard of living, there was still no program insuring citizens against disasters. The insurance program he envisioned "covering natural disaster risk over the entire fifty states, would probably reduce the cost to a point where the premiums could be afforded by everyone who could afford fire insurance."[77] In other words, if the risk of all natural disasters affecting the United States could be spread over the country's entire population, the individual premium cost would be so much reduced as to make disaster insurance affordable for everybody. By including *all* risks, rather than flood only, and spreading them over all U.S. citizens, not just residents in risk-zones, Lewis's argument effectively opposed the insurance industry's credo that flood insurance premiums would be so high that no one could be persuaded to pay them. His idea was based on his belief that disasters occurred in different areas all over the world and thus also implicitly on the notion of solidarity that is at the basis of such all-inclusive disaster insurance programs.

Despite the fact that the OEP was probably aware of the cost reduction that the spread over the entire U.S. population would bring, the office had not pointed out the benefits such an approach as clearly as Lewis in his essay.[78] Dryden, who ended up replying to the member of Congress, wrote that he found the businessman's proposal interesting and that the OEP agreed "that the ultimate solution to the problem may be all-risk disaster insurance available to everyone at reasonable rates."[79] What Lewis had not mentioned in his account was how he intended to persuade the whole U.S. population to actually *buy* his disaster insurance (i.e., how he would reach the blanket effect mentioned in Brewton's memorandum above). This was one of the critical reasons why the private insurance industry had rejected (single peril) flood insurance so far. For this problem the OEP had suggested making such insurance a requirement for obtaining federal or private mortgages.

So, two of the private insurance industry's strongest arguments against flood insurance could be disarmed by a different concept of cost bearing: the single package, broad-coverage approach propagated by the OEP. However, it appears that in particular the question of the mandatory character of such a new disaster insurance program proved to be an obstacle in the way of developing a viable alternative to federal disaster relief. It is here that perceptions of personal freedom and the federal state's role surfaced in the debate. They were to have a decisive influence on the outcome of the insurance program that was chosen for implementation and by extension on the future trajectory of adaptation and vulnerability to natural disasters of the U.S. population in general.[80]

The Issue of Mandatory Coverage

On 29 April 1966, Robert Weaver, secretary of HUD, sent a memorandum to the special assistant of the president that listed a number of policy issues on federal flood insurance. The issues had arisen from the study of flood and disaster insurance requested by the Betsy Bill, which his department had been entrusted to conduct in cooperation with agricultural economist and government official Robert Marion Clawson and with the American Insurance Association.[81] Under point 1, Weaver stated,

> Mandatory flood insurance, in the sense of a law requiring it, is surely not feasible. But should our agencies which supervise credit institutions require or encourage flood insurance as a condition to loans for buildings in flood prone areas? Should we take the view that property relief after a disaster will not be extended to the people who refused to take out flood insurance when it is available? Could we make such a position stick in the face of possible public sympathy for disaster victims?

Conspicuously, Secretary Weaver mentioned only flood insurance and not all-risk disaster insurance in the OEP's sense in his talking points. This was not a coincidence as we will see further into the HUD's correspondence. Unfortunately, Weaver did not specify why he thought a law requiring citizens to take out flood insurance was unfeasible. As in the OEP's memoranda, a way of enforcing the new insurance program was sought indirectly by ordering lending institutions to make insurance a requirement for loans.

What made a law mandating flood (or disaster) insurance seem so unfeasible as to be brushed aside with a single sentence in Weaver's communication? The documents of the National Archive's disaster insurance files give no direct answer to this question, yet we may derive clues from the structure of the U.S. insurance market as well as from a recent case where mandatory insurance was at stake. For a mandatory flood or disaster insurance program to work throughout the whole United States the federal government would have had to create new legislation superseding the fifty states' respective authority of insurance regulation. Yet this exact conflict over federal or state regulation of insurance had been at the center of *United States v. South-East Underwriters' Association*[82] in 1944 and was settled by the McCarran–Ferguson Act (34 Stat. 1937-1946, PL 15) in 1945. The latter had decreed that regulatory authority lay with the states. Any repeal of the McCarran–Ferguson Act is likely to have been unpopular and unable to pass Congress.[83]

G. Calvin Mackenzie and Robert Weisbrot have called "the American system of governance . . . by nature conservative" and described it as favoring the status quo because of its reliance on precedents.[84] Precedents were also called on to decide in favor of tradition in a present-day legislative example seeking to introduce a mandatory insurance program. I will briefly refer to this case since its (in many ways historical) argumentation may provide insights for the debate in 1968. One of the most recent conflicts about mandating insurance in the United States was the Patient Protection and Affordable Care Act. In 2010 Congress fought over whether this mandate was in fact constitutional under the Commerce and Necessary and Proper clauses.[85] While ultimately the Affordable Care Act was passed, the Supreme Court stripped it of its mandatory coverage requirement so that health insurance coverage was left merely an option and not a mandate. The Supreme Court's current chief justice Roberts had argued in an earlier case that Congress had never before attempted to "compel individuals not engaged in commerce to purchase an unwanted product."[86] That is, there was apparently no precedent to the congressional Democrats attempt at making health care mandatory for everyone in 2010. However, according to Roberts, under the Commerce clause Congress only had the authority to regulate commerce between states, it could not order *individuals* to engage in it. In other words, Roberts interpreted mandatory insurance coverage as "compulsion to engage in commerce," which he furthermore judged improper under the Necessary and Proper clause of the constitution. As a justification for this ruling, Roberts advanced that "granting the Congress this power [to mandate insurance coverage] would gravely limit the liberties of the people."[87] By deciding in this way, the Supreme Court effectively prevented creating a precedent that—from a conservative perspective—would have unduly enlarged Congress's powers. As I will show below, in 1968 as in 2010 considerations of people's liberty to take personal risks (even at the expense of the common good) overrode the logic of the law of large numbers.

Let us return to the confrontation between the two models of disaster insurance unfolding between the OEP and the HUD, in which the issue of mandatory coverage continued to be a subject of conflict. As mentioned above, Weaver's issues only considered flood insurance, allowing a preliminary glimpse of HUD's and the American Insurance Association's preferred program. In June 1966 the OEP phrased its counter position as "favor[ing] an all-natural disaster insurance program, rather than one limited to flood alone. If possible, such insurance should be handled by the insurance industry, supported by the government."[88] Toward the end of July 1966 OEP's assistant director Charles Brewton received memoranda from the heads of four government offices who had reviewed the apparently finished but as yet unpublished HUD report on *Insurance and Other Programs for Financial Assistance to Flood Victims*.[89] Three of them noted or even criticized that the study concentrated on flood insurance only and dismissed the research of other versions of disaster insurance by arguing that "floods are by a wide margin, the most serious of the natural disaster hazards facing the people of the United States; and efforts to provide insurance and other means of coping with flood hazards are difficult enough, at best. There are various kinds of relatively minor disaster hazards not covered by insurance such as mudflows, earth slippages, falling meteors or other materials, and others. . . . If programs of financial assistance to flood victims can be developed on a satisfactory basis, they can later be extended to the other disasters relatively easily."[90] In this way the HUD's proposal gave conscious preference to single-peril flood insurance, a decision that was likely influenced by the American Insurance Association, involved in the study. After all, the insurance industry had gathered experience with flood insurance at the beginning of the twentieth century, and the 1950s had laid a legislative foundation for thinking about flood insurance, while inclusive all-disaster insurance was completely new territory for the private companies. However, by concentrating exclusively on flood insurance, somewhat surprisingly even the private insurers disregarded the law of large numbers. According to the latter, "ideal risks" are those where potential losses are relatively small and not interrelated.[91] This was clearly not the case with single-peril flood insurance, where losses were usually large and highly interrelated (i.e., caused by the same loss event).

The same three authors, Charles Beal, Chief of the Government's Natural Disaster Division, Robert Y. Phillips, director of the Government Readiness Office and Robert A. Bowman of the Bureau of the Budged (BOB), agreed that all-risk disaster insurance was preferable to the HUD's single-peril flood insurance approach. For example, Bowman expressed his feeling "that it would be unfortunate for the government to enter into a purely flood insurance program rather than an all-disaster insurance program which could justify a greater spread of the risk."[92] Bowman was referring to the all-disaster approach's high improbability of incurring catastrophic loss, since it was rather unlikely that an earthquake, a landslide, a hurricane, and a river flood would occur simultaneously in the same area.

The fourth memorandum, sent under the letterhead of the OEP, criticized the HUD report for dismissing too lightheartedly the option of an insurance program operated entirely by the private industry based on their previous (negative) experience. The OEP's comment underlined the advantage of mandatory coverage in countering adverse selection and thus of possibly enabling such a program to be self-sustaining.[93] However, interestingly, the HUD report, which was published in September 1966, did not even discuss a "mandatory insurance program administered by the insurance industry."[94] Mandatoriness was discussed only in relation with different cost-bearing options. It was not mentioned in connection with the *private industry* at all but as part of a scenario where the public bears all costs. Because mandatory coverage would have to be introduced by the federal government, the study presumed this model to be administered by the government. Such a program would be financed from government funds—that is, from general tax money, or by levying a special tax for this purpose. The study's choice of vocabulary made clear the undesirability of this approach and, consequently, of the instrument of mandatory coverage by law. In derisive terms the authors of the study explained,

> The latter program has been proposed at times under the label of "flood insurance." Those who advocate it would require every homeowner or residential occupant to buy such "flood insurance" at a flat annual rate, regardless of his risk of flood damage, if any; the funds so raised would then be used to reimburse the victims of flood damage, wherever this might occur and regardless of how much he had paid for his "flood insurance." Those who argue for such a program emphasize the unpredictability of both the timing and geographical location of floods. . . . A program of this kind is not, in any reasonable sense of the term "insurance."[95]

Rather, it was compared to a simple system of taxation that could only be imposed on people by law. This and its proximity to taxation clearly was anathema to the HUD. Under their proposed scheme of a single-peril flood insurance program, this makes sense, since forcing people outside flood zones to subsidize those living in high-risk zones would have been inequitable indeed. However, it is quite evident that this was a misrepresentation of the logic of the all-risk model the OEP was considering.

Whether the HUD's sketch of mandatory coverage by law was a direct attack on the OEP's idea of single-package broad coverage all-risk disaster insurance is not entirely clear. Evidently, however, the HUD's conception of mandatory insurance was at best a misconception, or a gross distortion of the OEP's approach. Apart from projecting mandatory coverage on single-peril flood insurance and thus failing to consider any of the advantages of bundling the flood risk with other natural hazards in order to achieve balance, it neither discussed the benefits that spreading the risk of the few over the many might have for the national economy as a whole. Instead, the HUD's approach focused exclusively on inequities to the individual policyholder. Mandatory coverage did not reappear as a subject throughout the rest of the report. A line had been drawn with the "public bears all costs" scenario and the conclusion that such an approach—represented as introducing a new form of tax—could not, in earnest, be called "insurance." However, apart from economic considerations that made mandatoriness by law objectionable, the report also disclosed deeply rooted cultural values that influenced the rejection of this approach. For, "independence and self-reliance are deep-seated American traits, dating back to the extended pioneer period, when such traits were not only highly valued but essential for survival and success. Most people in this country today prefer to manage their own affairs, to receive the gains, if any, from their actions, and to take the consequences if things turn out badly."[96] Thus, flood insurance was to be left the property owner's free choice, regardless of whether this individual choice might bear heavily on the federal treasury (i.e., everyone's tax money).

The importance of the property owner's freedom of choice as an argument against mandatory coverage emerges more clearly from a contemporary article by economist Howard Kunreuther, who had been commissioned by the OEP to study the feasibility of all-risk disaster insurance in summer 1966.[97] In his opinion, "The simplest device . . . would be for the federal government to require all homeowners to take out a comprehensive disaster insurance policy offering protection against all natural hazards." However, like the HUD report—albeit without the latter's derision—Kunreuther remarked, "Premiums on each residence would thus be a type of property tax reflecting the risk of living in a certain area. This method has the undesirable characteristic of forcing individuals who own their home outright to purchase insurance even though they may prefer to gamble by not obtaining coverage."[98] Even in the eyes of the OEP's expert, the option of mandatory coverage by law was overruled by the individual's freedom of choice to take risks.

After rejecting an all-risk disaster insurance program, the report introduced four approaches to flood insurance, an all-private insurance program, two public–private partnership options, and an all-federal insurance program. The modes favored by the HUD were the intermediate ones, in other words, those in which the private industry partnered in some way with the federal government to provide coverage for policyholders and maximum protection for the insurance industry. Furthermore, the insurers' requirement of actuarially sound insurance rates entailed a demand for data that did not yet exist and that would be costly to collect. Had the gathering of information such as local flood depths and frequencies been the obligation of the private industry, the cost of such data collection would have had to be reflected in policyholders' insurance rates. Under the HUD's default setting of optional flood insurance, this additional cost would make it even less likely that property owners in high-risk zones would buy such policies. In a public–private partnership, on the other hand, such costly studies of local environmental conditions and of risk zoning could be carried out through the federal state's agencies so that their cost would not have to be burdened on policyholders.

The OEP Joint Resolution and the Merker Bill

A few weeks after the heads of the OEP, the Government Readiness Office, and the Natural Disaster Division had reviewed the HUD report, a joint resolution was drafted "to provide for insurance against property losses caused by natural disasters."[99] It presented an alternative to the single-peril flood insurance approach and clearly bore the OEP's handwriting.[100] The document declared in its preamble that "hundreds of thousands of Americans" lost their homes annually by exposure to a broad range of natural hazards, and that property destruction in major disasters in the United States exceeded the devastation wrought by the bombing of Hiroshima and Nagasaki. Natural disasters threatened the economic prosperity of the United States "by creating pockets of poverty, diluting the tax base and placing greater and greater strain on the financial reserves of the Federal Government." A program of inclusive nation-wide natural disaster insurance would therefore provide the means for effective recovery since it would achieve "the blanket effect essential for reasonable rates."[101]

Mandatory coverage was not mentioned in the joint resolution but was included in a bill drafted in December 1966, four months after the joint resolution.[102] This second legislative document was clearly authored by the OEP and assistant director Brewton's legal advisor Mordecai Merker.[103] The bill provided for automatic coverage which was the same as mandatory coverage. The bill required that in the states where it was made available, all-disaster insurance would be a requirement for all "properties covered by Federal loans and Federally guaranteed loans or financed from Federally insured savings or deposits."[104] Furthermore, the federal government would reinsure catastrophic losses that exceeded $200 million and would establish an all-disaster risk insurance fund or pool that would be administered by a board of governors representing the involved insurance companies and that would be chaired by the director of the OEP.

The Merker Bill obliged only property owners with *federally* financed or insured mortgages to acquire this insurance coverage. Those with privately financed mortgages were not affected by the OEP's legislative proposal and could consequently choose to remain uncovered. While the insurance program presented by the Merker Bill was clearly closer to reaching the desired blanket coverage, it was still not inclusive of all property owners. Mandatoriness by law apparently continued to be a non-option.

Comparing the points raised in the OEP joint resolution's preamble with the considerations of the HUD report, the perspectivity of the OEP and the HUD's position toward flood/disaster insurance emerges clearly. Even though the HUD was a government agency, the report had argued strongly from the point of view of the private insurance industry and the risk it would carry, were a flood insurance program to be enacted. This perspective was necessarily influenced by considerations of commercial competitiveness, financial profits, and the solvency of private companies—in short, by considerations of the survival of the private insurance industry. The OEP, on the other hand, had clearly argued from the point of view of the national economy and of the soaring costs inflicted on the federal government by the current disaster relief programs. As a government body the OEP had to consider factors of cost effectiveness and solvency as much as the private insurance industry, yet, evidently, on a rather different scale. Considerations of competitiveness in a specifically structured market did not apply to the OEP, neither did the question of profitability, beyond the point where a projected insurance program would be self-sufficient. This lack of entrepreneurial self-interest enabled the OEP to acquire a perspective that departed to quite some extent from the U.S. insurance industry's traditional approach, which was strongly reflected in the HUD study. "Single-peril" flood insurance was the field where the private companies had at least had some—albeit negative—experience. Added to this was the adherence to certain insurance principles, such as the reflection of risk in the pricing of policies. In the flood-only scenario the HUD study chose to pursue, this principle, which was to act as a (dis-)incentive for policyholders, made perfect sense. However, this principle at the same time became a stumbling block for the feasibility of a flood insurance program due to the problem of adverse selection. The strong focus on the actuarially sound pricing of risks seems to have prevented any consideration of the OEP's model of risk diversification and of expanding flood-only to all-disaster risk insurance. Clearly, this appeal of previous experience, knowledge, and expertise is highly significant in the context of adaptation/vulnerability since it generates a path dependence similar to that of built structures as we have seen in chapter 2. The gravity of existing knowledge and expertise is by no means intangible or abstract but very real in its entanglement with economic and political power structures. It is, therefore, possible to speak of a *path dependence of practice* that strongly influences decision-making and that may, more often than not, turn adaptive practices into vulnerability.[105]

The National Flood Insurance Program, 1968

Two years after the publication of the HUD report, the NFIP was enacted in August 1968.[106] It was closely modeled after the report. Most obviously, the program was to be administered and carried out under the authority of the secretary of HUD, Robert C. Weaver, who delegated it to the administrator of the Federal Insurance Administration (FIA).[107] The act contained two program options, an "industry program with Federal financial assistance" and a "Government program with industry assistance" that corresponded to the two intermediate approaches of the HUD report described above. The second, all-federal option could be adopted should the first variant, a public–private partnership, not work out.[108] The initial NFIP was entirely voluntary on the community as well as the individual level. That is, voluntary coverage to individuals became available only after an entire community had applied to take part and had confirmed to comply with the program's mitigation and land-use requirements. However, since no detailed data on local flood-risks were available at the time on which rates could be based, insurance rate studies and Flood Insurance Rate Maps had to be completed first. Since this was a time-consuming process, an emergency program was enacted in 1969 which enabled communities to buy limited insurance coverage until the completion of their Flood Insurance Rate Map. These maps were the basis for the actuarial pricing of a community's insurance rates as well as for its floodplain zoning in the flood-risk area that was required in exchange for insurance coverage.[109] The coupling of insurance with obligations to change land-use in a way that would reduce future flood losses and to elevate houses above a certain level of the flood plain could have been highly effective in reducing property owners' risk of loss, had the program been mandatory.

However, after the first five years of the NFIP, fewer than 20 percent of the local communities within identified flood-risk zones perceived flood insurance as an incentive to enforce the flood plain building regulations required by the program and only two hundred thousand individual policies were in force in 1973. This extent of disinterest (or ignorance) became evident after Hurricane Agnes struck the U.S. east coast in 1972 and the vast majority of the still uninsured residents had to rely once more on federal disaster relief.[110] An attempt to ameliorate this situation was undertaken with the Flood Disaster Protection Act in 1973.[111] The Act made it the NFIP's responsibility to identify all communities at risk of flooding. It also increased pressure on communities at risk to participate in the program by giving them the choice between the adoption of the NFIP's requirements or having cut the availability of certain disaster relief measures to their risk areas. Furthermore, it now required mandatory coverage—namely, that federal financial institutions require flood insurance on mortgages they issued.[112] Yet, the 1973 Flood Disaster Protection Act only mandated that lenders require flood insurance at the inception of the mortgage; after the first year, homeowners were in fact free not to renew or even to cancel their policy.[113] After the tremendous property losses occasioned by Hurricane Andrew in Florida in 1994, Congress passed the National Flood Insurance Reform Act, in which it concentrated on compliance of the federal lending institutions.[114] As opposed to the 1973 act, the 1994 Reform Act required lenders to oblige the borrower to take out flood insurance for the lifetime of their loan, in order to prevent them from cancelling their policies after the first year. In addition, lenders were allowed to force-place insurance coverage if a property owner failed to buy it.[115] Even this amendment of mandatory coverage seems not to have had the desired effect, judging by the program's market penetration, estimated to be at 26 percent in 1997.[116]

Yet, in order to be effective, the program obviously had to broaden its policy base as much as possible. Policy premiums are collected in the National

Flood Insurance Fund (Fund), which is used to pay flood losses, as well as operative costs and administrative expenses of the program. Theoretically, the Fund is intended to be self-sustaining—that is, it was expected to accumulate surpluses from which losses would be paid and that would enable it to balance loss indemnification. Since no initial capitalization of the Fund had been effected, it was authorized to borrow up to $1 billion from the federal treasury. As a result of continually low participation in the program, the Fund has had to borrow from the U.S. Treasury on a regular basis, incurring a total operating loss of $817.6 million between 1969 and 1980 (equivalent to $2.5 billion in 2016 dollars).[117] In other words, since its enactment in 1968 the program has been dysfunctional. This is in large part due to the failure of compliance of the money lending industry, which is used as the agent to enforce participation. However, the propensity of property owners to take the risk of loss (i.e., the abovementioned moral hazard), rather than paying insurance premiums adds to the difficulties of the system.[118] This problem of participation, and hence of the overall functionality of the program, theoretically could have been solved by making it mandatory by law.[119]

While many elements of the HUD report were transformed into the NFIP in 1968, what happened to the OEP's all-disaster insurance? The records discussing the inclusive disaster insurance approach continue into the early 1970s, and Howard Kunreuther, in particular, who had worked on the OEP's proposal of all-disaster insurance in 1966, continued studying and publishing on this alternative option. As late as 2006, in the aftermath of Hurricane Katrina (29 August 2005), Kunreuther pointed out that property owners did not voluntarily engage in cost-effective measures of loss-reduction. Despite the introduction and gradual improvement of the NFIP, what Kunreuther called the *natural disaster syndrome,* persisted in the United States. Kunreuther had coined this term to describe the perpetuation of the federal government's involvement in supporting individuals who had chosen not to buy the still largely voluntary flood insurance coverage prior to a disaster, despite the fact that the government had declared that such support would no longer be forthcoming.[120] After Hurricane Katrina, Kunreuther, again, presented the comprehensive all-disaster insurance program as an alternative to the persisting *natural disaster syndrome.* Apparently, Hurricane Katrina had created a window of opportunity to relaunch such a controversial idea as mandatoriness by law.

After its inception in 1968 the NFIP could not fully unfold its desired effect, namely, giving people the possibility of taking precautionary steps to protect their property and alleviating the burden of disaster relief costs of the federal state. Several complex and interrelated factors such as the absence of a market for natural hazard insurance, the exclusive focus on flood insurance, and the moral hazard created by the coexistence of federal disaster relief and an entirely optional insurance program are at the root of the fact that the principally adaptive measure of flood insurance was either ineffective or even increased vulnerability to flood loss.[121]

The central factor for this adaptive measure not to alleviate—or even to increase—vulnerability, and thus, to conform to McNeill's "conservation of catastrophe," is the issue of mandatory coverage. An insurance program mandated by law was considered unfeasible. The factor that was most frequently mentioned as a reason for this impossibility was the infringement on the personal freedom of individuals to take risks with their property. It is quite evident that the root of this problem lies in the United States' specific political culture and history regarding taxation and the perception that insurance mandated by law would be akin to a tax.

I have introduced the term *path dependence of practice* to describe the pull or gravity of previous knowledge and expertise, and the power structures connected with the latter when it comes to decision-making and innovation. Path dependence of practice, much like the path dependence created by the built environment discussed in chapter 2, restricts the course of action in such a way that small modifications of the existing structure are much more likely, while overhauling the system as a whole is almost impossible. Thus, apart from shedding light on the decision-making process that led to the introduction of the NFIP in 1968, this chapter has highlighted the difficulty and the complex factors involved in introducing an effective systems-change affecting adaptation to natural hazards at the level of the nation state. The analysis of the NFIP has underlined the multiplicity of contingent factors influencing the functionality of an insurance system and thus of whether adaptation to natural hazards, using the mechanism of insurance, is successful, or whether it turns into adaptation's flipside, vulnerability.[122]

Notes

1. United States Census Bureau, "1890 Census. Table 5: Population of States and Territories by Minor Civil Divisions, 1880 and 1890. Part I," http://www.census.gov/popula tion/www/censusdata/hiscendata.html; see also Campanella, *Dilemma*, graph insert.
2. Richard Campanella, "An Ethnic Geography of New Orleans," *Journal of American History* 94, no. 3 (2007), 709–10; Craig E. Colten, *An Unnatural Metropolis: Wresting New Orleans from Nature* (Baton Rouge: Louisiana State University Press, 2005), 83.
3. Kent B. Germany, "The Politics of Poverty and History. Racial Inequality and the Long Prelude to Katrina," *Journal of American History* 94, no. 3 (2007), 744.
4. Campanella, *Dilemma*, 152, 151–52.
5. Mackenzie and Weisbrot, *Liberal Hour*, 35–36.
6. Arsenault, "Storm," 278.
7. Five hundred thousand Gulf Coast residents evacuated in advance of Hurricane Carla in 1961. Lichtblau, "Hurricane Carla," 2.
8. Mackenzie and Weisbrot use the term "liberal hour" to describe the years between

1963 and 1966 that "yielded [a] policy explosion" beyond comparison in U.S. history. Mackenzie and Weisbrot, *Liberal Hour*, 79–83, 327.

9. Ibid., 99 ("elevating national", "advancing the quality"), 162.

10. The Civil Rights Act and the Voting Rights Act, in particular, caused the traditionally democratic, segregationist South to shift to the Republican party. See ibid., 354.

11. Ibid., 362 ("full power of"); ibid., 375, 377 (durable decade).

12. Some contemporary researchers in the field of climate change adaptation studies even go so far as to say that "insurance *is* adaptation." See Trevor Maynard, "Climate Change: Impacts on Insurers and How They Can Help with Adaptation and Mitigation," *Geneva Papers* 33 (2008), emphasis added.

13. Franz Mauelshagen, "Ungewissheit in der Soziosphäre. Risiko und Versicherung im Klimawandel," in *Unberechenbare Umwelt. Zum Umgang mit Unsicherheit und Nicht-Wissen*, ed. Roderich von Detten, Fenn Faber, and Martin Bemmann (Wiesbaden: Springer, 2013), 256–57.

14. The law of large numbers states that "with the increase of the number of exposed units, the actual loss experience will approach the expected loss experience." George E. Rejda, *Principles of Risk Management and Insurance*, 7th ed. (Boston: Addison Wesley, 2001), 4.; The term "catastrophic loss" describes the incurrence of large-scale loss at the same time by the same event, see ibid., 22; and Swiss Re, *Natural Catastrophes and Reinsurance*, Risk Perception (Zurich: Swiss Re, 2003), 11.

15. Zwierlein, *Prometheus*.

16. Unlike Hurricane Katrina, Hurricane Betsy has generated comparatively little (historical) scientific output so far. See, e.g., Colten, *Perilous Place*; Campanella, *Dilemma*, 321–24.; For meteorological facts see Keim and Muller, *Hurricanes*, 84–86; on race and Poverty in the United States, see Romain Huret, *Katrina, 2005. L'Ouragan, l'État et les Pauvres aux États-Unis*, Cas de Figure (Paris: Éditions EHESS, 2010), 110–23; Germany, "Poverty," 743–51.

17. Campanella, *Dilemma*, 321; Arsenault, "Storm," 275.

18. Augustin, "Lady on a Rampage (Hurricane Betsy)," 25 January 1979; LSM, Vertical File "Hurricanes," Folder 2, [1].

19. Ibid.

20. Campanella, *Dilemma*, 321. As pointed out in chapter 3, Campanella's finding stands in contrast to Zelinsky and Kosinski's account of the first mass evacuation by car after Hurricane Carla in 1961. Zelinsky and Kosinski, *Emergency Evacuation*, 43.

21. Oliver to Schiro, "Betsy, the Bête Noire," 23 November 1965; NOPL, Victor Schiro Collection (1957–1970), S 65–13, Hurricane Betsy 1965, Folder 5.

22. Victor Schiro, [TV/ Radio Broadcast Speech], n.d.; NOPL, Victor Schiro Collection (1957–1970), S 65- 12, Hurricane Betsy 1965, Folder 2.

23. Augustin, "Lady on a Rampage (Hurricane Betsy)"; U.S. Congress, House of Representatives, Committee on Public Works, *The Hurricane Betsy Disaster of September 1965: Report of the Special Subcommittee to Investigate Areas of Destruction of Hurricane Betsy* (Washington, DC: U.S. Government Printing Office, 1965), 1.

24. U.S. Congress, Office of Emergency Planning, *Hurricane Betsy, 27 August–10 September 1965: Federal Action in Disaster* (Washington, DC: Office of Emergency Planning, 1966), 4.

25. Colten, *Perilous Place*, 37.

26. Campanella, *Dilemma*, 322–23.

27. In the 1964 campaign Johnson lost Louisiana to the Republican candidate Barry Gold-water as a reaction to his pushing the Civil Rights Act (1964) and to his campaign speech in New Orleans, in which he called on the people of the South to end racial politics and to move toward a society in which everyone could prosper. See Mackenzie and Weisbrot, *Liberal Hour,* 171–72.

28. Kent B. Germany, "Presidential Recordings Program: LBJ and the Response to Hurricane Betsy. President Johnson and Russell Long, September 10, 1965," Miller Center, University of Virginia, Charlottesville. https://millercenter.org/the-presidency/educational-resources/lbj-and-senator-russell-long-on-hurricane-betsy.

29. Congress, *Hurricane Betsy, August 27–September 10, 1965,* 6; Huret, *Katrina,* 113.

30. The OEP was an operational unit created by Executive Order 11051 under the Kennedy administration in 1962. This Presidential initiative was "the culmination of a long-range plan to chart a new course for the management and mobilization of our national resources, continuity of government, and economic stabilization to meet all conditions of national emergency including attack on the United States." Executive Order 11051, September 27, 1962, NARA, RG 396, Records Relating to Emergency Preparedness—Office of the Director—Correspondence, Memorandums and other Records (1969–1971), A9/Entry 1005; 650: 41, 30, 02, Box 2.

31. Germany, "Recordings."

32. Huret, *Katrina,* 112–13 (including quotes).

33. Augustin, "Lady on a Rampage (Hurricane Betsy)," [3–4].

34. Congress, *Hurricane Betsy Disaster of September 1965,* 5.

35. Congress, *Federal Action,* inside cover.

36. McKeithen to Johnson, n.d., NARA, RG 311, Disaster Declaration Files (1965–1971), WW/Entry 2, (OEP 208 DR, Louisiana), 650–41, 21, 6, Box 7, Folder "Correspondence."

37. Ibid. In a hearing before the House Committee on Public Works on 13 October 1965, the director of the president's Government Readiness Office, Robert Phillips, estimated that the figure could be fifteen times larger. U.S. Congress, House of Representatives, Committee on Public Works, *Southeast Hurricane Disaster (Hurricane Betsy). Hearing. 89th Congress, 1st Session, on H. R. 11539 and Similar Bills. October 13, 1965* (Washington, DC: U.S. Government Printing Office, 1965), 27.

38. Under this act, the governor of a disaster stricken state could request the president to proclaim the calamity a major disaster, meaning "any flood, drought, fire, hurricane, earthquake, storm, or other catastrophe in any part of the United States which, in the determination of the President, is or threatens to be of sufficient severity and magnitude to warrant disaster assistance by the Federal Government to supplement the efforts and available resources of States and local governments in alleviating the damage, hardship, or suffering caused thereby." Federal Disaster Assistance Act (PL 81-875, 64 Stat. 1109).

39. Bruce R. Lindsay and Justin Murray, "Disaster Relief Funding and Emergency Supplemental Appropriations," *CRS Report for Congress* (2011), http://www.fas.org/sgp/crs/misc/R40708.pdf. Howard Kunreuther, "The Case for Comprehensive Disaster Insurance," *Journal of Law and Economics* April (1968), 143–44. The provision of disaster loans was introduced in the Small Business Act of 1953 (PL 85-536).

40. "The traditional position of insurance company underwriters is that specific flood insurance covering fixed location properties in areas subject to recurrent floods cannot feasibly be written." American Insurance Association, *Studies of Floods and Flood Damage, 1952–1955* (New York: Insurance Executives Association, 1956), 3.

41. Kunreuther, "Disaster Insurance," 145.

42. Maturity of SBA loans was first set at twenty years (PL 85-536), and was consequently augmented to thirty years after the Alaska earthquake in 1964. Small Business Act of 1965, § 1(a), 15 U.S.C. § 636 (b).

43. This is indicated in Hurricane Betsy victim's letters to President Johnson introduced on the next pages. Lower Ninth Ward resident Theresa Bourgeois, for example, refrained from going to the Red Cross for help because she felt that "we are not beggars." Bourgeois to Johnson, 18 November 1965, NARA, RG 311, Headquarters Disaster Declaration Files (1965–1971), WW/Entry 2; 650: 41, 21, 06, Box 7, Folder "Correspondence 3."

44. Lübken, "Gefahr," 12; Howard Kunreuther, "Has the Time Come for Comprehensive Natural Disaster Insurance?," in *On Risk and Disaster: Lessons from Hurricane Katrina*, ed. Ronald J. Daniels, Donald F. Kettl, and Howard Kunreuther (Philadelphia: University of Pennsylvania Press, 2006), 185.

45. Edwin S. Overman, "The Flood Peril and the Federal Flood Insurance Act of 1956," *Annals of the American Academy of Political and Social Science* 309 (1957), 99.

46. Federal Flood Insurance Act 70 Stat. 1078 1956, PL 84-1016, Sec. 2b) 1; ibid., 102.

47. Colten, *Perilous Place*, 39.

48. Edwin W. Kopf, "Notes on the Origin and Development of Reinsurance," *Proceedings of the Casualty Actuary Society* 16 (1933), 72.

49. Thomas to Johnson, 31 October 1965, NARA, RG 311, Headquarters Disaster Declaration Files (1965–1971), WW/Entry 2; 650: 41, 21, 06, Box 7, Folder "Correspondence 3." For the historical currency conversions see Officer and Williamson, "Measuring Worth."

50. Gully to Edson, November 17, 1965, in Thomas to Johnson, 31 October 1965, NARA, RG 311, Headquarters Disaster Declaration Files (1965–1971), WW/Entry 2; 650: 41, 21, 06, Box 7, Folder "Correspondence 3."

51. Hill to Johnson, 26 October 1965, NARA, RG 311, Headquarters Disaster Declaration Files (1965–1971), WW/Entry 2; 650: 41, 21, 06, Box 7, Folder "Correspondence 2"; Gully to Edson, November 17, 1965, in Hill to Johnson, 26 October 1965, NARA, RG 311, Headquarters Disaster Declaration Files (1965–1971), WW/Entry 2; 650: 41, 21, 06, Box 7, Folder "Correspondence 2."

52. Howard to Johnson, 22 October 1965, NARA, RG 311, Headquarters Disaster Declaration Files (1965–1971), WW/Entry 2; 650: 41, 21, 06, Box 7, Folder "Correspondence 3."

53. Finnin to Johnson, 21 September 1965, NARA, RG 311, Disaster Declaration Files (1965–1971), WW/Entry 2, (OEP 208 DR, Louisiana), 650-41, 21, 6, Box 7, Folder "Correspondence."

54. Congress, *Southeast Hurricane Disaster*, 2.

55. Ibid., 3; Southeast Hurricane Disaster Relief Act of 1965, PL 89–339, 79 Stat. 1301.

56. Southeast Hurricane Disaster Relief Act; Phillips to Alphonse, 21 October 1965, NARA, RG 311, Headquarters Disaster Declaration Files (1965–1971), WW/Entry 2;

650: 41, 21, 06, Box 7, Folder "Correspondence 2"; Phillips to Alphonse, November 3, 1965, NARA, RG 311, Headquarters Disaster Declaration Files (1965–1971), WW/ Entry 2; 650: 41, 21, 06, Box 7, Folder "Correspondence 2."

57.   Similar inequities existed in federal disaster relief programs before the Betsy Bill. For example, in the aftermath of the Alaska earthquake in 1964, people who owned their houses outright did not benefit from the disaster legislation, whereas people who had federally insured or guaranteed mortgages "received the bulk of Federal Assistance." Ellington to Johnson, Memorandum for the President. Disaster Insurance, 30 July 1965, NARA, RG 311, Headquarters Disaster Declaration Files (1965–1971). For a contemporary criticism of the federal disaster management program, see Kunreuther, "Disaster Insurance."

58.   In his 1957 study of the Flood Insurance Act, Edwin Overman stated that "if measured by the damage and destruction to the properties, facilities, and installations of industrial and commercial organizations, to say nothing of federal, state, and local governments and agriculture, flood peril would exceed all other natural causes of disaster." His argumentation was influenced by the losses of the devastating 1951 Southwest Floods. Overman, "Flood Peril," 98.

59.   David A. Moss, "Courting Disaster? The Transformation of Federal Disaster Policy since 1803," in *The Financing of Catastrophe Risk*, ed. Kenneth A. Froot (Chicago: University of Chicago Press, 1999), 335; Lindsay and Murray, "Disaster Relief Funding," 3.

60.   The term "moral hazard" is used in the insurance industry to describe the phenomenon that a policyholder, knowing that he is protected by insurance, might take greater risks or act imprudently, thus putting at risk the insurer who provides coverage. The same could also apply to the relationship between the insurer and a reinsurer. Carol Anne Heimer, *Reactive Risk and Rational Action: Managing Moral Hazard in Insurance Contracts*, California Series on Social Choice and Political Economy (Berkeley: University of California Press, 1985), 29; and Peter Liebwein, *Klassische und moderne Formen der Rückversicherung* (Karlsruhe: Verlag Versicherungswirtschaft, 2000), 167.

61.   The Flood Control Act of 1936, 49 Stat. 1570, P.L. 74-738, was the first step toward a national flood control program. See American Institutes for Research, "A Chronology of Major Events Affecting the National Flood Insurance Program. Completed for the Federal Emergency Management Agency Under Contract Number 282-98-0029," (2002), 3.

62.   Based on a systems theoretical perspective, a five-level risk model of the (re-) insurance system, illustrating the spread of risk between the involved institutions, was developed in Rohland, *Sharing the Risk*, 9–13.

63.   If a specialized reinsurer's risk portfolio were to coincide exactly with that of its cedent (the insurer), both would incur "catastrophic loss," hence the principle of reinsurance is to sign treaties with insurance companies worldwide to spread this risk of loss geographically as widely as possible. This principle was stated in Moritz Ignatz Grossmann's "Expertise on the Foundation of a Reinsurance Company," the founding document of Schweizerische Rückversicherungsgesellschaft (today *Swiss Re*). See Rohland, *Sharing the Risk*, 28.

64.   Insurance regulation as subject to state authority was confirmed by the McCarran-Ferguson Act of 1945, 59 Stat. 34 1937–1946, PL 15. See also Robert Klein, "Regulation and Catastrophe Insurance," in *Paying the Price: The Status and Role of Insurance*

Against Natural Disasters in the United States, ed. Howard Kunreuther and Richard J. Roth (Washington, DC: Joseph Henry Press, 1998), 173–74.

65. This point becomes evident from the debate about the different modes of disaster insurance where reinsurance is always discussed as granted by the federal government. See Kunreuther, "Disaster Insurance," 157; Howard Kunreuther, "Disaster Insurance: A Tool for Hazard Mitigation," *Journal of Risk and Insurance* 41, no. 2 (1974), 301; Howard Kunreuther, "The Changing Societal Consequences of Risks from Natural Hazards," *Annals of the American Academy of Political and Social Science* 443 (1979), 115.

66. As late as 1957 an article in the *Insurance Journal* noted the development of the U.S. insurance market toward multiple-multiple line insurance. However, this change was not seen in terms of risk diversification but rather as a development of expanding business. James Roland McPherson, "Multiple-Multiple Lines," *Journal of Insurance* 24, no. 1 (1957), 145.

67. Welf Werner, *Die späte Entwicklung der amerikanischen Rückversicherungswirtschaft. Eine Branchenstudie zur internationalen Wettbewerbsfähigkeit* (Berlin: Duncker & Humblot, 1993), 127–33, 29. In the 1913–14 session of the New York legislature, an amendment of the insurance law was debated which would have allowed insurance and reinsurance businesses licensed for that state to insure all kinds of risks, rather than being restricted to only one branch of underwriting. The bill was rejected with the argument it was not in line with the American system of insurance. Apart from the argument of tradition, nationalist overtones of the pre–World War I era had their own share in halting the endeavor to change the structure of the American insurance market when it was argued that the passage of this bill "might perhaps be a forerunner of the adoption in this country of a new system for the regulation of insurance companies, which had been vaguely referred to by advocates of the bill as the system obtaining in Europe." As quoted in Kopf, "Reinsurance," 72.

68. Meistrell, Speech at Convention of National Association of Insurance Commissioners, December 4, 1956, NARA, RG 207.7.5, General Records of the Dept. of HUD, Flood Insurance Studies of Dr. Marion Clawson (1966–68), Box 5, Folder "Miscellaneous Material"; Overman, "Flood Peril," 102.

69. In June 1965 a total of 240 disaster declarations had been made by the president since the enactment of the Federal Disaster Assistance Act of 1950 (PL 81-875) and some $305 million ($2.3 billion in 2016) relief funds had been allocated from the federal treasury. Dryden, Address, 30 June 1965, NARA, RG 396, Disaster Insurance Files (1967), A1/Entry 1052, 650:42, 8, 03, Box 1, Folder "Natural Disaster Insurance 1965."

70. Ellington to Johnson, Memorandum for the President. Disaster Insurance, 30 July 1965, NARA, RG 396, Disaster Insurance Files (1967), A1/Entry 1052, 650:42, 8, 03, Box 1, Folder 9 "Natural Disaster Insurance."

71. Brewton to Ellington, Memorandum for the Director. Disaster Insurance, 12 August 1965, NARA, RG 396, Disaster Insurance Files (1967), A1/Entry 1052, 650:42, 8, 03, Box 1, Folder 9 "Natural Disaster Insurance."

72. Ibid.; Brewton to Ellington, 23 July 1965, NARA, RG 396, Disaster Insurance Files (1967), A1/Entry 1052, 650:42, 8, 03, Box 1, Folder "Natural Disaster Insurance 1965."

73. Brewton to Ellington, Memorandum for the Director, Disaster Insurance, 12 August 1965, NARA, RG 396, Disaster Insurance Files (1967), A1/Entry 1052, 650:42, 8, 03, Box 1, Folder 9 "Natural Disaster Insurance."

74. Robert C. Bly, "The Prospects for a Federal Disaster Insurance Program," *Insurance Law Journal* October (1966), 601.

75. Ellington to Johnson, Memorandum for the President, Disaster Insurance, 30 July 1965, NARA, RG 396, Disaster Insurance Files (1967), A1/Entry 1052, 650:42, 8, 03, Box 1, Folder 9 "Natural Disaster Insurance."

76. Southeast Hurricane Disaster Relief Act.

77. Lewis, "Some Reflections," in Dryden to Rogers, 22 March 1966, NARA, RG 396, Disaster Insurance Files (1967), A1/Entry 1052, 650:42, 8, 03, Box 1, Folder 3 "Natural Disaster Insurance 1966," (original uppercase).

78. The memorandum stated that "by spreading the coverage to all hazard insurance throughout the nation the insurance premium rate will be very low." Anon., "All-Risk Hazard Insurance," 8 December 1969, NARA, RG 396, Disaster Insurance Files (1967), A1/Entry 1052, 650:42, 8, 03, Box 1, Folder 3 "Natural Disaster Insurance 1966."

79. Dryden to Rogers, 22 March 1966, NARA, RG 396, Disaster Insurance Files (1967), A1/Entry 1052, 650:42, 8, 03, Box 1, Folder 3 "Natural Disaster Insurance 1966."

80. In his comparison between the development of the German and the U.S. flood insurance systems, Uwe Lübken also briefly mentions the Swiss case, which is a working example of such an all-inclusive disaster insurance program (*Elementarschadenversicherung*, literally elementary damage insurance), see Lübken, "Gefahr," 16–17; and Thomas R. Ungern-Sternberg, *Efficient Monopolies: The Limits of competition in the European property insurance market* (Oxford, UK: Oxford University Press, 2004), 105–24.

81. The leading researcher of the study was Robert Marion Clawson (known as Marion Clawson), an agricultural economist and government official who had traveled internationally to advise countries on issues of environmental and natural resources. For the study he cooperated with the American Insurance Association, a trade organization representing the property/casualty sector of the insurance industry, see Forest History Society, "Inventory of the Marion Clawson Papers, 1927–1994," https://foresthistory.org/research-explore/archives-library/fhs-archival-collections/inventory-marion-clawson-papers-1927-1994/; and Congressional Record, Appendix, *Flood Protection Progress for our Area,* Extended Remarks by Hon. Hale Boggs, 23 May 1966, A2749-51, NARA, RG 200, Civilian Agency Records, Red Cross Central File, 200-85-33-100, 130: 79, 45, 3-4, Box 78.

82. Weaver to Califano, "Some notes . . . ," 29 April 1966, NARA, RG 396, Disaster Insurance Files (1967), A1/Entry 1052, 650:42, 8, 03, Box 1, Folder 3 "Natural Disaster Insurance 1966." This was the first time Congress was confronted with regulating insurance transactions across state borders, since the South-East Underwriters' Association infringed upon the Sherman Anti-Trust Act. The effect of the Supreme Court's decision on *U.S. v. South-East Underwriters' Association* was to withdraw from the states the authority to regulate insurance and confer it to the national government. U.S. Supreme Court, *United States v. Southeast Underwriters Association, 322 U.S. 533* (1944), http://supreme.justia.com/cases/federal/us/322/533/case.html., 581.

83. On insurance regulation and the federal government see Klein, "Regulation," 205.

84. Mackenzie and Weisbrot, *Liberal Hour,* 79.

85. The Commerce clause states that Congress shall have the power "to regulate Commerce with foreign Nations, and among the several States, and with the Indian

Tribes." House of Representatives, *The Constitution of the United States of America. As Amended. 110th Congress, 1st Session, Document No. 110-50* (Washington, DC: Government Printing Office, July 2007), Art I, §8, Clause 3. The Necessary and Proper clause provides that "the Congress shall have Power to make all Laws which shall be necessary and proper for carrying into Execution the foregoing Powers, and all other Powers vested by this Constitution in the Government of the United States, or in any Department or Officer thereof." Ibid., Art. I, §8, Clause 18.

86. Randy E. Barnett, "No Small Feat: Who Won the Obamacare Case (and Why Did So Many Law Professors Miss the Boat)?," *Georgetown Public Law and Legal Theory Research Paper,* no. 13-009 (2013), http://scholarship.law.georgetown.edu/fac pub/1176., 2, fn. 4 ("compel individuals not"); 3 ("compulsion to engage," "granting the Congress").

87. OEP, "OEP's Position on Disaster Insurance," June 16, 1966, NARA, RG 396, Disaster Insurance Files (1967), A1/Entry 1052, 650:42, 8, 03, Box 1, Folder "Natural Disaster Insurance 1966."

88. HUD and U.S. Congress, House Committee on Public Works, *Insurance and Other Programs for Financial Assistance to Flood Victims. A Report from the Secretary of the Department of Housing and Urban Development to the President, as Required by the Southeast hurricane Disaster Relief Act of 1965, Public law 89-339, 89th Congress, H.R. 11539, November 8, 1965* (Washington, DC: U.S. Government Printing Office, 1966).

89. Ibid., 14 ("floods are by"); Bowman to Brewton, Memorandum, 19 July 1966, NARA, RG 396, Disaster Insurance Files (1967), A1/Entry 1052, 650:42, 8, 03, Box 1, Folder "Natural Disaster Insurance 1966"; Beal to Philipps, Housing and Urban Development Report, n.d., NARA, RG 396, Disaster Insurance Files (1967), A1/Entry 1052, 650:42, 8, 03, Box 1, Folder "Natural Disaster Insurance 1966"; Phillips to Brewton, HUD Report on Insurance, 22 July 1966, NARA, RG 396, Disaster Insurance Files (1967), A1/Entry 1052, 650:42, 8, 03, Box 1, Folder "Natural Disaster Insurance 1966."

90. Kunreuther, "Natural Disaster Insurance," 180.

91. Bowman to Brewton, Memorandum, 19 July 1966, NARA, RG 396, Disaster Insurance Files (1967), A1/Entry 1052, 650:42, 8, 03, Box 1, Folder "Natural Disaster Insurance 1966."

92. Klein, "Regulation," 196.

93. Chapter 9 of the report discussed several approaches to flood insurance: all private industry, public–private partnership, the private industry operating a federal program, or an all-federal program. In none of these cases was mandatory coverage mentioned as an option of cost bearing. HUD and U.S. Congress, *Insurance,* 98–102.

94. Ibid., 38.

95. Ibid.

96. Stokley to Blee, Expanded Program in the Natural Disaster Field, 10 June 1966, NARA, RG 396, Disaster Insurance Files (1967), A1/Entry 1052, 650: 42, 8, 03, Box 1, Folder "Natural Disaster Insurance 1966."

97. Kunreuther, "Disaster Insurance," 152.

98. Joint Resolution (draft), 10 August 1966, NARA, RG 396, Disaster Insurance Files (1967), A1/Entry 1052, 650:42, 8, 03, Box 1, Folder "Natural Disaster Insurance 1966."

99. The draft of this joint resolution bears no office seal or other identification of authorship, but it is clear from the overall idea of disaster insurance, as well as from some of

the phrasing of the document (almost identical with that of earlier correspondence), that it was worked out by the OEP or in close collaboration with its officials.

100. Joint Resolution (draft), 10 August 1966, NARA, RG 396, Disaster Insurance Files (1967), A1/Entry 1052, 650:42, 8, 03, Box 1, Folder "Natural Disaster Insurance 1966," 1–3 ("by creating," "the blanket effect").

101. Bills and joint resolutions are the two forms most frequently used to introduce legislation into Congress. Either may originate in either the Senate or the House of Representatives. See LoC, "Laws."

102. Merker to Brewton, Draft of Proposed Legislation, 6 December 1966, NARA, RG 396, Disaster Insurance Files (1967), A1/Entry 1052, 650:42, 8, 03, Box 1, Folder "Flood Insurance Legislation." In a 1965 memorandum to OEP's director Buford Ellington, Charles Brewton had described Merker as his legal advisor who had helped to bring to life the Federal Employee's Group Life insurance program as well as the Federal Employee's Health Benefits program. See Brewton to Ellington, Memorandum, 23 July 1965, NARA, RG 396, Disaster Insurance Files (1967), A1/Entry 1052, 650:42, 8, 03, Box 1, Folder "Natural Disaster Insurance 1965."

103. Merker to Brewton, Draft of Proposed Legislation, 6 December 1966, NARA, RG 396, Disaster Insurance Files (1967), A1/Entry 1052, 650:42, 8, 03, Box 1, Folder "Flood Insurance Legislation," 2.

104. My notion of *path dependence of practice* is informed by Paul Pierson's discussion of power structures and path dependence within politics. Pierson, "Increasing Returns," 259–63; and Barry Barnes, "Practices as Collective Action," in *The Practice Turn in Contemporary Theory*, ed. Theodore R. Schatzki, Karin Knorr Cetina, and Eike von Savigny (London: Routledge, 2001).

105. National Flood Insurance Act, 82 Stat. 581 1968, P.L. 90-448.

106. In 1979 FIA was transferred to the newly set up Federal Emergency Management Agency (FEMA). Edward T. Pasterick, "The National Flood Insurance Program," in Kunreuther and Roth, *Paying the Price*, 128.

107. National Flood Insurance Act, 82 Stat. 581 1968, P.L. 90-448, 582, 584. The program started out as a public-private partnership with 125 private insurance companies forming the National Flood Insurance Association. They marketed the NFIP, collected premiums and paid indemnifications, while the federal government acted as a reinsurer. Due to a dispute over authority and financial control, the government decided to change the NFIP to become all-federal in 1977. Only in 1983 did private companies become involved again. See Pasterick, "Flood Insurance," 134.

108. Ibid., 128; Raymond J. Burby, "Flood Insurance and Floodplain Management: the US Experience," *Environmental Hazards* 3 (2001), 112.

109. Kunreuther, "Hazard Mitigation," 288.

110. Flood Disaster Protection Act, 87 Stat. 975 1973–1974, P.L. 93-234.

111. For comprehensive overviews over the NFIP's mandatory coverage requirement, see Ernest B. Abbott, "Floods, Flood Insurance, Litigation, Politics—and Catastrophe. The National Flood Insurance Program," *Sea Grant Law and Policy Journal* 1, no. 1 (2008), 138–42; and Richard J. Tobin, Corinne Calfee, "The National Flood Insurance Program's Mandatory Purchase Requirement. Policies, Processes, and Stakeholders," American Institutes for Research, Washington, DC (2005).

112. Burby, "Flood Insurance," 112. It took as long as 1998, for 18,760 out of 21,000 communities identified as at risk of flooding to join the NFIP. Pasterick, "Flood Insurance," 129, 141.

113. Flood Insurance Reform Act, 108 Stat. 2255 1994, P.L. 103-325.

114. Pasterick, "Flood Insurance," 141.

115. Burby, "Flood Insurance," 114.

116. Pasterick, "Flood Insurance," 138.

117. Burby, "Flood Insurance," 118. For further problems troubling the NFIP see ibid., 114–19, and Pasterick, "Flood Insurance," 140–53.

118. I am aware of the political implications such a statement may have in the United States. Yet, from the point of view of insurance as adaptation, mandatory all-risk disaster insurance appears to be the soundest program option. See also Howard Kunreuther and Erwann O. Michel-Kerjan, "Comprehensive Disaster Insurance. Will it Help in a Post-Katrina World?," in *Natural Disaster Analysis after Hurricane Katrina: Risk Assessment, Economic Impacts and Social Implications*, ed. Harry W. Richardson, Peter Gordon, and James E. Moore II (Cheltenham, UK: Edward Elgar, 2008), 28–29.

119. Howard Kunreuther, "Disaster Mitigation and Insurance: Learning from Katrina," *Annals of the American Academy of Political and Social Science* 604, no. 1 (2006), 208.

120. Raymond Burby identifies subsidized insurance premiums that do not reflect the actual risk of loss as one reason for further property development in flood zones. Burby, "Flood Insurance," 115.

121. In his article on insurance as part of human security, Cornel Zwierlein has pointed to the aura of progress and modernity that enveloped the insurance business emerging in late seventeenth-century Britain and Germany. Some of this enlightenment bias persists, in particular in the perception that insurance would be a boon to developing countries in the grip of climate change. See Cornel Zwierlein, "The Production of Human Security in Premodern and Contemporary History," *Historical Social Research* 35, no. 4 (2010), 257; and Cornel Zwierlein, "Security, Nature and Mercantilism in the Early British Empire," *European Journal for Security Research* (2017).

CHAPTER 7

Adaptive Practices, Past and Present

The choice to follow adaptation across three hundred years through the history of New Orleans was based on the premise that adaptive practices evolve over time in environments in which natural extreme events are endemic and, hence, will challenge societies repeatedly. Throughout, the relativist conception of adaptation has revealed some of the complexity of human life in a hazard-prone environment. For any historical study of adaptation, it is crucial to conceive of adaptation as a process involving cultural practices of interaction with the environment. In varying temporal cuts through history, we have followed the adaptive practices of levee building, disaster migration, evacuation, disaster relief, and flood insurance, as well as the factor of political vulnerability. In the history of New Orleans these practices had their own temporality and emerged in a specific cultural, sociopolitical, and economic context that shaped them in a particular way.

The most striking facets of levee-building technology as a means to adapt to New Orleans's flood-prone environment are, on the one hand, the fact that it was an imported technology with its own history of problems in France, and on the other hand, the path dependence connected with introducing this technology in an unfamiliar environment. However, once the levees were a reality it was difficult to change them on a large scale. This path dependence of French levee technology on the Mississippi led to a reduplication of the Colbert-era discussion of spillways. In the United States the debate unfolded some two hundred years later, before and after the Great Mississippi Flood of 1927, under the keyword "levees only." While the problems and constraints of the levee technology were of relatively minor consequence in a sparsely populated colonial setting, they were of a different order in a more populous, more industrialized, and more interconnected world in the nineteenth and twentieth centuries.

In other words, the crucial point is not whether levee building was a successful adaptive practice in the first place. Rather, the central factor in technological adaptation and vulnerability is time. Even if colonial authorities had had a reason for wanting to foresee New Orleans's urban growth, they could not have imagined the size and layout of the city as it emerged in the twentieth or twenty-first century. Yet, the city's present-day and future generations will have to deal with the accumulated legacy of those early French colonial decisions. The longevity of adaptive structures such as levees and their innate entanglements with the sociopolitical and institutional level may prompt rethinking the meaning of long-term urban planning in the present.

While I have concentrated on disaster migration and its effects during the eighteenth century, this practice continued throughout the nineteenth, the twentieth, and, with Hurricane Katrina (2005) and the recent Hurricanes Harvey, Irma, and Maria (2017), even during the twenty-first century. During the eighteenth century disaster migration as a form of nonadaptation to New Orleans and its environs was a factor that made both the French and the Spanish colonial governments vulnerable. This vulnerability was a result of the loss of population in specific areas around New Orleans where it was needed either for strategic purposes—as a buffer against enemy invasions—or for the agricultural and economic development of the colony. Even general migration, unrelated to natural hazards, could have a detrimental effect on New Orleans when it came to adapting to the flood hazard. Levees on abandoned properties upriver from the city would breach eventually, flooding the neighbors' properties and sometimes even the city territory, thus causing the loss of crops and creating a health hazard for the whole community.

However, post-disaster migration continued to affect New Orleans beyond the colonial period. Even if it was not New Orleanians who left the city after the Cheniere Caminada Hurricane in 1893, the fact that the island's inhabitants abandoned their destroyed homes worried the city's merchant class. In the perception of its members, the loss of this fishing community threatened the city's trade in seafood and thus appeared to be a setback in an era that saw the progress of the city through the introduction of its modern drainage system.[1] Disaster migration occurred again in the aftermath of Hurricane Katrina in 2005. However, since for many evacuees leaving New Orleans for sometimes far-away cities in the United States was not voluntary, this process in many cases must be called displacement.[2] The slow return of residents to the city, often owing to financial inability to return and rebuild, reduced the city's tax base and in turn made it difficult to restart infrastructural services basic to a city's existence, such as gas and electricity, garbage disposal, hospitals, public transport, schools, and postal services. In a vicious circle this kept more people from returning and hence from stabilizing the tax base.[3] Though the French and Spanish colonial cases of disaster migration occurred on a different scale and in a technologically less interconnected urban environment, ultimately the effect of losing important parts of the citizenry put the economic development and societal cohesion of the city at risk, at least temporarily. So, while there are differences across time, the similarities with the present and well-known cases may help us appreciate the severity of the historical situations.

As opposed to disaster migration, evacuation is an adaptive practice geared only toward a temporary removal from a hazardous area but with a clear intention of returning to the hazard-prone place of settlement after the danger for human life has passed. Evacuation in New Orleans meant moving to sturdier buildings within the city until long after Hurricane Betsy in 1965.[4] It seems that intra-urban site evacuation sufficed as a practice to protect one's life against hurricanes into the 1990s, when an increase in active hurricane seasons, soil subsidence, and rising sea levels started impacting the city.[5] As hurricanes have remained uncontrollable natural extreme events to this day—despite attempts at hurricane seeding (dissolving hurricanes with silver iodide) in the 1960s[6]— evacuation has remained the only real adaptive practice capable of moderating harm to life on an increasingly densely populated Louisiana Gulf Coast and in New Orleans. Yet, with reference to Katrina, it is also evident that as long as out-of-town evacuation is dependent on private transportation and funds, an element of social inequality emerges that makes this practice more adaptive for the wealthier part of the population while it renders the less affluent vulnerable. In particular in an urban environment where on-site evacuation may be increasingly insufficient with rising sea levels due to global warming.

Rising population numbers and a turnover in social, racial, and ethnic composition of the population in and around New Orleans due to (forced) migration revealed the political vulnerability of an economic and governance system based on the institution of slavery in the hurricane of 1812. The coincidence with a war and with the integration process of the new Louisiana territory, peopled by a culturally "foreign" society, amplified this vulnerability. This amplification was expressed by a heightened concern about national and internal security that was not only directed against the white, francophone population of Louisiana but also very specifically against the substantial numbers of enslaved Africans and free people of color who had taken refuge in New Orleans in the aftermath of the Haitian Revolution. The amplified political vulnerability furthermore found its expression in the installation of the first territorial police force and in an increased military presence in New Orleans.

Colonial governments had granted disaster relief in monetary form as early as the eighteenth century. This becomes evident during New Orleans's Spanish period, when Governor Carondelet requested 3,000 pesos of disaster relief money from the government in Havana and Intendant Rendon distributed alms among the stricken farmers below New Orleans (see chapter 3). Early post-hurricane emergency management largely consisted in organizing emergency food provisions, often through the illicit Caribbean trade network, in order to overcome food shortages caused by destroyed crops. At the beginning of the nineteenth century federal disaster relief to communities—rather than to individuals—started taking shape in the context of war, namely in the aftermath of the War of 1812.[7] However, organized local hurricane disaster relief and concerted search-and-rescue operations in New Orleans only developed between the Last Island Hurricane in 1856 and the Cheniere Caminada Hurricane of 1893. After this hurricane we see a change in the institutionalization of disaster relief. Where, during the yellow fever epidemic of 1878, as many as forty benevolent societies had been providing relief to victims, activities were centralized and streamlined through the CCSRC in the aftermath of the Cheniere Caminada Hurricane.

Evidence from the historical record suggests that New Orleans's CCSRC was an ad hoc, local, and voluntary committee that was formed as occasion arose and disassembled when its work was done. The tasks the committee had acquired out of necessity ranged from search and rescue operations, raising and distributing funds, to the distribution of building materials and food stuffs, to helping to rebuild destroyed houses. Today those tasks are divided between various governmental and private organizations such as FEMA, the Coast Guard, the Army, and different local and national volunteer groups. Although in 1893 the CCSRC was not the only organization involved in the relief of the Cheniere Caminada Hurricane victims, it clearly had taken on the central responsibility for the local relief organization. The Louisiana Red Cross Society, which one might think would have been the obvious agent for disaster relief operations, was not at the head of the local organization but rather was subsumed under the structure that emerged from the CCSRC's relief efforts.

If the CCSRC remained an ad hoc institution that formed in the aftermath of disasters, tasks that had a preventative character could, by definition, not figure among the possible actions of the committee. Only a permanent institution for which "after the hurricane" could become "before the hurricane" could have started pressuring for the adoption of safer building codes or, possibly, land use regulations on the local government level. However, it is unlikely that different institutional structures alone would have changed the adaptive capacity of the CCSRC and, consequently, of New Orleans and the downriver parishes. With a committee manned by the city's prominent merchants in whose interest it was that the fishing trade and tourist industry below New Orleans continued, introducing prohibitive land-use or zoning measures would have been counterproductive. Not least, the establishment of a local disaster relief institution during the second half of the nineteenth century is also connected with the general population growth in the parishes below New Orleans and is linked to the increased economic dependence of the city on the deltaic fishing communities and summer resorts toward the end of the nineteenth century.

None of the actions taken by the CCSRC involved the federal government in the month after the hurricane. Senator Donleson Caffery did attempt to acquire relief appropriations for Louisiana from Congress in November 1893, but apparently failed. Arguments against appropriating federal disaster relief for South Carolina and Louisiana underlined the difficult economic situation of the United States in the 1893 depression and the widespread hardship due to unemployment. The 1893 congressional debate revealed the importance of the national economic context for local adaptation, and again highlights the contingent combination of factors involved in adaptation.

The realization of a national disaster or flood insurance program, was closely connected to the long tradition of federal disaster relief appropriations by Congress. An increasing "socialization" of hurricane (and other) risk evolved as a consequence of the development of the United States as a polity. That is, between the mid-nineteenth and mid-twentieth centuries a shift occurred, from local adaptation and coping to involving state and federal level authorities on a large and institutional scale. The increased interconnectedness of the levels of disaster relief, on the one hand, also led to increased resilience against large-scale natural disasters, since federal financial back-up could save cities or regions from failing recovery in the aftermath of a disaster. On the other hand, the increased interconnectedness of the modern nation state could also create new forms of vulnerability, as large-scale, local disasters now also affected federal politics with their rising costs. The NFIP of 1968 was an attempt at spreading those costs more evenly at a point when the economic costs of appropriating disaster relief after the fact had become so high that a change in practice became pressing. However, the public–private NFIP that was introduced after Hurricane Betsy never fully replaced the disaster relief appropriated by Congress, nor has it ever become fully self-sustaining during its forty-year lifespan. On the contrary, the coexistence of both systems has undermined the functionality of the NFIP by creating a moral hazard.

In 1893 at the time of the Cheniere Caminada Hurricane, as well as in 1965 after Hurricane Betsy, the United States' national economy was strained, albeit to different degrees. In the nineteenth-century case it was because of a nationwide financial crisis; in the twentieth-century case a coincidence of several large-scale natural disasters made politicians feel they were restricted regarding the relief appropriations that were likely to be administered by Congress. Both of these case studies illustrate the effect of a strained national economy on local adaptation. This is an important point with regard to the mounting costs of natural disasters in present-day Western industrialized countries and their interconnectedness in national and global financial crises.

With regard to the connection between knowledge, technology, and adaptation it can be said that while there is a certain congruence of adaptation with industrialization and mechanization, there is no linearity to the co-emergence of adaptation with the industrialization process. Whether or not adaptation options were chosen or declined often depended on political decisions that were unrelated to technological progress. That is, building a hurricane port in New Orleans after the 1722 hurricane would have been technologically feasible, yet the directors of the Company of the West decided not to incur the costs of such a project. In other words, though certain adaptation options are dependent on technological development, the latter does not guarantee successful adaptation. Furthermore, the study of the NFIP has underlined that the outcome of adaptive practices on the systemic level is strongly related to ideas about the role of the federal state, political decisions, and the economic and legal underpinnings political systems rest on.

On the whole, adaptation to hurricanes in New Orleans has been characterized by ruptures and continuity alike. Ruptures in adaptation are expressed most strongly in the aspect of the untranslatability of environmental and hurricane knowledge across different political regimes. This is not to say that each of those successive political governments (and its populations) adapted less successfully than the preceding one. Rather, the knowledge gap and inexperience of newcomers created a lag in adaptation to the environment, and in turn, to hurricanes. This has been most evident in the case of Bernardo de Gálvez who came to New Orleans as the new Louisiana governor in 1777 and who strategically placed seven hundred Canary Islanders in the marshes below the city where they were swept consecutively by the 1779 and 1780 hurricanes. Though the placement of new settlers may have been strategically advantageous, it was not from an environmental perspective and with regard to the sustainability of the Spanish military strategy.

The example of the fort La Balize at the mouths of the Mississippi is further evidence of the difficulty of passing environmental knowledge from one governing system to another. It must remain open, however, how much of the resettlement attempts of the Spanish colonial regime and of the American period can really be attributed to environmental inexperience, or whether they would rather have to figure under sheer human tenacity to persist in a place considered economically or strategically valuable.

Transfer of hurricane knowledge occurred between indigenous populations and Spanish and French colonists in the sixteenth- and seventeenth-century Caribbean, as we have seen in chapter 1. At the beginning of the eighteenth century exchange of environmental knowledge between the native Americans and the French colonists in Louisiana focused on the Mississippi's flood levels. Yet, my sources have not allowed for a glimpse of such communication between the colonial and/or the American regimes that governed Louisiana throughout the researched period. It is quite possible that such communication did not exist (at least not in writing) since the knowledge of geographical specificities (including maps) remained well-guarded for strategic reasons and was not shared with competitor colonial powers. This discrepancy in the exchange of environmental knowledge between the different colonial and native agents in New Orleans and the Caribbean points to the importance of communication for adaptation. Local environmental knowledge, whether native American or French Creole, was crucial for each wave of newcomers. Hence, the relationship between those different groups and the dissemination of environmental knowledge could influence the ease and rapidity of adaptation to the new environment. Ruptures in environmental knowledge and adaptation went hand in hand with the political caesurae, the changing governments, that affected Louisiana and New Orleans.

On the whole, the 1890s brought an increase in vulnerability to hurricanes for the U.S. Gulf Coast population due to the death of Padre Viñes (1893) and the disruption of the connection between his hurricane warning system and the U.S. Weather Bureau. Though Viñes's successor continued his observations after the hurricane priest's death in July 1893, these data were apparently not available at the time of the Cheniere Caminada Hurricane, contributing to the high death toll on the barrier island and the Louisiana Gulf Coast. After the Spanish–American War in 1898, the connection between the Belen observatory and the U.S. Weather Bureau was severed for good. The Galveston Hurricane of 1900 became sad and stark proof of this increased vulnerability and for the loss and untranslatability of hurricane knowledge and science between different cultural and political systems. However, as in the example of the NFIP of the twentieth century, there could also be disrupting factors that prevented smooth or successful adaptation *within* one political system.

In contrast to caesurae in adaptation, processes of technological path dependence and the path dependence of practice emerged, both implying continuity albeit not necessarily in the positive sense that the term evokes. The continuity in path dependence could turn into an obstacle for adaptation processes by gradually forming patterns from which it became increasingly difficult to break free. I have already mentioned the technological path dependence the French created by importing their levee building tradition to Louisiana. The *path dependence of practice* emerged from negotiating the NFIP, and from the fact that the political stakeholders chose the familiar option of single-peril flood insurance, rather than spreading the insurance risk more broadly over all kinds of disasters and opting for an all-risk disaster insurance program. An even deeper layer of path dependence of practice emerged from the dispute about whether federal disaster or flood insurance could be mandated by law. The United States' specific historical relationship with taxation and the consequent evolution of legal practice around that subject significantly preconfigured the unfolding debate. In addition, the HUD report mentioned the "deep-seated American traits" of independence and self-reliance, which it traced back to the "extended pioneer period," hence showing how factors of cultural identity also influenced decision-making in a realm as seemingly rational as disaster insurance.[8] These cultural, sociopolitical, and legal traditions significantly shaped the field in the search for the best way to distribute the disaster risk, and hence to adapt on the level of the nation state. The path dependence of technology is, in fact, often connected to the path dependence of practice, for example in the case of institutions that emerge around levee building such as the Deichgräfe (dyke overseer) in early modern Germany, or the Mississippi River Commission.

Clearly, both sociopolitical and economic contexts with long periods of continuity as well as such without continuity affected adaptation to natural disasters. But also, with regard to the role of knowledge and technology adaptation processes were often slow and contingent. For example, none of the technologies helping to predict hurricanes since the 1940s, such as radiosondes, airplanes, radar, satellites, and computer technology was developed specifically *for* that purpose. The same is true for cars, television, and the mass use of which has enabled twentieth- and twenty-first-century coastal societies in the United States to evacuate in case of impending hurricane landfalls.

However, apart from contingent and comparatively slow processes in technological adaptation, moments of socioeconomic pressure acted as push-factors for the relatively rapid institutional adaptation in (local) disaster relief and (federal) flood insurance that culminated in 1893 and in 1965. After the Cheniere Caminada Hurricane in 1893, the CCSRC formed in part for charitable and humane reasons to help out the inhabitants of the downriver parishes. Yet, economic and social reasons loomed in the background. The fishing trade with settlements below the city had become important for New Orleans so that helping the hurricane victims to rebuild—or in the case of Cheniere arguing with them not to leave—was in the economic interest of the city. In addition, the prospect of hundreds of destitute disaster victims flocking to New Orleans seeking shelter, food, and employment acted as a further incentive to organize the CCSRC that enabled most of the storm sufferers to rebuild their livelihoods and continue their lives. The extent of disaster relief appropriations authorized by the Southeast Hurricane Disaster Relief Act after Hurricane Betsy in 1965 made clear to federal politicians that a different mode of cost-bearing for flood disasters in the United States had to be sought. The repeated expansion of federal disaster relief payments had reached a limit in 1965 and pushed federal agencies to come up with an alternative way of distributing the costs of hurricane/flood disasters in America.

More generally and in relation to the present, adaptation to natural hazards and their potentially disastrous effects may occur on different timescales that intersect in various ways but are not synchronized. Furthermore, adaptation to disasters is influenced by social, political, legal, and economic developments that need not be linked directly to adaptation. The emergence of adaptive practices is, hence, in many ways contingent and—in the case of technological adaptation—often dependent on coincidence. Nevertheless, the emergence of adaptive practices is not arbitrary but highly contextual, often depending on political, legal, or cultural traditions. This point is significant with regard to the research on limits and barriers to adaptation. Among other factors, such as biophysical, economic, social, and cultural constraints, this field also recognizes path dependence as one of the major criteria that limit adaptation to climate change. The longevity of the historical, cultural, and legal entanglement in the path dependence of practice that has emerged from the study of the NFIP may hence inform research on limits and barriers. The systemic aspect created by political and legal culture, influences the shape of political programs and forms a sort of background noise. This systemic fabric is often not visible at first sight when it comes to identifying limits and barriers to adaptation. Recognizing the contextuality and historicity of adaptive practices is also a crucial point when exporting such practices as insurance in the context of climate change adaptation policy. A historically informed and self-reflexive stance is called for by the Western/industrialized nations suggesting such programs to be implemented in countries of the global South.[9]

With regard to the different time scales, contingency, and coincidence mentioned above, it seems, therefore, that it is difficult or impossible to plan certain aspects of adaptation in a policy process, while others, pertaining to institutions, may be more easily projectable. Yet it has become evident throughout this study that adaptive practices have developed over time periods that lie beyond the usual scope of political institutions and the electoral cycle. Considering that we currently shift from adaptation as a contingent historical-driven to adaptation as a policy-driven planning process, this last point is crucial because it raises a variety of questions regarding democratic processes of decision-making, and regarding the maintenance of institutions and political programs across periods of thirty, fifty, or even one hundred years or longer. These periods are the windows projected by current climate change scenarios within which societies around the globe need to adapt and change their energy regimes to keep global warming within manageable bounds.

The emergence of adaptive practices across time depends on choices that are often neither rational nor determined by the environment. Those choices are made within sociocultural contexts in correspondence with specific environments. That is, adaptive practices are always embedded in those sociocultural-natural contexts and they change together with those contexts. In other words, adaptive practices coevolve with environment and society over time. This is why studying the history and genealogy of these practices is indispensable for understanding adaptation in the present. This holds true even at a moment in time when the temporal horizon that is opened between past experience and future projections has not only become shortened and uncertain regarding processes within society, as suggested by Koselleck for the age of modernity, but when the element of anthropogenic climate change puts the whole concept of "future of the past" in question.[10] Such a fundamental watershed moment in the applicability of past experience to the present and future might compel one to renounce history lightheartedly. However, if we only have a fragmentary understanding of complex human-environment interactions in the past, how are we to move forward into a possibly radically different future?

Notes

1. Colten, *Metropolis,* 83–89.
2. Oliver-Smith, "Disasters."
3. Amy Liu, Matt Fellowes, and Mia Mabanta, "Special Edition of the Katrina Index: A One-Year Review of Key Indicators of Recovery in Post-Storm New Orleans," *Brookings Institution Metropolitan Policy Program* (2006), http://www.brookings.edu/research/reports/2006/08/metropolitanpolicy-liu, 6–8.
4. So far, no historical evidence has come to light that could help date the beginning of intra-urban evacuation in New Orleans.
5. Campanella, *Dilemma,* 61, 321.
6. James Rodger Fleming, *Fixing the Sky: The Checkered History of Weather and Climate Control,* Columbia Studies in International and Global History (New York: Columbia University Press, 2010), 177–79. See also Joanne Simpson, Glenn W. Brier, and R. H. Simpson, "Stormfury Cumulus Seeding Experiment 1965: Statistical Analysis and Main Results," *Journal of the Atmospheric Sciences* 24, no. 5 (1967); Willoughby et al., "Project STORMFURY."
7. Dauber, *Sympathetic State,* 20, 23.
8. HUD and U.S. Congress, *Insurance,* 38.
9. On the "geopolitics of knowledge" and persisting, colonial structures in Climate Change Adaptation research see George Adamson, Matthew J. Hannaford, and Eleonora Rohland, "Re-thinking the Present: The Role of a Historical Focus in Climate Change Adaptation Research," *Global Environmental Change* (2018), 201.
10. Dipesh Chakrabarty described the implications of anthropogenic climate change for the academic field of history in Dipesh Chakrabarty, "The Climate of History: Four Theses," *Critical Inquiry* 35, no. 2 (2009).

Bibliography

Archival Sources

Archdiocesan Archives of New Orleans (AANO), New Orleans
Folder "Hurricanes"

Archives Nationales d'Outre-Mer (ANOM), Aix-en-Provence
Archives des Colonies (AC)
Série A: register 23, *Actes du Pouvoir Souverain*
Série C: registers 13 A and C, *Correspondance à l'arrivée en provenance de la Louisiane*

Archivo General de Indias (AGI), Sevilla
Papeles de Cuba
Audiencia de Santo Domingo

Historic New Orleans Collection (HNOC), New Orleans
Late Colonial and Early Territorial Louisiana Collection
Dominic You Papers 1812–13

Howard Tilton Memorial Library (HTML), Tulane University, New Orleans
Newspapers online database
Boston Gazette (Boston, MA)
Commercial Advertiser (New York, NY)
Lancaster Journal (Lancaster, PA)
National Gazette (Philadelphia, PA)
New York Herald (New York, NY)

Library of Congress, Washington, DC
Clara Barton Papers
Newspaper Collection: New Orleans Daily Picayune (New Orleans, LA)
U.S. Statutes at Large: Hein Online Database

Louisiana State Museum (LSM), New Orleans
Vertical File "Hurricanes"
James Parkerson Kemper Papers

National Archives and Records Administration I (NARA), Washington, DC
Records of the United States House of Representatives
RG 233 House of Representatives, 53rd Congress, 1st session, August 7, 1893-November 3, 1893

National Archives and Records Administration II (NARA), College Park (MD)
Records of the Office of Emergency Planning (OEP)
RG 311 Disaster Declaration Files (1965–71)
RG 311 Headquarters Disaster Declaration Files (1965–71)
RG 396 Records Relating to Emergency Preparedness, Office of the Director, Correspondence, Memorandums and other Records (1969–71)
RG 396 Disaster Insurance Files (1967)

General Records of the Department of Housing and Urban Development
RG 207.7.5 Flood Insurance Studies of Dr. Marion Clawson (1966–68)

Civilian Agency Records
RG 200 Red Cross Central File

New Orleans Public Library (NOPL), New Orleans
Acts and Deliberations of the Cabildo
August 18, 1769 to August 27, 1779
September 8, 1779 to June 25, 1784
January 1, 1788 to May 18, 1792
May 25, 1792 to April 10, 1795

Conseil de Ville de la Nouvelle Orléans
Official Proceedings, 1803–36
Messages from the Mayor, 1805–36
Letters, Petitions, and Reports, 1804–35

Victor Schiro Collection (1957–70)
Hurricane Betsy 1965

Literature

***, M. *Mémoires sur la Louisiane et la Nouvelle Orléans.* Paris: Ballard, 1804.
Abbott, Ernest B. "Floods, Flood Insurance, Litigation, Politics—and Catastrophe. The National Flood Insurance Program." *Sea Grant Law and Policy Journal* 1, no. 1 (2008): 129–55.
Abel, Wilhelm. *Massenarmut und Hungerkrisen im vorindustriellen Europa. Versuch einer Synopsis.* Hamburg, Germany: Parey, 1974.
Acosta Rodríguez, Antonio. *La Población de Luisiana española, 1763–1803.* Madrid: Ministerio de Asuntos Exteriores, 1979.
Adamson, George. "Institutional and community adaptation from the archives: A study of drought in western India, 1790–1860." *Geoforum* 55 (2014): 110–19.
Adamson, George, Matthew J. Hannaford, and Eleonora Rohland. "Re-thinking the Present: The Role of a Historical Focus in Climate Change Adaptation Research." *Global Environmental Change* (2018): 195–205.
Adger, W. Neil, Nigel W. Arnell, and Emma L. Tompkins. "Adapting to Climate Change: Perspectives across Scales." *Global Environmental Change* 15, no. 2 (2005): 75–76.
Adger, W. Neil, Jon Barnett, Nadine Marshall, and Karen L. O'Brien. "Cultural Dimensions of Climate Change Impacts and Adaptation." *Nature Climate Change* 3, February (2013), 112–117.

Adger, W. Neil, Suraje Dessai, Marisa Goulden, Mike Hulme, Irene Lorenzoni, Donald R. Nelson, Lars Otto Naess, Johanna Wolf, and Anita Wreford. "Are There Social Limits to Adaptation to Climate Change?" *Climatic Change* 93 (2009): 335–54.

Agamben, Giorgio. *State of Exception*. Chicago: University of Chicago Press, 2005.

Albrecht, Andrew C. "Indian-French Relations at Natchez." *American Anthropologist* 48, no. 3 (1946): 321–54.

Allain, Mathé. "French Emigration Policies. Louisiana, 1699–1715." In Conrad, *French Experience*, 106–14.

———. *Not Worth a Straw: French Colonial Policy and the Early Years of Louisiana*. Lafayette: Center for Louisiana Studies, University of Southwestern Louisiana, 1988.

Allemeyer, Marie Luisa. "'Dass man dem grausam Toben des Meeres nicht etwa kann Widerstand thun mit Gewalt.' Kontroversen um den Küstenschutz im 17. und 18. Jahrhundert." In *Inszenierungen der Küste*, edited by Norbert Fischer, Susan Müller-Wusterwitz and Brigitta Schmidt-Lauber, 87–106. Berlin: Reimer Verlag, 2007.

———. *"Kein Land ohne Deich . . . !" Lebenswelten einer Küstengesellschaft in der Frühen Neuzeit*. Veröffentlichungen des Max-Planck-Instituts für Geschichte 222. Göttingen: Vandenhoeck & Ruprecht, 2006.

American Institutes for Research. "A Chronology of Major Events Affecting the National Flood Insurance Program. Completed for the Federal Emergency Management Agency Under Contract Number 282-98-0029." American Institutes for Research, Washington, DC, 2002.

American Insurance Association. *Studies of Floods and Flood Damage, 1952–1955*. New York: Insurance Executives Association, 1956.

Aristotle. *Meteorologica*. Translated by Erwin Wentworth Webster. Oxford, UK: Oxford University Press, 1923.

Arsenault, Raymond. "The Public Storm. Hurricanes and the State in Twentieth Century America." In *American Public Life and the Historical Imagination*, edited by Wendy Gamber, Michael Grossberg, and Hendrik Hartog, 262–92. Notre Dame, IN: University of Notre Dame Press, 2003.

Bankoff, Greg. *Cultures of Disaster: Society and Natural Hazard in the Philippines*. London: Routledge Curzon, 2003.

Bardsley, Douglas K. "Limits to Adaptation or a Second Modernity? Responses to Climate Change Risk in the Context of Failing Socio-ecosystems." *Environment, Development and Sustainability* 17, no. 1 (1 February 2015): 41–55.

Barnes, Barry. "Practices as Collective Action." In *The Practice Turn in Contemporary Theory*, edited by Theodore R. Schatzki, Karin Knorr Cetina, and Eike von Savigny, 17–28. London: Routledge, 2001.

Barnett, Jon, Louisa S. Evans, Catherine Gross, Anthony S. Kiem, Richard T. Kingsford, Jean P. Palutikof, Catherine M. Pickering, et al. "From Barriers to Limits to Climate Change Adaptation: Path Dependency and the Speed of Change." *Ecology and Society* 20, no. 3 (2015).

Barnett, Randy E. "No Small Feat: Who Won the Obamacare Case (and Why Did So Many Law Professors Miss the Boat)?" *Georgetown Public Law and Legal Theory Research Paper* no. 13-009 (2013). http://scholarship.law.georgetown.edu/facpub/1176, accessed 29 August 2018.

Barnshaw, John. "Evacuation, Types of." In Penuel and Statler, *Encyclopedia of Disaster Relief*, 186–87.

Barry, John M. *Rising Tide: The Great Mississippi Flood of 1927 and How it Changed America*. New York: Simon & Schuster, 1997.

Barton, Clara. *The Red Cross in Peace and War*. Washington, DC: American Historical Press, 1910.

———. *The Red Cross: A History of This Remarkable International Movement in the Interest of Humanity*. Washington, DC: J. B. Lyon & Comp., 1898.

Bea, Keith. "The Formative Years. 1950–1978." In *Emergency Management: The American Experience, 1900–2010*, edited by Claire B. Rubin, 83–113. Boca Raton: CRC Press, 2012.

Beik, William. *A Social and Cultural History of Early Modern France*. Cambridge, UK: Cambridge University Press, 2009.

Bénard de La Harpe, Jean Baptiste. *Journal historique de l'établissement des Français à la Louisiane*. New Orleans: A.-L. Boimare, 1831.

Bennett, John William. *The Ecological Transition: Cultural Anthropology and Human Adaptation*. New York: Pergamon Press, 1976.

Berlin, Ira. *Many Thousands Gone: The First Two Centuries of Slavery in North America*. Cambridge, MA: Belknap Press, 1998.

Berube, Alan, and Steven Raphael. "Access to Cars in New Orleans." In *The Brookings Institution* (2005). Published electronically December 15, 2005. http://www.columbia .edu/itc/journalism/cases/katrina/Brookings%20Institution/2005-09-15%20Brook ings%20Transportation.pdf, accessed 30 July 2018.

Biet, Père Antoine. *Voyage de la France Equinoxiale en l'Île de Cayenne, Entrepris par les Francais en l'Année 1652*. Paris: Francois Clouzier, 1664.

"Biographical Directory of the United States Congress, 1774 to Present." http://bioguide .congress.gov/biosearch/biosearch.asp, accessed 2 February 2018.

Blassingame, John W. *Black New Orleans, 1860–1880*. Chicago: University of Chicago, 1973.

Bly, Robert C. "The Prospects for a Federal Disaster Insurance Program." *Insurance Law Journal* October (1966): 598–604.

Bohun, Ralph. *A Discourse Concerning the Origine and Properties of Wind with an Historicall Account of Hurricanes, and other Tempestuous Winds*. Oxford, UK: Printed by W. Hall for Tho. Bowman, 1671.

Bond, Bradley G., ed. *French Colonial Louisiana and the Atlantic World*. Baton Rouge: Louisiana State University Press, 2005.

Brasseaux, Carl A. "The Image of Louisiana and the Failure of Voluntary French Emigration, 1683–1731." In *Proceedings of the Fourth Meeting of the French Colonial Historical Society, April 6–8, 1978*, edited by Alf Andrew Heggoy and James J. Cooke. Washington, DC: Universtiy Press of America, 1979.

———. "A New Acadia. The Acadian Migrations to South Louisiana, 1764–1803." *Acadiensis* 15, no. 1 (1985): 123–32.

Buffon, Georges-Louis Leclerc, Compte de. "Preuves de la Théorie de la Terre. Article XV [15]. Des Vents Irréguliers, des Ouragans, des Trombes, et de Quelques Autres Phénomènes Causez par l'Agitation de la Mer et de l'Air." In Buffon, *Histoire Naturelle, Générale Et Particulière, Avec La Déscription Du Cabinet Du Roy*, 44 vols. Vol. 1. Paris:

Imprimerie Royale, 1749, 478–501. http://visualiseur.bnf.fr/ark:/12148/bpt6k97490d/
f8.image, accessed 30 July 2018.

Bull, Elias B. "Storm Towers of the Santee Delta." *South Carolina Historical Magazine* 81,
no. 2 (1980): 95–101.

Burby, Raymond J. "Flood Insurance and Floodplain Management: The US Experience."
Environmental Hazards 3 (2001): 111–22.

Büschges, Christian, ed. *Das Ende des alten Kolonialsystems,* Dokumente zur Europäischen
Expansion, vol. 8. Munich: C.H. Beck, forthcoming.

Butzer, Karl W., and Georgina H. Endfield. "Critical Perspectives on Historical Collapse."
Proceedings of the National Academy of Sciences 109, no. 10 (March 6, 2012): 3628–
31.

Calvert, Edgar B. "The Hurricane Warning Service and Its Reorganization." *Monthly
Weather Review* March (1935): 85–88.

Campanella, Richard. *Bienville's Dilemma: A Historical Geography of New Orleans.* Lafayette: Center for Louisiana Studies, University of Louisiana at Lafayette, 2008.

———. "Disaster and Response in an Experiment Called New Orleans, 1700s–2000s." *Oxford Research Encyclopedias: Natural Hazard Science* (2016).

———. "An Ethnic Geography of New Orleans." *Journal of American History* 94, no. 3
(2007): 704–15.

———. "The Evolution of Creole Architecture." *Times Picayune,* Friday, 8 April 2016.

———. *Geographies of New Orleans: Urban Fabrics Before the Storm.* Lafayette: Center for
Louisiana Studies, University of Southwestern Louisiana, 2006.

———. *Time and Place in New Orleans: Past Geographies in the Present Day.* Gretna, LA:
Pelican, 2002.

Carleton, Eleanor Beatrice. "The Establishment of the Electric Telegraph in Louisiana and
Mississippi." *Louisiana Historical Quarterly* 31, no. 2 (1948): 425–54.

Casas, Bartolomé de las, Feliciano Ramírez de Arellano Fuensanta del Valle, and José León
Sancho Rayón. *Historia de las Indias,* 5 vols. Vol. 2. Madrid: Imprenta de Miguel Ginesta, 1575/1875.

Castree, Noel, William M. Adams, John Barry, Daniel Brockington, Bram Büscher, Esteve
Corbera, David Demeritt, et al. "Changing the Intellectual Climate." *Nature Climate
Change* 4 (2014): 763.

Chakrabarty, Dipesh. "The Climate of History: Four Theses." *Critical Inquiry* 35, no. 2
(2009): 197–222.

Chambers, Henry E. *History of Louisiana.* Vol. 3. Chicago: American Historical Society,
1925.

Chaplin, Joyce E. *The First Scientific American: Benjamin Franklin and the Pursuit of Genius.*
New York: Basic Books, 2006.

Chávez, Thomas E. *Spain and the Independence of the United States: An Intrinsic Gift.* Albuquerque: University of New Mexico Press, 2002.

Chenoweth, Michael. "A Reasessment of Historical Atlantic Basin Tropical Cyclone Activity, 1700 to 1855." *Climatic Change* 76 (2006): 169–240.

Clark, Emily. "Refracted Reformations and the Making of Republicans." In Kastor and Weil,
Empires of the Imagination, 180–203.

Clark, John G. *New Orleans, 1718–1812: An Economic History.* Baton Rouge: Louisiana
State University Press, 1970.

———. "The Role of the City Government in the Economic Development of New Orleans. Cabildo and City Council, 1783–1812." In *The Spanish in the Mississippi Valley, 1762–1804,* edited by John Francis McDermott, 133–48, 1974.

Cline, Isaac Monroe. *Storms, Floods and Sunshine.* New Orleans: Pelican, 1945.

Colten, Craig E. *Perilous Place, Powerful Storms: Hurricane Protection in Coastal Louisiana.* Jackson: University Press of Mississippi, 2009.

———. *Southern Waters: The Limits to Abundance.* Baton Rouge: Louisiana State University Press, 2014.

———. *An Unnatural Metropolis: Wresting New Orleans from Nature.* Baton Rouge: Louisiana State University Press, 2005.

Conrad, Glenn R., ed. *The French Experience in Louisiana.* The Louisiana Purchase Bicentennial Series in Louisiana History. Lafayette: Center for Louisiana Studies, University of Southwestern Louisiana, 1995.

———. *The German Coast: Abstracts of the Civil Records of St. Charles and St. John the Baptist Parishes, 1804–1812.* Lafayette: Center for Louisiana Studies, University of Southwestern Louisiana, 1981.

Conte, René Le, and Glenn R. Conrad. "The Germans in Louisiana in the Eighteenth Century." *Louisiana History: Journal of the Louisiana Historical Association* 8, no. 1 (1967): 67–84.

Coumou, Dim, and Stefan Rahmstorf. "A Decade of Weather Extremes." *Nature Climate Change* 2 (2012): 491–96.

Cummins, Light Townsend. *Spanish Observers and the American Revolution, 1775–1783.* Baton Rouge: Louisiana State University Press, 1991.

Dart, Henry P. "The First Cargo of African Slaves for Louisiana, 1718." *Louisiana Historical Quarterly* 14, no. 2 (1931): 163–77.

Dart, Sally. "French Incertitude in 1718 as to a Site for New Orleans." *Louisiana Historical Quarterly* 15 (1932): 37–43.

Dauber, Michele Lenore Landis. "Helping Ourselves. Disaster Relief and the Origins of the American Welfare State." PhD Thesis, Northwestern University, 2003.

———. *The Sympathetic State: Disaster Relief and the Origins of the American Welfare State.* Chicago: University of Chicago Press, 2013.

David, Paul A. "Clio and the Economics of QWERTY." *American Economic Review* 75, no. 2 (1985): 332–37.

Dawdy, Shannon Lee. *Building the Devil's Empire? French Colonial New Orleans.* Chicago: University of Chicago Press, 2008.

DeGrummond, Jane Lucas. "Cayetana Susana Bosque y Fanqui. 'A Notable Woman.'" *Louisiana History* 22 (1982): 277–94.

Delsalle, Paul. *Vocabulaire Historique de la France Moderne. XVIe—XVIIe—XVIIIe Siècles.* 2nd ed. Paris: Armand Colin, 2007.

Derrida, Jacques. "Force of Law: The Mystical Foundation of Authority." Translated by Mary Quaintance. In *Deconstruction and the Possibility of Justice,* edited by Cornell Drucilla, Michael Rosenfeld, and David Gray Carlson, 3–67. New York: Routledge, 1992.

Dessens, Nathalie. "From Saint Domingue to Louisiana. West Indian Refugees in the Lower Mississippi Region." In Bond, *French Colonial Louisiana,* 244–64.

———. *From Saint-Domingue to New Orleans: Migration and Influences.* Gainesville: University Press of Florida, 2007.

————. "The Saint-Domingue Refugees and the Preservation of Gallic Culture in Early American New Orleans." *French Colonial History* 8 (2007): 53–69.

d'Iberville, Pierre Le Moyne. "Mémoire de D'Iberville sur le pays du Mississipi, La Mobile et ses environs, leurs rivières, les peuples qui les habitent, et du commerce qui se pourra faire dans moins de cinq ou six années, en établissant ce pays." In Magry, *Découverte par Mer,* "Quatrième Partie."

Diderot, Denis, and Jean le Rond d'Alembert. *Encyclopédie, ou Dictionnaire Raisonné des Sciences, des Arts et des Métiers, etc.* Chicago: University of Chicago, ARTFL Encyclopédie Project (Spring 2011 edition): 1751–80. http://encyclopedie.uchicago.edu/, accessed 2 February 2018.

Din, Gilbert. *Spaniards, Planters, and Slaves: The Spanish Regulation of Slavery in Louisiana, 1763–1803.* College Station: Texas A&M University Press, 1999.

Din, Gilbert C. "The Canary Islander Settlements of Spanish Louisiana. An Overview." *Louisiana History: Journal of the Louisiana Historical Association* 27, no. 4 (1986): 353–73.

————. "Carondelet, the Cabildo, and Slaves. Louisiana in 1795." *Louisiana History: Journal of the Louisiana Historical Association* 38, no. 1 (1997): 5–28.

Din, Gilbert, and John E. Harkins. *The New Orleans Cabildo: Colonial Louisiana's First City Government 1769–1803.* Baton Rouge: Louisiana State University Press, 1996.

Dinges, Martin. "Pest und Staat." In *Neue Wege in der Seuchengeschichte,* edited by Martin Dinges and Thomas Schlich, 71–103. Stuttgart, Germany: Steiner, 1995.

Dion, Roger. *Histoire des levées de la Loire.* Paris: CNRS Editions, 1961.

————. *Le Val de Loire. Étude de Géographie Régionale.* Tours, France: Arrault et Cie, 1933.

Ditchy, Jay K. "Census of Louisiana in 1721." *Louisiana Historical Quarterly* (1930): 214–29.

Donnelly, Jeffrey P., Andrea D. Hawkes, Philip Lane, Dana MacDonald, Bryan N. Shuman, Michael R. Toomey, Peter J. van Hengstum, and Jonathan D. Woodruff. "Climate Forcing of Unprecedented Intense Hurricane Activity in the Last 2000 Years." *Earth's Future* 3, no. 2 (2015): 49–65.

Dormon, James H. "The Persistent Specter: Slave Rebellion in Territorial Louisiana." *Louisiana History: Journal of the Louisiana Historical Association* 18, no. 4 (1977): 389–404.

Drum, Walter Mary. *The Pioneer Forecasters of Hurricanes.* Havana: Stormont & Jackson, 1905.

du Tertre, Jean-Baptiste. *Histoire générale des Antilles, habitées par les François,* 2 vols. Vol. 2. Paris: Thomas Iolly, 1667.

Dumont de Montigny, Jean-Francois-Benjamin. *Mémoires historiques sur la Louisiane.* 2 vols. Paris: Cl. J. G. Bauche, 1753.

Dunbar, William. "Meteorological Observations, Made by William Dunbar, Esq, at the Forest, Four Miles East of the River Mississippi, in Lat. 31 degrees 28 minutes North, and in Long. 91 degrees 30 minutes West of Greenwich, for the Year 1800." *Transactions of the American Philosophical Society* 6 (1809): 43–55.

Ellen, Roy F., and Holly Harris. "Introduction." In *Indigenous Environmental Knowledge and its Transformations: Critical Anthropological Perspectives,* edited by Roy F. Ellen, Peter Parkes, and Alan Bicker, 1–33. Amsterdam: Harwood, 2000.

Emanuel, Kerry. "A Century of Scientific Progress. An Evaluation." In Simpson et al., *Coping with Disaster,* 177–216.

———. *Divine Wind: The History and Science of Hurricanes.* Oxford: Oxford University Press, 2005.

———. "Downscaling CMIP5 Climate Models Shows Increased Tropical Cyclone Activity over the 21st Century." *Proceedings of the National Academy of Sciences* 110, no. 30 (July 23, 2013): 12219–24.

Encyclopedia Britannica Online. "Buys Ballot's Law." http://www.britannica.com/EB-checked/topic/86881/Buys-Ballots-Law, accessed 10 February 2018.

Endfield, Georgina H., and Isabel Fernández Tejedo. "Decades of Drought, Years of Hunger: Archival Investigations of Multiple Year Droughts in Late Colonial Chihuahua." *Climatic Change* 75, no. 4 (2006): 391.

Engler, Steven, Franz Mauelshagen, J. Werner, and Jürg Luterbacher. "The Irish Famine of 1740–1741: Famine Vulnerability and 'Climate Migration.'" *Climate of the Past* 9 (2013): 1161–79.

Ernest, John. *A Nation within a Nation: Organizing African-American Communities Before the Civil War.* The American Ways Series. Lanham, MD: Rowman & Littlefield, 2011.

Espy, James P. "Essays on Meteorology. Examination of Hutton's, Redfield's and Olmsted's theories." *Journal of the Franklin Institute of the State of Pennsylvania* 18, no. Aug (1836): 100–8.

———. *The Philosophy of Storms.* Boston: C.C. Little and J. Brown, 1841.

Falconer, Thomas, Robert Cavelier La Salle, and Henri de Tonti. *On the Discovery of the Mississippi, and on the South-western, Oregon, and North-Western Boundary of the United States.* London: S. Clarke, 1844.

Falls, Rose C. *Cheniere Caminada, or, The Wind of Death: The Story of the Storm in Louisiana.* New Orleans: Hopkins' Printing Office, 1893.

Favier, René. "Bordelais et Aquitains Face aux Inondations à la Fin du XVIIIe Siècle." In *Les Passions d'un Historien. Mélanges en l'Honneur de J.-P. Poussou*, 159–72. Paris: Presses de l'Université Paris-Sorbonne, 2010.

———. "Sociétés Urbaines et Culture du Risque. Les Inondations Dans la France d'Ancien Régime." In *Les Cultures du Risque (XVIe–XXIe siècle)*, edited by François Walter, B. Fantini, and Paul Delvaux, 49–86. Geneva: Presses d'Histoire Suisse, 2006.

Favier, René, and Anne-Marie Granet-Abisset. "Society and Natural Risks in France, 1500–2000. Changing Historical Perspectives." In Mauch and Pfister, *Natural Disasters*, 103–36.

Favier, René, and Christian Pfister. *Solidarité et Assurance. Les Sociétés Européennes Face aux Catastrophes (17e–21e Siècles).* Grenoble, France: CNRS MSH-Alpes, 2008.

Fleming, James Rodger. *Fixing The Sky: The Checkered History of Weather and Climate Control.* Columbia Studies in International and Global History. New York: Columbia University Press, 2010.

———. *Meteorology in America, 1800–1870.* Baltimore, MD: Johns Hopkins University Press, 1990.

Flink, James. *The Automobile Age.* Cambridge, MA: MIT Press, 1988.

Forest History Society. "Inventory of the Marion Clawson Papers, 1927–1994." http://www.foresthistory.org/ead/Clawson_Marion.html, accessed 8 February 2018.

Foret, Michael J. "The Failure of Administration: The Chickasaw Campaign of 1739–1740." In Conrad, *French Experience.*

Foucault, Michel. "Governmentality." In *The Foucault Effect: Studies in Governmentality*, edited by Graham Burchell, Colin Gordon and Peter Miller, 87–104. Chicago: Univeristy of Chicago Press, 1991.

Freemon, Frank R. "American Colonial Scientists Who Published in the 'Philosophical Transactions' of the Royal Society." *Notes and Records of the Royal Society of London* 39, no. 2 (1985): 191–206.

Fuchs, Karl, and Friedemann Wenzel. *Erdbeben. Instabilität von Megastädten. Eine wissenschaftlich-technische Herausforderung für das 21. Jahrhundert*. Schriften der Mathematisch-naturwissenschaftlichen Klasse der Heidelberger Akademie der Wissenschaften. Berlin: Springer-Verlag, 2000.

García Acosta, Virginia. "Building on the Past. Disaster Risk Reduction Including Climate Change Adaptation in the Longue Durée." In Kelman, Mercer, and Gaillard, *The Routledge Handbook*, 203–13.

García-Herrera, Ricardo, Luis Gimeno, Pedro Ribera, and Emiliano Hernández. "New Records of Atlantic Hurricanes from Spanish Documentary Sources." *Journal of Geophysical Research* 110 (2005). https://doi.org/10.1029/2004JD005272.

Geggus, David Patrick. "Saint-Domingue on the Eve of the Haitian Revolution." In *The World of the Haitian Revolution*, edited by David Patrick Geggus and Norman Fiering, 3–20. Bloomington: Indiana University Press, 2009.

Gergis, Joelle L., Don Garden, and Claire Fenby. "The Influence of Climate on the First European Settlement of Australia. A Comparison of Weather Journals, Documentary Data, and Paleoclimate Records, 1788–1793." *Environmental History* 15, no. July (2010): 485–507.

Germany, Kent B. "The Politics of Poverty and History. Racial Inequality and the Long Prelude to Katrina." *Journal of American History* 94, no. 3 (2007): 743–51.

———. "Presidential Recordings Program. LBJ and Senator Russell Long on Hurricane Betsy." Miller Center. University of Virginia, https://millercenter.org/the-presidency/educational-resources/lbj-and-senator-russell-long-on-hurricane-betsy, accessed 30 August 2018

Geschwind, Carl-Henry. *California Earthquakes: Science, Risk, and the Politics of Hazard Mitigation*. Baltimore, MD: Johns Hopkins University Press, 2001.

Giraud, Marcel. *Histoire de la Louisiane Française. L'Époque de John Law (1717–1720)*, 1st ed. 4 vols. Vol. 3, Paris: Presses Universitaires de France, 1953.

———. *Histoire de la Louisiane Française. Le Règne de Louis XIV*. 1 ed. 4 vols. Vol. 1, Paris: Presses universitaires de France, 1953.

———. "The Official Initiative." In Conrad, *French Experience*, 54–63.

Grand Dictionnaire Encyclopédique Larousse. "Lettre de Marque," 10 vols. Vol. 6. Paris: Librairie Larousse, 1984: 6245.

Green, Elna. "National Trends, Regional Differences, Local Circumstances. Social Welfare in New Orleans, 1870s–1920s." In *Before the New Deal: Social Welfare in the South, 1830–1930*, edited by Elna Green, 81–99. Athens: University of Georgia Press, 1999.

Greenwood, Isaac. "A New Method for Composing a Natural History of Meteors Communicated in a Letter to Dr. Jurin, R. S. & Coll. Med. Lond. Soc. By Mr. Isaac Greenwood, Professor of Mathematicks at Cambridge, New-England." *Philosophical Transactions* 35 (1727): 390–402.

Gutiérrez-Lanza, Mariano. *Apuntes Historicos Acerca del Observatorio del Colegio de Belén.* Havana: Avisador Comercial, 1904.

Hall, Gwendolyn Midlo. *Africans in Colonial Louisiana: The Development of Afro-Creole Culture in the Eighteenth Century.* Baton Rouge: Louisiana State University Press, 1992.

Halley, Edmund. "An Historical Account of the Trade Winds, and Monsoons, Observable in the Seas between and Near the Tropicks, with an Attempt to Assign the Phisical Cause of the Said Winds, By E. Halley." *Philosophical Transactions* 16, no. 179–91 (1686): 153–68.

Hannaford, Matthew J., and David J. Nash. "Climate, history, society over the last millennium in southeast Africa." *Wiley Interdisciplinary Reviews: Climate Change* (2016): 195–205.

Head, Lesley. "Cultural Ecology: Adaptation—Retrofitting a Concept?" *Progress in Human Geography* 34, no. 2 (2010): 234–42.

Heimer, Carol Anne. *Reactive Risk and Rational Action: Managing Moral Hazard in Insurance Contracts.* California Series on Social Choice and Political Economy. Berkeley: University of California Press, 1985.

Hickey, Donald R. *The War of 1812: A Forgotten Conflict.* Urbana: University of Illinois Press, 1989.

Higginbotham, Jay. *Old Mobile: Fort Louis de la Louisiane, 1702–1711.* Mobile, AL: Museum of the City of Mobile, 1977.

Hinshaw, Robert E. *Living with Nature's Extremes: The Life of Gilbert Fowler White.* Boulder, CO: Johnson Books, 2006.

Hoffmann, Charles. *The Depression of the Nineties: An Economic History.* Westport: Greenwood, 1970.

Hogue, James K. *Uncivil War: Five New Orleans Street Battles and the Rise and Fall of Radical Reconstruction.* Baton Rouge: Louisiana State University Press, 2006.

Holmes, Jack D. L. "The Abortive Slave Revolt at Pointe Coupée, Louisiana, 1795." *Louisiana History: Journal of the Louisiana Historical Association* 11, no. 4 (1970): 341–62.

———. "Indigo in Colonial Louisiana and the Floridas." *Louisiana History: Journal of the Louisiana Historical Association* 8, no. 4 (1967): 329–49.

House of Representatives. *The Constitution of the United States of America: As Amended.* 110th Congress, 1st Session, Document No. 110-50. Washington, DC: Government Printing Office, July 2007.

Hughes, J. Donald. "New Orleans: An Environmental History of Disaster." In *Natural Resources, Sustainability and Humanity: A Comprehensive View,* edited by Angela Mendonca, Ana Cunha and Ranjan Chakrabarti, 17–28. Dordrecht, Netherlands: Springer, 2012.

Humphreys, Margaret. *Yellow Fever and the South.* Baltimore, MD: Johns Hopkins University Press, 1992.

Huret, Romain. *Katrina, 2005. L'Ouragan, l'État et les Pauvres aux États-Unis.* Cas de Figure. Paris: Éditions EHESS, 2010.

Ingvar, David H. "'Memory of the Future': An Essay on the Temporal Organization of Conscious Awareness." *Human Neurobiology* 4, no. 3 (1985): 127–36.

Intergovernmental Policy on Climate Change (IPCC). "IPCC Factsheet. What is the IPCC." World Meteorological Organization (WMO), accessed 3 April 2018.

Irwin, Julia F. *Making the World Safe: The American Red Cross and a Nation's Humanitarian Awakening*. Oxford, UK: Oxford University Press, 2013.

Janku, Andrea, Gerrit Jasper Schenk and Franz Mauelshagen, eds. *Historical Disasters in Context: Science, Religion, and Politics*. New York: Routledge, 2012

Johnson, Sherry. *Climate and Catastrophe in Cuba and the Atlantic World in the Age of Revolution*. Envisioning Cuba. Chapel Hill: University of North Carolina Press, 2011.

Kadetz, Paul, and Nancy B. Mock. "Problematizing Vulnerability: Unpacking Gender, Intersectionality, and the Normative Disaster Paradigm." In *Creating Katrina, Rebuilding Resilience*, 215–30. Oxford, UK: Butterworth-Heinemann, 2018.

Kastor, Peter J. *The Nation's Crucible: The Louisiana Purchase and the Creation of America*. New Haven, CT: Yale University Press, 2004.

———. "'They Are All Frenchmen': Background and Nation in an Age of Transformation." In Kastor and Weil, *Empires of the Imagination*, 239–67.

Kastor, Peter J., and François Weil, eds. *Empires of the Imagination: Transatlantic Histories of the Louisiana Purchase*. Charlottesville: University of Virginia Press, 2009.

Keim, Barry D., and Robert A. Muller. *Hurricanes of the Gulf of Mexico*. Baton Rouge: Louisiana State University Press, 2009.

Kelman, Ari. *A River and Its City: The Nature of Landscape in New Orleans*. Berkeley: University of California Press, 2003.

Kelman, Ilan, Jessica Mercer, and J. C. Gaillard, eds. *The Routledge Handbook of Disaster Risk Reduction Including Climate Change Adaptation*. New York: Routledge, 2017.

Kemper, James Parkerson. *A.B.C. of the Flood Problem: A Discussion By J.P. Kemper, C.E. Consulting Engineer of the National Flood Prevention and River Regulation Commission*. New Orleans: National Flood Prevention and River Regulation Commission, 1927.

Klein, Robert. "Regulation and Catastrophe Insurance." In *Paying the Price: The Status and Role of Insurance Against Natural Disasters in the United States*, edited by Howard Kunreuther and Richard J. Roth, 171–207. Washington, DC: Joseph Henry Press, 1998.

Kopf, Edwin W. "Notes on the Origin and Development of Reinsurance." *Proceedings of the Casualty Actuary Society* 16 (1933): 22–91.

Koselleck, Reinhart. *Futures Past: On the Semantics of Historical Time*. Studies in Contemporary German Social Thought. Cambridge: MIT Press, 1985.

———. *Vergangene Zukunft. Zur Semantik geschichtlicher Zeiten*. Frankfurt am Main: Suhrkamp, 1989.

Kühn, Hans Joachim. *Die Anfänge des Deichbaus in Schleswig-Holstein*. Heide, Germany: Boyens, 1992.

Kuhn, Thomas S. "The Caloric Theory of Adiabatic Compression." *Isis* 49, no. 2 (1958): 132–40.

Kunkel, Paul A. "The Indians of Louisiana, about 1700: Their Customs and Manner of Living." In Conrad, *French Experience*, 248–68.

Kunreuther, Howard. "The Case for Comprehensive Disaster Insurance." *Journal of Law and Economics* April (1968): 133–63.

———. "The Changing Societal Consequences of Risks from Natural Hazards." *Annals of the American Academy of Political and Social Science* 443 (1979): 104–16.

———. "Disaster Insurance. A Tool for Hazard Mitigation." *Journal of Risk and Insurance* 41, no. 2 (1974): 287–303.

———. "Disaster Mitigation and Insurance. Learning from Katrina." *Annals of the American Academy of Political and Social Science* 604, no. 1 (2006): 208–27.

———. "Has the Time Come for Comprehensive Natural Disaster Insurance?." In *On Risk and Disaster: Lessons from Hurricane Katrina,* edited by Ronald J. Daniels, Donald F. Kettl, and Howard Kunreuther, 175–202. Philadelphia: University of Pennsylvania Press, 2006.

Kunreuther, Howard, and Erwann O. Michel-Kerjan. "Comprehensive Disaster Insurance. Will it Help in a Post-Katrina World?" In *Natural Disaster Analysis after Hurricane Katrina: Risk Assessment, Economic Impacts and Social Implications,* edited by Harry W. Richardson, Peter Gordon, and James E. Moore II, 8–33. Cheltenham, UK: Edward Elgar, 2008.

Kupperman, Karen Ordahl. "Apathy and Death in Early Jamestown." *Journal of American History* 66, no. 1 (1979): 24–40.

Kutzbach, Gisela. *The Thermal Theory of Cyclones: A History of Meteorological thought in the Nineteenth Century.* Historical Monograph Series. Edited by Society American Meteorological. Lancaster, PA: Lancaster Press, 1979.

Lachance, Paul. "The 1809 Immigration of Saint Domingue Refugees to New Orleans. Reception, Integration and Impact." *Louisiana History* 29 (1988): 109–41.

———. "The Louisiana Purchase in the Demographic Perspective of Its Time." In Kastor and Weil, *Empires of the Imagination,* 143–79.

———. "Repercussions of the Haitian Revolution in Louisiana." In *The Impact of the Haitian Revolution in the Atlantic World,* edited by David Patrick Geggus, 209–30. Columbia: University of South Carolina Press, 2001.

Lamb, Simon, and Paul Davis. "Cenozoic Climate Change as a Possible Cause for the Rise of the Andes." *Nature* 425 (2003): 792.

Langford, Captain, and Mr Bonavert. "Captain Langford's Observations of His Own Experience upon Huricanes, and Their Prognosticks. Communicated by Mr. Bonavert." *Philosophical Transactions (1683–1775)* 20 (1698): 407–16.

Larson, Erik. *Isaac's Storm: A Man, A Time, and the Deadliest Hurricane in History.* 1st ed. New York: Crown, 1999.

———. *Isaac's Storm: Isaacs Sturm.* Swiss Re Special ed. Zurich: Swiss Re, 1999.

Le Glaunec, Jean-Pierre. "Slave Migrations in Spanish and Early American Louisiana: New Sources and New Estimates." *Louisiana History: Journal of the Louisiana Historical Association* 46, no. 2 (2005): 185–209.

Le Page du Pratz, Antoine Simon. *Histoire de la Louisiane.* Paris: De Bure, la Veuve Delaguette, et Lambert, 1758.

Le Roy Ladurie, Emmanuel. *Histoire Humaine et Comparée du Climat. Canicules et Glaciers, XIIIe–XVIIIe Siècles.* Paris: Fayard, 2004.

———. *Histoire Humaine et Comparée du Climat. Disettes et Révolutions, 1740–1860.* Paris: Fayard, 2004.

Lewis, James E. "A Tornado on the Horizon: The Jeffersonian Administration, the Retrocession Crisis, and the Louisiana Purchase." In Kastor and Weil, *Empires of the Imagination,* 117–40.

Lewis, Peirce F. *New Orleans: The Making of an Urban Landscape.* Santa Fe, NM: Center for American Places, 2003.

Lichtblau, Stephen. "Preliminary Report—Hurricane Carla." Weather Bureau, http://www
.nhc.noaa.gov/archive/storm_wallets/atlantic/atl1961/carla/preloc/new03.gif, accessed
13 May 2013.

Liebwein, Peter. *Klassische und moderne Formen der Rückversicherung.* Karlsruhe: Verlag
Versicherungswirtschaft, 2000.

Lindsay, Bruce R., and Justin Murray. "Disaster Relief Funding and Emergency Supplemental Appropriations." In *CRS Report for Congress* (2011). Published electronically April
12, 2011. http://www.fas.org/sgp/crs/misc/R40708.pdf, accessed 30 August 2018.

Littlefield, Daniel C. "Colonial and Revolutionary United States." In *The Oxford Handbook
of Slavery in the Americas,* edited by Robert L. Paquette and Mark M. Smith, 201–26.
Oxford: Oxford University Press, 2010.

Liu, Amy, Matt Fellowes, and Mia Mabanta. "Special Edition of the Katrina Index. A One-
Year Review of Key Indicators of Recovery in Post-Storm New Orleans." *Brookings
Institution Metropolitan Policy Program* (2006): 1–15. https://www.brookings.edu/
research/special-edition-of-the-katrina-index-a-one-year-review-of-key-indicators-
of-recovery-in-post-storm-new-orleans/, accessed 30 August 2018.

Lopez Medel, Tomás. *De los Tres Elementos. Tratado Sobre la Naturaleza y el Hombre del
Nuevo Mundo,* edited by Berta Ares Quejia. 1570 ed. Madrid: Quinto Centenario, 1990.

Lowrey, Walter M. "The Engineers and the Mississippi." *Louisiana History: Journal of the
Louisiana Historical Association* 5, no. 3 (1964): 233–55.

Lübken, Uwe. *Die Natur der Gefahr. Überschwemmungen am Ohio River im neunzehnten
und zwanzigsten Jahrhundert.* Göttingen, Germany: Vandenhoeck & Ruprecht, 2014.

———. "Die Natur der Gefahr. Zur Geschichte der Überschwemmungsversicherung in
Deutschland und den USA." *Behemoth: A Journal on Civilisation* 1, no. 3. Special Issue:
Surviving Catastrophes (Anne Dölemeyer, Hg.) (2008): 4–20.

Ludlum, David McWilliams. *Early American Hurricanes, 1492–1870.* Boston: American
Meteorological Society, 1963.

Mackenzie, G. Calvin, and Robert Weisbrot. *The Liberal Hour: Washington and the Politics
of Change in the 1960s.* New York: The Penguin Press, 2008.

Maduell, Charles R. *The Census Tables for the French Colony of Louisiana from 1699 Through
1732.* Baltimore, MD: Genealogical Pub. Co., 1972.

Mann, Michael E., Jonathan D. Woodruff, Jeffrey P. Donnelly, and Zhihua Zhang. "Atlantic
Hurricanes and Climate over the Past 1500 Years." *Nature* 460, no. August 13 (2009):
880–85.

Margry, Pierre. "Découvertes et établissements des Français dans l'ouest et dans le sud de
l'Amérique septentrionale (1614–1754). Mémoires et documents originaux." In Magry,
*Découverte par Mer des Bouches du Mississippi et Établissments de Le Moyne D'Iberville
sur Le Golfe Du Mexique (1694–1703),* 6 vols. Vol. 4. Paris: Maisonneuve, 1881.

———. *Découvertes et établissements des Français dans l'ouest et dans le sud de l'Amérique
septentrionale (1614–1754): Mémoires et documents originaux. Première formation
d'une chaine de postes entre le fleuve Saint Laurent et le Golfe du Méxique (1683–1724),*
6 vols. Vol. 5. Paris: Maisonneuve, 1887.

Martin, Paulette Guilbert. "Les Ouragans de Louisiane de 1717 à 1750 et Leurs Effets sur la
Vie des Colons." *Revue de Louisiane/Louisiana Review* 4, no. 2 (1975): 29–36.

Mauch, Christof, and Christian Pfister, eds. *Natural Disasters, Cultural Responses: Case
Studies toward a Global Environmental History.* Lanham, MD: Lexington Books, 2009.

Mauelshagen, Franz. "Disaster and Political Culture in Germany since 1500." In Mauch and Pfister, *Natural Disasters*, 41–75.

———. *Klimageschichte der Neuzeit 1500—1900.* Geschichte kompakt. Darmstadt: WBG, 2010.

———. "Natural Disasters and Legal Solutions in the History of State Power." *Solutions* 4, no. 2 (2013): 65–68.

———. "Ungewissheit in der Soziosphäre. Risiko und Versicherung im Klimawandel." In *Unberechenbare Umwelt. Zum Umgang mit Unsicherheit und Nicht-Wissen,* edited by Roderich von Detten, Fenn Faber and Martin Bemmann, 252–69. Wiesbaden: Springer, 2013.

Mavrogenis, Stavros, Petros Theodorou, and Rory Walshe. "Climate Change Adaptation. A Critical Approach." In Kelman, Mercer, and Gaillard, *The Routledge Handbook,* 24–34.

Maynard, Trevor. "Climate Change. Impacts on Insurers and How They Can Help With Adaptation and Mitigation." *Geneva Papers* 33 (2008): 140–46.

McNeill, John R. *Mosquito Empires: Ecology and War in the Greater Caribbean, 1620–1914.* Cambridge, UK: Cambridge University Press, 2010.

McNeill, William Hardy. *The Global Condition: Conquerors, Catastrophes, and Community.* Princeton, NJ: Princeton University Press, 1992.

McPherson, James Roland. "Multiple-Multiple Lines." *Journal of Insurance* 24, no. 1 (1957): 145–50.

McSeveney, Samuel T. *The Politics of Depression: Political Behavior in the Northeast, 1893–1896.* New York: Oxford University Press, 1972.

Meier, Mischa. "Roman Emperors and 'Natural Disasters' in the First Century A.D." In Janku, Schenk, and Mauelshagen, *Historical Disasters in Context,* 15–30.

Menier, Marie-Antoinette, Etienne Taillemite, and Gilberte de Forges, eds. *Inventaire des Archives Coloniales. Correspondance à l'Arrivée en Provenance de la Louisiane.* 2 vols. Vol. 1. Paris: Archives Nationales, 1976.

Mereness, Newton Dennison. "Travels in the American Colonies." edited by National Society of the Colonial Dames of America. New York: Macmillan, 1916.

Meyer, William B. "Appendix A: Climate and Migration." In *The Role of Migration in the History of the Eurasian Steppe: Sedentary Civilization vs. "Barbarian" and Nomad,* edited by Andrew Bell-Fialkoff, 287–94. New York: St. Martin's Press, 2000.

Micelle, Jerry A. "From Law Court to Local Government. Metamorphosis of the Superior Council of French Louisiana." *Louisiana History: Journal of the Louisiana Historical Association* 9, no. 2 (1968): 85–107.

Millás, José Carlos, and Leonard Pardue. *Hurricanes of the Caribbean and adjacent regions, 1492–1800.* Miami, Fla.: Academy of the Arts and Sciences of the Americas, 1968.

Miller Surrey, Nancy M. "The Commerce of Louisiana During the French Regime, 1699–1763." Ph.D. thesis, Columbia University, New York, 1916.

Mitchem, Jamie D. "Hurricanes/Typhoons." In Penuel and Statler, *Encyclopedia of Disaster Relief,* 327–33.

Mock, Cary J. "Tropical Cyclone Reconstructions from Documentary Records. Examples for South Carolina, United States." In *Hurricanes and Typhoons: Past, Present, and Future,* edited by R. J. Murnane and K.-B. Liu, 121–48. New York: Columbia University Press, 2004.

Mock, Cary J., Michael Chenoweth, Isabel Altamirano, Matthew D. Rodgers, and Ricardo García-Herrera. "The Great Louisiana Hurricane of August 1812." *Bulletin of the American Meteorological Society* 91, no. 12 (2010): 1653–63.

Mooney, Chris. *Storm World: Hurricanes, Politics, and the Battle over Global Warming*. Orlando, FL: Harcourt, 2007.

Moore, John Preston. *Revolt in Louisiana: The Spanish Occupation, 1766–1770*. Baton Rouge: Louisiana State University Press, 1976.

Morris, Christopher. *The Big Muddy: An Environmental History of the Mississippi and its Peoples, from Hernando de Soto to Hurricane Katrina*. Oxford: Oxford University Press, 2012.

Moss, David A. "Courting Disaster? The Transformation of Federal Disaster Policy since 1803." In *The Financing of Catastrophe Risk*, edited by Kenneth A. Froot, 307–62. Chicago: University of Chicago Press, 1999.

Mouhot, Jean-Francois. *Les Réfugiés Acadiens en France, 1758–1785. L'Impossible Réintegration?* Paris, France: Septentrion, 2010.

Mulcahy, Matthew. *Hurricanes and Society in the British Greater Caribbean, 1624–1783*. Early America. Baltimore, MD: Johns Hopkins University Press, 2006.

Munich Re. *Topics Geo. Natural Catastrophes 2011. Earthquake, Flood, Nuclear Accident. Analyses, Assessments, Positions*. Munich, Germany: Munich Re, 2011.

Myers, Mary Frances, and Gilbert F. White. "Social Choice in Dealing with Hurricanes." In Simpson et al., *Coping with Disaster*, 141–53.

Nalau, Johanna, and Walter Leal Filho. "Introduction: Limits to Adaptation." In *Limits to Climate Change Adaptation*, 1–8. Cham, Switzerland: Springer, 2018.

Nelson, Louis P. *Architecture and Empire in Jamaica*. New Haven ; London: Yale University Press, 2016.

Noble, I.R., S. Huq, Y.A. Anokhin, J. Carmin, D. Goudou, F.P. Lansigan, B. Osman-Elasha, and A. Villamizar. "Adaptation needs and options." In *Impacts, Adaptation, and Vulnerability. Part A: Global and Sectoral Aspects. Contribution of Working Group II to the Fifth Assessment Report of the Intergovernmental Panel on Climate Change*, edited by C. B. Field, V. R. Barros, D. J. Dokken, K. J. Mach, M. D. Mastrandrea, T. E. Bilir, M. Chatterjee, et al., 833–68. Cambridge: Cambridge University Press, 2014.

Officer, Lawrence H., and Samuel H. Williamson. "Measuring Worth." http://www.measuringworth.com/index.html, accessed 13 February 2018.

Oliver-Smith, Anthony. "Anthropological Research on Hazards and Disasters." *Annual Review of Anthropology* 25 (1996): 303–28.

———. "Disasters and Forced Migration in the 21st Century." On *Understanding Katrina: Perspectives from the Social Sciences* [website] (2006). http://understandingkatrina.ssrc.org/Oliver-Smith/, accessed 30 August 2018.

———. "Global Changes and the Definition of Disaster." In *What Is a Disaster: Perspectives on the Question*, edited by Enrico L. Quarantelli, 177–94. London: Routledge, 1998.

———. "Peru's Five Hundred Year Earthquake: Vulnerability in Historical Context." In *Disasters, Development and Environment*, edited by Ann Varley, 31–48. Chichester, UK: John Wiley & Sons, 1994.

Ortiz Fernández, Fernando. *El Huracán, su Mitología y sus Símbolos*, 1st ed. Mexico City, Mexico: Fondo de Cultura Económica, 1947.

Overman, Edwin S. "The Flood Peril and the Federal Flood Insurance Act of 1956." *Annals of the American Academy of Political and Social Science* 309 (1957): 98–106.

Padilla Lozoya, Raymundo, and Myriam de la Parra Arellano. "Metodología, métodos, técnicas. Sistematización de la recurrencia de amenazas naturales y desastres en el estado de Colima, México." *Estudios sobre las Culturas Contemporáneas* 21, no. 3 (2015): 143–65.

Palmén, Erik. "On the Formation and Structure of Tropical Hurricanes." *Geophysica* 3, no. 1 (1948): 26–39.

Paquette, Robert L. "Revolutionary Saint Domingue in the Making of Territorial Louisiana." In *A Turbulent Time: The French Revolution and the Greater Caribbean,* edited by David Barry Gaspar and David Patrick Geggus, 204–25. Bloomington: Indiana University Press, 1997.

Parrish, Susan Scott. *The Flood Year 1927: A Cultural History.* Princeton, NJ: Princeton University Press, 2016.

Parry, Martin, Osvaldo Canziani, Jean Paultikof, Paul van der Linden, and Clair Hanson, eds. *Climate Change 2007: Impacts, Adaptation and Vulnerability. Contribution of Working Group II to the Fourth Assessment Report of the Intergovernmental Panel on Climate Change.* Cambridge, UK: Cambridge University Press, 2007.

Pasterick, Edward T. "The National Flood Insurance Program." In Kunreuther and Roth, *Paying the Price,* 125–54.

Pena y Camara, José de la, Ernest J. Burrus, Charles Edwards O'Neill, and María Teresa García Fernández, eds. *Catálogo de Documentos. Archivo General de Indias, Sección V, Audiencia de Santo Domingo.* New Orleans: Loyola University, 1968.

Penuel, K. Bradley, and Matt Statler, eds. *Encyclopedia of Disaster Relief.* Los Angeles: SAGE, 2011.

Pfister, Christian. "Disasters, Interregional Solidarity and Nation-Building. Reflections on the Case of Switzerland, 1806–1914." In *Solidarité et Assurance. Les Sociétés Européennes Face aux Catastrophes (17e–21e Siècles),* edited by René Favier and Christian Pfister, 117–42. Grenoble, France: CNRS MSH-Alpes, 2008.

———. "Learning from Nature-Induced Disasters. Theoretical Considerations and Case Studies from Western Europe." In Mauch and Pfister, *Natural Disasters,* 17–40.

———. "'The Monster Swallows You': Disaster Memory and Risk Culture in Western Europe, 1500–2000." *RCC Perspectives* 1 (2011): 2–22.

———. "Von Goldau nach Gondo. Naturkatastrophen als identitätsstiftende Ereignisse in der Schweiz des 19. Jahrhunderts." In *Katastrophen und ihre Bewältigung. Perspektiven und Positionen,* edited by Christian Pfister and Stephanie Summermatter, 53–78. Bern, Switzerland: Haupt, 2003.

Pfister, Christian, and Rudolf Brázdil. "Social Vulnerability to Climate in the 'Little Ice Age': An Example from Central Europe in the Early 1770s." *Climate of the Past Discussions* 2 (2006): 123–55.

Philosophical Transactions of the Royal Society of London. "Supplement: A General Index to the Philosophical Transactions, from the First to the End of the Seventieth Volume." *Philosophical Transactions of the Royal Society of London* 70 (1780).

Piddington, Henry. *The Sailor's Horn-Book for the Law of Storms.* 7th ed. London: Frederic Norgate, 1848.

Pierson, Paul. "Increasing Returns, Path Dependence, and the Study of Politics." *American Political Science Review* 94 (2000): 251–68.

Pittman, Philip. *The Present State of the European Settlements on the Mississippi*. London: J. Nourse, 1770.

Prieto, M., D. Gallego, R. García-Herrera, and N. Calvo. "Deriving Wind Force Terms from Nautical Reports Through Content Analysis. The Spanish and French Cases." *Climatic Change* 73, no. 1 (2005): 37–55.

Poey y Aguirre, Andrés. "A Chronological Table Comprising 400 Cyclonic Hurricanes Which Have Occurred in the West Indies and in the North Atlantic within 362 years, from 1493 to 1855." *Journal of the Royal Geographical Society (London)* 25 (1855): 291–328.

Porteous, Laura L. "Governor Carondelet's Levee Ordinance of 1792." *Louisiana Historical Quarterly* 10, no. 4 (1927): 513–16.

Pritchard, James. "Population in French America, 1670–1730. The Demographic Context of Colonial Louisiana." In Bond, *French Colonial Louisiana*, 175–203.

———. *In Search of Empire: The French in the Americas, 1670–1730*. New York: Cambridge University Press, 2004.

Pritchard, Walter. "The Last Island Disaster of August 10, 1856: Personal Narrative of His Experiences by One of the Survivors." *Louisiana Historical Quarterly* 20, no. 3 (1937): 690–737.

Pyne, Stephen J. *Fire in America: A Cultural History of Wildland and Rural Fire*. Princeton, NJ: Princeton University Press, 1982.

Rahmstorf, Stefan, and Dim Coumou. "Increase of Weather Extremes in a Warming World." *Proceedings of the National Academy of Sciences* 108, no. 44 (2011): 17905–9.

Rappaport, Edward N., and Robert H. Simpson. "Impact of Technologies from two World Wars." In Simpson et al., *Coping with Disaster*, 39–61.

Rasmussen, Daniel. *American Uprising: The Untold Story of America's Largest Slave Revolt*. New York: Harper Collins, 2011.

———. "Remarks on the Prevailing Storms of the Atlantic Coast of the North American States." *American Journal of Science and Arts* 20, no. July (1831): 17–51.

Reclus, Élisée. "Fragment d'un Voyage à la Nouvelle Orléans," *Le Tour du Monde* 1, no. 12 (1860): 177–92.

Redfield, William Charles. "Hurrcane of August 1831." *American Journal of Science and Arts* 21, no. Oct (1832): 191–93.

Reed, Andra J., Michael E. Mann, Kerry Emanuel, Ning Lin, Benjamin P. Horton, Andrew C. Kemp, and Jeffrey P. Donnelly. "Increased Threat of Tropical Cyclones and Coastal Flooding to New York City during the Anthropogenic Era." *Proceedings of the National Academy of Sciences* 112, no. 41 (2015): 12610–15.

Rejda, George E. *Principles of Risk Management and Insurance*. 7th ed. Boston: Addison Wesley, 2001.

Riehl, Herbert. *Tropical Meteorology*. New York: McGraw-Hill, 1954.

Rochefort, Charles de. *Histoire Naturelle et Morale des Iles Antilles de l'Amerique. Enrichie de Plusieurs Belles Figures des Raretez les Plus Considerables Qui y Sont d'écrites. Avec un Vocabulaire Caraïbe*, 1st ed. Rotterdam, Netherlands: Arnout Leers, 1658.

Rockman, Marcy. "Knowledge and Learning in the Archaeology of Colonization." In *Col-*

onization of Unfamiliar Landscapes: The Archaeology of Adaptation, edited by Marcy Rockman and James Steele, 3–24. New York: Routledge, 2003.

———. "New World with a New Sky. Climatic Variability, Environmental Expectations, and the Historical Period Colonization of Eastern North Carolina." *Historical Archaeology* 44 (2010): 4–20.

Rogers, Dale P. *Cheniere Caminada Buried at Sea.* Thibodaux, LA: D.P. Rogers, 1981.

Rohland, Eleonora. "Adapting to Hurricanes. A Historical Perspective on New Orleans from Its Foundation to Hurricane Katrina, 1718–2005." *Wiley Interdisciplinary Reviews: Climate Change.* OnlineFirst (2017): doi:10.1002/wcc.488.

———. "Beschwerde der Bürger von Louisiana: Der 'Louisiana Purchase' 1803 und die lokale Opposition gegen die amerikanische Territorialregierung." In Büschges, *Das Ende des alten Kolonialsystems.*

———. "Earthquake versus Fire. The Struggle over Insurance in the Aftermath of the 1906 San Francisco Disaster." In Janku, Schenk, and Mauelshagen, *Historical Disasters in Context.*

———. *Sharing the Risk: Fire, Climate and Disaster: Swiss Re, 1864–1906.* Lancaster, UK: Crucible Books, 2011.

Rohland, Eleonora, Maike Böcker, Gitte Cullmann, Ingo Haltermann, and Franz Mauelshagen. "Woven Together: Attachment to Place in the Aftermath of Disaster. Perspectives from Four Continents." In *Listening on the Edge,* edited by Stephen Sloan and Mark Cave, 183–206. New York: Oxford University Press, 2014.

Rowland, Dunbar, ed. *The Letter Books of William C.C. Claiborne, 1801–1816.* 6 vols. Vol. 1. Jackson: Mississippi State Library Archive, 1917.

———, ed. *The Letter Books of William C.C. Claiborne, 1801–1816.* 6 vols. Vol. 2. Jackson: Mississippi State Library Archive, 1917.

———, ed. *The Letter Books of William C.C. Claiborne, 1801–1816.* 6 vols. Vol. 6. Jackson: Mississippi State Library Archive, 1917.

Rowland, Dunbar, and Albert G. Sanders, eds. *Mississippi Provincial Archives (1701–1763): French Dominion.* 3 vols. Vol. 2. New York: AMS Press, 1973.

Russell, Sarah. "Ethnicity, Commerce, and Community on Lower Louisiana's Plantation Frontier, 1803–1828." *Louisiana History* 40 (1999): 389–405.

Saffir, Herbert S. "Communicating Damage Potentials and Minimizing Hurricane Damage." In Simpson et al., *Coping with Disaster,* 155–73.

Sauvé, Pierre, Jean-Noel Destrehan, and Pierre Derbigny. "Remonstrance of the People of Louisiana." *Annals of Congress* 8th Congress, 2nd session (1804): 1597–606.

Sauvole, Commander. "Journal Historique de l'établissement des Francais à la Louisiane. Recueil que j'ai pris sur mon journal de ce qui s'est passé de plus remarquable depuis le départ de M. d'Iberville du 3 mai 1699 jusqu'en 1700. [Lettre de Sauvole. Commandant au Biloxi, sur ce qui s'est passé dans l'intervalle du 1er au 2ème voyage de D'Iberville, et Instructions qui lui sont laissées par ce dernier en Mai 1700.]." In Magry, *Découverte par Mer.*

Schenk, Gerrit Jasper. "Managing Natural Hazards: Environment, Society, and Politics in Tuscany and the Upper Rhine Valley in the Renaissance (ca. 1270–1570)." In Janku, Schenk, and Mauelshagen, *Historical Disasters in Context,* 31–53.

Schwartz, Stuart B. *Sea of Storms: A History of Hurricanes in the Greater Caribbean from Columbus to Katrina.* Princeton, NJ: Princeton University Press, 2015.

Sealander, Judith. "Curing the Evils at their Source: The Arrival of Scientific Giving." In *Charity, Philanthropy, and Civility in American History,* edited by Lawrence J. Friedman and Mark D. McGarvie, 217–39. Cambridge: Cambridge University Press, 2003.

Shallat, Todd. *Structures in the Stream: Water, Science, and the Rise of the U.S. Army Corps of Engineers.* Austin: University of Texas Press, 1994.

Simpson, Joanne, Glenn W. Brier, and R. H. Simpson. "Stormfury Cumulus Seeding Experiment 1965: Statistical Analysis and Main Results." *Journal of the Atmospheric Sciences* 24, no. 5 (1967): 508–21.

Simpson, Joanne, R. H. Simpson, J. R. Stinson, and J. W. Kidd. "Stormfury Cumulus Experiments. Preliminary Results 1965." *Journal of Applied Meteorology* 5, no. 4 (1966/08/01 1966): 521–25.

Simpson, Robert, Richard A. Anthes, Michael Garstang, and Joanne Simpson, eds. *Hurricane! Coping with Disaster: Progress and Challenges since Galveston, 1900.* Washington, DC: American Geophysical Union, 2003

Smith, S.D. "Storm Hazard and Slavery: The Impact of the 1831 Great Caribbean Hurricane on St. Vincent." *Environment and History* 18, no. 1 (2012): 97–123.

Stagg, J. C. A. *Mr. Madison's War: Politics, Diplomacy, and Warfare in the Early American Republic 1783–1830.* Princeton, NJ: Princeton University Press, 1983.

———. *The War of 1812: Conflict for a Continent.* New York: Cambridge University Press, 2012.

Sturgill, Claude C., and Charles L. Price. "On the Present State of the Province of Louisiana in the Year 1720, by Jean-Baptiste Bernard de La Harpe." *Louisiana Historical Quarterly* 54, no. 3 (1971): 28–48.

Swiss Re. *Natural Catastrophes and Reinsurance. Risk Perception.* Zurich: Swiss Re, 2003.

———. *Sigma: Natural Catastrophes and Man-Made Disasters in 2012. A Year of Extreme Weather Events in the US,* Vol. 2. Zurich, Switzerland: Swiss Re, 2013.

Taleb, Nassim Nicholas. *The Black Swan: The Impact of the Highly Improbable.* 1st ed. New York: Random House, 2007.

Taylor, Joe Gray. *Louisiana Reconstructed, 1863–1877.* Baton Rouge: Louisiana State University Press, 1974.

Thompson, Thomas Marshall. "National Newspaper and Legislative Reactions to Louisiana's Deslondes Slave Revolt of 1811." *Louisiana History: Journal of the Louisiana Historical Association* 33, no. 1 (1992): 5–29.

Thrasher, Albert. *On to New Orleans! Louisiana's Heroic 1811 Slave Revolt.* 2nd ed. New Orleans: Cypress Press, 1996.

Tobin, Richard J., Corinne Calfee, and American Institutes for Research. "The National Flood Insurance Program's Mandatory Purchase Requirement. Policies, Processes, and Stakeholders." 2005.

Tolstoy, Maya. "Mid-ocean Ridge Eruptions as a Climate Valve." *Geophysical Research Letters* 42, no. 5 (2015): 1346–51.

Towers, Frank. *The Urban South and the Coming of the Civil War.* Charlottesville: University of Virginia Press, 2004.

Tregle, Joseph G. "Creoles and Americans." In *Creole New Orleans: Race and Americanization,* edited by Arnold Hirsch and Joseph Logsdon, 131–85. Baton Rouge: Louisiana State University Press, 1992.

U.S. Census Bureau. "1890 Census. Table 5: Population of States and Territories by Minor Civil Divisions, 1880 and 1890. Part I." http://www.census.gov/population/www/cen susdata/hiscendata.html, accessed 20 February 2018.

U.S. Congress. House of Representatives. Committee on Public Works. *The Hurricane Betsy Disaster of September 1965: Report of the Special Subcommittee to Investigate Areas of Destruction of Hurricane Betsy.* Washington, DC: U.S. Government Printing Office, 1965.

U.S. Congress. House. Committee on Public Works. *Southeast Hurricane Disaster (Hurricane Betsy): Hearing. 89th Congress, 1st Session, on H. R. 11539 and Similiar Bills. October 13, 1965.* Washington, DC: U.S. Government Printing Office, 1965.

U.S. Department of Housing and Urban Development (HUD), and U.S. Congress. House Committee on Public Works. *Insurance and Other Programs for Financial Assistance to Flood Victims: A Report from the Secretary of the Department of Housing and Urban Development to the President, as Required by the Southeast hurricane Disaster Relief Act of 1965, Public law 89–339, 89th Congress, H.R. 11539, November 8, 1965.* Washington, DC: U.S. Government Printing Office, 1966.

U.S. Green Building Council. "Dutch Dialogues: New Orleans architects look to the Netherlands for ideas on living with water." http://plus.usgbc.org/dutch-dialogues/, accessed 19 March 2017.

U.S. Office of Emergency Planning. *Hurricane Betsy, August 27-September 10, 1965: Federal Action in Disaster.* Washington, DC: Office of Emergency Planning, 1966.

U.S. Supreme Court. *United States v. Southeast Underwriters Association, 322 U.S. 533* 1944. http://supreme.justia.com/cases/federal/us/322/533/case.html, accessed 2 February 2018.

Udías, Agustín. "Jesuits' Contribution to Meteorology." *Bulletin of the American Meteorological Society* 77, no. 10 (1996): 2307–15.

Ungern-Sternberg, Thomas R. *Efficient Monopolies: The Limits of Competition in the European Property Insurance Market.* Oxford, UK: Oxford University Press, 2004.

Usner, Daniel H. *Indians, Settlers & Slaves in a Frontier Exchange Economy: The Lower Mississippi Valley before 1783.* Chapel Hill: Published for the Institute of Early American History and Culture, Williamsburg, Virginia, by the University of North Carolina Press, 1992.

Usner, Daniel H., Jr. "From African Captivity to American Slavery. The Introduction of Black Laborers to Colonial Louisiana." *Louisiana History: Journal of the Louisiana Historical Association* 20, no. 1 (1979): 25–48.

Vidal, Cécile. "Antoine Bienvenu, Illinois Planter and Mississippi Trader. The Structure of Exchange Between Lower and Upper Louisiana Under French Rule." In *Colonial Louisiana and the Atlantic World,* edited by Bradley G. Bond, 111–33. Baton Rouge: Louisiana State University Press, 2005.

———. "French Louisiana in the Age of the Companies, 1712–1731." In *Constructing Early Modern Empires: Proprietary Ventures in the Atlantic World, 1500–1750,* edited by Lou H. Roper and Bertrand van Ruymbeke. Leyde, Netherlands: Brill, 2006.

———. "Les Autorités et les Colons Face aux Catastrophes Naturelles (Inondantions et Ouragans) en Basse-Louisiane sous le Régime Français." Unpublished paper presented at the Conference: La Louisiane à la Dérive. Louisiana Adrift, EHESS Paris, 2005.

Vidal, Cécile, and Gilles Havard, eds. *Histoire de l'Amérique Française*. revised ed. Paris: Flammarion, 2008.

Viñes, Benito. *Apuntes Relativos a los Huracanes de las Antillas en Setiembre y Octubre de 1875 y 76*. Havana: Tipografía y Papeleria El Iris, 1878.

———. *Investigaciones Relativas a la Circulación y Traslación Cyclónica en las Huracanes de las Antillas*. Havana: de Pulido y Diaz, 1895.

———. *Investigation of the Cyclonic Circulation and the Translatory Movement of West Indian Hurricanes*. Washington, DC: Weather Bureau, 1898.

———. *Practical Hints in Regard to West Indian Hurricanes*. Washington, DC: Government Printing Office, 1886.

Walker, William O. *National Security and Core Values in American History*. New York: Cambridge University Press, 2009.

Walsh, Kevin J. E., John L. McBride, Philip J. Klotzbach, Sethurathinam Balachandran, Suzana J. Camargo, Greg Holland, Thomas R. Knutson, et al. "Tropical Cyclones and Climate Change." *Wiley Interdisciplinary Reviews: Climate Change* 7, no. 1 (2016): 65–89.

Warshauer, Matthew. *Andrew Jackson and the Politics of Martial Law: Nationalism, Civil Liberties and Partisanship*. Knoxville: University of Tennessee Press, 2006.

Watts, M. "On the Poverty of Theory: Natural Hazards Research in Context." In *Interpretations of Calamity from the Viewpoint of Human Ecology*, edited by Kenneth Hewitt, 231–62. Boston: Allen and Unwin, 1983.

Weber, David J. *The Spanish Frontier in North America*. Yale Western Americana Series. New Haven: Yale University Press, 1992.

Weber, Gustavus A. *The Weather Bureau: Its History, Activities and Organization*. Vol. 9, New York: Appleton, 1922.

Weddle, Robert S. *Changing Tides: Twilight and Dawn in the Spanish Sea, 1763–1803*. College Station: Texas A&M University Press, 1995.

Weems, John Edward. *A Weekend in September*. College Station: Texas A&M University Press, 1957.

Weinberger, Rachel. "Rebuilding Transportation." In *Rebuilding Urban Places after Disaster: Lessons from Hurricane Katrina*, edited by Eugenie Birch and Susan M. Watcher, 117–31. Philadelphia: University of Pennsylvania Press, 2006.

Werner, Welf. *Die späte Entwicklung der amerikanischen Rückversicherungswirtschaft. Eine Branchenstudie zur internationalen Wettbewerbsfähigkeit*. Berlin: Duncker & Humblot, 1993.

Wescoat, James L. "Water, Climate, and the Limits of Human Wisdom: Historical-Geographic Analogies Between Early Mughal and Modern South Asia." *Professional Geographer* 66, no. 3 (2014): 382–89.

Wheeler, Dennis. "An Examination of the Accuracy and Consistency of Ships' Logbook Weather Observations and Records." *Climatic Change* 73, no. 1 (2005): 97–116.

Wheeler, Dennis, and Clive Wilkinson. "The Determination of Logbook Wind Force and Weather Terms: The English Case." *Climatic Change* 73, no. 1 (2005): 57–77.

White, Sam. "'Shewing the Difference betweene Their Conjuration, and Our Invocation on the Name of God for Rayne': Weather, Prayer, and Magic in Early American Encounters." *William and Mary Quarterly* 72, no. 1 (2015): 33–56.

Willoughby, H. E., D. P. Jorgensen, R. A. Black, and S. L. Rosenthal. "Project STORMFURY. A Scientific Chronicle 1962–1983." *Bulletin of the American Meteorological Society* 66, no. 5 (1985/05/01 1985): 505–14.

Willoughby, Urmi Engineer. *Yellow Fever, Race, and Ecology in Nineteenth-Century New Orleans.* The Natural World of the Gulf South. Baton Rouge: Louisiana State University Press, 2017.

Wilson, Steven G., and Thomas R. Fischetti. "Coastline Population Trends in the United States: 1960–2008." In *Current Population Reports* (2010): 1–27. Published electronically May 2010. https://www.census.gov/prod/2010pubs/p25-1139.pdf, accessed 30 July 2018.

Woods, Patricia D. "The French and the Natchez Indians in Louisiana. 1700–1731." In Conrad, *French Experience,* 278–95.

———. *French-Indian Relations on the Southern Frontier, 1699–1762.* Ann Arbor, MI: UMI Research, 1980.

Zelinsky, Wilbur, and Leszek A. Kosinski. *The Emergency Evacuation of Cities: A Cross-National Historical and Geographical Study.* Savage, MD: Rowman & Littlefield, 1991.

Zwierlein, Cornel. *Der gezähmte Prometheus. Feuer und Sicherheit zwischen Früher Neuzeit und Moderne.* Göttingen, Germany: Vandenhöck und Ruprecht, 2011.

———. "The Production of Human Security in Premodern and Contemporary History." *Historical Social Research* 35, no. 4 (2010): 7–21.

———. "Security, Nature and Mercantilism in the Early British Empire." *European Journal for Security Research* 3 (2018): 15–34.

Index